TECHNICAL COMMUNICATION

A READER-CENTERED APPROACH

Sixth Edition

商务沟通
以读者为中心的方法（上）

（第6版）

Paul V. Anderson
Miami University (Ohio)

汪 红 选译

北京市版权局著作权合同登记号 图字 [01-2010-4300] 号

图书在版编目 (CIP) 数据

商务沟通：以读者为中心的方法：第 6 版·上 / Technical Communication: A Reader-Centered Approach (Sixth Edition) / （美）安德森 (Anderson, P. V.) 著. —北京：北京大学出版社，2011.3
（商务英语写作系列丛书）
ISBN 978-7-301-18605-3

Ⅰ. 商… Ⅱ. 安… Ⅲ. 商务—英语—写作—高等学校—教材 Ⅳ. H315

中国版本图书馆 CIP 数据核字（2011）第 030959 号

Technical Communication: A Reader-Centered Approach (Sixth Edition)
Paul V. Anderson
Copyright © 2007 by Wadsworth, a part of Cengage Learning.
Original edition published by Cengage Learning. All rights reserved.
本书原版由圣智学习出版公司出版。版权所有，盗印必究。

Peking University Press is authorized by Cengage Learning to publish and distribute exclusively this edition. This edition is authorized for sale in the People's Republic of China only (excluding Hong Kong SAR, Macao SAR and Taiwan). Unauthorized export of this edition is a violation of the Copyright Act. No part of this publication may be reproduced or distributed by any means, or stored in a database or retrieval system, without the prior written permission of the publisher.
本书由圣智学习出版公司授权北京大学出版社独家出版发行。此版本仅限在中华人民共和国境内（不包括中国香港、澳门特别行政区及中国台湾）销售。未经授权的本书出口将被视为违反版权法的行为。未经出版者预先书面许可，不得以任何方式复制或发行本书的任何部分。

Cengage Learning Asia Pte. Ltd.
5 Shenton Way, # 01-01 UIC Building, Singapore 068808

本书封面贴有 Cengage Learning 防伪标签，无标签者不得销售。

书　　　名：	Technical Communication: A Reader-Centered Approach (Sixth Edition) 商务沟通：以读者为中心的方法（第 6 版）（上）
著作责任者：	［美］Paul V. Anderson 著
责 任 编 辑：	黄瑞明
标 准 书 号：	ISBN 978-7-301-18605-3/H·2771
出 版 发 行：	北京大学出版社
地　　　址：	北京市海淀区成府路 205 号　100871
网　　　址：	http://www.pup.cn
电　　　话：	邮购部 62752015　发行部 62750672　编辑部 62754382　出版部 62754962
电 子 邮 箱：	zbing@pup.pku.edu.cn
印 　刷 　者：	河北滦县鑫华书刊印刷厂
发 　行 　者：	新华书店
	787 毫米×960 毫米　16 开本　22.25 印张　350 千字
	2011 年 3 月第 1 版　2011 年 3 月第 1 次印刷
定　　　价：	45.00 元

未经许可，不得以任何方式复制或抄袭本书之部分或全部内容。

版权所有，侵权必究　举报电话：010-62752024
　　　　　　　　　　　电子邮箱：fd@pup.pku.edu.cn

专家委员会

顾问　文秋芳

主任　王立非

委员　（按姓氏笔画排序）

丁言仁	于兰祖	卫乃兴	马广惠	王东风	王俊菊
文 旭	文 军	方 琰	邓鹂鸣	朱 源	刘世生
许德金	严明秦	苏 刚	杨永林	杨达复	杨鲁新
李小华	李文中	李正栓	李生禄	李炳林	李霄翔
肖德法	吴红云	汪 红	张世耘	张佐成	陈法春
陈新仁	周 平	郑 超	封一函	赵永青	胡一宁
胡 健	战 菊	俞洪亮	洪 刚	袁洪庚	晓 晴
徐 珺	郭海云	黄国文	常玉田	梁茂成	程幼强
程晓堂	程朝翔	傅似逸	蔡金亭		

总 序

北京大学出版社继《英语写作原版引印系列丛书》之后，2010年，又专题引进商务英语写作原版系列教材。这套教材体系完整，应用性强，商务内容丰富，十分贴近英语教学改革的需要和广大学生提升未来就业能力的需求，填补了我国商务英语写作领域内没有高质量商务英语写作教材的空白，并得到15所商务英语专业院校教学协作组和中国英语写作教学专业委员会相关专家的联合推荐。

随着我国对外开放的不断深入，高水平的商务英语写作人才一将难求，能用地道规范的英文起草法律合同、撰写咨询报告的专业写作人才更是凤毛麟角，部分国际咨询机构提供的一份英文公司咨询报告价格高达百万美元，如此激烈的竞争值得我们认真反思现有的写作教学。即将出台的《高等学校商务英语专业本科教学要求》（试行）明确指出，商务英语写作是学生的核心能力，商务英语专业应加大毕业设计的比重，鼓励学生采用商务报告（如市场调研报告、商业计划书、营销方案等）多种形式。而全面提升商务英语写作能力，按照过去传统的写作教学模式，已无法适应，必须要有新的改革思路，要改变"费时低效"的困境，就必须做到以下几个转变：(1) 从重写作技能转向技能与内容并重；(2) 从传统写作教学转向机辅写作教学模式；(3) 从开设单一写作课转向开设写作课程群；(4) 从大班课堂写作教学转向个性化写作教学中心。通过对美国普林斯顿大学、英国华威大学等世界名校的考察，我们建议，可分阶段分层次为不同水平的学生开设商务英语写作课程群（Writing Portfolio），具体可包括：基础英语写作、国际贸易写作、国际营销写作、金融英语写作、法律英语写作、学术英语写作、财经新闻写作、商务函电写作、商务报告写作、职业应用文写作等，全面提升学生的写作能力。

本套系列教材在国外畅销经久不衰，多次再版或重印，此次由北京大学出版社首批引进出版10本：《商务沟通：以读者为中心的方法》（上、下册）、《商务沟通与写作》（上、下册）、《最新商务报告写作》（上、下册）、《职场英语写作》（上、下册）、《成功商务英语写作》（上、下册），由对外经济贸易大学商务英语写作教学团队的教师魏明博士、冯海颖博士、杨颖莉博士、李玉霞博士、尹珏林博士分别撰写导读。

本套丛书既是职场英语写作的优质教材，又是商务写作的经典教材，教材深入浅出，语言简明，可帮助学生理解、记忆和应对多种国际商务场合下的写作需求。通过本丛书的学习和训练，学生可提高写作水平，为踏入职场做好准备。本套丛书可用作全国大专院校的商务英语学生和教师的写作课教材和参考书，还可供经管类学生学习商务英语写作之用，同时也可供爱好商务英语写作的广大社会读者和各类公司企业人员提高英语写作使用。

中国英语写作教学专业委员会主任
对外经济贸易大学英语学院院长
教授、博士生导师
王立非
2010年国庆节于北京

导 读

一、本书的特色

1. 作者简介

Paul V. Anderson 是美国迈阿密大学英语系教授,多年来一直从事有关技术写作方面的写作和研究工作,并且成立了该校的技术与科学交流专业,担任第一任主任。他为该校技术交流专业的发展争取到了上百万美元的校外资助,同时,在美国、欧洲、亚洲、澳洲,以及非洲各地为公司以及政府部门举办了多次工作坊和讲座。他在技术交流的理论和实践,跨课程写作、研究方法,教学法以及评估等方面有多部著作和多篇论文,并且获得了技术交流学会以及美国全国英文教师理事会等机构颁发的多个奖项。此外,他还当选为技术交流学会和技术写作教师协会的成员。

2. 本书特色

《商务沟通:以读者为中心的方法》于1987年首次出版,已再版五次,深受读者欢迎。本书紧密结合现代学习和工作的发展和需求,全面体现了技术交流领域的标准惯例以及最新发展。全书始终突出以读者为中心,紧紧围绕着写作的实际目的(即可用性和说服力)。本书不仅涉及传统的文本写作,同时凸显了时代性,讲授了如何进行口头演示、版面设计、平面设计、团队合作,以及使用新技术通过电子媒介(如电子邮件,网站和网页)进行交流。本书采用第二人称,语言流畅,简单易读,辅以大量实际工作中的实例和场景,有助于学习者轻松、透彻的掌握主要内容。每一章都附有一览表,主要学习内容一目了然,方便学习者在实际交流时拿来使用。同时,每一章都有练习,帮助学习者巩固所学内容。

本书的另一个亮点是辅有丰富的网络资源,相应的链接上提供了大量的案例、练习、样本、补充材料、测验以及本书主要内容的幻灯片演示,使得学习内容和形式多样化。本书的版面设计十分新颖,清晰,大量的图示有助于学习者了解实际的工作情形,视觉上非常直观,使学习过程更为活泼生动。值得一提的,书中的页边注释标注了书中其他部分的相关内容或相应的网络资源,使学习者能够融会贯通。

3. 使用对象与方法

本书对于写作教师以及各个专业的在校学生都是非常好的教材。教师在讲授完主要章节后,可以给学生布置附录中配套的课题。由于书中内容较多,时间以两学期为宜。同时,职场人士在实际工作中也可以用作参考手册和自学教材。

二、本书内容

本书共有23章,分为八大部分。

第一部分 引言(第1-2章)

第一部分主要是让学习者了解技术交流的特点以及本书的使用方法。

第一章 交流,职业,以及本书

帮助学习者了解工作与读书期间所进行的交流的不同之处,以及本书所讲授的工作中进行交流所需要的专门知识。对于学生,写作有助于学习课程,并向教师展示自己对课程的掌握情况,读者主要为教师。而在工作上,写作是一种行动,服务于现实性的目的,读者为同事、客户或其他需要通过写作者所提供的信息达成特定目标的人。我们在写作中要时刻考虑到自己的读者。工作中有效的交流具有两个特性，即可用性以及说服力。在交流中要时时与读者进行积极的交流；同时，还应当遵循一定的道德标准。此外，作者还提醒学习者，要灵活使用这本书所提供的指南。

第二章 以读者为中心的交流过程综述：获得一份工作

通过带领读者体验撰写有效的简历以及求职申请信，详细阐释了以读者为中心的交流方式。该章强调了此方式的核心原则，并以简历以及求职申请信的撰写为例进行了具体讲解，在写作方法上给予了详细的指导。该章还特别指出了创建和使用电子版简历所应当注意的事项，提醒学习者注意技术道德层面的一些问题。此外，作者还指出不同的文化之间在简历以及求职信的书写上存在差异。

第二部分 界定交流目标（第3章）

这一部分讨论了界定交流目标的重要性，提供了界定交流目标所需的多项指导原则，并通过具体事例加以详细说明。

第三部分 计划（第4-6章）

这一部分讲解如何以读者为中心，为实现界定的交流目标而做出计划。

第四章 为可用性做出计划

作者指出可用性有三条标准：从读者的角度来说要完整；以读者需要完成的任务为中心；能使读者迅速找到所需信息。该章就这三条标准提供了九个指导原则，最后一个原则帮助学习者确保所策划的交流活动合乎道德规范。

第五章 制订说服策略

该章阐释了两种相互关联但又有所不同的说服，一种是以影响他人态度和行为为目的，一种是以使团队在寻求知识和想法时进行协作为目的。举例说明了说服力发挥作用的过程。随后，该章提供了一系列相应的指导原则。

第六章 进行以读者为中心的调研

在工作中，为了有效地进行交流，还需要进行一定的调研。该章提供的指导原则，能够帮助学习者高效的收集目标读者所需要的信息。作者还给出了相关的道德和法律问题方面所应当遵循的原则。最后，"写作者参考指南"就五种研究方法的使用做出了详细说明。

第四部分 草拟文本（第7-11章）

通过这一部分，可以学习在草拟交流的文本、图示以及平面设计方面，如何实施所做的计划。

第七章 起草段落、节和章

该章所提供的指导原则可以帮助学习者草拟具有很强可用性和说服力的文本，适用于段落、段落群、章节直至整个交流活动等各个层次。作者还讨论了所草拟的文件对他人可能产生的道德层面的影响，并提出需要注意的事项。"写作者参考指南"提供了七种文本的结构模式。

第八章 形成有效的风格

在写作时，要时时考虑到读者对可用性以及说服力的看法。通过遵循该章的原则，可学习到构成写作风格的三方面主要内容：语气、句法结构，以及措辞。作者还提醒学习者在语言使用上要注意到读者的文化背景以及性别、称呼等道德层面的问题。

第九章 开始交流

该章讲授了开始进行交流的八种策略，均是以读者为中心，围绕着有用性以及说服力展开。最后，作者指出在决定是否尝试交流时所应考虑到的道德方面的问题。

第十章　结束交流

结尾对交流的有效性会产生很大影响，能够产生强调的效果，加深读者印象，为读者解答应当去做什么的问题。该章的九条指导原则就如何有效的结尾提供了具体的策略。

第十一章　以读者为中心写作正文之前和之后的部分

许多文书正文之前包括标题页、摘要、目录以及表格目录等，正文之后有附录、参考文献、尾注、词汇表或符号目录以及索引等。这些内容对于提高文书的有用性以及说服力都有很大的作用。该章提供了总体原则以及具体建议，并辅以许多实例进行阐释。

第五部分　草拟视觉效果（第12-13章）

此部分对如何设计视觉效果给出建议。

第十二章　制作以读者为中心的图表

图表包括图片、绘画、流程图、表格以及其他视觉表现。图表信息量大，一目了然，易于理解，能够提高书面交流的清晰度和效果。该章就此提供了九条指导原则，并使用了大量的图表举例说明。此外，作者还在最后使用图表加以总结。"写作者参考指南"就如何创建十一种常用的图表提供了详细的补充性建议。

第十三章　设计以读者为中心的页面和文件

在构建交流文件时，每一个环节都会涉及到视觉效果。好的页面设计能够帮助读者更好地理解作者所要传递的信息，并产生良好印象。该章的八个指导原则帮助学习者逐步学习页面设计；此外，该章还指导学习者通过使用文字处理程序对这些原则进行应用。

第六部分　修改（第14-15章）

第十四章　修改草稿

修改的一个重要环节是找出可能改进的地方。有两种应用最为广泛的方法，一是自我检查，二是得到他人的评论。该章就这两种方法提供了指导原则，并阐释了如何判断何种修改会对文书产生最好的效果。

第十五章　对草稿的可用性和说服力进行测试

只有通过得到读者的反馈才能得知文书是否需要进一步改进。通过测试，能够提高交流的有效性。该章介绍了对测试进行策划、执行，以及解释的方法。

第七部分　以读者为中心的方法的应用（第16-19章）

这一部分讲授如何将以读者为中心的方法应用于四种场景，即，通过电子邮件以及创建网站进行交流；与团队协作进行创建交流；进行口头演示；从事了解客户以及服务的项目。

第十六章　与团队一起创建交流

该章举例说明了团队在创建交流时的作用和重要性。团队有两种结构：一种是指定领导者；另一种是将任务进行分配。该章的指导原则讲授了如何使得这两种团队在交流过程的不同阶段有效并高效的运作。

第十七章　准备和进行以听者为中心的口头演示

与书面交流相比，口头演示更为个性化，互动性更强。该章的指导原则紧紧围绕着以听者为中心的原则，讲授策划以及进行口头宣讲的各个环节。

第十八章　创建以听者为中心的网页和网站

随着网站数量增加和使用范围的扩大，在工作中的需求也随之增加。在该章，会学习到如何将以读者为中心的方法应用于网站创建上（主要是使用微软的文字处理系统来创建网站）。该章所提供的指导原则涉及到创建网站的四个主要环节，即确定交流目标、策划、草拟以及修改。

第十九章　管理客户项目和服务学习项目

该章介绍了准备客户沟通项目的一系列技巧，包括为咨询公司、智囊团、设计公司以及其他企业和政府客户撰写研究报告、可行性报告及说明书、培训计划、市场营销材料、网站等商务沟通资料。

第八部分　总体结构（第20-23章）

第八部分仍然采用以读者为中心的角度，阐释工作中如何处理最为常见的四类交流形式：函电、报告、提案和说明书，提供了十分详尽的指导。

第二十章　以读者为中心的函电写作：信函、备忘录和电子邮件

人们常常通过信函、备忘录和电子邮件等函电进行工作。虽然简短，其应用范围非常广泛。该章首先强调了三者通用的一些原则；随后，提供了这三类函电的写作所涉及到的具体惯例和注意事项。

第二十一章　撰写以读者为中心的报告

报告是工作中最为常见的交流形式之一。该章从读者角度出发，探讨了报告的基本特征。这些特征与报告的框架密切相关。该章解释了基本框架，并随后举例说明。

第二十二章　撰写以读者为中心的提案

提案有两个主要目的：说服读者，保护自己。在写作中，一方面要考虑如何使得自己的提议对读者具有吸引力；另一方面，还要确保提议没有超出自己的能力范围。该章通过实例讲解了提案写作的几种主要情景，介绍了提案的常规结构，最后以实例解释了提案的写作策略。

第二十三章　撰写以读者为中心的说明书

说明书的形式和长度不尽相同，应用范围非常广泛。该章所提供的指导适用于各种题材和长度，打印版和电子版。作者还就电子版提供了补充性建议。

附录 A　引证资料

简要介绍了常见的两种引证格式，即 APA 和 MLA。

附录 B　项目

提供了教师可以布置给学生的作业。涵盖了本书所讲授的主要内容。这些项目都对交流对象、目的等方面有明确的说明。

三、推荐相关参考书

1. 马林，2007，英语技术写作与交流，哈尔滨工业大学出版社。
2. Alfred, Gerald, 2007, *Handbook of Technical Writing*, 中国人民大学出版社。
3. Gerson, Sharon, 2004, *Technical Writing: Process and Product*, 高等教育出版社。
4. Lannon, John, 2007, *Technical Communication (11th Edition)*, Longman.
5. Markel, Michael H., 2009, *Technical Communication (9th Edition)*, Bedford/St. Martin's.
6. Jean Wyrick, 2008,《成功写作入门》（英文版）（第10版），北京大学出版社。
7. Bonnie L. Tensen, 2008,《数字时代写作研究策略》（英文版）（第2版），北京大学出版社。
8. Steven H. Gale, 2008,《公司管理写作策略》（英文版），北京大学出版社。
9. David Rosrnwasser, 2008,《分析性写作》（英文版）（第5版），北京大学出版社。
10. Edward P. Bailey, 2010,《实用写作》（英文版）（第9版），北京大学出版社。

对外经济贸易大学
魏　明

Brief Contents 简短目录

PART I INTRODUCTION 引言   1

1 Communication, Your Career, and This Book
交流，职业，以及本书   3

2 Overview of the Reader-Centered Communication Process: Obtaining a Job
以读者为中心的交流过程综述：获得一份工作   25

PART II DEFINING YOUR COMMUNICATION'S OBJECTIVES 界定交流目标   63

3 Defining Your Communication's Objectives
界定交流目标   65

PART III PLANNING 计划   97

4 Planning for Usability 为可用性做出计划   99

5 Planning Your Persuasive Strategies
制订说服策略   118

6 Conducting Reader-Centered Research
进行以读者为中心的调研   151

Writer's Reference Guide to Using Five Reader-Centered Research Methods
写作者参考指南：使用五个以读者为中心的研究方法   165

PART IV DRAFTING PROSE ELEMENTS 草拟文本   197

7 Drafting Paragraphs, Sections, and Chapters
起草段落、节和章   199

Writer's Reference Guide to Using Seven Reader-Centered Organizational Patterns
写作者参考指南：使用七个以读者为中心的组织模式   229

8 Developing an Effective Style
形成有效的风格   257

9 Beginning a Communication 开始交流   280

10 Ending a Communication 结束交流   297

11 Writing Reader-Centered Front and Back Matter
以读者为中心写作正文之前和之后的部分   305

PART V DRAFTING VISUAL ELEMENTS 草拟视觉效果   323

12 Creating Reader-Centered Graphics
制作以读者为中心的图表   325

Writer's Reference Guide to Creating Eleven Types of Reader-Centered Graphics
写作者参考指南：制定十一种以读者为中心的图表   351

13 Designing Reader-Centered Pages and Documents
设计以读者为中心的页面和文件   372

PART VI REVISING 修改   399

14 Revising Your Drafts 修改草稿   401

15 Testing Drafts for Usability and Persuasiveness
对草稿的可用性和说服力进行测试   421

PART VII APPLICATIONS OF THE READER-CENTERED APPROACH
以读者为中心的方法的应用   437

16 Creating Communications with a Team
与团队一起创建交流   439

17 Creating and Delivering Listener-Centered Oral Presentations
准备和进行以听者为中心的口头演示   459

18 Creating Reader-Centered Web Pages and Websites
创建以读者为中心的网页和网站   484

19 Managing Client and Service-Learning
Projects　管理客户项目和服务学习项目　507

PART VIII　SUPERSTRUCTURES　总体结构　523

20 Writing Reader-Centered Correspondence:
Letters, Memos, and E-mail　以读者为中心的
函电写作：信函、备忘录和电子邮件　525

21 Writing Reader-Centered Reports
撰写以读者为中心的报告　539

**Writer's Reference Guide to Creating Three
Types of Special Reports**
写作者参考指南：创建三种特殊类型的报告　557

22 Writing Reader-Centered Proposals
撰写以读者为中心的提案　618

23 Writing Reader-Centered Instructions
撰写以读者为中心的说明书　642

APPENDICES　附录

Appendix A: Documenting Your Sources
引证资料　671

Appendix B: Projects　项目　686

Credits　致谢　699

References　参考书目　705

Contents 目录

Preface xix

PART I INTRODUCTION 引言 1

Chapter 1 Communication, Your Career, and This Book 交流，职业，以及本书 3

Communication Expertise Will Be Critical to Your Success 交流技能对成功至关重要 4

Writing at Work Differs from Writing at School 工作中的写作不同于学校中的写作 5

At work, Writing Is an Action 工作中，写作是种行动 10

The Main Advice of This Book: Think Constantly about Your Readers 本书的主要建议：始终为读者着想 10

Qualities of Effective On-the-Job Communication: Usability and Persuasiveness 有效的职场交流特点：可用性及说服力 11

The Dynamic Interaction between Your Communication and Your Readers 交流与读者间的互动 12

Some Reader-Centered Strategies You Can Begin Using Now 可以从现在开始采取的一些以读者为中心的策略 18

Communicating Ethically 交流应符合职业道德 19

What Lies Ahead in This Book 本书的构成 21

Guidelines, Your Creativity, and Your Good Judgment 指导方针、创造能力和判断力 22

Exercises 练习 23

Case: Selecting the Right Forklift Truck 案例：选择正确的铲车 23

Chapter 2 Overview of the Reader-Centered Communication Process: Obtaining a Job 以读者为中心的交流过程综述：获得一份工作 25

Central Principles of the Reader-Centered Approach 以读者为中心的方法的主要原则 26

A Reader-Centered Approach to Writing Your Résumé 用以读者为中心的方法写简历 26

Writer's Tutorial: Using Tables to Design a Résumé 写作者指南：用表格设计简历 40

Electronic Résumés: Special Considerations 电子简历：需要考虑的特别因素 45

A Reader-Centered Approach to Writing Your Job Application Letter 用以读者为中心的方法写职位申请信 49

Ethical Issues in the Job Search 求职中的道德因素 58

Writing for Employment in Other Countries 撰写去其他国家的求职材料 59

Conclusion 总结 59

Exercises 练习 59

Case: Advising Patricia 案例：给 Patricia 建议 60

PART II DEFINING YOUR COMMUNICATION'S OBJECTIVES 界定交流目标 63

Chapter 3 Defining Your Communication's Objectives 界定交流目标 65

The Importance of Defining Objectives 界定目标的重要性 66

GUIDELINE 1: Focus on What You Want to Happen While Your Readers Are Reading 指导方针 1：集中关注读者的阅读过程 66

GUIDELINE 2: Define Your Usability Goal: Analyze Your Readers' Reading Tasks 指导方针 2：界定可用性目标：分析读者的阅读任务 68

GUIDELINE 3: Define Your Persuasive Goal: Analyze Your Readers' Attitudes 指导方针 3：界定说服力目标：分析读者的态度 71
GUIDELINE 4: Learn Your Readers' Personal Characteristics 指导方针 4：了解读者的个人特点 73
GLOBAL GUIDELINE 5: Learn Your Readers' Cultural Characteristics 整体指导方针 5：了解读者的文化特点 76
GUIDELINE 6: Study the Context in Which Your Readers Will Read 指导方针 6：研究读者的阅读语境 82
GUIDELINE 7: Ask Others to Help You Understand Your Readers and Their Context 指导方针 7：请他人帮助你了解读者和他们的语境 82
GUIDELINE 8: Learn Who *All* Your Readers Will Be 指导方针 8：了解你所有的目标读者 83
GUIDELINE 9: Identify Any Constraints on the Way You Write 指导方针 9：找出写作方式的任何限制 87
ETHICS GUIDELINE 10: Identify Your Communication's Stakeholders 道德指导方针 10：明确交流过程中的参与者 87
Expertise in Action: An Example 89
Conclusion 总结 93
Exercises 练习 93
Case: Announcing the Smoking Ban 案例：宣布禁烟令 94

PART III PLANNING 计划 97

Chapter 4 Planning for Usability 为可用性做出计划 99
Your Goal When Planning for Usability 计划可用性的目标 100
GUIDELINE 1: Identify the Information Your Readers Need 指导方针 1：明确读者所需的信息 101
GUIDELINE 2: Organize around Your Readers' Tasks 指导方针 2：根据读者任务组织内容 101
GUIDELINE 3: Identify Ways to Help Readers Quickly Find What They Want 指导方针 3：确定帮助读者快速找到所需信息的方法 106

GUIDELINE 4: For a Complex Audience, Plan a Modular Communication 指导方针 4：针对复杂的读者群，制订一个模块式交流 106
GUIDELINE 5: Look for a Technical Writing Superstructure You Can Adapt 指导方针 5：找到一个可供你改编的写作模式 108
GUIDELINE 6: Plan Your Graphics 指导方针 6：制订图表 108
GLOBAL GUIDELINE 7: Determine Your Readers' Cultural Expectations about What Makes a Communication Usable 指导方针 7：确定不同文化背景的读者对于交流可用性的期待 109
GUIDELINE 8: Outline, If This Would Be Helpful 指导方针 8：如果有帮助的话，可列提纲 111
GUIDELINE 9: Check Your Plans with Your Readers 指导方针 9：与读者核查计划 112
ETHICS GUIDELINE 10: Investigate Stakeholder Impacts 道德指导方针 10：调查参与者影响 112
Conclusion 总结 114
Exercises 练习 116
Case: Filling the Distance Learning Classroom 案例：参与远程学习 116

Chapter 5 Planning Your Persuasive Strategies 制订说服策略 118
Persuasion to Influence Attitudes and Action 说服力影响态度和行为 119
Persuasion to Help a Team Develop Knowledge and Ideas Collaboratively 说服力帮助团队扩充知识和想出好点子 119
How Persuasion Works 说服力是怎样发挥作用的 120
The Sources of This Chapter's Advice 本章建议的来源 121
GUIDELINE 1: Listen—And Respond Flexibly To What You Hear 指导方针 1：听——并灵活回应你所听到的 121
GUIDELINE 2: Focus on Your Readers' Goals and Values 指导方针 2：关注读者的目标和价值 121
GUIDELINE 3: Address—And Learn From—Your Readers' Concerns and Counterarguments 指导方针 3：说——并从中了解读者的顾虑和反对观点 125

GUIDELINE 4: Reason Soundly
指导方针 4：正确地推论 　　127

GUIDELINE 5: Organize to Create a Favorable Response
指导方针 5：组织思路创造良好的回应 　　132

GUIDELINE 6: Build an Effective Relationship with Your Readers　指导方针 6：与读者建立有效关系 　　134

GUIDELINE 7: Determine Whether To Appeal to Your Readers' Emotions　指导方针 7：确定是否需要激发读者的情感 　　137

GLOBAL GUIDELINE 8: Adapt Your Persuasive Strategies to Your Readers' Cultural Background
总体指导方针 8：调整说服策略使其适用于读者的文化背景 　　139

ETHICS GUIDELINE 9: Employ Ethical Persuasive Techniques
道德指导方针 9：采用符合道德规范的说服技巧 144

Conclusion　总结 　　145
Exercises　练习 　　147
Case: Debating a Company Drug-Testing Program
案例：讨论一个公司的药物测试项目 　　150

Chapter 6　Conducting Reader-Centered Research　进行以读者为中心的调研 　　151

Special Characteristics of On-the-Job Research
工作中研究的特点 　　152

GUIDELINE 1: Define Your Research Objectives
指导方针 1：确定研究目标 　　152

GUIDELINE 2: Create an Efficient and Productive Research Plan
指导方针 2：制定有效的研究计划 　　153

GUIDELINE 3: Check Each Source for Leads to Other Sources
指导方针 3：检查每条资源，寻求更多线索 　　155

GUIDELINE 4: Carefully Evaluate What You Find
指导方针 4：仔细评估你所找到的信息 　　155

GUIDELINE 5: Begin Interpreting Your Research Results Even as You Obtain Them
指导方针 5：得到研究成果即开始分析 　　156

GUIDELINE 6: Take Careful Notes
指导方针 6：仔细作笔记 　　157

ETHICS GUIDELINE 7: Observe Intellectual Property Law and Document Your Sources　道德指导方针 7：遵守知识产权法并记录信息来源 　　157

Conclusion　总结 　　161
Exercises　练习 　　161

WRITER'S REFERENCE GUIDE: Using Five Reader-Centered Research Methods
写作者参考指南：使用五个以读者为中心的研究方法 　　165

Exploring Your Own Memory and Creativity
开发自己的记忆力与创造力 　　166
Searching the Internet　网上查询 　　172
Writer's Tutorial: Three ways to Search Efficiently on the Internet
写作者指南：三种网上查询的有效方式 　　178
Using the Library　利用图书馆 　　180
Interviewing　采访 　　185
Writer's Tutorial: Conducting Efficient Library Research
写作者指南：利用图书馆进行有效的研究 　　186
Conducting a Survey　开展问卷调查 　　190

PART IV　DRAFTING PROSE ELEMENTS　草拟文本 　　197

Chapter 7　Drafting Paragraphs, Sections, and Chapters　起草段落、节和章 　　199

Drafting Usable, Persuasive Prose
起草可用的、有说服力的文章 　　200

GUIDELINE 1: Begin by Announcing Your Topic
指导方针 1：从主题入手 　　201

GUIDELINE 2: Present Your Generalizations before Your Details
指导方针 2：在考虑细节前先考虑总体框架 　　204

GUIDELINE 3: Move from Most Important to Least Important　指导方针 3：从最重要到最不重要 　　206

GUIDELINE 4: Consult Conventional Strategies When Having Difficulties Organizing　指导方针 4：组织文章出现困难时借鉴常用策略 　　206

GLOBAL GUIDELINE 5: Consider Your Readers' Cultural Background When Organizing　指导方针 5：组织文章时考虑读者的文化背景 　　207

GUIDELINE 6: Reveal Your Communication's Organization
指导方针 6：展示交流的组织模式　　208
GUIDELINE 7: Smooth the Flow of Thought from Sentence to Sentence　指导方针 7：逐句调整理顺思路　219
ETHICS GUIDELINE 8: Examine the Human Consequences of What You're Drafting　道德指导方针 8：在起草文章时考虑读者感受　　222
Conclusion　总结　　223
　Exercises　练习　　224
　Case: Increasing Organ Donations
　案例：增加器官捐赠活动　　226

WRITER'S REFERENCE GUIDE: Using Seven Reader-Centered Organizational Patterns
写作者参考指南：使用七个以读者为中心的组织模式　　229

Formal Classification (Grouping Facts)
正式分类（事实归类）　　230
Informal Classification (Grouping Facts)
非正式分类（事实归类）　　233
Comparison　对比　　236
Description of an Object (Partitioning)
描述一个物体（分割）　　240
Description of a Process (Segmenting)
描述一个过程（分段）　　242
Cause and Effect　原因和结果　　246
Problem and Solution　问题和解决方法　　251
Combinations of Patterns　模式合并　　254
　Exercises　练习　　255

Chapter 8 Developing an Effective Style
形成有效的风格　　257

Creating Your Voice　有自己的想法和见解　　258
GUIDELINE 1: Find Out What's Expected
指导方针 1：确定读者期待看到的成果　　258
GUIDELINE 2: Consider the Roles Your Voice Creates for Your Readers and You　指导方针 2：考虑文章语气为你和读者确立的角色　　260
GUIDELINE 3: Consider How Your Attitude Toward Your Subject Will Affect Your Readers　指导方针 3：考虑你对主题的态度将如何影响读者　　261

GUIDELINE 4: Say Things in Your Own Words
指导方针 4：用自己的话阐述　　261
GLOBAL GUIDELINE 5: Adapt Your Voice To Your Readers' Cultural Background　整体指导方针 5：根据读者的文化背景调整语气　　262
ETHICS GUIDELINE 6: Avoid Stereotypes
道德指导方针 6：避免成见　　262
Constructing Sentences　造句　　263
GUIDELINE 1: Simplify Your Sentences
指导方针 1：简化句子　　264
GUIDELINE 2: Put the Action in Your Verbs
指导方针 2：运用动词　　265
GUIDELINE 3: Use the Active Voice Unless You Have a Good Reason to Use the Passive Voice
指导方针 3：尽量使用主动语态　　266
GUIDELINE 4: Emphasize What's Most Important
指导方针 4：强调重点　　267
GUIDELINE 5: Vary Your Sentence Length and Structure　指导方针 5：句子长度和结构不应一成不变　　268
GLOBAL GUIDELINE 6: Adapt Your Sentences For Readers Who Are Not Fluent in Your Language
整体指导方针 6：为不熟悉你的语言的读者调整语句　　269
Selecting Words　选词　　269
GUIDELINE 1: Use Concrete, Specific Words
指导方针 1：使用具体的词　　270
GUIDELINE 2: Use Specialized Terms When—And Only When—Your Readers Will Understand Them
指导方针 2：使用专业术语——当且仅当读者能够理解时　　271
GUIDELINE 3: Use Words Accurately
指导方针 3：使用精确的词　　272
GUIDELINE 4: Choose Plain Words over Fancy Ones
指导方针 4：选择平实的语言而不是华丽的辞藻　　273
GUIDELINE 5: Choose Words with Appropriate Associations
指导方针 5：选用含义恰当的词　　274
GLOBAL GUIDELINE 6: Consider Your Readers' Cultural Background When Choosing Words
整体指导方针 6：选词时考虑读者的文化背景　　275

ETHICS GUIDELINE 7: Use Inclusive Language
道德指导方针 7：使用总括性的语言　276
Conclusion　总结　277
　Exercises　练习　277

Chapter 9　Beginning a Communication
开始交流　280

Introduction to Guidelines 1 Through 3
介绍指导方针 1 至 3　281
GUIDELINE 1: Give Your Readers a Reason to Pay Attention
指导方针 1：给读者一个关注的理由　281
GUIDELINE 2: State Your Main Point
指导方针 2：说出主要观点　285
GUIDELINE 3: Tell Your Readers What to Expect
指导方针 3：向读者介绍结构及内容　286
GUIDELINE 4: Encourage Openness to Your Message
指导方针 4：鼓励对信息的开放性　287
GUIDELINE 5: Provide Necessary Background Information
指导方针 5：提供必要的背景知识　289
GUIDELINE 6: Include a Summary Unless Your Communication Is Very Short
指导方针 6：要有总结——除非篇幅很短　290
GUIDELINE 7: Adjust the Length of Your Beginning to Your Readers' Needs
指导方针 7：根据读者的需要调整开头的长度　291
GLOBAL GUIDELINE 8: Adapt Your Beginning to Your Readers' Cultural Background　整体指导方针 8：根据读者的文化背景调整开头　294
ETHICS GUIDELINE 9: Begin to Address Unethical Practices Promptly—And Strategically　道德指导方针 9：迅速并有策略地揭示不道德行为　294
Conclusion　总结　295
　Exercises　练习　296

Chapter 10　Ending a Communication
结束交流　297

GUIDELINE 1: After You've Made Your Last Point, Stop　指导方针 1：在说清最后一点后，停止　298
GUIDELINE 2: Repeat Your Main Point
指导方针 2：重复主要观点　299
GUIDELINE 3: Summarize Your Key Points
指导方针 3：总结重要观点　299
GUIDELINE 4: Refer to a Goal Stated Earlier in Your Communication
指导方针 4：提及在沟通前期设定的目标　300
GUIDELINE 5: Focus on a Key Feeling
指导方针 5：抓住情感基调　301
GUIDELINE 6: Tell Your Readers How to Get Assistance or More Information　指导方针 6：告诉读者如何获得帮助以及更多的信息　302
GUIDELINE 7: Tell Your Readers What to Do Next
指导方针 7：告诉读者下一步该做什么　302
GUIDELINE 8: Identify Any Further Study That Is Needed
指导方针 8：明确任何需要的进一步研究　302
GUIDELINE 9: Follow Applicable Social Conventions
指导方针 9：遵循恰当的社会规约　303
Conclusion　总结　303
　Exercises　练习　303

Chapter 11　Writing Reader-Centered Front and Back Matter
以读者为中心写作正文之前和之后的部分　305

How Transmittal Letters, Covers, and Front and Back Matter Increase Usability and Persuasiveness
介绍函、封面和文前、文后资料如何增加可用性和说服力　306
GUIDELINE 1: Review The Ways Your Readers Will Use the Communication
指导方针 1：考虑读者将如何使用文章　307
GUIDELINE 2: Review Your Communication's Persuasive Goals
指导方针 2：考虑文章的说服力目标　307
GUIDELINE 3: Find Out What's Required
指导方针 3：找出所要求的　307
GUIDELINE 4: Find Out What's Expected
指导方针 4：找出所期望的　308
GUIDELINE 5: Evaluate and Revise Your Front and Back Matter
指导方针 5：评价和修改文前及文后部分　308
Conventions and Local Practice
传统及当地习俗　308

Writing a Reader-Centered Transmittal Letter
写以读者为中心的介绍函　308
Writing a Reader-Centered Cover
写以读者为中心的封面　309
Writing Reader-Centered Front Matter
写以读者为中心的文前部分　309
Writing Reader-Centered Back Matter
写以读者为中心的文后部分　317

PART V DRAFTING VISUAL ELEMENTS
草拟视觉效果　323

Chapter 12 Creating Reader-Centered Graphics 制作以读者为中心的图表　325
A Reader-Centered Approach to Creating Graphics
以读者为中心的方法制作图表　327
GUIDELINE 1: Look for Places Where Graphics Can Increase Your Communication's Usefulness and Persuasiveness 指导方针1：寻找图表的恰当位置以增强文章的可用性及说服力　327
Writer's Tutorial: Graphics Help Readers Understand and Use Information
写作者指南：图表帮助读者理解和使用信息　328
GUIDELINE 2: Select the Type of Graphic That Will Be Most Effective at Achieving Your Objectives 指导方针2：选择可以达到目标的最有效的图表　330
GUIDELINE 3: Make Each Graphic Easy to Understand and Use 指导方针3：使每个图表易于理解和使用　333
GUIDELINE 4: Use Color to Support Your Message 指导方针4：用颜色辅助信息传达　338
GUIDELINE 5: Use Graphics Software and Existing Graphics Effectively 指导方针5：有效使用图表软件和现有图表　341
GUIDELINE 6: Integrate Your Graphics with Your Text 指导方针6：使图表与文本结合　342
GUIDELINE 7: Get Permission and Cite the Sources for Your Graphics 指导方针7：得到使用允许注明图表来源　343

Writer's Tutorial: Creating Reader-Centered Graphs with a Spreadsheet Program
写作者指南：使用电子制表软件制作以读者为中心的图表　344
GLOBAL GUIDELINE 8: Adapt Your Graphics When Writing to Readers in Other Cultures 整体指导方针8：为具有其他文化背景的读者调整图表　346
ETHICS GUIDELINE 9: Avoid Graphics That Mislead 道德指导方针9：避免误导性图表　347
Conclusion　总结　349
　Exercises　练习　349

WRITER'S REFERENCE GUIDE: Creating Eleven Types of Reader-Centered Graphics
写作者参考指南：制定十一种以读者为中心的图表　351
Tables　图表　352
Line Graphs　折线图　354
Bar Graphs　条形图　356
Pictographs　统计图表　358
Pie Charts　饼图　360
Photographs　相片　362
Drawings　图画　364
Screen Shots　抓屏　366
Flowcharts　流程图　368
Organizational Charts　组织结构图　370
Schedule Charts　日程表　371

Chapter 13 Designing Reader-Centered Pages and Documents
设计以读者为中心的页面和文件　372
A Reader-Centered Approach to Design
以读者为中心的设计方法　374
Design Elements of a Communication
交流中的设计元素　374
GUIDELINE 1: Begin by Considering Your Readers and Purpose 指导方针1：从考虑读者和目的开始　374
GUIDELINE 2: Create a Grid to Serve as the Visual Framework for Your Pages 指导方针2：制定一个网格作为页面的视觉框架　375

Writer's Tutorial: Designing Grid Patterns for Print
写作者指南：设计打印模式 376
GUIDELINE 3: Align Related Elements with One Another
指导方针 3：匹配相关元素 380
GUIDELINE 4: Group Related Items Visually
指导方针 4：分类相关视觉元素 382
GUIDELINE 5: Use Contrast to Establish Hierarchy and Focus 指导方针 5：利用对比分级和聚焦 385
Using Word Processors to Create Page Designs
使用文字处理器制定页面设计 388
GUIDELINE 6: Use Repetition to Unify Your Communication Visually
指导方针 6：利用重复保持视觉上的统一 389
GUIDELINE 7: Select Type That Is Easy to Read
指导方针 7：选择易读的字体 391
GUIDELINE 8: Design Your Overall Document for Ease of Use and Attractiveness
指导方针 8：从易于使用和有吸引力的角度出发设计文件 392
Conclusion 总结 393
Exercises 练习 393

PART VI REVISING 修改 399

Chapter 14 Revising Your Drafts
修改草稿 401
The Three Activities of Revising 修改的三个方式 402
Checking Your Draft Yourself 自己检查草稿 403
GUIDELINE 1: Check from Your Readers' Point of View
指导方针 1：从读者角度检查 403
GUIDELINE 2: Check from Your Employer's Point of View
指导方针 2：从雇主的角度检查 403
GUIDELINE 3: Distance Yourself from Your Draft
指导方针 3：让自己保持客观 404
GUIDELINE 4: Read Your Draft More Than Once, Changing Your Focus Each Time 指导方针 4：
不止一遍读草稿，每次改变关注点 404
GUIDELINE 5: Use Computer Aids to Find (But Not to Cure) Possible Problems 指导方针 5：
利用电脑辅助寻找（而不是更正）可能的问题 405

ETHICS GUIDELINE 6: Consider the Stakeholders' Perspective
道德指导方针 6：考虑参与者的观点 406
Reviewing 审读 407
GUIDELINE 1: Discuss the Objectives of the Communication and the Review
指导方针 1：讨论沟通和审读的目标 408
GUIDELINE 2: Build a Positive Interpersonal Relationship with Your Reviewers or Writer 指导方针 2：
与审读者或作者建立良好的人际关系 408
GUIDELINE 3: Rank Suggested Revisions—and Distinguish Matters of Substance from Matters of Taste
指导方针 3：分析修改建议——
区分实质性修改和风格上的改动 410
GUIDELINE 4: Explore Fully the Reasons for All Suggestions
指导方针 4：充分探究所有修改建议的原因 410
GUIDELINE 5: Use Computer Aids for Reviewing in a Reader-Centered Way 指导方针 5：
利用电脑的帮助按以读者为中心的方式审读 411
ETHICS GUIDELINE 6: Review from the Stakeholders' Perspective
道德指导方针 6：从参与者的角度审读 412
Guidelines for Managing Your Revising Time
控制修改时间的指导方针 414
GUIDELINE 1: Adjust Your Effort to the Situation
指导方针 1：根据情况调整修改工作 414
GUIDELINE 2: Make the Most Significant Revisions First
指导方针 2：先做最重要的调整 416
GUIDELINE 3: Be Diplomatic
指导方针 3：灵活变通 418
GUIDELINE 4: To Revise Well, Follow the Guidelines for Writing Well 指导方针 4：
想要修改得好就要遵循写作的指导方针 418
GUIDELINE 5: Revise to Learn
指导方针 5：以学习为目的的修改 418
Conclusion 总结 419
Exercises 练习 419

Chapter 15 Testing Drafts for Usability and Persuasiveness
对草稿的可用性和说服力进行测试 421

The Logic of Testing　测试逻辑　423
GUIDELINE 1: Establish Your Test Objectives
　指导方针1：确定测试目标　423
GUIDELINE 2: Pick Test Readers Who Truly Represent Your Target Readers　指导方针2：挑选真正能代表目标读者的人受测　424
GUIDELINE 3: Focus on Usability: Ask Your Test Readers to Use Your Draft the Same Way Your Target Readers Will
　指导方针3：专注于可用性：让受测读者按照与目标读者同样的方式使用草稿　425
GUIDELINE 4: Focus on Persuasiveness: Learn How Your Draft Affects Your Readers' Attitudes
　指导方针4：专注于说服力：了解草稿如何影响读者的态度　429
GUIDELINE 5: Interview Your Test Readers after They Have Read and Used Your Draft　指导方针5：在受测读者阅读和使用草稿后采访他们　430
GUIDELINE 6: Avoid Biasing Your Test Results
　指导方针6：避免对测试结果有偏见　430
GUIDELINE 7: Interpret Your Test Results Thoughtfully
　指导方针7：深刻解读测试结果　431
GUIDELINE 8: Test Early and Often
　指导方针8：尽早和经常性地测试　432
GLOBAL GUIDELINE 9: With Communications for Readers in Other Cultures, Choose Test Readers from the Culture
　整体指导方针9：针对与其他文化背景的读者交流，从该文化背景中选取受测读者　432
ETHICS GUIDELINE 10: Obtain Informed Consent from Your Test Readers
　道德指导方针10：取得受测读者的同意　433
Conclusion　总结　433
　Exercises　练习　436

PART VII APPLICATIONS OF THE READER-CENTERED APPROACH
以读者为中心的方法的应用　437

Chapter 16 Creating Communications with a Team　与团队一起创建交流　439

Varieties of Team Structures　不同的团队结构　440
GUIDELINE 1: Develop a Shared Understanding of the Communication's Objectives
　指导方针1：培养对于交流目标的共同理解　441
GUIDELINE 2: Make and Share Detailed Plans
　指导方针2：制定和分享具体计划　424
GUIDELINE 3: Make a Project Schedule
　指导方针3：制定计划进度表　444
GUIDELINE 4: Share Leadership Responsibilities
　指导方针4：分享领导职责　445
GUIDELINE 5: Make Meetings Efficient
　指导方针5：高效会议　447
GUIDELINE 6: Encourage Discussion, Debate, and Diversity of Ideas　指导方针6：鼓励讨论、辩论和多种意见的产生　448
GUIDELINE 7: Use Computer Tools for Collaboration
　指导方针7：利用电脑工具合作　451
GLOBAL GUIDELINE 8: Be Sensitive to Possible Cultural and Gender Differences in Team Interactions
　整体指导方针8：对团队互动中可能出现的文化和性别差别保持敏感　454
Conclusion　总结　456
　Exercises　练习　456

Chapter 17 Creating and Delivering Listener-Centered Oral Presentations
准备和进行以听者为中心的口头演示　459

GUIDELINE 1: Define Your Presentation's Objectives
　指导方针1：确定演示目标　460
GUIDELINE 2: Plan the Verbal and Visual Parts of Your Presentation as a Single Package　指导方针2：把演示的口头和视觉部分计划为一个整体　461
Writer's Tutorial: Creating a Listener-Centered Presentation
　写作者指南：制定以听者为中心的演示　464
GUIDELINE 3: Focus on a Few Main Points
　指导方针3：专注于几个要点　467
GUIDELINE 4: Use a Simple Structure—and Help Your Listeners Follow It
　指导方针4：采用简单结构——听众易懂　469
GUIDELINE 5: Speak in a Conversational Style
　指导方针5：以谈话的方式讲解　470

GUIDELINE 6: Create Easy-to-Read, Understandable Graphics
指导方针 6：制作易读易理解的图表　　　471
GUIDELINE 7: Involve Your Audience in Your Presentation
指导方针 7：让听众参与到演示中　　　474
GUIDELINE 8: Prepare for Interruptions and Questions—and Respond Courteously
指导方针 8：准备好面对被打断或提问的情况——并有礼貌地作答　　　476
GLOBAL GUIDELINE 9: Adapt Your Presentation Strategies to Your Audience's Cultural Background
整体指导方针 9：根据听众的文化背景调整演示策略　　　477
GUIDELINE 10: Rehearse　指导方针 10：排练　　　479
GUIDELINE 11: Accept Your Nervousness—and Work with It
指导方针 11：允许自己紧张——坦然面对　　　479
Making Team Presentations
准备和进行团队演示　　　480
Conclusion　总结　　　482
Exercises　练习　　　482

Chapter 18 Creating Reader-Centered Web Pages and Websites
创建以读者为中心的网页和网站　　　484

How the World Wide Web Works
万维网如何工作　　　485
Guideline for Defining Objectives
确定目标的指导方针　　　486
GUIDELINE 1: Learn about Your Site's Readers and Define Its Purpose　指导方针 1：了解你网站的读者并确立网站目标　　　486
Guidelines for Planning　计划方针　　　487
GUIDELINE 2: Create the Map for a Site That Includes What Your Readers Want and Enables Them to Get It Quickly
指导方针 2：创建包括读者的各种需求信息在内的网站导航图，使其能够迅速找到所需信息　　　487
GUIDELINE 3: Gather the Information Your Readers Need
指导方针 3：搜集读者所需的信息　　　487

Writer's Tutorial: Creating a Web Page in HTML Code
写作者指南：创建 HTML 格式的网页　　　488
ETHICS GUIDELINE 4: Respect Intellectual Property and Provide Valid Information
道德指导方针 4：尊重知识产权，提供有效信息　　　490
Guidelines for Drafting　草拟的指导方针　　　491
GUIDELINE 5: Design Pages That Are Easy to Use and Attractive
指导方针 5：设计美观实用的网页　　　491
Writer's Tutorial: Designing Grid Patterns for Web Pages
写作者指南：设计网页网格图案　　　492
GUIDELINE 6: Provide Navigational Aids That Help Your Readers Move Quickly Through Your Site to the Information They Want
指导方针 6：为读者提供网站导航服务，帮助其快速找到所需信息　　　497
GUIDELINE 7: Unify Your Site Verbally and Visually
指导方针 7：统一网站的文字和图像　　　500
GUIDELINE 8: Construct a Site That Readers with Disabilities Can Use　指导方针 8：建立一个残障人士可以使用的网站　　　500
GLOBAL GUIDELINE 9: Design Your Site for International and Multicultural Readers　整体指导方针 9：为国际化和多元文化的读者设计网站　　　502
GUIDELINE 10: Help Readers Find Your Site on the Internet　指导方针 10：帮助读者找到网站　　　503
Revising Guideline　修改方针　　　504
GUIDELINE 11: Test Your Site Before Launching It
指导方针 11：发布之前测试网站　　　504
Exercises　练习　　　504

Chapter 19 Managing Client and Service-Learning Projects
管理客户项目和服务学习项目　　　507

Overall Project Management Strategy
项目管理总体策略　　　509
GUIDELINE 1: Determine Exactly What Your Client Wants and Why
指导方针 1：明确客户需求和需求原因　　　509

GUIDELINE 2: Develop Your Own Assessment of the Situation
指导方针2：自己评估项目 510
GUIDELINE 3: Create a Project Management Plan
指导方针3：创建项目管理计划 511
GUIDELINE 4: Submit a Written Proposal to Your Client—and Ask for a Written Agreement 指导方针4：向客户递交书面提议——并征得书面同意 513
GUIDELINE 5: Communicate with Your Client Often—Especially at All Major Decisions 指导方针5：经常与客户沟通——尤其是所有重大决策 514
GUIDELINE 6: Advocate and Educate, but Defer to Your Client
指导方针6：提议，劝说，但服从客户 519
GUIDELINE 7: Hand Off the Project in a Helpful Way
指导方针7：以一种有助的方式移交项目 520
Conclusion 总结 520
Exercises 练习 520

PART VIII SUPERSTRUCTURES
总体结构 523

Chapter 20 Writing Reader-Centered Correspondence: Letters, Memos, and E-mail
以读者为中心的函电写作：信函、备忘录和电子邮件 525

GUIDELINE 1: Adopt a Reader-Centered "You-Attitude"
指导方针1：采用以读者为中心的态度 526
GUIDELINE 2: State Your Main Point Up Front—Unless Your Readers Will React Negatively
指导方针2：首先陈述主要观点——除非读者反对 527
GUIDELINE 3: Keep It Short
指导方针3：陈述简短 527
GUIDELINE 4: Give Your Readers the Background They Need
指导方针4：提供读者所需的背景信息 528
GUIDELINE 5: Use Headings, Lists, and Graphics
指导方针5：利用标题、清单和图表 528

GLOBAL GUIDELINE 6: Learn the Customs of Your Readers' Culture
整体指导方针6：了解读者的文化风俗 528
GUIDELINE 7: Follow Format Conventions
指导方针7：遵循格式惯例 529
Writing Reader-Centered Letters
撰写读者为中心的信函 529
Writer's Tutorial: Writing Letters
写作者指南：写信 530
Writing Reader-Centered Memos
以读者为中心的备忘录写作 532
Writing Reader-Centered E-mail
以读者为中心的电子邮件写作 533
Writer's Tutorial: Writing Memos
写作者指南：写备忘录 534
Writer's Tutorial: Writing E-mail
写作者指南：写电子邮件 535

Chapter 21 Writing Reader-Centered Reports
撰写以读者为中心的报告 539
Your Readers Want to Use the Information You Provide 读者想要使用你提供的信息 540
Readers' Six Basic Questions
读者的六个基本问题 540
General Superstructure for Reports
报告的一般结构 541
Sample Outlines and Report
提纲和报告样本 546

WRITER'S REFERENCE GUIDE: Creating Three Types of Special Reports
写作者参考指南：创建三种特殊类型的报告 557
　Empirical Research Reports　实证研究报告 558
　Feasibility Reports　可行性报告 586
　Progress Reports　进度报告 607

Chapter 22 Writing Reader-Centered Proposals 撰写以读者为中心的提案 618
The Variety of Proposal-Writing Situations
撰写提案的各种情况 619
Proposal Readers Are Investors
提案的读者是投资者 621

The Questions Readers Ask Most Often	
读者最常问的问题	622
Strategy of the Conventional Superstructure for	
Proposals 传统形式提案的结构策略	622
Superstructure for Proposals 提案结构	624
Sample Proposal 提案样本	633

Chapter 23 Writing Reader-Centered Instructions 撰写以读者为中心的说明书   642

Four Important Points 四个要点	643
Superstructure for Instructions 说明书的结构	644
Physical Construction of Instructions	
说明书的物理结构	658
Online Instructions 在线说明书	659
Sample Instructions 说明书样本	659
Exercises 练习	669

Appendix A Documenting Your Sources 引证资料   671

Choosing a Format for Documentation	
选择一种引证格式	672
Deciding Where to Place In-Text Citations	
决定文中加注的位置	672
Writing APA In-Text Citations	
写 APA 格式的文中加注	673
Writing an APA References List	
写 APA 格式的参考文献	674
Writing MLA In-Text Citations	
写 MLA 格式的文中加注	679
Writing a MLA Works Cited List	
写 MLA 格式的参考文献	680

Appendix B Projects 项 目   686

Project 1 Résumé and Job Application Letter	
项目 1：简历和工作申请信	687
Project 2 Informational Website	
项目 2：信息网站	688
Project 3 Informational Page	
项目 3：信息页面	689
Project 4 Unsolicited Recommendation	
项目 4：主动建议	689
Project 5 Brochure	
项目 5：手册	691
Project 6 Instructions	
项目 6：说明书	691
Project 7 User Test and Report	
项目 7：用户测试和报告	692
Project 8 Project Proposal	
项目 8：项目提案	693
Project 9 Progress Report	
项目 9：进度报告	694
Project 10 Formal Report or Proposal	
项目 10：正式报告和提案	694
Project 11 Oral Briefing I: Project Plans	
项目 11：口头简报 I：项目计划	696
Project 12 Oral Briefing II: Project Results	
项目 12：口头简报 II：项目结果	697
Credits 致谢	699
References 参考书目	705

Preface

前 言

Welcome to the sixth edition of *Technical Communication: A Reader-Centered Approach*. Technical communication continues to change in substantial ways, and research has produced new insights into effective communication practices and pedagogy. This edition, building on the many strengths of previous editions, offers updated treatment of core topics, coverage of additional topics, and new pedagogical features that make it even more effective for teaching and learning.

Most importantly, this edition retains the book's distinctive reader-centered approach, whose hallmarks are that it:

- **Teaches highly transferable strategies.** Through its uniquely strong emphasis on teaching a flexible set of research-based strategies, the reader-centered approach helps students learn how to take a thoughtful, resourceful, creative approach to all the communications they will prepare in their careers.
- **Provides in-depth coverage in an easy-to-learn manner.** Because all of this book's advice grows directly from a common set of basic reader-centered principles and processes, the book is able to help students understand, remember, and apply unusually sophisticated discussions on a wide array of topics.
- **Benefits students in many fields.** The strategic emphasis and wide applicability of the reader-centered approach mean that the book is very well suited to students majoring in a broad range of technical, engineering, scientific, business, and other specialized fields.

MAJOR CHANGES IN THIS EDITION

Among the many new features introduced in this edition, the following are particularly notable because of the special ways they increase the book's breadth and effectiveness for teaching and learning.

- A new, **wider trim size** allows for a more usable, more attractive page design. Capitalizing on this new page design, innovative **new two-page spreads** are provided to enhance student learning, and more detailed annotations explain the key rhetorical features of sample documents (see pages 138, 140, and 362–363 for examples).
- New **Writer's Tutorials,** many of which utilize the new two-page spread design, have been added to many chapters in the sixth edition to help guide

students as they create their own technical documents (see pages 40–42 and 344–345).

- The text's margin notes have been revised and reorganized for greater ease-of-use. **Learn More** margin notes point students to other areas of the text they can read to supplement the text discussion at hand. **Web** margin notes direct students to material on the text's companion website.

- The **Planning Guides** and **Revision Checklists,** which assist students as they work on their course projects and professional communications, have been redesigned for the sixth edition. Downloadable versions of these are available at the text's companion website.

In revising the content for the sixth edition, the author has focused his attention on the following areas:

- **Integration.** The author has more fully integrated the themes of usability and persuasiveness as focal points that enable writers to apply the reader-centered approach more effectively.

- **Updating.** The author has updated many areas of the text, including those relating to technology. Newly revised Chapter 18 (*Creating Reader-Centered Web Pages and Websites*) combines material from several chapters in the last edition into one comprehensive presentation.

- **New Examples.** Many of the sample documents have been replaced for the sixth edition.

- **New Topics/Chapters:**
    - The *Reference Guides* from the last edition are now called *Writer's Reference Guides* in the sixth edition, to better reflect their usefulness to writers/creators of technical communication documents. These have also been thoroughly revised.
    - Coverage of international communication has been strengthened and updated throughout the text, including new or revised *Global Guidelines* in many chapters and a new discussion of intercultural communication in Chapter 3 (*Defining Your Communication's Objectives*).
    - Chapter 11 (*Writing Reader-Centered Front and Back Matter*) is completely new to the sixth edition.
    - Chapter 5 (*Planning Your Persuasive Strategies*) has been expanded and emphasizes the *cooperative* persuasion that writing teams can use to develop knowledge and ideas collaboratively.
    - The *Writer's Reference Guide to Creating Eleven Types of Reader-Centered Graphics* has been made more user-friendly through the extensive use of the new two-page-spread design that makes highlighting elements of sample documents clearer and easier for students to follow.
    - Chapter 14 (*Revising Your Drafts*) now combines material formerly found in two separate chapters. Chapter 15 (*Testing Drafts for Usability and Persuasiveness*) now follows the new chapter.

- A new chapter, *Writing Reader-Centered Correspondence: Letters, Memos, and E-mail* (Chapter 20), has been added.
- New discussions of copyright and intellectual property law have been added to Chapter 6 (*Conducting Reader-Centered Research*) and Chapter 18 (*Creating Reader-Centered Web Pages and Websites*).
- The expanded Chapter 18 (*Creating Reader-Centered Web Pages and Websites*) provides more guidance for creating highly effective online communications.
- Coverage of MLA and APA documentation styles has been revised and updated (see Appendix A).

ORGANIZATION AND COVERAGE OF THIS EDITION

This book's four major parts combine attention to communication processes and products. Throughout, the book tells students how to apply effective, reader-centered strategies in the practical situations they will encounter in their careers.

- **Introduction.** Chapter 1 helps students understand the differences between communicating at work and at school, as well as the kinds of expertise this book will help them develop so they can communicate successfully in their careers. Chapter 2 provides a detailed overview of the reader-centered approach by leading students through the process of creating highly effective résumés and job application letters.
- **Communication Process.** Chapters 3 through 15 guide students through each activity in the writing process, helping them become confident, resourceful writers. In addition, three reference guides help students use a variety of research methods, employ seven organizational patterns that are often useful in career-related communications, and create eleven types of graphics, including tables, charts, drawings, and photographs. Richly annotated examples enable students to see the book's advice in action.
- **Applications.** Chapters 16 through 19 provide detailed advice for applying the reader-centered approach in four situations: when communicating with e-mail and creating websites; when creating a communication collaboratively with a team; when making oral presentations; and when working on client and service-learning projects.
- **Superstructures.** Chapters 20 through 23 take a reader-centered approach to four of the most common types of career-related communications: correspondence, reports, proposals, and instructions. Detailed advice helps students learn how to craft each element of these communications in ways that meet their readers' needs and also achieve the writers' goals.

In addition, Appendix A explains the APA and MLA documentation styles. Appendix B includes a variety of effective projects for student assignments. Downloadable and editable versions of projects are available at the book's website.

ADDITIONAL ENHANCEMENTS IN THIS EDITION

The sixth edition provides new and revised discussions of many other critically important topics.

- **Communication expertise.** Chapter 1 foregrounds the major results of two decades of research into the kinds of expert knowledge possessed by successful on-the-job communicators. This discussion helps students understand the differences between the communication skills and strategies needed to succeed in college and in their careers.
- **Résumé and job application letters.** Revisions to Chapter 2 increase students' ability to write successful résumés, and they provide an enriched overview of the reader-centered approach.
- **Intellectual property and copyright.** Chapter 6 includes an updated discussion that helps students understand the most relevant aspects of intellectual property and copyright law.
- **Internet research.** The *Writer's Reference Guide to Using Five Reader-Centered Research Methods* includes updated information for conducting research on the Internet and for using the electronic resources now available in most libraries.
- **Organization of communication teams.** Chapter 16's revised and updated discussion of various ways that collaborative teams are structured helps students understand the advantages of each alternative.
- **Ethics.** The discussion of ethics is presented in special "ethics guidelines" that fully integrate ethics into the fabric of the book. Most chapters have special exercises that focus on ethical issues particular to the topic of those chapters. This treatment helps instructors include ethics as a consistent theme throughout their courses, rather than as the topic for one day's reading.
- **Exercises.** The exercises at the end of chapters promote students' ability to apply the book's advice. Most chapters include exercises on four topics: developing expertise, communicating online, collaborating, and communicating ethically.
- **Superstructures.** Revisions to Chapters 21, 22, and 23 fully integrate these chapters into the book's unifying emphasis on usability and persuasiveness.
- **Updated MLA and APA documentation style.** Appendix A contains examples of the latest MLA and APA documentation styles.

ENHANCED WEB RESOURCES FOR STUDENTS AND INSTRUCTORS

The book's website provides many additional resources that promote broader, deeper teaching and learning. Chapter-by-chapter and topical links provide ready access to the site's contents.

- **Web links.** Carefully selected links in the Web notes in the margins throughout the text provide students with Internet access to sample communications and additional information related to each chapter.
- **Additional annotated sample documents.** A library of fully annotated sample documents provides additional examples of reader-centered communications for the students' study.
- **Planning Guides and Revision Checklists.** Downloadable Planning Guides and Revision Checklists help students navigate through the process of creating many kinds of communication. Instructors can download and edit these handouts in order to tailor the handouts to their courses and assignments.
- **Exercises.** Downloadable copies of selected exercises from the book enable students to work with them in convenient, electronic form. Additional exercises provide students with further opportunities to apply the book's advice.
- **Projects.** All projects from Appendix B appear on the website so students can consult their assignments even when their book isn't handy. Additional projects provide instructors with a wider selection from which to choose assignments that are most appropriate for their students.
- **Cases.** The website also offers a library of cases, some suitable for homework or class discussion, others appropriate for course projects. All can be downloaded by instructors for revision to suit their courses and students.
- **Style and usage guide.** This concise reference source enables students to extend their study of style and usage in on-the-job communications.
- **Chapter quizzes.** Online, interactive quizzes help students test themselves to determine whether they have gathered central concepts and advice from each chapter.
- **Grammar quizzes.** Keyed to the style and usage guide, these quizzes enable students to test their knowledge of grammar and usage.
- **PowerPoint® Presentations.** PowerPoint® presentations for every chapter may be used by students for review and by instructors for discussion of chapter content.
- **Sample syllabi.** Instructors can gain ideas for their courses by consulting the site's collection of sample syllabi.
- **E-mail link to Paul Anderson.** Using this e-mail link, faculty and students can contact Paul with comments, questions, and suggestions.

- **Instructor's Manual.** Accompanying this edition of *Technical Communication* is a new instructor's manual prepared by Professor Lisa McClure of Southern Illinois University. It includes a thorough introduction to the course, information on how to integrate supplemental materials into the class, advice on teaching the exercises and cases in the textbook, alternative cases, projects and exercises, and more. Instructors may request printed copies by calling 1-800-354-9706 and requesting ISBN 1-4130-2749-0, ordering a copy online at http://www.thomson.com/learning/learning_order_samples.jsp, or by downloading a PDF version from the book's website: www.thomsonedu.com/english/anderson.

AUTHOR'S ACKNOWLEDGMENTS

Writing a textbook is truly a collaborative effort to which numerous people make substantial contributions. I take great pleasure in this opportunity to thank the many people who generously furnished advice and assistance while I was working on this sixth edition of *Technical Communication: A Reader-Centered Approach.*

I am grateful to the following individuals, who prepared extensive and thoughtful reviews of the fifth edition and my preliminary plans for the sixth edition: Anne Bliss, University of Colorado-Boulder; Adam Collins, Grambling State University; Suzanne Karberg, Purdue University; Karen R. Schnakenberg, Carnegie Mellon University; Elizabeth Wardle, University of Dayton.

I would also like to thank the following people, who, by participating in a survey, expanded my understanding of the many ways technical communication is taught and helped me identify changes I could make in this edition to more fully support them and other technical communication instructors: Joyce Adams, Brigham Young University; Jacob Agatucci, Central Oregon Community College; Heidi E. Ajrami, Victoria College; Heather J. Allman, University of West Florida; Gillian F. Andersen, Eastern New Mexico University; Ken Andersen, Milwaukee School of Engineering; Joyce Anderson, Millersville University; Bim Angst, Pennsylvania State University–Schuylkill; Susan Baack, Montana State University--Billings; Sandy Balkema, Ferris State University; Brian Ballentine, Case Western Reserve University; Robert Barrier, Kennesaw State University; Nancy Barron, Northern Arizona University; Howard Benoist, Our Lady of the Lake University; Melinda Benton, Umpqua Community College; Thomas Beery, Rhodes State College; Laura Bennett-Kimble, Montcalm Community College; Bruce Bickley, Florida State University; Jennie Blankert, Purdue University; Janet M. Bodner, New Jersey Institute of Technology; Maureen Bogdanowicz, Kapiolani Community College; Michele Bresso, Bakersfield College; CarolAnn Britt, San Antonio College; Jane Gibson Brown, North Carolina Agricultural and Technical State University; Patrick Brown, Indiana University Northwest; Beatrice Capen, State University of New York–Ulster; Brady Carey, Kendall College; Diljit K Chatha, Prairie View A&M University; M. Chesin, John Jay College; Beth Collins, Iowa State University; Janice Cooke, University of New Orleans; Nancy W.

Coppola, New Jersey Institute of Technology; Ken Cox, Florence-Darlington Technical College; Michelle Cox, University of New Hampshire; Huey Crisp, University of Arkansas at Little Rock; Sally Crisp, University of Arkansas at Little Rock; Susan Cunningham, Ohlone College; Waneta Davis, Coffeyville Community College; Rose Day, Albuquerque Technical Vocational Institute Community College; David Dayton, Towson University; Betty Dennison, Marshall Community & Technical College; Bonnie Devet, College of Charleston; Emily Dial-Driver, Rogers State University; Anthony Di Renzo, Ithaca College; Mike Donaghe, Eastern New Mexico University; Matthew Drumheller, McMurry University; Crystal Edmonds, Robeson Community College; Stacie Egan, Weber State University; Dawn Elmore-McCrary, San Antonio College; Ernest Enchelmayer, Louisiana State University; Bonnie W. Epstein, Plymouth State University; Heidi Erickson, Northwestern College; Wendy Erman, Lewis-Clark State College; Henry A. Etlinger, Rochester Institute of Technology; Donna Faber, Miles Community College; Michael A. Fairley, Richmond Community College; Joyce Fisher, Henry Ford Community College; Eileen Fitzsimmons, Sage College of Albany; Phyllis Fleming, Patrick Henry Community College; M. L. Flynn, South Dakota State University; Marge Freking, Minnesota State University, Mankato; Alexander Friedlander, Drexel University; Duke Fuehrer, Concordia University, St. Paul; Elizabeth Giddens, Kennesaw State University; Tim Giles, Georgia Southern University; June Griffin, University of Georgia; Karen Gulbrandsen, Iowa State University; Sue Hagedorn, Virginia Polytechnic Institute and State University; Darryl E. Haley, East Tennessee State University; Donna Halford, Texas A&M University–Kingsville; Larry D. Hansen, Madison Area Technical College; Lila Harper, Central Washington University; M. Suzanne Harper, Pennsylvania State University–Worthington Scranton; Sheryl Harrell, Roanoke-Chowan Community College; Carey Harrington, University of Colorado at Colorado Springs; Dawn Hayden, Thomas Nelson Community College; Pat Heintzelman, Lamar University; Pat Herb, North Central State College; David Howell, Milwaukee School of Engineering; Michael Hricik, Westmoreland County Community College; Dollie Hudspeth, St. Philip's College; Carolyn Robbins Hyde, Roanoke-Chowan Community College; Dawnelle Jager, Syracuse University; Ann Jagoe, North Central Texas College; Florence Johnson, North Dakota State College of Science; Kathy Johnston, Iowa State University; Amy Jurrens, Northwest Iowa Community College; Suzanne Karberg, Purdue University; Erin Karper, Niagara University; Carolyn J. Kelly, Iowa State University; Sandra Kelly, Roanoke College; Millard Kimery, Howard Payne University; Charles Klingensmith, Pennsylvania State University–New Kensington; Benedda Konvicka, Terleton State University; Tracy Lassiter, Eastern Arizona College; Susan Latta, Indiana State University; Barbara L'Eplattenier, University of Arkansas at Little Rock; Tom Lewis, Oklahoma Panhandle State University; Rhonda Linseman, Northwood University; Keming Liu, Medgar Evers College; Richard Lombardo, University of Nebraska–Lincoln; Ralph Maass, Nebraska Indian Community College; Anna Maheshwari, Schoolcraft College; David Major, Austin Peay State University; Ana R. Malitzke-Goes, Northern Virginia Community College; Mickey Marsee, University of New Mexico–Los

Alamos; Joseph McCallus, Columbus State University; Michael A. McCord, Minnesota State University–Moorhead; Karen L. McCullough, Georgia Southern University; Jeannine McDevitt, Pennsylvania Highlands Community College; Nancy McGee, Macomb Community College; Hawkinson Melkun, University of Mary Washington; Robert Milde, Eastern Kentucky University; Christine Miller, Davenport University; Christine Mitchell, Southeastern Louisiana University; Andrea Modica, University of Colorado at Denver; Dorothy Morrison, University of Minnesota–Duluth; Mary Ellen Muesing, University of North Carolina at Charlotte; Teresa Murden, The University of Texas at Brownsville; Kris Muschal, Richland Community College; Laju Nankani, Centralia College; Kathy Neal, York Technical College; Lisa R. Neilson, State University of New York–Ulster; Marguerite Newcomb, University of Texas at San Antonio; Chari Norgard, University of Houston–Victoria; Matthew S. Novak, California Polytechnic State University; Nancy Nygaard, University of Wisconsin–Milwaukee; Kristen L. Olson, Pennsylvania State University–Beaver; Erin O'Neill, School of Arts and Humanities/UAM; Scott Orme, Spokane Community College; Andrew Otieno, Northern Illinois University; Pratul Pathak, California University of Pennsylvania; Jeni Patton, Cochise College; Felicity Pearson, University of Tennessee; Joe Pellegrino, University of South Carolina Upstate; David Phillips, Charleston Southern University; Kerry Phillips, California State University–Sacramento; Katharine Pionke, Harper College; Roxanna Pisiak, Morrisville State College; Liza Pots, Rensselaer Polytechnic Institute; Tamara Powell, Louisiana Tech University; Pete Praetorius, Matanuska-Susitna College; Kenneth Price, University of Alaska–Anchorage; Linda Pridgen, Richmond Community College; Cheryl Raleigh, University of Maryland University College; Nora E. Ransom, Kansas State University; Timothy D. Ray, West Chester University of Pennsylvania; James W. Richardson Jr., Morehouse College; Renee Riess, Hill College; Charles Riley, Baruch College, The City University of New York; Sherry Robertson, Arizona State University; Judith Rosenberg, College of Lake County; John Rothfork, Northern Arizona University; Mary R. Ryder, South Dakota State University; Penny Stockman Sansbury, Florence-Darlington Technical College; Jennifer Santos, Arizona State University; Dave Sawyer, North Hennepin Community College; Patrick Scanlon, Rochester Institute of Technology; Jane Schreck, Bismarck State College; Holly Schullo, University of Louisiana at Lafayette; Alan B. Sevison, Brigham Young University; Kristi Shackelford, James Madison University; Seema Shrikhande, Oglethorpe University; William Sprunk, Lake Michigan College; Caroline Stern, Ferris State University; Brent L. Stiles, Troy University; Brenda Stubbs, Navarro College; Lee Tesdell, Minnesota State University, Mankato; Shelley Thomas, Weber State University; Charlotte Thralls, Western Michigan University; Katherine Tirabassi, University of New Hampshire; Donna Townsend, Baker College of Clinton Township; Lisa Veasey, Washtenaw Community College; Molly Voorheis, Syracuse University; Janice R. Walker, Georgia Southern University; Joel Westwood, California Polytechnic State University–San Luis Obispo; Deanna White, University of Texas at San Antonio; Mary W. White, Lees-McRae College; Melanie Whitebread, Luzerne County Community College; Russell Willerton,

Texas Tech University; Matt Willen, Elizabethtown College; Richard Williamson, Muskingum College; Delinda Wunder, Community College of Aurora; Michael Young, La Roche College; Bo Yu, North Hennepin Community College.

As I began writing this edition, I received an abundance of helpful suggestions from the following individuals, who meticulously reviewed evolving drafts of key chapters: Janice Cooke, University of New Orleans; Dawnelle Jager, Syracuse University; Amber Lancaster, Texas Tech University; John Rothfork, Northern Arizona University.

While developing this edition, I have benefited from the thoughtful and energetic assistance of an extraordinary group at Wadsworth/Thomson Higher Learning. Dickson Musselwhite helped me define this edition's goals. Lianne Ames and Ed Dodd skillfully shepherded the book through the many phases of development and production. I am very grateful to Kathy Smith for her exceptional support during production. Christina Micek contributed abundant resourcefulness and tenacity while conducting photo research. I owe special thanks to Lisa McClure (Southern Illinois University) for her outstanding work on the instructor's manual for the book. Michael Rosenberg's confidence that this edition would turn out well has been indispensable.

For this edition, Betty Marak, who has read this book more than anyone else over the years, assisted me again in preparing the manuscript. Kirsten Anderson of Turnstone Design helped me plan this edition's spreads for the Writer's Tutorials and the Writer's Reference Guides. Jeff Mahrt, Rachel Marht, and Melissa Steckhahn provided user testing (see Chapter 15) of several Writer's Tutorials. All my work in technical communication benefits from many conversations with and numerous examples of excellent teaching provided by Jean Lutz. I am deeply indebted to all of these individuals.

I am also grateful to David Bruce, who has written and e-mailed many times over the years to share suggestions he has developed while teaching with the various editions of this book at Ohio University.

Finally, I thank my family. Their encouragement, kindness, and good humor have made yet another edition possible.

PAUL V. ANDERSON
Oxford, Ohio

PART I INTRODUCTION 引言

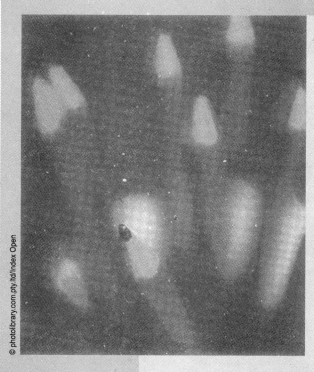

Chapter 1 Communication, Your Career, and This Book

Chapter 2 Overview of the Reader-Centered Communication Process: Obtaining a Job

Communication, Your Career, and This Book
交流，职业，以及本书

CHAPTER OVERVIEW

- Communication Expertise Will Be Critical to Your Success **4**
- Writing at Work Differs from Writing at School **5**
- At work, Writing Is an Action **10**
- The Main Advice of This Book: Think Constantly about Your Readers **10**
- Qualities of Effective On-the-Job Communication: Usability and Persuasiveness **11**
- The Dynamic Interaction between Your Communication and Your Readers **12**
- Some Reader-Centered Strategies You Can Begin Using Now **18**
- Communicating Ethically **19**
- What Lies Ahead in This Book **21**
- Guidelines, Your Creativity, and Your Good Judgment **22**

From the perspective of your professional career, communication is one of the most valuable subjects you will study in college.

Why? Imagine what your days at work will be like. If you are majoring in an engineering, technical, or other specialized field, you will spend much of your time using the special knowledge and skills you learned in college to answer questions asked by coworkers and complete projects assigned by managers. Furthermore, you will generate many good ideas on your own. Looking around, you'll discover ways to make things work better or do them less expensively, to overcome problems that have stumped others, or to make improvements others haven't begun to dream about.

Yet all your knowledge and ideas will be useless unless you communicate them to someone else. Consider the examples of Sarah Berlou and Larry Thayer. A recent college graduate who majored in metallurgy, Sarah has spent three weeks analyzing pistons that broke when her employer tested an experimental automobile engine. Her analysis has been skillful. Her conclusions are valid. However, the insights she gained about why the pistons failed will be useless to her employer unless she communicates them clearly and usefully to the engineers who must redesign the pistons. Similarly, Larry, a nutritionist newly hired by a hospital, has several ideas for improving the efficiency of the hospital's kitchen. However, his ideas will reduce costs and improve service to patients only if he presents his recommendations persuasively to the people who have the power to implement them.

> For additional information, examples, and exercises related to this chapter, visit this book's website (www.thomsonedu.com/english/anderson) and click on Chapter 1.

COMMUNICATION EXPERTISE WILL BE CRITICAL TO YOUR SUCCESS
交流技能对成功至关重要

College graduates typically spend one day a week — or more — writing.

Like Sarah and Larry, you will be able to make your work valuable to others only if you communicate it effectively. Numerous studies indicate that the typical college graduate spends about 20 percent of his or her on-the-job time writing (Beer & McMurrey, 1997). That's one day out of every five-day work week! And it doesn't include the additional time spent talking — whether on the phone or in person, whether in groups and meetings or one-on-one. Writing is so important to employers that they spend an estimated $3.1 billion annually on writing instruction for their employees (National Commission on Writing, 2004).

The ability to write well increases your promotabilty.

Moreover, your ability to write well can significantly increase the success you enjoy in your career. Researcher Stephen Reder discovered that college graduates judged to be in the top 20 percent of writing ability earn, on average, more than three times as much as workers rated in the bottom 20 percent of writing ability (Fisher, 1998). In a survey of leading employers, the National Commission on Writing (2004) found that writing skills is a major consideration for promotion. As one employer stated, "You can't move up without writing skills." Of course, good writing is equally important as you search for the job that will begin your career.

This book's goal is to help you develop the communication expertise you must have in order to realize the full potential of your expertise in your specialized field.

Developing your communication expertise will be even more important if you have chosen a career as a technical, scientific, medical, or professional communicator. Work in these fields is ideal for persons who love to learn and communicate about technical and scientific advances. Employed by private corporations, non-profit organizations, and government agencies, these communication specialists typically create print and online multimedia communications on topics that match their personal interests, such as computers, health, and environmental science.

In addition to being essential to your career, communication expertise will enable you to make valuable contributions to your campus or community. Volunteer organizations, service clubs, and committees of local government will welcome your assistance in writing clear and compelling reports, proposals, and other documents. When confronting complex decisions about environmental standards, economic policy, and other issues, the citizens of your community will be grateful for your ability to explain technical, scientific, and other specialized subjects in ways they can understand.

> For more information on careers in technical communication and related fields, go to **www.thomsonedu.com/english/anderson** and click on Chapter 1.

WRITING AT WORK DIFFERS FROM WRITING AT SCHOOL
工作中的写作不同于学校中的写作

This book assumes you already know many things about effective communication that will be indispensable to you in your career. It also assumes you must learn new skills — and even new ways of thinking about communication — in order to develop the expertise required on the job. That's because writing in the workplace differs from writing at school in many important ways. The following sections discuss the key differences with respect to writing. Similar differences exist for oral communication.

Serves Practical Purposes

As a student, you write for *educational* purposes. Instructors ask you to compose term papers, prepare laboratory reports, and take written exams to help you learn the course material and enable you to demonstrate your mastery of a subject. They read your papers, projects, and tests primarily to assess your knowledge and assign a grade. They are unlikely to rely on what you say as a guide for their own beliefs or actions. On the job, in contrast, people write for *practical* purposes, such as helping their employer improve a product or increase efficiency. Readers are coworkers, customers, or other individuals who *need* the writer's information and ideas in order to pursue their own practical goals.

These different purposes profoundly affect the kinds of communication you need to produce. Consider just one example. In college, where your aim is to show how much you know, one of your writing strategies is probably to say as much as you can about your subject. At work, where you will write to support or influence other people's actions, your strategy should be to include only the information your readers require — no matter how much more you know. Extra information will only clog your readers' paths to what they need, thereby decreasing their efficiency and creating frustration. Developing skill at determining exactly what your readers need is one of the major steps in acquiring expertise in workplace communication.

Addresses Complex Audiences

When you write a paper in college, you most often write to a single person: your instructor. At work, however, you will often create a single communication that addresses a wide variety of people who differ from one another in many important ways, including their familiarity with your specialty, the way they will use your information, and their professional and personal concerns. The audience for Larry's report recommending changes to the hospital kitchen is complex in this way. His readers include his supervisor, who will want to know how operations in her area would have to change if Larry's recommendations were adopted; the vice president for finance, who will want to analyze Larry's cost estimates; the director of personnel, who will want to know how job descriptions will need to be rewritten; and members of the labor union, who will want assurances that the new work assignments will treat them fairly. When you are writing in situations like Larry's, you will need expertise at constructing one communication that simultaneously satisfies an array of individuals who will each read it with a different set of concerns and goals in mind.

Addresses International and Multicultural Audiences

> **Learn More**
>
> To learn strategies for addressing international and intercultural communication audiences, read the Global Guidelines included in most of the other chapters.

Also, when writing at work, you may often address readers from other nations and cultural backgrounds. Many organizations have clients, customers, and suppliers in other parts of the world. Thirty-three percent of U.S. corporate profits are generated by international trade (Lustig & Koester, 1993), and the economies of many other nations are similarly linked to distant parts of the globe. Corporate and other websites are accessed by people around the planet. Even when communicating to coworkers at your own location, you may address a multicultural audience — persons of diverse national and ethnic origins.

Uses Distinctive Types of Communication

In addition, people create a wide variety of job-related communications that aren't usually prepared at school, including memos, business letters, instructions, project proposals, and progress reports. Each of these types of communication has its own conventions, which you must follow to write successfully.

Employs Graphics and Visual Design to Increase Effectiveness

When writing at school, you may be accustomed to writing assignments that involve only words. At work, however, tables, charts, drawings, photographs, and other graphics are as important as written text in communicating facts and shaping attitudes. To write effectively, you will need expertise in creating graphics and in arranging your graphics and text on a page or computer screen in ways that make your communications visually appealing, easy to understand, and easy to navigate. Figure 1.1 shows a page from an instruction manual that illustrates the importance of graphics and visual design.

> **Learn More**
>
> To learn strategies for using graphics and visual design to achieve your communication objectives on the job, see Chapters 12 and 13.

Requires Collaboration

You are much more likely to write collaboratively at work than at school. Eighty-seven percent of the college graduates studied by researchers Lisa Ede and Andrea Lunsford (1990) reported that they write with cowriters at least some of the time. For long documents, the number of cowriters is sometimes astonishingly large. Martin Marietta Corporation's multivolume proposal to build the international space station contained text and drawings by more than 300 engineers (Mathes & Stevenson, 1991). Even when you prepare communications alone, you may consult your coworkers, your boss, and even members of your intended audience as part of your writing process.

In one common form of collaboration, you will need to submit drafts of some of your communications for review by managers and others who have the power to demand changes. The number of reviewers may range from one to a dozen or more, and some drafts go through many cycles of review and revision before obtaining final approval. Communication expert Carolyn Boiarsky (1993) describes one memo that went through more than a hundred drafts!

© Anton Vengo/SuperStock

On the job, groups of employees often work together to plan, draft, and revise proposals, reports, and other printed, online, and oral communications.

Shaped by Social and Political Factors

Every communication situation has social dimensions. In the writing done at school, the key social relationship is that of a student to the teacher who assigned the paper or project. At work, you will have a much wider variety of relationships with your readers, such as manager and subordinate, customer and supplier, coworker and coworker. Sometimes these relationships will be characterized by cooperation and goodwill. At others, they will be fraught with competitiveness as people strive for recognition, power, or money for themselves and their departments.

FIGURE 1.1
Page that Illustrates the Importance of Graphics and Visual Design

The visually prominent heading explains what readers will learn from this page.

The drawings show exactly what a reader needs to do to clean the printer; they even show a hand performing these tasks.

The drawings include arrows to indicate the direction of movement.

Each numbered drawing corresponds to the step with the same number.

The numbers for the drawings and steps are visually prominent to help readers match each drawing with its corresponding step.
- In the steps, the numbers are bold and placed in a column of their own.
- In the drawings, the numbers are large and bold.

The cautions are highlighted visually.
- Horizontal lines (called rules) set the cautions off from the text.
- The word *Caution* is printed in bold and blue.

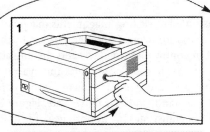

To Clean the Printer

1. Turn the printer off and unplug the power cable, and then open the printer's top cover by pressing the top cover release on the side of the printer.

2. Remove toner cartridge.

Caution
Because light damages the cartridge's photosensitive drum, do not expose the cartridge to light for more than a few minutes.

3. With a dry lint-free cloth, wipe any residue from the paper path area and the toner cartridge cavity as shown.

4. Remove the cleaning brush from the shoulder above the toner cartridge area. Place the flat part of the brush on the shoulder while allowing the brush to be inserted below the shoulder where the mirror is located. Move the brush from side to side several times to clean the mirror.

5. Replace the brush and toner cartridge, close the top cover, plug in the power cable, and then turn the printer on.

Caution
Do not touch the transfer roller (shown in the illustration) with your fingers. Skin oils on the roller can cause print quality problems.

Caution
If toner gets on your clothes, wipe it off with a dry cloth and wash your clothes in **cold** water. Hot water sets toner into fabric.

Troubleshooting and Maintenance 4-19

At the side of this and every page in the manual is a colored rectangle that gives the section number and title. These rectangles help readers flip quickly to the specific information they need.

This page from an instruction manual for a computer printer illustrates the way graphics and visual design work together with words in technical communications.

CHAPTER 1 **Communication, Your Career, and This Book**

You will need to attune the style, tone, and overall approach of each communication to these social and political considerations.

Shaped by Organizational Conventions and Culture

In addition, each organization has a certain style that reflects the way it perceives itself and presents itself to outsiders. For example, an organization might be formal and conservative or informal and innovative. Individual departments within organizations may also have their own styles. On the job, you will be expected to understand the style of your organization and employ it in your writing.

Must Meet Deadlines

At work, your deadlines for completing communications are much more significant — and changeable — than the deadlines for the papers you write at school. For example, when a company prepares a proposal or sales document, it must reach the client on time. Otherwise, it may not be considered at all — no matter how good it is. Employers sometimes advise that "it's better to be 80 percent complete than 100 percent late."

Produced with Advanced Computer Technology

On the job, writers often use advanced computer programs and employ advanced features of less specialized software. For example, advanced features of Microsoft Word enable you to compare drafts to identify every change and to work on a communication at the same time that other writers are also working on it. Similarly, you can link an online report or a PowerPoint presentation to an Excel spreadsheet so that when the data in the spreadsheet are changed (perhaps through the automatic operation of a database), the report changes as well.

Sensitive to Legal and Ethical Issues

Under the law, most documents written by employees represent the position and commitments of the organization itself. Company documents can even be subpoenaed as evidence in disputes over contracts and in product liability lawsuits. These are among the reasons certain documents are carefully reviewed before being sent to their intended readers.

Even when the law does not come into play, many communications written at work have moral and ethical dimensions. The decisions and actions they advocate can affect many people for better or worse. Because of the importance of the ethical dimension of workplace writing, this book incorporates in most chapters a discussion of ethical issues that may arise in your on-the-job communications.

> For more on the legal and ethical dimensions of workplace communication, go to www.thomsonedu.com/english/anderson and click on Chapter 1.

Ethics are discussed further on page 19.

AT WORK, WRITING IS AN ACTION
工作中，写作是种行动

As you can infer from the preceding section, there is tremendous variety among communications written on the job, depending on such variables as their purposes and readers; organizational conventions and cultures; and the political, social, legal, and ethical contexts in which they are prepared. Some people are hindered in their ability to write effectively in these multifaceted, shifting situations because they mistakenly think of writing as an afterthought, as merely recording or transporting information they developed while acting as specialists in their chosen fields.

Nothing could be further from the truth.

When you write at work, you act. You exert your power to achieve a specific result, to change things from the way they are now to the way you want them to be. Consider, again, the examples of Sarah and Larry. Sarah wants to help her team develop a successful engine. Acting as a metallurgical specialist, she has tested the faulty pistons to determine why they failed. Her ultimate purpose is to help her employer design and produce pistons without flaws. To contribute to the success of the engine, she must perform a writing act. She must compose sentences, construct tables of data, and perform other writing activities in order to present her results in a way the engineers will find useful. Similarly, Larry believes that the hospital kitchen is run inefficiently. Acting as a nutrition specialist, he has devised a plan for improving its operation. For his plan to be put into effect, however, Larry must perform an act of writing. He must write a proposal that will persuade the hospital's decision makers to implement his plan.

The most important thing to remember about the "writing acts" you will perform at work is that they are social actions. Every communication you write will be an interchange between particular, individual people: you and your readers. Perhaps you will be a supervisor telling a coworker what you want done, an adviser trying to persuade your boss to make a certain decision, or an expert helping another person operate a certain piece of equipment. Your reader may be an experienced employee who is uncertain of the purpose of your request, a manager who has been educated to ask certain questions when making a decision, or a machine operator who has a particular sense of personal dignity and a specific amount of knowledge about the equipment to be operated.

Even when writing to a large group of people, your communication will establish an individual relationship between you and each person in the group. Each person will read with his or her own eyes, react with his or her own thoughts and feelings.

THE MAIN ADVICE OF THIS BOOK: THINK CONSTANTLY ABOUT YOUR READERS
本书的主要建议：始终为读者着想

The observation that writing is a social action leads to the main advice of this book: When writing, think constantly about your readers. Think about what they want from you — and why. Think about how you want to help or influence them and how they will react to what you have to say. Think about them as if they were standing right there in front of you while you talked together.

You may be surprised that this book emphasizes the personal dimension of writing more than such important characteristics as clarity and correctness. Although clarity and correctness are important, they cannot, by themselves, ensure that something you write at work will be successful.

For example, if Larry's proposal for modifying the hospital kitchen is to succeed, he will have to explain the problems created by the present operation in a way that his readers find compelling, address the kinds of objections his readers will raise to his recommendations, and deal sensitively with the possibility that his readers may feel threatened by having a new employee suggest improvements to a system they themselves set up. If his proposal fails to do these things, it will not succeed, no matter how "clear and correct" the writing is. A communication may be perfectly clear, perfectly correct, and yet be utterly unpersuasive, utterly ineffective.

The same is true for all the writing you will do at work: What matters is how your readers respond. That's the reason for taking the reader-centered approach described in this book. This approach focuses your attention on the ways you want to help and influence your readers and teaches specific strategies that you can use to achieve those goals.

The importance of thinking constantly about your readers is highlighted by studies in which researchers compared the ways students approach their college assignments with the ways successful workplace communicators approach their writing tasks (Beaufort, 1999; Bereiter & Scardamalia, 1993; Dias & Paré, 2000; Spilka, 1993). These studies reveal that the distinctive feature of the experts' approach is that they consider their readers while deciding about nearly every detail of their communications. When they aren't thinking specifically about the readers themselves, the experts are thinking about the conventions, expectations, and situations that influence their readers' responses to their writing. This book will assist you in developing the same reader-centered approach that is used by these expert communicators.

QUALITIES OF EFFECTIVE ON-THE-JOB COMMUNICATION: USABILITY AND PERSUASIVENESS
有效的职场交流特点：可用性及说服力

A first step in developing your expertise in on-the-job writing is to focus your attention on the two qualities that a workplace communication must have in order to be successful: usability and persuasiveness. Both qualities, of course, must be defined from the readers' perspective.

Usability refers to a communication's ability to help its readers. As explained above, people read at work to gain information they need in order to *do something*. Their tasks may be physical, such as installing a new memory card in a computer. Or their tasks may be mental, as when Sarah's readers use her report to redesign the

Usability defined

pistons and Larry's readers compare his recommended procedures with those currently used in the hospital kitchen. No matter what the readers' task, a workplace communication is highly usable if it enables them to:

- Locate quickly the information they need in order to accomplish their goal.
- Understand the needed information easily and accurately.
- Use the information to complete their task with minimum effort.

If readers have difficulty locating, understanding, or using the information they need, the communication is not as usable, not as helpful, as it should be.

Persuasiveness defined

A communication's persuasiveness is its ability to influence its readers' attitudes and actions. It's easy to imagine why persuasiveness is important in proposals and recommendation reports. However, persuasiveness is also an indispensable quality in *all* on-the-job communications, including ones we often think of as purely informational. For example, experience shows that many people are impatient with instructions. They read them carelessly, if at all. Thus, an instruction manual must persuade potential readers to consult it rather than try things out on their own, possibly damaging products, fouling the equipment, or harming themselves.

As the preceding paragraphs suggest, every communication written at work must have *both* usability and persuasiveness to succeed. In most communications, one of these qualities dominates: usability in instructions, for example, and persuasiveness in proposals. However, the two are always inextricably intertwined. Instructions are effective only if the intended readers are persuaded to use them. A proposal can persuade only if its readers can easily find, understand, and analyze its content. To see how you can combine usability and persuasiveness in a single communication, look at the web page and memo shown in Figures 1.2 and 1.3.

> To view other websites and print documents that combine usability and persuasiveness, go to www.thomsonedu.com/english/anderson and click on Chapter 1.

THE DYNAMIC INTERACTION BETWEEN YOUR COMMUNICATION AND YOUR READERS
交流与读者间的互动

Of course, the people who actually decide whether your on-the-job communications are usable and persuasive will be your readers. Therefore, the more you know about how your readers will read your communications, the better prepared you will be. Consequently, the detailed suggestions in this book are based, in large part, on what researchers have learned about how people read. The following paragraphs describe the three research findings that will be the most useful to you.

- Readers construct meaning.
- Readers' responses are shaped by the situation.
- Readers react moment by moment.

All three research findings stress that writing is not a passive activity for readers but a dynamic interaction between readers and texts.

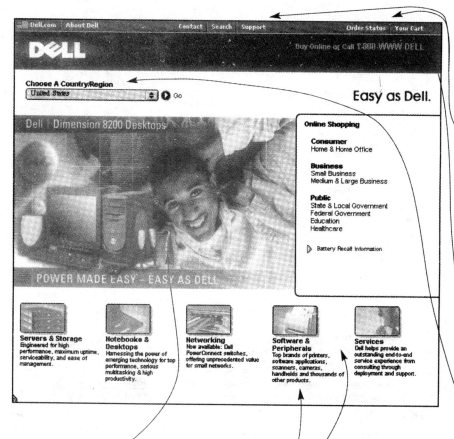

FIGURE 1.2
Web Page that Combines Usability and Persuasiveness

Usability strategies

At the top of the page, the writers provide several links that enable people to find specific information quickly.
- A link to the mailing address and phone number for various company offices.
- A link to a search engine that enables people to locate specific information without navigating through multiple screens.
- A link to support.
- A link that enables people to check the status of orders they've made.

To help people who prefer to buy on the phone rather than online, the writers include the number for Dell's sales agents.

For users around the world, the writers provide links to Dell sites in many countries.

The writers organize their links in ways that help users quickly find the information they want.
- Links on the right-hand side are organized around types of customers.
- Links across the bottom are organized around the products and services people might want.

Persuasive Strategies

To emphasize customer satisfaction with Dell, the writers included a large photograph that shows a smiling, relaxed, and unstressed person.

At the bottom of the page, the writers describe Dell's products in highly favorable ways.

They use bright colors against a white background to create an upbeat, appealing design.

By using large amounts of white space, the writers create an uncrowded, orderly design that reinforces the slogan, "Easy as Dell."

In this homepage, writers at Dell met the challenge of creating a site that would be both usable and persuasive to a wide variety of persons, including consumers and business people, novice and expert computer users, new visitors and longtime customers, as well as persons in the United States and other countries around the world.

FIGURE 1.3
Memo that Combines Usability and Persuasiveness

Usability strategies

In the subject line, Frank tells Alyssa exactly what the memo is about.

Frank uses the first sentence to tell Alyssa how the memo relates to her: It reports on tests she requested.

In the next two sentences, Frank presents the information that Alyssa most needs: The new plastic won't work. She doesn't have to read the entire memo to find this key information.

Using headings and topic sentences, Frank helps Alyssa locate specific details quickly.

He uses bold type to make the headings stand out visually.

By presenting the test results in a list, he enables Alyssa to read through them quickly.

Frank states clearly the significance of each test result.

Persuasive strategies

To build credibility for his results, Frank describes the test method in detail.

To establish the credibility of the conclusion he draws, Frank presents specific details concerning each of the three major problems discovered in the storage tests.

By using lively active verbs (highlighted in color), he creates a vivid, action-oriented writing style.

By preparing a neat and carefully proofread memo, Frank bolsters confidence in the care he takes with his work.

PIAGETT HOUSEHOLD PRODUCTS
Intracompany Correspondence

October 12, 2004

To Alyssa Wyatt
From Frank Thurmond
Subject Test of Salett 321 Bottles for Use with StripIt

We have completed the tests you requested to find out whether we can package StripIt Oven Cleaner in bottles made of the new plastic, Salett 321. We conclude that we cannot, chiefly because StripIt attacks and begins to destroy the plastic at 100°F. We also found other significant problems.

Test Methods
To test Salett 321, we used two procedures that are standard in the container industry. First, we evaluated the storage performance of filled bottles by placing them in a chamber for 28 days at 73°F. We stored other sets of 24 bottles at 100°F and 125° for the same period. Second, we tested the response of filled bottles to environmental stress by exposing 24 of them for 7 days to varying humidities and varying tremperatures up to 140°F.

We also subjected glass bottles containing StripIt to the same test conditions.

Results and Discussion
In the 28-day storage tests, we discovered three major problems:

- StripIt attacked the bottles made from Salett 321 at 100°F and 125°F. At 125°F, the damage was particularly serious, causing localized but severe deformation. Most likely, StripIt's ketone solvents weakened the plastic. The deformed bottles leaned enough to fall off shelves in retail stores.

- The sidewalls sagged slightly at all temperatures, making the bottles unattractive.

- StripIt yellowed in plastic bottles stored at 125°F. No discoloration occurred in glass bottles at this temperature. We speculate that StripIt interacted with the resin used in Salett 321, absorbing impurities from it.

In the environmental test, StripIt attacked the bottles at 140°F.

Conclusion
Salett 321 is not a suitable container for StripIt. Please call me if you want additional information about these tests.

In this memo, Frank, a chemist, uses many usability and persuasive strategies while reporting test results to his boss, Alyssa. The results he reports will help her decide whether to use a newly developed plastic to bottle an oven cleaner manufactured by their employer. This product is sold on supermarket shelves.

Readers Construct Meaning

When researchers say that readers *construct* meaning, they are emphasizing the fact that the meaning of a written message doesn't leap into our minds solely from the words we see. Instead, to derive meaning from the message, we actively interact with it. In this interaction, we employ a great deal of knowledge that's not on the page, but in our heads. Consider, for example, the knowledge we must possess and apply to understand this simple sentence: "It's a dog." To begin, we must know enough about letters and language to decipher the three printed words (*it's*, *a*, and *dog*) and to understand their grammatical relationships. Because they do not possess this knowledge, young children and people from some other cultures cannot read the sentence. Often, we must also bring other kinds of knowledge to a statement in order to understand it. For instance, to understand the meaning of the sentence "It's a dog," we must know whether it was made during a discussion of Jim's new pet or during an evaluation of ABC Corporation's new computer.

In addition to constructing the meanings from individual words and sentences, we build these smaller meanings into larger structures of knowledge. These structures are not merely memories of words we have read. They are our own creations. To demonstrate this point, write a sentence that explains the following heading, which you read earlier in this chapter: "At work, writing is an action." Next, look for a sentence in the book that exactly matches yours. Most likely, you won't find one. The sentence you wrote is not one you remembered. Rather, it is the meaning you constructed through your interaction with the text.

The fact that readers construct the meaning they derive from a communication has many implications for writers that are explored later in this book. An especially important one is this: You should learn as much as possible about the knowledge your readers will bring to your communication so you can create a communication that helps them construct the meanings you want them to build.

Readers' Responses Are Shaped by the Situation

A second important fact about reading is that people's responses to a communication are shaped by the context in which they read — including such things as their purpose for reading, their perception of the writer's purpose, their personal stake in the subject discussed, and their past relations with the writer.

For example, Kate has finished investigating several brands of notebook computers to determine which one would be best for her company to purchase for each of its fifty field engineers. Opening her e-mail, she finds a message asserting that the ABC computer is "a dog." Her response to this statement will depend on many things. Did the information she gathered support this assessment? Was the statement made by a computer specialist, a salesperson for one of ABC's competitors, or the president of Kate's company? Has she already announced publicly her own assessment of the computer, or is she still undecided about it? Depending on the answers to these questions, Kate's response might range anywhere from pleasure that her own judgments have been supported by a well-respected person to embarrassment that her publicly announced judgment has been called into question.

The range of situational factors that can affect a reader's response is obviously unlimited. The key point is that in order to predict how your readers might respond, you must understand thoroughly the situation in which they will read your message.

Readers React Moment by Moment

The third important fact about reading is that readers react to communications moment by moment. When we read a humorous novel, we chuckle as we read a funny sentence. We don't wait until we finish the entire book. Similarly, people react to each part of a memo, report, or proposal as soon as they come to it. Consider the following scenario.

Imagine that you manage a factory's personnel department. A few days ago, you discussed a problem with Donald Pryzblo, who manages the data processing department. Recently, the company's computer began issuing some payroll checks for the wrong amount. Your department and Pryzblo's work together to prepare each week's payroll in a somewhat antiquated way. First, your clerks collect a time sheet for each employee, review the information, and transfer it to time tickets, which they forward to Pryzblo's department. His clerks enter the information into a computer program that calculates each employee's pay and prints the checks. The whole procedure is summarized in the diagram shown here.

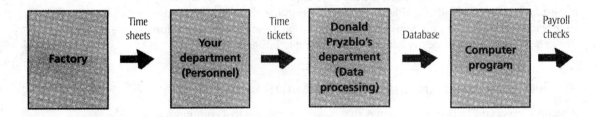

In your discussion with Pryzblo, you proposed a solution he did not like. Because you two are at the same level in the company, neither of you can tell the other what to do. When you turn on your computer this morning, you find an e-mail message from Pryzblo.

Your task in this demonstration is to read the memo *very slowly*— so slowly that you can focus on the way you react, moment by moment, to each statement. First, turn to the e-mail message shown in Figure 1.4 on page 17. Cover it with a sheet of paper. Then slide the paper down the page, stopping after you read the first sentence. Immediately record your reactions (in your role as manager of the personnel department). Proceed in this way through the rest of the message.

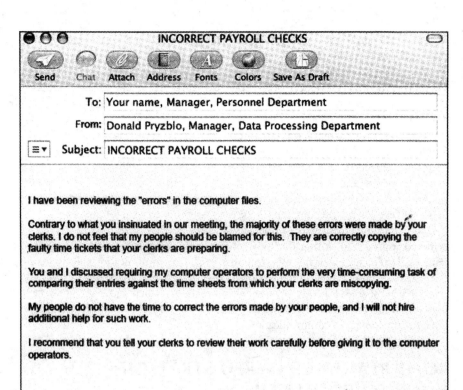

FIGURE 1.4
E-mail Message for Demonstration

Finished? Now look over your notes. Most people who participate in this demonstration find themselves responding strongly to almost every sentence. For example, they react to the quotation marks that surround the word *errors* in the first sentence. The word *insinuated* in the second sentence also draws an immediate response from most readers. (They laugh if they forget to play the role of personnel manager; they cringe if they remember to play the role.)

The fact that readers respond to a communication moment by moment is important to you as a writer because your readers' reaction to any one sentence in a communication you write will influence their reaction to everything they read from that point forward. For example, most people who read Donald Pryzblo's memo while playing the role of personnel manager grow defensive the moment they see the quotation marks around the word *errors,* and they become even more so when they read the word *insinuated.* After they read the third paragraph, their defensiveness hardens into a grim determination to resist any recommendation Pryzblo may make.

A few readers are more even tempered. Instead of becoming defensive, they become skeptical. As they read the first two sentences, they realize Pryzblo is behaving emotionally rather than intellectually, so they evaluate his statements very carefully. When they read his accusation that the personnel department clerks are miscopying the time sheets, they want to know what evidence supports that claim. When the

Readers respond on a moment-by-moment basis.

Readers' reactions in one moment shape their subsequent reactions.

When writing, keep your readers foremost in mind.

next sentence fails to provide any evidence, they feel disinclined to go along with any recommendations from Pryzblo.

Thus, even though individual readers react to the first few sentences of this memo differently, their early reactions shape their responses to the sentences that follow. Consequently, even though Pryzblo's recommendation seems sensible enough, no reader I've met feels inclined to accept it.

Of course, Pryzblo may have had some other purpose in writing his memo. For example, he may have wanted to inflame the personnel manager into responding rashly so he or she would get in trouble with the boss. For that purpose, his memo might have worked very well. But even in that case, the basic points of this demonstration would remain unchanged: People react to what they read on a moment-by-moment basis, and their reactions at each moment shape their reactions to what follows.

The preceding discussion underscores the importance of taking a reader-centered approach to writing, one in which you think constantly about your readers. Each reader creates his or her own response to your communications. To write effectively, you must predict these responses and design your messages accordingly. You will be best able to do this if you keep your readers — their needs and goals, feelings and situations, preferences and responsibilities — foremost in mind throughout your work on each communication.

SOME READER-CENTERED STRATEGIES YOU CAN BEGIN USING NOW
可以从现在开始采取的一些以读者为中心的策略

Despite the many ways readers' goals, concerns, feelings, and likely responses can vary from situation to situation, readers approach almost all on-the-job communications with several widely shared aims and preferences. The following list briefly introduces several reader-centered strategies you can begin using immediately that address these common aims and preferences. All are discussed more fully later in this book. Many are illustrated in the web page and memo shown in Figures 1.2 and 1.3.

- **Help your readers find the key information quickly.** State your main points at the beginning rather than middle or end of your communications. Use headings, topic sentences, and lists to guide your readers to the specific information they want to locate. Eliminate irrelevant information that can clog the path to what your readers want.
- **Use an easy-to-read writing style.** Trim away unnecessary words. Use the active voice rather than the passive. Put action in verbs rather than other parts of speech. To test the effectiveness of these three techniques, researchers James Suchan and Robert Colucci (1989) created two versions of the same report. The high-impact version used the techniques. The low-impact one did not. The high-impact version reduced reading time by 22 percent, and tests showed that readers understood it better.
- **Highlight the points your readers will find to be persuasive.** Present the information your readers will find more persuasive before you present the

information they will find to be less persuasive. Show how taking the actions you advocate will enable them to achieve their own goals. When selecting evidence to support your arguments, look specifically for items you know your readers will find to be credible and compelling.
- **Talk with your readers.** Before you begin work on a report or set of instructions, ask your readers, "What do you want in this communication? How will you use the information it presents?" When planning the communication, share your thoughts or outline, asking for their reaction. After you've completed a first draft, ask for their feedback.

If you cannot speak directly with your readers, talk with them imaginatively. Think of your communication as a conversation in which you make a statement and your reader responds. Write each sentence, each paragraph, and each chapter to create the interaction that will bring about the final outcome that you desire. When following this strategy, it's crucial that you talk *with* your readers, not *to* them. When you talk *to* other people, you are like an actor reciting a speech: You stick to your script without regard to the way your audience is responding. When you talk *with* other people, you adjust your statements to fit their reactions. Does someone squeeze his brows in puzzlement? You explain the point more fully. Does someone twist her hands impatiently? You abbreviate your message. Figure 1.5 on page 20 shows how one writer benefited from "talking" with her reader in this way while drafting one step in a set of instructions.

COMMUNICATING ETHICALLY
交流应符合职业道德

So far, this chapter has introduced concepts and strategies that will serve as the springboard from which you can understand and apply the rest of this book's advice for creating effective communications at work. Because effective communications create change — they make things happen — they also have an important ethical dimension. When things happen, people are affected. Their happiness and even their health and well-being may be impacted. For example, you may write a proposal for a new product that can cause physical harm — at least if not handled properly. You may prepare a report that managers will use to make other people's jobs significantly more — or less — desirable, or even determine whether these people will continue to be employed. Ethical considerations can also apply to impacts on people outside your employer's organization, even future generations, and the environment.

Because technical communications have an important ethical dimension, in addition to providing advice for creating usable, persuasive communications, this book also provides advice for creating ethical ones.

What Is Ethical?

To act ethically, you must first have a sense of what is ethical. At work, you have three major sources for guidance.

FIGURE 1.5
How One Writer Used an Imaginary Conversation with Her Reader to Improve Her Instructions

After writing Step 15, Marti imagined her reader asking, "What should the reading be?" So she revised the direction to answer her reader's question.

Marti then imagined that her readers would ask, "Where is the Table of Values?" So she added more information.

Next, Marti imagined her reader discovering in the Table of Values that the reading on Gauge E was wrong. Her imaginary reader asked, "What should I do now?" Marti answered in her final version.

Marti's Imaginary Conversation with a Reader

Marti's initial direction
15. Check the reading on Gauge E.

Her revised direction
15. Determine whether the reading on Gauge E matches the appropriate value listed in the Table of Values.

Her next revision
15. Determine whether the reading on Gauge E matches the appropriate value listed in the Table of Values (page 38).

Marti's final direction
15. Determine whether the reading on Gauge E matches the appropriate value listed in the Table of Values (page 38).
  • If the value does not match, follow the procedure for correcting imbalances (page 27).

As Marti, a mechanical engineer, wrote instructions for calibrating an instrument for testing the strength of steel beams and other building materials, she imagined how a reader would react to each of her directions. This example shows how Marti used the questions asked by an imaginary reader to revise one step so that it fully met her reader's needs.

To view professional and corporate codes of ethics, go to **www.thomsonedu.com/english/anderson** and click on Chapter 1.

- Professionals in your specialty have probably developed a code of ethics.
- Your employer may also have developed an ethics code. Some companies have even hired professional ethics specialists whom employees may consult.
- Your own sense of values, the ones you developed in your home, community, and studies.

Some students wonder whether it will really be necessary for them to think about their values at work. In your career will you actually be asked to write unethically? The answer depends largely on the company you work for and the managers to whom you report. Based on interviews with top executives, Charles E. Watson (1991) reports that 125 of the largest companies in the United States have a strong commitment to ethical behavior. Employees of these companies, one assumes, receive support and guidance when facing an ethical conflict. Similarly, in *Companies with a Conscience*, Mary Scott and Howard Rothman (1992) describe many instances of values-minded management. And the Center for Business Ethics has a file with hundreds of ethics codes that corporations throughout the United States have adopted as their official policies (see page 124 for an example). Still, we all have read stories about companies that engage in bribery, price gouging, dumping of toxic wastes in public waterways, and other unethical practices. Further, even a company that has adopted an ethics code may have employees who act unethically. A nationwide survey indicates that 50 percent of U.S. employees have felt pressure on the job to act in ways they consider to be unethical (Golen, Powers, & Titkemeyer, 1985).

Because they want to avoid conflicts over values in their careers, some employees have decided that their personal values have no place on the job. But that is a dangerous course. It can lead you into going along with actions at work that you would condemn at home. Furthermore, as companies decide what to do in certain situations, they sometimes discuss quite explicitly the ethical dimensions of the actions they might take. In these discussions, you can influence your employer's organization to act in accordance with your own ethical views, but only if you have brought your values with you to work — and only if you have the communication expertise required to present your view in ways that others find persuasive.

This Book's Approach to Ethics

A basic challenge facing anyone addressing ethical issues in workplace settings is that different people have different values and, consequently, different views of the right actions to take in various situations. This fact should not surprise you. For thousands of years, philosophers have offered various incompatible ethical systems. They have yet to reach agreement. Moreover, people from different cultural backgrounds and different nations adhere to different values. On your own campus, you surely know other students with whom you disagree on ethical issues.

The same thing happens in the workplace. Consequently, this book won't tell you what your values ought to be. Instead, it seeks to help you act in accordance with your own values. Toward that end, it seeks to enhance your sensitivity to often subtle and difficult-to-detect ethical implications so that you don't inadvertently end up preparing a communication that affects people in ways you would wish it hadn't. This book also presents some ways of looking at the ethical aspects of various writing decisions — such as the way you use colors in graphs — that you may not have considered before. Ultimately, however, the book's goals are to help you communicate in ways that, after careful consideration, you believe to be ethical and to enable you to build the communication expertise needed to influence others when you want to raise ethical questions.

These corporations are among the thousands worldwide that have adopted ethics codes to guide employee and company conduct.

Learn More

To learn strategies for recognizing and addressing the ethical issues that arise on the job, read the Ethics Guidelines included in most of the other chapters.

WHAT LIES AHEAD IN THIS BOOK
本书的构成

Throughout this book, you'll find detailed advice and information to help you create highly usable, highly persuasive, and thoroughly ethical communications on the job. Its contents are divided into three major parts.

Major Parts of This Book

- **The Reader-Centered Writing Process.** Chapters 1 through 15 provide reader-centered advice for performing each of the four major activities of writing:
  - Defining your communication's objectives.
  - Planning your communication.
  - Drafting its text and visual elements.
  - Revising your draft.
- **Applications of the Reader-Centered Writing Process.** Chapters 16 through 19 explain how to apply the reader-centered writing process in order to do the following:
  - Create a communication collaboratively.
  - Prepare and deliver oral presentations.
  - Create web pages and websites.
  - Prepare a communication for a client, whether on the job or as a course project.
- **Superstructures.** Chapters 20 though 23 introduce you to the general frameworks, called *superstructures,* and conventions used in the workplace for correspondence (including e-mail), reports, proposals, and instructions.

GUIDELINES, YOUR CREATIVITY, AND YOUR GOOD JUDGMENT
指导方针、创造能力和判断力

This book's guidelines are not rules.

Many of the chapters offer guidelines—brief summary statements designed to make the book's suggestions easy to remember and use. As you read the guidelines, remember that the guidelines are merely that: guidelines. They are not rules. Each one has exceptions, and some of them may even seem to conflict. An essential part of your communication expertise will be your ability to use your creativity and good judgment, guided always by thoughts of your readers and the specific ways you want them to respond to your communication.

To help you learn how to apply the guidelines, the chapters describe many sample situations and show sample communications. These samples reflect typical workplace communication practices. However, what's *typical* is not what's universal. The readers and circumstances you encounter in your job will certainly differ to some extent from those described here. In fact, you may work for a boss or client whose regulations, values, or preferences are very untypical. To write successfully, then, you may need to ignore one or more of this book's guidelines.

No matter what situation you find yourself in, however, the book's overall advice will guide you to success: Whenever you write, focus on your readers and the way you want to affect them, use your knowledge of your readers to shape your message in a way they will find highly usable and highly persuasive, and treat ethically all persons who might be affected by your message. If you learn how to apply this advice with ingenuity and good sense to the typical situations described here, you will have mastered the strategies needed to write successfully in any atypical situation you encounter.

In your effort to develop expertise at communicating in your career, I wish you good luck.

EXERCISES 练习

For additional exercises, go to www.thomsonedu.com/english/anderson. *Instructors:* The book's website includes suggestions for teaching the exercises.

EXPERTISE

1. Interview someone who holds the kind of job you might like to have. Ask about the types of communications the person writes, the readers he or she addresses, the writing process and technology the person uses, and the amount of time the person spends writing. Supplement these questions with any others that will help you understand how writing fits into this person's work. According to your instructor's directions, bring either notes or a one-page report to class.

2. Find a communication written by someone who has the kind of job you want, perhaps by asking a friend, family member, or your own employer. Explain the communication's purposes from the point of view of both writer and readers. Describe some of the writing strategies the writer has used to achieve these purposes.

ONLINE

Explore websites created by two organizations in the same business (airlines, computers, museums, etc.) or two employers for whom you might like to work. Compare the strategies used to make the sites usable and persuasive. Note ways their usability and persuasiveness might be increased.

COLLABORATION

Working with another student rewrite the e-mail message by Donald Pryzblo (Figure 1.4, page 17) so that it will be more likely to persuade the personnel manager to follow Pryzblo's recommendation. Assume that Pryzblo knows that the manager's clerks are miscopying because he has examined the time sheets, time tickets, and computer files associated with 37 incorrect payroll checks; in 35 cases, the clerks made the errors. Take into account the way you expect the personnel manager to react upon finding an e-mail from Pryzblo in his or her in-box. Make sure that the first sentence of your revision addresses a person in that frame of mind and that your other sentences lead effectively from there to the last sentence, which you should leave unchanged.

ETHICS

As a first step in bringing your personal values to your on-the-job communication, list those values that you think will be especially important in your career. Explain situations in which you think it may be especially important for you to be guided by them.

CASE   SELECTING THE RIGHT FORKLIFT TRUCK   选择正确的铲车

For additional cases, go to www.thomsonedu.com/english/anderson. *Instructors:* The book's website includes suggestions for teaching the cases.

It has been two weeks since you received this assignment from your boss, Mickey Chelini, who is the Production Engineer at the manufacturing plant that employs you. "We've been having more trouble with one of our forklift trucks," he explained. You are not surprised. Some of those jalopies have been breaking down regularly for years. "And Ballinger's finally decided to replace one of them," Mickey continued. Ballinger is Mickey's boss and the top executive at the plant. His title is Plant Manager.

"What finally happened to make him decide that?" you asked. "I thought he was going to keep trying to repair those wrecks forever."

"Actually, he wants to replace one of the newer ones that we bought just two years ago," Mickey replied. "That particular forklift was manufactured by a company that has since gone bankrupt. Ballinger's afraid we won't be able to get replacement parts. I think he's right."

"Hmm," you commented.

"Anyway," Mickey said, "Ballinger wants to be sure he spends the company's money more wisely this time. He's done a little investigation himself and has narrowed the choice to two machines. He's asked me to figure out which one is the best choice."

You could see what was coming. You've had a hundred assignments like this before from Mickey.

"I'd like you to pull together all the relevant information for me. Don't make any recommendation yourself; just give me all the information I need to make my recommendation. Have it to me in two weeks."

"Will do," you said, as you started to think about how you could squeeze this assignment into your already tight schedule.

Your Assignment

It's now two weeks later. You've gathered the information given below in the "Notes on Forklifts." First, plan your final report by performing the following activities:

- List the specific questions Mickey will want your report to answer. Note: Your boss does not want you to include a recommendation in your report.
- Underline the facts in your notes that you would include in your report; put an asterisk by those you would emphasize.
- Decide how you would organize the report.
- Explain which techniques from the list on pages 18–19 you would use when writing this report. What other things would you do to assist your readers?

Second, imagine that you have been promoted to Mickey's job (Production Engineer). Tell how you would write the report that you would send to Ballinger about the purchase of a new forklift. It must contain your recommendation.

Notes On Forklifts

Present Forklift. The present forklift, which is red, moves raw material from the loading dock to the beginning of the production line and takes finished products from the Packaging Department back to the loading dock. When it moves raw materials, the forklift hoists pallets weighing 600 pounds onto a platform 8 feet high, so that the raw materials can be emptied into a hopper. When transporting finished products, the forklift picks up and delivers pallets weighing 200 pounds at ground level. The forklift moves between stations at 10 mph, although some improvements in the production line will increase that rate to 15 mph in the next two months. The present forklift is easy to operate. No injuries and very little damage have been associated with its use.

Electric Forklift. The electric forklift carries loads of up to 1,000 pounds at speeds up to 30 mph. Although the electric forklift can hoist materials only 6 feet high, a 2-foot ramp could be built beneath the hopper platform in three days (perhaps over a long weekend, when the plant is closed). During construction of the ramp, production would have to stop. The ramp would cost $1,600. The electric forklift costs $37,250, and a special battery charger costs $1,500 more. The forklift would use about $2,000 worth of electricity each year. Preventive maintenance costs would be about $700 per year, and repair costs would be about $800 per year. While operating, the electric forklift emits no harmful fumes. Parts are available from a warehouse 500 miles away. They are ordered by phone and delivered the next day. The electric forklift has a good operating record, with very little damage to goods and with no injuries at all. It comes in blue and red.

Gasoline Forklift. The gasoline forklift is green and carries loads of up to 1 ton as rapidly as 40 mph. It can hoist materials 12 feet high. Because this forklift is larger than the one presently being used, the company would have to widen a doorway in the cement wall separating the Packaging Department from the loading dock. This alteration would cost $800 and would stop production for two days. The gasoline forklift costs $49,000 but needs no auxiliary equipment. However, under regulations established by the Occupational Safety and Health Administration, the company would have to install a ventilation fan to carry the exhaust fumes away from the hopper area. The fan costs $870. The gasoline forklift would require about $1,800 of fuel per year. Preventive maintenance would run an additional $400 per year, and repairs would cost about $600 per year. Repair parts are available from the factory, which is 17 miles from our plant. Other owners of this forklift have incurred no damage or injuries during its operation.

Overview of the Reader-Centered Communication Process: Obtaining a Job

以读者为中心的交流过程综述：获得一份工作

CHAPTER OVERVIEW

- Central Principles of the Reader-Centered Approach *26*
- A Reader-Centered Approach to Writing Your Résumé *26*
- Electronic Résumés: Special Considerations *45*
- A Reader-Centered Approach to Writing Your Job Application Letter *49*
- Ethical Issues in the Job Search *58*
- Writing for Employment in Other Countries *59*

As explained in Chapter 1, this book aims to help you develop your communication expertise by teaching you the strategies used by successful workplace communicators. At the heart of these communicators' success is the reader-centered way they approach their communications.

This chapter's purpose is to provide you with an overview of the reader-centered approach, which is described in detail throughout the rest of this book. The chapter shows how to take a reader-centered approach in preparing two communications that will play important roles in your career: your résumé and job application letter.

The résumé and job application letter are ideal communications to use in an overview of the reader-centered process because they illustrate with special clarity that the success of your work-related communications depends on your readers' response to them. If your résumé and letter persuade employers to invite you for an interview or offer you a job, they have succeeded. If they don't produce such a response in their readers, they haven't been effective. Thus, in addition to helping you understand how to employ the reader-centered approach to your own on-the-job writing, this chapter will help you see *why* it is important for you to do so.

> To read additional information, see more examples, and access links related to this chapter, go to www.thomsonedu.com/english/anderson and click on Chapter 2.

CENTRAL PRINCIPLES OF THE READER-CENTERED APPROACH
以读者为中心的方法的主要原则

To gain the maximum value from reading this chapter, take a moment to review the central principles of the reader-centered approach. As explained in Chapter 1, this approach's key strategy is simple: Throughout all your work on a communication, think constantly about your readers.

- **As you make each writing decision, consider your readers' characteristics, goals, expectations, situation, and other factors that will shape their response to what you say.**
- **Concentrate on crafting a communication that will be persuasive and usable in your readers' eyes.** Persuasiveness and usability are indispensable qualities of all successful work-related communications.
- **Focus specifically on the ways your readers will respond, moment by moment, while they are reading your communication.** These moments are the only opportunity your communication has to influence your readers directly.

A READER-CENTERED APPROACH TO WRITING YOUR RÉSUMÉ
用以读者为中心的方法写简历

The following sections explain how to apply the central principles of the reader-centered approach to all four activities of the résumé-writing — and communication — process:

- **Defining objectives** for your résumé
- **Planning** what you will say in your résumé and how you will organize it
- **Drafting** your résumé's text, graphics, and visual design
- **Revising** your draft by reviewing it from your readers' perspective and then making the improvements your review suggests

A special section provides advice for preparing web and scannable résumés, which many employers request.

Defining Your Résumé's Objectives

When writing your résumé—or any other workplace communication—you must make many decisions about such things as what to say, how to organize, how to design pages, and so on. The most effective basis for making these decisions is to think about your readers in the act of reading. What will they be looking for? How will they look for this information? How will they use it when they find it? What are their attitudes about your subject and what do you want their attitudes to be when they have finished reading? The answers to these questions will help you create a communication that, during each reading moment, leads readers closer to taking the action you desire. With your résumé, this action is to invite you for an interview or offer you a job.

Identifying Employers

To understand your readers, you must know who they are. When writing a résumé, start by naming the employers to whom you will apply. If you haven't identified the jobs, internships, or co-op positions you'd like, you might talk with instructors in your major and with staff at the college placement office. You might also network by asking family members, friends, former employers, and others to help you spot opportunities. As you speak with each person, ask him or her to suggest others who can assist. Other good sources for leads are newspapers, professional organizations, and professional publications directed to people who have graduated in your major. You can also use the web, consulting such sites as America's Job Bank (www.ajb.dni.us), sponsored by the U.S. Department of Labor; commercial boards such as Monster (www.monster.com); and state and local job listings. If you don't know what kind of job you want, there are resources on the web and, most likely, at your college that can help.

For assistance in deciding what kind of career you would like, go to at **www.thomsonedu.com/english/anderson** and click on Chapter 2.

Defining Your Résumé's Persuasive Objectives

Having identified employers to whom you will apply, create as accurate a mental portrait as you can of the way they will read the résumé you submit to them. Because your résumé's primary objective is to persuade employers that you possess the qualifications they are looking for, begin by determining what these qualifications are.

Learn More

To learn more about creating a portrait of your reader in the act of reading, turn to pages 19 and 24.

At a general level, these qualifications fall into the following three categories:

> **WHAT EMPLOYERS SEEK IN NEW EMPLOYEES**
>
> - **Technical expertise.** Employers want to hire people who can perform their jobs adeptly with a minimum of on-the-job training.
> - **Supporting abilities.** Most jobs require a wide range of abilities beyond the purely technical ones of your degree or specialty. Among others, these often include communication, interpersonal, time management, and project management skills.
> - **Favorable personal qualities.** Employers want to hire motivated, self-directed, and responsible individuals. They also want people who will work well with their other employees as well as with customers, vendors, and others outside the organization.

Of course, for any particular job, employers seek specific technical know-how, supporting abilities, and personal attributes. Instead of asking, "Does this applicant have technical expertise?" an employer will ask, "Can this person analyze geological samples?" "Write computer programs in Linux?" "Manage a consumer electronics store?" Your task is to find out the precise set of technical know-how, supporting abilities, and personal attributes that is sought by the employers to whom you are applying.

To identify these specific qualifications, learn as much as you can about the daily work of people in the position you would like to hold. Interview someone who holds such a position, talk with instructors in your major, and read materials about careers at your library or campus employment center. If you have an advertisement or job description from the employer to whom you are applying, study it carefully. As you identify qualifications the employer wants, put them in a list. The longer and more detailed your list, the better prepared you will be to write a résumé that achieves its persuasive objective, which is to demonstrate you have the knowledge, skills, and personal qualities that employers are seeking.

> **Learn More**
>
> For detailed advice about conducting interview and library research, turn to the Writer's Reference Guide: Using Five Reader-Centered Research Methods, page 165.

Defining Your Résumé's Usability Objectives

In order to succeed, your résumé must not only highlight your qualifications, but also present these facts in a manner that employers find to be highly usable. For résumé readers, the key factor in usability is the speed with which they can find the information they want about you.

Résumés are read in a three-stage process by most employers. At all three stages readers perform the same moment-by-moment reading activity: They compare the information each applicant supplies against the requirements of the job and against the qualifications of the other applicants. However, at each stage they perform this activity in somewhat different ways:

- **Initial screening.** Many employers receive hundreds, even thousands, of applications a week. Faced with this deluge of applications, one person may be charged with scanning quite quickly through résumés, hoping to spot promising candidates. Often such initial readers are employees in a personnel office, not specialists in the area where you are seeking a position. Faced with stacks of résumés to evaluate, these readers spend less than a minute deciding whether to devote additional time examining any particular résumé closely. Unless they can rapidly spot clear, relevant information about an applicant's qualifications, they set the résumé aside and pick up the next one. To reduce this screening workload, an increasing number of employers submit all résumés to a computer first; only those that meet predefined criteria are read by a human.

- **Detailed examination of the most promising applications.** Résumés that pass the initial screening are forwarded to managers and others in the department that wishes to hire a new employee. These readers know exactly what qualifications they desire, and they look specifically for them.
- **Preparation for in-depth interviewing.** Applicants whose résumés are persuasive to second-stage readers are invited for interviews. Their résumés are usually read with great care at this stage. Often managers and others will use the résumé as the basis for questions to ask during the interview.

The differing needs of the readers at these three stages means that you must address the challenge of preparing a résumé that satisfies a first-stage reader's need to find information quickly while also meeting the second- and third-stage readers' need for a substantial amount of specific details about your qualifications.

Planning

In the reader-centered writing process, you first put your objectives to use as you plan the overall strategies you will use in your communication. In this planning stage, you decide what you will include and how you will organize and present this content.

Think Creatively about Your Qualifications

Many people don't realize how many qualifications they have for the position they are applying for. To develop a rich pool of possible contents for your résumé, try beginning with the list you created when detailing the qualifications desired by the employer. Next to each item, put down the course, activity, previous job, or other experience through which you gained or demonstrated the desired knowledge or ability. You might also create a list of your accomplishments and areas of knowledge, noting the connection each item may have with a qualification for the job you want. Talking with someone who holds the job now could spark additional ideas. Later sections in this chapter suggest some other possibilities. As you work at creating a reader-centered résumé, you may decide at some point not to include some of the ideas you have generated, but don't hold back on possibilities now.

Decide How Long Your Résumé Should Be

In planning, people often ask, "How long should my résumé be?" The answer is that it should be as short as possible while still presenting the facts about you that employers will find most persuasive. For most undergraduates, this is one page. However, some undergraduates have extensive qualifications that justify a second page. Many experienced workers do as well. Don't misunderstand this advice, however. Your résumé shouldn't exceed one page unless you are certain you have the qualifications to justify the extra length. If yours runs past one page by a small amount, redesign your layout, edit your content, or delete something to make it fit it on a single page.

Choose the Type of Résumé You Will Prepare

There are two types of résumés from which you can choose:

- **Experiential résumé.** In an experiential résumé, you organize information about yourself around your experiences, using headings such as "Education," "Employment," and "Activities." Under these headings, you describe your experiences in ways that demonstrate that you possess the qualifications the employers want. An experiential résumé is the best choice for most college students and persons new in their careers. Figures 2.1 and 2.2 (pages 34 and 35) show examples of an experiential résumé.
- **Skills résumé.** In a skills résumé, you create key sections around your abilities and accomplishments, using such headings as "Technical Abilities," "Management Experience," and "Communication Skills." Later, you list the college you attended and jobs you've held. Skills résumés work best for people with enough professional experience to be able to list several on-the-job responsibilities and accomplishments in each of several categories. Figure 2.3 (page 39) shows a skills résumé.

Drafting the Text

For many people, drafting the text is the most challenging part of writing a résumé. Because employers must find information quickly and because they want specific, relevant details, every word counts. The following sections provide advice about your general style and about how you can present your qualifications effectively in each section of your résumé.

Writing Style for Résumés

Your writing style, like every other feature of your résumé, should help employers quickly find detailed information about your qualifications that match the qualifications for the job the employer has open.

- **Write concisely.** Typically résumés contain lists of sentence fragments and phrases, not full sentences. Eliminate every word that you can without losing essential information.

Conducted an analysis of the strength of the load-bearing parts	Wordy
Analyzed strength of load-bearing parts	Concise
Member, PreMed Club, 2005–2006 Vice President, PreMed Club, 2006–2007	Wordy
PreMed Club, 2005–2007; Vice President, 2006–2007	Concise

- **Be specific.** Employers find generalities to be ambiguous and unimpressive. Give precise details.

Proficient on the computer	General
Program in Linux, SQL, CAD, and php	Specific
Reduced breakage on the assembly line	General
Reduced breakage on the assembly line by 17%	Specific

- **Watch your verb tenses.** Use the past tense for activities completed. Use the present tense for those you continue to perform.

| Designed automobile suspensions | Completed activity |
| Design aircraft landing gear | Continuing activity |

By convention, the word "I" is not used in résumés.

Name and Contact Information

Help your readers locate your résumé in a stack of applications by placing your name prominently at the top of your page. Enable them to contact you quickly for an interview or with a job offer by including your postal address, e-mail address, and phone number. If you will live at another address during the summer or other part of the year, give the relevant information.

Professional Objective

The statement of your objective serves two important purposes. It provides a focus for your résumé and it tells employers what job you want. Your goal in the rest of your résumé is to make a compelling case that you have the qualifications necessary to do an outstanding job in the position you describe in your objective.

When drafting your objective, take the reader-centered approach of telling what you will *give* to your future employer rather than the writer-centered approach of telling what you want to gain from the employer. Here's a simple, two-step procedure for doing this:

1. **Identify the results sought by the department or unit in which you wish to work.** If you don't know what they are, ask a professor, talk with someone in

the kind of job you want, or contact your campus employment center for assistance.

2. State that your objective is to help achieve those results.

Howard, a senior in sports studies, and Jena, a computer science major, used this process to improve the first drafts of their objectives. Their initial drafts read as follows:

Writer-centered vague objectives

> **Howard:** A position where I can extend my knowledge of nutrition and sports studies
>
> **Jena:** A position as a computer systems analyst in the field of software development with an innovative and growing company

When Howard and Jena considered their statements from their readers' perspective, they realized that they were merely stating what they wanted to gain from their jobs. They said nothing about how they would use their knowledge to benefit their employers. Howard and Jena revised their objectives to read as follows:

Reader-centered, results-oriented revisions

> **Howard:** To develop nutrition and exercise programs that help athletes achieve peak performance
>
> **Jena:** To create software systems that control inventory, ordering, and billing

If you are applying for an internship, co-op, or summer job, tell what you will "help" or "assist" the employer to do.

Objective for internship

> An internship helping design high-quality components for the electronics industry

Some job seekers ask whether they really need to include an objective statement. In fact, an objective may be unnecessary for people advanced in their careers who begin their résumés with a summary of their qualifications and accomplishments that indicate clearly the specific kind of job they are seeking. For people seeking an entry-level job, the objective is essential. However, as résumé expert Susan Ireland (2003) says, for a new college graduate to omit an objective is like saying, "Here's what I've done. Now tell me what I should do next." As you know from the earlier discussion of the way employers read résumés, they are looking for applicants whose qualifications meet their needs. They are not trying to find jobs for applicants.

Education

Place your education section immediately after your identifying information, unless you have had enough work experience to make the knowledge you gained at work more impressive to employers than the knowledge you gained in classes. Name your college, degree, and graduation date. If your grade point average is good, include it. If your average in your major is higher, give it. But don't stop there. Provide additional details about your education that employers will see as relevant to the job you want. Here are some examples.

> **FACTS TO HIGHLIGHT ABOUT YOUR EDUCATION**
> - Advanced courses directly relevant to the job you want (give titles, not course numbers)
> - Courses outside your major that broaden the range of abilities you would bring to an employer
> - Internships, co-op assignments, or other on-the-job academic experiences
> - Special projects, such as a thesis or a design project in an advanced course
> - Academic honors and scholarships
> - Study abroad
> - Training programs provided by employers

You can highlight any of these credentials by giving it a separate heading (for example, "Honors" or "Internship").

The résumés of Jeannie Ryan (Figure 2.1) and Ramón Perez (Figure 2.2) show how two very different college seniors elaborated on the ways their education qualifies them for the jobs they are seeking.

Work Experience

When drafting your work experience section, list the employers, their cities, your job titles, and your employment dates. Then present facts about your work that will impress employers.

> **FACTS TO HIGHLIGHT ABOUT YOUR WORK EXPERIENCE**
> - **Your accomplishments.** Describe projects you worked on, problems you addressed, goals you pursued, products you designed, and reports you helped write. Where possible, emphasize specific results—number of dollars saved, additional units produced, or extra customers served.
> - **Knowledge gained.** Be resourceful in highlighting things you learned that increased your ability to contribute to your future employer. Realizing that her duties of stacking ice cream packages neatly in supermarket freezers might not seem relevant to a job in marketing, Jeannie describes the insight she gained in that job: "Learned to see consumer marketing from the perspectives of both the manufacturer and the retailer" (Figure 2.1).
> - **Responsibilities given.** If you supervised others, say how many. If you controlled a budget, say how large it was. Employers will be impressed that others have entrusted you with significant responsibility.

FIGURE 2.1
Experiential Résumé

Jeannie tells where she can be reached before and after graduation.

She includes her e-mail address.

Jeannie states her specific career objective.

Jeannie emphasizes her thorough preparation by listing many relevant courses.

Jeannie describes a special course related to her career objective.

She provides specific details when highlighting her accomplishment.

She uses bullet lists throughout her résumé to enable her readers to scan her qualifications quickly.

Jeannie tells what she learned that would help her succeed in the job she desires.

Jeannie lists references who can verify her knowledge in each of her areas of expertise that is related to the job she wants.

Jeannie Ryan

Present Address
325 Foxfire Drive, Apt 214
Denver, Colorado 70962
(303) 532-1401

ryanja@acs.udenver.edu

After May 29, 2006
85 Deitrich Court
Flint, Colorado 73055
(303) 344-7329

Objective To conduct market research in a full-service marketing firm with clients in the electronics industry

Education B.S. in Marketing, Minor in Computer Science, University of Denver, May 2006

Specialized Courses
- Analytical Methods for Marketing
- Strategic Marketing Management
- Stochastics
- Programming Computer Games
- Architecture of Small Computers
- Managing Data Sets

Project for Real Client In Advanced Marketing, we used a telephone survey and focus groups to estimate the potential market for a new hand-held learning game for pre-school children.

Work Experience
Interim Manager, Stan's Electronics, Redvale, Colorado, Summer 2005
- Collaborated with buyer to project product sales and advertising
- Sales increased 15% over the previous year

Sales Intern, Ali Ice Cream Company, Wilke, Colorado, Summer 2004
- Built backroom inventories, stocked cases, and secured endcap displays
- Learned to see consumer marketing from the perspectives of manufacturers and retailers

Tels Marquart, Inc., Redvale, Colorado, Summer 2000
- Receptionist
- Learned to work in a fast-paced office environment

Activities Synchronized Swim Team 2002–2006
- Vice President (Senior Year)
- Planned and directed an hour-long public program for this 50-member club

References
Harlan Betrus-Holloway, Professor, Marketing Department, University of Denver, 199 S. University Blvd., Denver, Colorado 80208, 303-871-3418
Sheila Cortez, Professor, Computer Science Department, 199 S. University Blvd., Denver, Colorado 80208, 303-871-1547
Raphael Tedescue, President, Stan's Electronics, 1176 Sunnyside Avenue, Redvale, Colorado 79638, 303-461-9872.

To see how Jeannie designed her résumé in a word-processing program, go to **www.thomsonedu.com/english/anderson.**

FIGURE 2.2
Résumé of a Person Who Completed College While Working Full-Time

---

Ramón Perez
16 Henry Street
Brooklyn, New York 11231
Work: (212) 374-7631
Home: (718) 563-2291

Ramón tells how he can be reached at work and home.

Professional Objective
A position as a systems analyst where I can use my knowledge of computer science and business to develop customized systems for financial institutions

He tells what he will do to help the employer achieve its goals.

Education
New York University. *B.S. in Computer Science*
December, 2006
GPA 3.4 overall; 3.7 in major

Ramón includes his excellent GPA.

Computer classes include artificial intelligence and expert systems, computer security, data communication, deterministic systems, and stochastics

Business classes include accounting, banking, finance, and business law

He emphasizes his preparation in both computers and business.

Worked full-time while completing last half of course work

Ramón highlights his achievement in completing his degree while working full-time.

Honors
Dean's List three times
Golden Key National Honor Society

He emphasizes his honors by giving them their own heading.

Related Work
Miller Health Spas, New York City, 2004–Present
Data Entry Clerk
- Helped convert to a new computerized accounting system
- Served on the team that wrote user documentation for the system
- Trained new employees
- Earned Employee of the Month Award twice

Ramón lists specific on-the-job accomplishments.

He establishes that he was recognized as a good employee.

Meninger Bank, New York City, 2000–2004
Teller
- Performed all types of daily, night-deposit, and bank-by-mail transactions
- Proved the vault, ordered currency, and handled daily cash flow
- Learned how financial computer systems look from tellers' viewpoint

Ramón notes substantial responsibilities he was assigned; he uses a technical term of the field ("proved the vault").

Activities
Juvenile Diabetes Foundation, 2003–Present
Volunteer
- Helped design a major fundraising event two years in a row
- Successfully solicited two million dollars in contributions from sponsors

References

Professor Max Dobric	Professor R. Paul Berg	Wilson Meyerhoff
Computer Science Department	Finance Department	Senior Accountant
New York University	New York University	Miller Health Spas
New York, NY 12234	New York, NY 12234	3467 Broadway
(212) 998-1212	(212) 998-7635	New York, NY 12232
		(212) 671-9007

He includes his references in his résumé.

Ramón emphasizes a specific achievement, naming the amount of money involved.

To see how Ramón designed his résumé in a word-processing program, go to www.thomsonedu.com/english/anderson.

A Reader-Centered Approach to Writing Your Résumé

When organizing and describing your work experience, follow these guidelines for achieving high impact.

ORGANIZING AND DESCRIBING YOUR WORK EXPERIENCE

- **List your most impressive job first.** If your most recent job is your most impressive, list your jobs in reverse chronological order. To highlight an older job, create a special heading for it, such as "Related Experience." Then describe less relevant jobs in a later section entitled "Other Experience."
- **Put your actions in verbs, not nouns.** Verbs portray you in action. Don't say you were responsible for the "analysis of test data" but that you "analyzed test data." Avoid such weak phrases as "responsibilities included" or "duties were."
- **Use strong verbs.** When choosing your verbs, choose specific, lively verbs, not vague, lifeless ones. Avoid saying simply that you "made conceptual engineering models." Say that you "designed" or "created" the models. Don't say that you "interacted with clients" but that you "responded to client concerns."
- **Use parallel constructions.** When making parallel statements, use a grammatically correct parallel construction. Nonparallel constructions slow reading and indicate a lack of writing skill.

NOT PARALLEL	PARALLEL
• Trained new employees	• Trained new employees
• Correspondence with customers	• Corresponded with customers
• Prepared loan forms	• Prepared loan forms

Learn More

For more information about putting actions in verbs, see Chapter 8, page 265.

Changing *correspondence* to *corresponded* makes it parallel with *trained* and *prepared*.

Activities

At the very least, participation in group activities indicates that you are a pleasant person who gets along with others. Beyond that, it may show that you have acquired certain abilities that are important in the job you want. Notice, for instance, how Jeannie Ryan describes one of her extracurricular activities in a way that emphasizes the essentially managerial responsibilities she held (Figure 2.1):

Emphasis on management responsibilities

Synchronized Swim Team
Vice President (Senior Year)
• Planned and directed an hour-long public program for this 50-member club.

Special Abilities

Let employers know about exceptional achievements and abilities of any sort, using such headings as "Foreign Languages" or "Certifications."

Interests

If you have interests such as golf or skiing that could help you build relationships with coworkers and clients, you may wish to mention them, although a separate section for interests is unnecessary if the information is provided in your activities section.

Personal Data

Federal law prohibits employers from discriminating on the basis of sex, religion, color, age, or national origin. It also prohibits employers from inquiring about matters unrelated to the job for which a person has applied. For instance, employers cannot ask if you are married or plan to marry. Many job applicants welcome these restrictions because they consider such questions to be personal or irrelevant. On the other hand, federal law does not prohibit you from giving employers information of this sort if you think it will help to persuade them to hire you. If you include such information, place it at the end of your résumé, just before your references. It is almost certainly less impressive than what you say in the other sections.

References

Many job applicants omit their references from their résumés, including instead a line that reads, "References available upon request." This is a mistake. Research shows that most employers want applicants to include references with their résumés (Bowman, 2002). By including your references, you increase your résumé's usability by enabling employers to contact them immediately and directly without having to write to you and then wait for your reply. You also increase your résumé's persuasiveness by letting readers see the names and titles of the impressive people who will speak favorably about you. If your references won't fit on your page, create a separate page entitled "References" and enclose it with your résumé.

Employers expect three to five references, so include this many. Select a mix of people who, taken together, can describe the range of your qualifications. As appropriate, choose instructors in your major and other key courses, former employers, and advisers of campus organizations. Avoid listing your parents and their friends, who (an employer might feel) are going to say nice things about you no matter what. Provide titles, business addresses, phone numbers, and e-mail addresses. If one of your references has changed jobs so that his or her business address doesn't indicate how the person knows you, provide the needed information: "My supervisor while at Sondid Company." Obtain permission from the people you want to list as references so they aren't taken by surprise by a phone call. Give your résumé to your references so they can quickly review your qualifications when they receive an inquiry from an employer.

Tailoring Résumés to Specific Employers

The preceding discussion has emphasized the importance of tailoring every feature of a communication to the needs and goals of the specific readers you are addressing. But what if you are going to apply to more than one employer?

If you are seeking the same type of position with both employers and if both employers are seeking the same qualifications, the same résumé will probably work equally well with both.

However, the farther apart the two positions are, the more adjustments you should make. In addition to rewriting your objective, you may need to reshape the descriptions of your education, experience, and activities; reorder your résumé's contents; and even change the information you include about yourself.

Drafting the Text for a Skills Résumé

A skills résumé has the same aims as an experiential one. The chief difference is that in a skills résumé you consolidate the presentation of your accomplishments and experience in a special section located near the beginning rather than weave this information into your sections on education, work experience, and activities. Figure 2.3 shows an example.

For this special section, use a title that emphasizes its contents, such as "Skills" or "Skills and Achievements." Within the section, use subheadings that identify the major areas of ability and experience you would bring to an employer. Typical headings include "Technical," "Management," "Financial," and "Communication." However, the specific headings that will work best for you depend on what employers seek when recruiting people for the kind of job you want. For example, the headings in George Shriver's résumé (Figure 2.3) focus specifically on skills required of managers of technical communication departments.

Because you aggregate your skills and accomplishments in a special "Skills" section, the other sections of your skills résumé should be brief in order to avoid redundancy.

Designing Your Résumé's Appearance

At work, good visual design is crucial to achieving communication goals. Nowhere is that more true than with a résumé, where design must support rapid reading, emphasize your most impressive qualifications, and look attractive. The résumés shown in this chapter achieve these objectives through a variety of methods you can use.

DESIGNING YOUR RÉSUMÉ'S VISUAL APPEARANCE

SHORT, INFORMATIVE HEADINGS	DIFFERENT TYPEFACES FOR HEADINGS THAN FOR TEXT
■ Lists	■ White space to separate sections
■ Bullets	■ Ample margins (3/4" to 1")
■ Italics	■ Visual balance
■ Variety of type sizes	■ Bold type for headings and key information

FIGURE 2.3
Skills Résumé

GEORGE SHRIVER

Objective

Senior management position where I can lead a technical communication department that assists a computer manufacturer in achieving high quality and productivity

George names the goal that he will help the employer achieve.

Skills and Accomplishments

In this skills résumé, George highlights his special qualifications in a separate section.

Management — Supervise a team of six specialists who create print and on-line user documentation and also develop and deliver training programs for in-house use

Innovation — Proposed and oversaw the development of an interactive videodisc training program for process engineers in a small factory that manufactures computer components

Technical Expertise — Familiar with latest developments in both hardware and software. Programming knowledge of Visual C++, Java, and various proprietary computer languages

Budgetary Responsibility — Manage an annual budget of nearly one-half million dollars

George uses the present tense in his "Management" and "Budgetary" entries because these are continuing duties; he uses the past tense in his entry about "Innovation" because it describes a completed project.

He describes a major accomplishment.

He provides information about the budget's size.

Employment History

Training Director, Saffron Computer Technology, Inc., Anaheim, CA, 2001–Present
Training Specialist, Calpon Software Systems, Deer Park, NJ, 1997–2001

Because he presented information about substantial on-the-job responsibilities and achievements above, he does not elaborate on his jobs here.

Education

B.A. in Technical and Scientific Communication, Miami University (OH), 1997
Numerous professional development courses

Because he has substantial professional experience, George de-emphasizes his college experiences by giving only basic facts.

Professional Societies

Society for Technical Communication (Chapter President, 2004)
American Society for Training and Development

George shows commitment to continued professional development.

Special Qualifications

Fluent in German   Trained in conflict resolution   Certified to teach CPR

References available upon request

1734 Everet Avenue   Pasadena, CA 91101   (314) 417-7787
GShriver@nettlink.com

George lists additional qualifications that may interest an employer.

George creates a distinctive design for his résumé by putting his address and phone number at the bottom.

He names a leadership position in his professional society.

To see how George designed his résumé in a word-processing program, go to www.thomsonedu.com/english/anderson.

A Reader-Centered Approach to Writing Your Résumé

Writer's Tutorial
Using Tables to Design a Résumé 写作者指南：用表格设计简历

This tutorial tells how to design a multicolumn résumé with Word for Windows 2003. For instructions on using Word for Macintosh, go to www.thomsonedu.com/english/anderson and click on Chapter 2. If you use a different word processor or get stuck, click on your program's **Help** menu for assistance.

After learning the basic strategies described below, use your creativity to create a résumé that employers will find informative and persuasive.

MAKE A TABLE TO SERVE AS THE VISUAL FRAMEWORK FOR YOUR RÉSUMÉ
1. Create a new Word document.
2. From the pull-down **File** menu, choose **Page Setup**.
3. Set all margins at one inch.
4. From the pull-down **Table** menu, choose **Insert**.
5. Slide the cursor to **Table** in the new menu that appears.
6. In the popup menu, give the table 3 columns and 7 rows.
   - You can add or delete rows as necessary later.
7. Click **OK**.

ADJUST THE WIDTHS OF THE COLUMNS
1. Move the cursor over the vertical line that separates the left and center columns so that the cursor changes to this: ◄║►
2. Press the left mouse button.
3. Slide the vertical line to left until it is at 1.5 inches on the ruler.
   - This narrow column is for your topic headings.
4. Follow the same procedure to the vertical line between the center and right-hand columns as far left as you can.
   - This thin column is a gutter between the heading and text columns.

HIDE THE TABLE'S BORDERS SO THEY WON'T SHOW WHEN YOU PRINT YOUR RÉSUMÉ
1. Highlight the entire table (but not anything else).
2. From the **Format** menu, select **Borders and Shading**.
3. For **Borders**, click **None** (the box near the top left).
4. Click **OK**.
   - The borders will show in light gray on screen, but will not print.

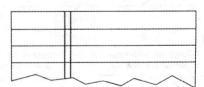

> **Learn More at the Web Site**
> To see tables used to make a variety of résumés, go to www.thomsonedu.com/english/anderson

CHAPTER 2 Overview of the Reader-Centered Communication Process

CREATE A HEADING FOR YOUR RÉSUMÉ

1. Highlight all three columns in the top row.
2. Under the **Table** menu, select **Merge Cells**.
   - If Merge Cells doesn't appear at first, continue to hold down the mouse button and place the cursor over the two arrowheads (two v's) at the bottom of the menu.
3. In this wide cell, enter your name and contact information.
4. Change your name to a larger type and bold.
5. Center all the text.

BE CREATIVE

This tutorial's purpose is to teach you to how to use a word-processing program to create an effective résumé, not to suggest that your résumé should look one particular way. Use your creativity.

For example, here are two alternative headings you can make if you don't merge the three cells in the first row. In the bottom example, grid lines for the gutter are moved to the right in the first row only.

ENTER YOUR TOPIC HEADINGS

1. In each cell in the left column, enter a topic heading.
   - If the heading has two words, put a **Return** between them.
   - If the column isn't wide enough for the longest word, enlarge it slightly.
2. Change all the topic headings to bold.
3. Align the headings on the right side of the column.
   - Highlight all the headings.
   - From the pull-down **Format** menu, choose **Paragraph**.
   - On the popup menu, pull down the menu next to **Alignment**.
   - Choose **Right**.

(continued)

Writer's Tutorial *(continued)*

Using Tables to Design a Résumé

ENTER TEXT

1. In the right-hand column of each row, enter the appropriate text.
2. At the end of each entry, type one **Return**.
   - The **Return** will create a blank line between this entry and the next.
3. If you want to enter multicolumn text in the right-hand column, do the following:
   - Put the cursor in the cell that you want to have columns.
   - Follow the procedure for making a table that is given on the first page of this tutorial.
4. Use bold, italics, bullets, indentation and other design elements to create an attractive, easy-to-read design that emphasizes your qualifications.

EXPERIMENT WITH YOUR DESIGN

- Try using a different typeface for your name and the headings.
- Try aligning the headings on the right side of their column.
- Try adding a vertical rule (line).
   1. Highlight the text cells in the right-hand column.
   2. From the pull-down **Format** menu, choose **Borders and Shading.**
   3. On the left-hand side of the window that appears, click on **None.**
   4. On the right-hand side of the window, click on the small square that has the darker line on the left side:
   5. Click **OK.**
- Try adding one or more horizontal rules (lines).
   1. Highlight the cell that has your heading.
   2. From the pull-down **Format** menu, choose **Borders and Shading.**
   3. On the left-hand side of the window that appears, click on **None.**
   4. On the right-hand side of the window, click on the small square that has the darker line on the bottom:
   5. Click **OK.**

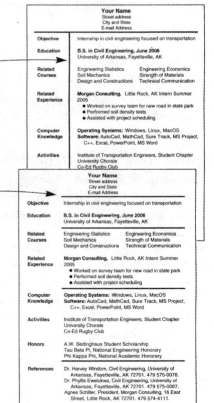

---

42   ■ CHAPTER 2 Overview of the Reader-Centered Communication Process

To check visual balance, fold your résumé vertically. Both sides should have a substantial amount of type. Neither should be primarily blank.

You will probably need to make adjustments to the design of your résumé so that your content and design work together to create a balanced, attractive page — one that visually emphasizes your most impressive qualifications and makes your résumé seem neither too packed nor too thin.

Do not rely on a computer program's templates or wizards to design your résumé for you. They are generic packages that don't let you create the most favorable presentation of your qualifications. Each of the various designs shown in this chapter's examples are easy to create using the tables in Microsoft Word. The tutorial on pages 40–42 will get you started. Use knowledge of your readers and your creativity to shape your résumé into a highly persuasive communication.

Revising

After drafting your résumé, but before sending it to the employer, take time to revise. Read it over carefully, trying to see it as the employer would. Then show your draft to other people. Tell them about the job you want so they can read from your readers' perspective, imagining what the employer will look for and how the employer will respond to each feature. Good reviewers for your résumé include classmates, your writing instructor, and instructors in your major department.

After you've made all of your revisions, run your spellchecker again, then proofread carefully for errors that spellcheckers don't catch. Employers say repeatedly that even a single error in spelling or grammar can eliminate a résumé from further consideration. The programs some employers use for initial screening of résumés kick out those with errors.

Check, too, for consistency in the use of italics, boldface, periods, bullets, and abbreviations as well as in the format for dates and other parallel items. Finally, check for consistency in the vertical alignment of information that isn't flush against the margin.

Adapting Your Résumé for Different Employers

The reader-centered process emphasizes the importance of tailoring every feature of a communication to the needs and goals of the specific readers you are addressing. This approach is the key to developing expertise at communicating in your career. Does this mean that you should write a new résumé for every application? Not really. In fact, if you are applying for the same type of position in two very similar organizations, you can probably use the same résumé for both. However, if you are applying to dissimilar positions or employers, make the changes needed to target each résumé to its readers. Even when sending the same résumé to different organizations, tailor each job application letter to one specific employer; see page 56.

Figure 2.4 shows a revision checklist you can use as you prepare your résumé.

> To see how one student adapted her résumés when applying for two different kinds of jobs, go to www.thomsonedu.com/english/anderson and click on Chapter 2.

FIGURE 2.4 Revision Checklist for Résumés
To download a copy of this checklist, go to at www.thomsonedu.com/english/anderson.

REVISION CHECKLIST FOR RÉSUMÉS

The following checklist describes the basic elements of a résumé. Some of the elements would be organized differently in a chronological résumé than in a skills résumé; see page 38.

Preliminary Research
- _____ Determined as exactly as possible what the employer wants?
- _____ Learned enough about the job and employer to tailor your résumé to them
- _____ Created a keyword list?

Name and Contact Information
- _____ Enables employers to reach you by mail, phone, and e-mail?

Objective
- _____ Tailored to the specific job you want?
- _____ Emphasizes what you will give rather than what you would like to get?

Education
- _____ Tells your school, major, and date of graduation?
- _____ Provides additional information that shows you are well-qualified for the job you want: academic honors and scholarships, specialized courses and projects, etc.?
- _____ Uses headings such as "Honors" and "Related Courses" to highlight your qualifications?

Work Experience
- _____ Identifies each employer's name and city, plus your employment dates?
- _____ Provides specific details about your previous jobs that highlight you qualifications: accomplishments, knowledge gained, equipment and programs used, responsibilities, etc.?

Activities
- _____ Describes your extracurricular and community activities in a way that shows you are qualified, responsible, and pleasant?

Interests
- _____ Mentions personal interests that will help the reader see you as a well-rounded and interesting person?

References
- _____ Lists people who will be impressive to your readers?
- _____ Includes a mix of references who can speak about your performance in different contexts?
- _____ Includes title, business address, phone, and e-mail address for each reference?

FIGURE 2.4 *(continued)*

> **REVISION CHECKLIST FOR RÉSUMÉS**
> *(continued)*
>
> _____ Includes only people who've given permission to be listed?
> _____ Omits personal references (family, friends, etc.)?
>
> **Prose**
> _____ Presents the most impressive information first?
> _____ Expresses the action in verbs, not nouns?
> _____ Uses strong verbs?
> _____ Uses parallel constructions?
> _____ Omits irrelevant information?
> _____ Uses correct spelling, grammar, and punctuation?
>
> **Visual Design**
> _____ Looks neat and attractive?
> _____ Highlights the facts that will be most impressive to employers?
> _____ Uses headings, layout, and other design features to help readers to find specific facts quickly?
>
> **Ethics**
> _____ Lists only experiences, accomplishments, degrees, and job titles you've actually had?
> _____ Avoids taking sole credit for things you did with a team?
> _____ Avoids statements intended to mislead?

ELECTRONIC RÉSUMÉS: SPECIAL CONSIDERATIONS
电子简历：需要考虑的特别因素

Increasingly, job applicants and employers are using electronic résumés rather than paper ones. The following sections provide advice about three types: scannable résumés, résumés submitted via e-mail or the Internet, and web page résumés.

Scannable Résumés

Many employers ask computers, not people, to be the first readers of your résumé. They feed your résumé to a scanner, which enters it into a computer's database. To find applicants who might be invited for a job interview, the employers ask the computer to search its database for résumés that have words — *keywords* — that the employers believe would appear in the résumés of good candidates for the opening they want to fill. The computer displays a list of the résumés with the most matches, called *hits*. These are the only résumés a person would read.

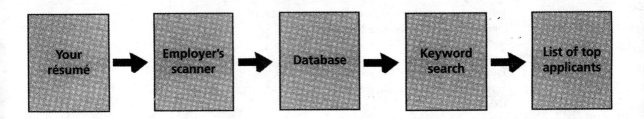

If you suspect that your résumé might be scanned, call the employer to check or else enclose both a regular résumé and a scannable one. To increase the number of hits your résumé will receive, make a list of keywords that employers are likely to ask their computers to look for. Here are some suggestions.

KEYWORDS FOR RÉSUMÉS

- Words in the employer's ad or job description
- All degrees, certifications, and licenses you've earned: B.A., B.S., R.N. (registered nurse), P.E. (professional engineer license), C.P.A. (certified public accountant)
- Advanced topics you've studied.
- Computer programs and operating systems you've mastered: Excel, AutoCAD II, C++, Linux
- Specialized equipment and techniques you've used in school or at work: X-ray machine, PK/PD analysis, ladderlogic
- Job titles and the specialized tasks you performed
- Buzzwords in your field: client server, LAN, low-impact aerobics, TQM (total quality management)
- Names of professional societies to which you belong (including student chapters)
- Other qualifications an employer would desire: leadership, writing ability, interpersonal skills, etc.

To increase the chances that the computer will select your résumé as one a human should read, do the following.

INCREASING THE NUMBER OF HITS YOUR RÉSUMÉ RECEIVES

- Put your keywords in nouns, even if your scannable résumé becomes wordy as a result.
- Be redundant. For instance, write "Used Excel spreadsheet program" rather than "Used spreadsheet program" or "Used Excel." You don't know which term an employer will use, and if both terms are used, you will have two hits.
- Create a "Keywords" section for keywords you can't easily work into any of your résumé's other sections.
- Proofread carefully. Computer programs don't match misspellings.
- Use 12-point type.
- Use a standard typeface (e.g., Times, Arial, or Helvetica).
- Avoid italics, underlining, and decorative elements such as vertical lines, borders, and shading. Boldface, all caps, and bullets are okay.
- Use blank lines and boldface headings to separate sections.
- Use a single column of text.
- Put your name at the top of every page, on a line of its own.
- Use laser printing or high-quality photocopying on white paper.
- Mail your résumé flat and without staples.

Figure 2.5 shows Ramón Perez's résumé in a scannable form. It is longer than his print résumé, but computers don't care how much they read. Notice how different it looks from the résumé he designed to be read first by a person (Figure 2.2).

Résumés Submitted Via E-mail

More than one-third of human resource managers prefer e-mailed résumés, according to a survey by the Society for Human Resource Managers. The following advice is based on suggestion by certified career coach Kirsten Dixon (2001).

- Follow the employer's directions about whether to include your résumé in an attachment or in the e-mail itself. In either case, follow the advice for scannable résumés because yours may be read by a computer.
- If you are sending your résumé as an attachment, save it as a pdf file so that it will retain the appearance you designed regardless of the computer and printer used by the employer.
- If you are sending your résumé in the e-mail itself, design it the way you would design a scannable résumé. The formatting you create using your own e-mail program may create an eyesore in the employer's program.
- Write a simple subject line. For example: Résumé—Kelly Borowitz-Rioja: CivilEng Major. Abbreviations are fine. If you don't include a subject line, the employer may mistake your e-mail for spam and discard it unread.

FIGURE 2.5
Scannable Résumé

Ramón includes a list of keywords that don't appear elsewhere in his résumé.

To assure that a scanner could read his résumé, Ramón uses a single-column format rather than the two-column format he created for his print résumé.

He also eliminates the italics that appeared in his print resume (see page 35).

Throughout this résumé, Ramón uses 12-point Times, a typeface scanners can read without difficulty.

To make his résumé easy for humans (as well as scanners) to read, Ramón relies on:
- capital letters
- bold
- bullets
- blank lines

To be read by a scanner, Ramón's résumé requires two pages, but that is fine because scanners don't care how many pages they read.

RAMÓN PEREZ
16 Henry Street
Brooklyn, New York 11231
Work: (212) 374-7631
Home: (718) 563-2291

KEYWORDS
Responsible, financial management, banking experience, accounting, auditing, high motivation, communication ability

PROFESSIONAL OBJECTIVE
A position as a systems analyst where I can use my knowledge of computer science and business to develop customized systems for financial institutions

EDUCATION
New York University
B.S. in Computer Science
December 2006
GPA 3.4 overall; 3.7 in major

Computer classes include artificial intelligence and expert systems, computer security, data communication, deterministic systems, and stochastics

Business classes include accounting, banking, finance, and business law

Worked full-time while completing last half of course work

HONORS
Dean's List three times
Golden Key National Honor Society

RELATED WORK
Miller Health Spas, New York City, 2004–Present
Data Entry Clerk
- Helped convert to a new computerized accounting system
- Served on the team that wrote user documentation for the system
- Trained new employees
- Earned Employee of the Month Award twice

Meninger Bank, New York City, 2001–2004
Teller
- Performed all types of daily, night-deposit, and bank-by-mail transactions
- Proved the vault, ordered currency, and handled daily cash flow
- Learned how financial computer systems look from tellers' viewpoint

ACTIVITIES
Juvenile Diabetes Foundation, 2003–Present
Volunteer
- Helped design a major fund-raising event two years in a row
- Successfully solicited two million dollars in contributions from sponsors

(Ramón uses a second page for his references)

- Use a straightforward e-mail address for yourself. Avoid cute names. If necessary, set up a free e-mail account at Hotmail, Yahoo, or a similar service.

Résumés Submitted Via Websites

Some employers ask applicants to submit their résumés by completing online forms at the employers' websites. These résumés will almost surely be read into a computer, so follow the advice, given above, for scannable résumés. To complete an online application form, draft your text in a word processing program, then review and proofread it carefully before pasting it into the employer's form.

Web Page Résumés

Although most employers do not read web page résumés, a few do. If you create a résumé accessible via the World Wide Web, consider the following advice:

- **Link to samples of your work and fuller descriptions of your experiences and capabilities.**
- **Keep your design simple, uncluttered.** Don't let fancy embellishments distract employers' attention from your qualifications.
- **Include a "mail-to" link to your e-mail address.**
- **Post your online résumé only at secure services.** Some services have no security, making it possible for other people to alter your résumé.

> For additional advice about creating web page résumés, go to www.thomsonedu.com/english/anderson and click on Chapter 2.
>
> **Learn More**
>
> Chapter 18 provides additional advice about creating effective web pages.

A READER-CENTERED APPROACH TO WRITING YOUR JOB APPLICATION LETTER
用以读者为中心的方法写职位申请信

Your job application letter can be a powerfully persuasive part of the package you submit to employers. In response to a survey of 150 executives from the nation's 1,000 largest employers, 60 percent indicated that a job application letter is just as or more important than the résumé (Patterson, 1996).

Reflecting the approach of many employers, corporate recruiter Richard Berman reports that if a letter doesn't grab him, he merely gives the enclosed résumé a quick scan to see if it might turn his opinion around. In contrast, when he discovers a particularly effective letter, he goes immediately to colleagues to announce that he's "found a good one" (Patterson, 1996).

Defining Your Letter's Objectives

Your job application letter has somewhat different work to do than does your résumé. Although the readers are the same, the usability and persuasive objectives differ.

The usability objectives are different because readers look for different information in a letter than in a résumé. Their major letter-reading questions are as follows.

> **WHAT EMPLOYERS ASK WHEN READING APPLICATION LETTERS**
>
> - **Why do you want to work for me instead of someone else?** Employers are more responsive to applicants who know about their organization and can express specific reasons for wanting to work for it.
> - **How will you contribute to my organization's success?** In the Wells, Spinks, and Hargrave survey, 88 percent of the personnel directors "agreed" or "strongly agreed" that job application letters should tell how the jobseeker's qualifications match the organization's needs.
> - **Will you work well with my other employees and the persons with whom we do business?** Because every job involves extensive interactions with coworkers, employers want to hire people who excel in these relationships. Of course, interactions with clients, vendors, and others outside the employer's organization are also important.

The persuasive objectives of your letter also differ from those of your résumé:

Your job application letter's persuasive objectives

- To respond to the employer's questions listed above in ways that make the employer want to hire you.
- To convey a favorable sense of your enthusiasm, creativity, commitment, and other attributes that employers value but can't be communicated easily in your résumé.

Planning

Begin planning your job application letter by conducting the research necessary to answer the reader's first question, "Why do you want to work for me instead of someone else?" Seek things you can praise. You'll find it helpful to categorize the facts you discover as either writer-centered or reader-centered. Examples of *writer-centered facts* are the benefits the organization gives employees or the appealing features of its co-op program. You won't gain anything by mentioning writer-centered facts in your letter because whenever you talk about them you are saying, in essence, "I want to work for you because of what you'll give me." When employers are hiring, they are not looking for people to give things to.

In contrast, *reader-centered facts* concern things the organization is proud of: a specific innovation it has created, a novel process it uses, a goal it has achieved. These are facts you can build on to create a reader-centered letter.

For advice about finding employers you might want to work for, go to www.thomsonedu.com/english/anderson and click on Chapter 2.

CHAPTER 2 **Overview of the Reader-Centered Communication Process**

In addition, research the goals and activities of people who hold the job you want. The more you know about that job, the more persuasively you will be able to answer the reader's second question, "How will you contribute to my organization's success?"

Here are several ways to obtain specific, reader-centered information about an employer.

LEARNING ABOUT EMPLOYERS

- **Draw on your own knowledge.** If you've already worked for the company, you may already know all you need to know. Remember, however, that you need information related to the specific area of activity in which you'd like to work.
- **Ask an employee, professor, or other knowledgeable person.** People often have information that isn't available in print or online.
- **Contact the company.** It might send publications about itself.
- **Search the web.** Start with the employer's own website. Also use resources such as Business Week Online (http://www.businessweek.com), LexisNexis (http://lexisnexis.com), and the sites for other major newspapers and magazines.
- **Consult your campus's placement office.**
- **Visit the library.** Business newspapers and magazines, as well as trade and professional journals, are excellent sources of information.

Learn More

For more detailed advice about how to conduct research, see Chapter 6 and the Writer's Reference Guide: Using Five Reader-Centered Research Methods (page 165).

For links to other online resources for researching employers, go to www.thomsonedu.com/english/anderson and click on Chapter 2.

Drafting

Business letters have three parts: introduction, body, and conclusion. Within this general framework, an effective job application letter does the following:

1. Identifies the job you want
2. Demonstrates your knowledge of the employer's company or organization
3. Explains why you have chosen to apply to this employer
4. Explains how your qualifications enable you to contribute to the employer's success
5. Indicates the next step that you will take

There is no single best way to combine these five elements within the three-part framework of a letter. Use your creativity to make your letter distinctive. The following advice will help you write an original letter that observes the general conventions of business correspondence. Figures 2.6 and 2.7 show how Jeannie Ryan and Ramón Perez applied this advice in their letters.

FIGURE 2.6

Letter of Application to Accompany the Résumé Shown in Figure 2.1

Jeannie addresses a specific person.

She shows specific knowledge of the company and offers praise related to it.

Jeannie states that she wishes to pursue a goal that the employer pursues.

Jeannie explains the relevance of her courses to the job she is seeking.

She describes one way her job experience will benefit the employer.

Jeannie tells how abilities she developed in a college activity will benefit the employer.

She highlights a specific accomplishment.

Jeannie politely requests an interview.

---

325 Foxfire Drive, Apt. 214
Denver, Colorado 70962
February 8, 2006

Ms. Nancy Zwotny, Manager
Employment and Employee Relations
Burdick Marketing
650 Broadway
Denver, Colorado 70981

Dear Ms. Zwotny:

I was very impressed to read in *Marketing News* that last year Burdick added seven national accounts to its client list. I was especially interested to learn that this success is built upon the power and rapid response of computerized tools for marketing analysis developed by your personnel. Moreover, two of these new accounts are in the electronics industry, a special interest of mine. As a senior marketing major at the University of Denver, I would very much like to work for Burdick as a research assistant, helping clients maximize sales. In particular, I would like to contribute to the success of clients in the electronics industry.

To develop a solid background in computerized decision making, I have taken several classes in data analysis, including two classes in quantitative methods, one in data management, and one in survey sampling. In addition, through my minor in computer science, I have gained technical knowledge to work effectively with Burdick's clients selling computer games and similar consumer products.

To learn the practical application of concepts I've studied in school, I have worked in selling to consumers and to retailers. Both jobs taught me how unreliable our intuitive predictions about consumer behavior can be and how important it is to research the market before introducing a new product. In addition, my service as vice president of the university's synchronized swim team has helped me develop my leadership and communication skills that will help me work effectively with other Burdick clients and employees. Last year, I helped this diverse group of fifty students prepare programs that they presented proudly to the public.

I'm sure you realize that a letter and résumé (which I've enclosed) can convey only a limited sense of a person's motivation and qualifications. Next week, I will call your assistant to see if you are able to grant me an interview. I hope that I may look forward to meeting you to discuss my credentials more fully.

Sincerely yours,

Jeannie Ryan

Jeannie Ryan

Enclosure: Résumé

FIGURE 2.7
Letter of Application to Accompany the Résumé Shown in Figure 2.2

16 Henry Street
Brooklyn, New York 11231
March 24, 2006

Estelle Ritter
Financial Systems Division
Medallion Software, Inc.
1655 Avenue of the Americas
New York, New York 11301

Dear Ms. Ritter:

About a year ago, I met David Yang, a systems analyst in your department, who told me about Medallion's highly successful efforts to create integrated computer systems for banks and other financial institutions. I was particularly intrigued when he explained that many of the programs you design for international corporations must conform to government banking regulations—which differ from country to country. What a challenge! As a systems analysis major with a considerable interest in meeting the needs of clients in the financial services industry, I would like to be considered for a position in your division.

Since talking with David, I have sought out courses that would prepare me for exactly the kind of work your division performs. This semester, for example, I am taking a course in computer security and another in international finance. In addition, I have gained considerable insight into the structure and uses of two sophisticated financial systems while working as a data entry clerk for the Miller Health Spas chain and as a teller for the Meninger Bank. I have also completed several classes in written and oral communication, which would help me present Medallion effectively to clients. You will find additional details about my qualifications in the enclosed résumé.

I feel that I am a well-disciplined, highly motivated person with a strong desire to excel. I have taken the last half of my college courses while working full-time to support my wife and young son. After I become settled into a permanent job, I plan to begin graduate study in computer science so that I continue to develop my skills in systems analysis and design.

Would it be possible for me to meet with you to discuss what I have to contribute to Medallion? If so, please call me at (212) 374-7631 during the day.

Sincerely,

Ramón Perez
Ramón Perez

Enclosure

- Ramón addresses a specific person.
- He demonstrates a specific knowledge of the company and conveys his enthusiasm for it.
- Ramón states that he wishes to achieve results that the employer desires to achieve.
- Ramón conveys his determination to prepare for the job for which he is applying.
- Ramón explains how his job experience would benefit the employer.
- He also tells how two classes he took would benefit the employer.
- He provides specific evidence of personal characteristics he thinks the employer will view favorably.
- Ramón asks for an interview.

A Reader-Centered Approach to Writing Your Job Application Letter

Introduction

By identifying the job you want in the introduction, you accommodate the employer's desire to know why you have written. When naming the position, convey your enthusiasm for it.

> I was delighted to see your ad for a chemical engineer in Sunday's newspaper.

To make your enthusiasm credible, explain the *reason* for it. In the following examples, Harlan shaped his explanations to the positions he applied for. To an environmental consulting company, he wrote:

> As an environmental engineering major who will graduate in May, I am eager to help companies assess and remediate hazards.

To a company that makes industrial lubricants, he wrote

> In my capstone course as a chemical engineering student, I am studying the synthesis of molecules for the same industrial uses that your company's products serve.

Another effective way to begin your letter is to praise an accomplishment, project, or activity you learned about during your research. Praise is almost always welcomed by a reader, provided that it seems sincere. In the following example, Shawana combines the praise with an explanation of her reason for applying to this employer and with her statement of the job she is applying for.

Shawana gives specific praise related to the job she wants.

She introduces herself and expresses her desire to contribute.
She identifies the job she wants.

> While reading the August issue of *Automotive Week*, I learned that you needed to shut down your assembly line for only 45 minutes when switching from making last year's car model to this year's model. This 500 percent reduction in shutdown time over last year is a remarkable accomplishment. As a senior in manufacturing engineering at Western University, I would welcome a chance to contribute to further improvements in the production processes at your plant. Please consider me for the opening in the Production Design Group that you advertised through the University's Career Services Center.

Note that Shawana isn't praising the features of the car or the huge profit the company made. That would be superficial praise anyone could give without having any real understanding of the organization. Instead, Shawana focuses on a specific accomplishment, discovered through her research, that is directly related to her own specialty.

If you have a connection with a current employee or representative of the employer, you might mention it, especially if you can combine this reference with evidence that you are knowledgeable about the organization.

> At last month's Career Fair at the University of Missouri, I spoke with AgraGrow's representative Raphael Ortega, who described your company's novel approaches to no-till agriculture. As an agronomy major, I would welcome the chance to work in your research department.

Body (Qualifications Section)

Sometimes called the *qualifications section,* the body of your letter is the place to explain how your knowledge and experience prepare you to contribute significantly to the employer's organization. Some job applicants divide this section into two parts: one on their education and the other on their work experience or personal qualities. Other applicants devote a paragraph to their knowledge and skills in one area, such as engineering, and a second paragraph to their knowledge and skills in another area, such as communication. Many other methods of organizing are also possible.

No matter how you organize this section, indicate how the specific facts you convey about yourself relate to the demands of the position you want. Don't merely repeat information from your résumé. Instead of merely listing courses you've taken, show also how the knowledge you gained will help you to do a good job for the employer. Rather than listing previous job titles and areas of responsibility, indicate how the skills you gained will enable you to succeed in the job you are seeking.

In my advanced physical chemistry course, I learned to conduct fluoroscopic and gas chromatographic analyses similar to those your laboratory uses to detect contaminants in the materials provided by your vendors.	What the student learned
In one course, we designed a computer simulation of the transportation between three manufacturing facilities, two warehouses, and seventeen retail outlets. Through this class, I gained substantial experience in designing the kinds of systems used by your company.	How this will enable the student to contribute

Conclusion

In the conclusion of your letter, look ahead to the next step. If you are planning to follow up your letter with a phone call, indicate that. In some situations, such a call can be helpful in focusing an employer's attention on your résumé. If you are planning to wait to be contacted by the employer, indicate where you can be reached and when.

Using a Conventional Format

Finally, when you draft a letter of application, be sure to use a conventional format. Standard formats are described in Chapter 20 and used in this chapter's sample letters.

Revising

A job application letter is an especially challenging communication to write. Look it over very carefully yourself, and ask others to help you determine whether your letter is coming across in the way you intend. The following paragraphs discuss some of the most important things to look for.

Review the Personality You Project

Employers will examine everything you say for clues to your personality. When you say what appeals to you about the organization and explain why you are well suited for the job, you are revealing important things about yourself. Notice, for instance, how the first sentence of the second paragraph of Jeannie Ryan's letter (Figure 2.6) shows her to be a goal-oriented person who plans her work purposefully. Also, notice how the first paragraph of Ramón's letter (Figure 2.7) shows him to be an enthusiastic person with a firm sense of direction. When reviewing your own draft, pay special attention to the personality you project. An attribute employers especially value is enthusiasm for their organization and for the work you would do there.

> To see other application letters that follow the advice given in this chapter, go to www.thomsonedu.com/english/anderson and click on Chapter 2.

Review Your Tone

Some people have difficulty indicating an appropriate level of self-confidence. You want the tone of your letter to suggest to employers that you are self-assured but not brash or overconfident. Avoid statements like this:

Overconfident tone
> I am sure you will agree that my excellent education qualifies me for a position in your Design Department.

The phrase "I am sure you will agree" will offend some readers. And the sentence as a whole seems presumptuous. It asserts that the writer knows as much as the reader about how well the writer's qualifications meet the reader's needs. The following sentence is more likely to generate a favorable response:

More effective tone
> I hope you will find that my education qualifies me for a position in your Design Department.

Achieving just the right tone in the conclusion of a letter is also rather tricky. You should avoid ending your letter like this:

Ineffective, demanding tone
> I would like to meet with you at your earliest convenience. Please let me know when this is possible.

To sound less demanding, the writer might revise the second sentence to read, "Please let me know *whether* this is possible" and add "I *look forward* to hearing from you."

Finally, remember that you must assure that each sentence states your meaning clearly and precisely. And you must eradicate *all* spelling and grammatical errors.

Adapting Your Application Letter for Different Employers

If you are applying to different employers for the same type of position, you may be able to adapt your application letter by altering only places where you demonstrate your knowledge of each specific company and tell why you are applying to it. However, if you are applying for different kinds of jobs, revise also your explanations of the match between your qualifications and the job you want.

Figure 2.8 shows a checklist you can use as you prepare your job application letters.

> To see the different letters one student wrote when applying for two different jobs, go to www.thomsonedu.com/english/anderson and click on Chapter 2.

FIGURE 2.8 Revision Checklist for Job Application Letters

To download a copy of this checklist, go to at www.thomsonedu.com/english/anderson.

REVISION CHECKLIST FOR JOB APPLICATION LETTERS

Preliminary Research
- _____ Determined as exactly as possible what the employer wants?
- _____ Learned enough about the job and employer to tailor your letter to them?

Address
- _____ Addresses a specific individual, if possible?

Introduction
- _____ Tells clearly what you want?
- _____ Persuades that you know specific, relevant things about the reader's organization?
- _____ Conveys that you like the company?

Qualifications
- _____ Explains how the knowledge, abilities, and experiences described in your résumé are relevant to the specific job for which you are applying?

Closing
- _____ Sounds cordial, yet clearly sets out a plan of action?

Prose
- _____ Uses clear sentences with varied structures?
- _____ Uses an easy-to-follow organization?
- _____ Uses a confident but modest tone?
- _____ Expresses the action in verbs, not nouns?
- _____ Uses strong verbs?
- _____ Uses correct spelling, grammar, and punctuation?

Appearance
- _____ Looks neat and attractive?
- _____ Includes all the elements of a business letter?

Ethics
- _____ Describes your qualifications honestly?
- _____ Avoids statements intended to mislead?

Overall
- _____ Shows that you are aware of your reader's goals and concerns when hiring?
- _____ Demonstrates that you are a skilled communicator?

ETHICAL ISSUES IN THE JOB SEARCH
求职中的道德因素

One of the most interesting—and perplexing—features of workplace writing is that the ethical standards differ from one situation to another. The résumé and job application letter illustrate this point because the expectations that apply to them are significantly different from those that apply to other common types of on-the-job writing.

For instance, when writing a résumé you are permitted to present facts about yourself in a very selective way that would be considered unethical in most other kinds of workplace writing. For example, imagine that you have suggested that your company reorganize its system for keeping track of inventory. Several managers have asked you to investigate this possibility further, then write a report about it. In this report, your readers will expect you to include unfavorable information about your system as well as favorable information. If you omit the unfavorable information, your employer will judge that you have behaved unethically in order to win approval of your idea. If you were to submit your résumé to these same readers, however, they would not expect you to include unfavorable information about yourself. In fact, they would be surprised if you did.

Furthermore, these readers would expect you to present the favorable information about yourself in as impressive a language as possible, even though they might feel you were ethically bound to use cooler, more objective writing in your proposal about the inventory system. Here are the ethical guidelines that *do* apply to résumés and job application letters.

GUIDELINES FOR AN ETHICAL RÉSUMÉ AND JOB APPLICATION LETTER

- Don't list degrees you haven't earned, offices you haven't served in, or jobs you haven't held.
- Don't list awards or other recognition you haven't actually received.
- Don't take sole credit for things you have done as a team member.
- Don't give yourself a job title you haven't had.
- Don't phrase your statements in a way that is intended to mislead your readers.
- Don't list references who haven't agreed to serve as references for you.

If you are unsure whether you are writing ethically in some part of your résumé, check with your instructor or someone else who is familiar with workplace expectations about this type of communication. (You might also ask for advice from more experienced people whenever you are unsure about the ethical expectations that apply to *any* communication you write at work.)

WRITING FOR EMPLOYMENT IN OTHER COUNTRIES
撰写去其他国家的求职材料

In other countries, résumés and job application letters may look very different from those used in the United States. The traditional Japanese job application, the *rirekisho*, includes a significant amount of personal information to indicate that the applicant comes from an environment that makes it likely the person will enjoy long-term success in the organization (Lofving & Kennedy-Takahashi, 2000). Although Japanese employers expect less personal information in applications from persons in other cultures, they still want to know the applicant's nationality, age, and marital status. In France, many employers want job application letters written by hand so they can subject the letters to handwriting analysis (Pensot, 2000). French employers believe that this analysis enables them to learn about the applicant's personal traits, which they weigh heavily when making employment decisions. Employers in many countries, including South Africa, want applications to include grades, copies of diplomas, and reference letters, called *testimonials* (Woodburn Mann, 2000).

Because expectations differ so significantly from country to country, conduct reader-centered research about the country to which you will send applications. Among others, Mary Ann Thompson's *Global Résumé and CV Guide* (2000) is an excellent source.

For links to websites with information about preparing resumes for jobs in specific countries, go to www.thomsonedu.com/english/anderson and click on Chapter 2.

CONCLUSION
总 结

This chapter has demonstrated how the reader-centered approach used by successful workplace communicators can help you create a highly effective résumé and letter of application. The strategies you saw in action here are ones you can use for all your work-related writing:

- Think continuously about your readers.
- Use your knowledge of your readers to guide all your writing decisions.

The rest of this book is devoted to developing your communication expertise by providing detailed reader-centered advice you can use whenever you write at work.

EXERCISES 练 习

EXPERTISE

1. Find a sample résumé at your college's Career Services Center or in a book about résumé writing. Evaluate it from the point of view of its intended reader. How could it be improved?

2. Using the web, newspapers, or journal articles, locate four or more openings that appeal to you. Create a unified list of the qualifications they specify. Then identify your skills and experiences that match each item on the employers' list.

3. Complete the assignment in Appendix B on writing a résumé and a letter of application.

ONLINE

Using the web, find an employer or online job board that asks you to fill out an online résumé form. Evaluate the extent to which the form helps or hinders you from presenting your qualifications in the most persuasive manner.

COLLABORATION

Collaborating with another student in your class, work together on developing a keyword list for each of you that you could use when creating a scannable résumé.

ETHICS

Using the library or web, read an article that discusses the attitudes of employers toward unethical résumés. Take notes you can share with your class.

CASE — ADVISING PATRICIA 案例：给 Patricia 建议

For additional cases, visit www.thomsonedu.com/english/anderson. Instructors: The book's website includes suggestions for teaching the cases.

This morning you stopped outside the library to talk with Patricia Norman, a senior who is majoring in marketing. She told you with a mixture of excitement and anxiety that she has finally decided to join the many other seniors who are busily looking for a job. She's even drafted a résumé and begun writing letters to employers listed in a publication she picked up at the Career Services Center.

"Look," she exclaimed. "One of the department store chains I'm writing to is mentioned in this article that Professor Schraff asked us to read." She held out an article from *Retail Management*. "They've begun opening freestanding specialty shops in their stores. The managers order their own merchandise and run their own advertising campaigns. It's been a huge success. This sounds like such a great place to work — a big chain that welcomes innovators." Then her excitement turned to anxiety. "I'm worried they won't like my résumé and application letter, though. I've gone over both again and again, and my roommate has, too. But I'm still worried."

As you tried to reassure her, she pulled out her drafts and put them into your hand. "Take a look at them and tell me what you really think. I need all the help I can get." You had to leave for an appointment, but you agreed to look over her drafts and meet her again this evening.

Now it's afternoon, and you've started to read Patricia's résumé and letter. As you do, you think back over some of the things you know about her. She's an active and energetic person, talkative, and fun to be with. Throughout her years in college, she has spent lots of time with a group called Angel Flight, a volunteer organization that sponsors service activities on campus and off. In fact, this past year you've seen less of her because she has spent so much time serving as the organization's president. "As president, I'm responsible for everything," she once told you. "Everything from running meetings, to getting volunteers, to seeing that the volunteers have done what they said they would." While a junior she held some other office, you recall — also a time-consuming one. But she's like that. In the Marketing Club, she edited the newsletter and handled lots of odd jobs, like putting up posters announcing speakers and meetings. She was also treasurer of the Fencing Club, another of her interests. Once when you marveled at how many things she was able to do, she responded, "It's not so much, if you're organized."

Despite all the time she spends on such activities, Patricia earns good grades, a 3.6 average, she told you once. Although she's had to take lots of business courses, she's also squeezed in a few electives in one of her favorite subjects: art history. One Saturday last year, she even got you to travel 200 miles with her to see an art exhibit — a "major" exhibit, she had assured you.

But the trip you most enjoyed with her was to a shopping center, where she spent more time commenting on how the merchandise was displayed than looking for things to buy. She talked a lot about the way they did things at a Dallas department store where she's worked the past three summers. She must have some interesting opportunities there, you note; after all, one of the people she lists as a reference is the store manager. Her other references are professors who've taught classes that you and Patricia have taken together. They were fun. Everything's fun with Patricia.

YOUR ASSIGNMENT

Decide what you will say to Patricia about her letter (Figure 2.9) and résumé (Figure 2.10). What strengths will you praise? What changes will you suggest? What questions will you ask to determine whether she might include additional information? Assume that her résumé will be read first by a person, not by a scanner.

FIGURE 2.9
Letter of Application for Use with Case

Box 88
Wells Hall
University of Washington
Seattle, Washington 98195
February 12, 2006

Kevin Mathews, Director
Corporate Recruiting
A. L. Lambert Department Stores, Inc.
Fifth and Noble Streets
San Diego, California 92103

Dear Mr. Mathews:

I saw A. L. Lambert's advertisement in the *College Placement Annual.* I was very impressed with your company. I hope that you will consider me for an opening in your Executive Develepment Program.

In June, I will graduate from the University of Washington's retailing program, where I have focused my study on marketing management. I have learned a great deal about consumer behavior, advertising, and innovative sales techniques. Furthermore, I have gained a through overview of the retailing industry, and I have studied successful and unsuccessful retailing campaigns through the case-study method.

In addition to my educational qualifications, I have experience both in retail sales and in managing volunteer organizations. While working in a Dallas department store for the past four summers, I had many opprtunities to apply the knowledge and skills that I have learned in college. Likewise, in my extracurricular activities, I have gained experience working and communicating with people. For instance, I have been the president of Angel Flight, a volunteer service organization at the University of of Washington. Like a manager, I supervised many of the organization's activities. Similarly, while holding offices in two campus organizations, I have developed my senses of organization and responsibility.

I would like to talk with you in person about my qualifications. Please tell me how that can be arranged.

Sincerely yours,

Patricia Norman

Exercises

FIGURE 2.10
Résumé for Use with Case

PATRICIA NORMAN
Box 80, Wells Hall
University of Washington
Seattle, Washington 98195
(206) 529-5097

PERSONAL
Born: March 17, 1985
Health: Excellent
Willing to relocate

PROFESSIONAL OBJECTIVE
To work for an innovative and growing retailer.

EDUCATION
University of Washington, Seattle, Washington, B.S. in Retailing, May 2006.

Earned 23 credit hours in marketing management, obtaining a working knowledge of the factors motivating today's consumer. Also learned how a product is marketed and distributed to the consumer. Took eight credit hours of study focused specifically on principles and problems of retail management.

WORK EXPERIENCE
Danzig's Department Store, Dallas, Texas,
Summers 2002–2005.

Worked as a sales clerk. Helped customers choose their purchases and listened politely to their complaints. Cash register operation. Stocked shelves and racks. Provided assistance to several department managers.

ACTIVITIES
Fencing Club, served as treasurer.
Angel Flight, President.
Marketing Club, member.

REFERENCES
Derek Yoder, *Store Manager*
Danzig's Department Store
11134 Longhorn Drive
Dallas, Texas 75220

Gregory Yule
Pinehurst Hall
University of Washington 98195
(206) 579-9481

Lydia Zelasko
Putnam Hall
University of Washington
Seattle, Washington 98195

PART II DEFINING YOUR COMMUNICATION'S OBJECTIVES 界定交流目标

Chapter 3 Defining Your Communication's Objectives

Defining Your Communication's Objectives
界定交流目标

3

GUIDELINES

1. Focus on what you want to happen while your readers are reading *66*
2. Define your usability goal: Analyze your readers' reading tasks *68*
3. Define your persuasive goal: Analyze your readers' attitudes *71*
4. Learn your readers' personal characteristics *73*
5. **Global Guideline:** Learn your readers' cultural characteristics *76*
6. Study the context in which your readers will read *82*
7. Ask others to help you understand your readers and their context *82*
8. Learn who *all* your readers will be *83*
9. Identify any constraints on the way you write *87*
10. **Ethics Guideline:** Identify your communication's stakeholders *87*

CHAPTER 3

DEFINING OBJECTIVES

PLANNING

DRAFTING

REVISING

You are now beginning a new portion of this book. It includes thirteen chapters that will help you gain expertise at the four major activities of the writing process:

- Defining your communication's objectives
- Planning your communication
- Drafting your prose and graphics
- Revising

This chapter focuses on the first of these activities: defining your communication's objectives.

THE IMPORTANCE OF DEFINING OBJECTIVES
界定目标的重要性

All four writing activities are important, but defining objectives deserves your special attention. To see why, consider Todd's situation.

> For additional information and examples related to this chapter's guidelines, go to www.thomsonedu.com/english/anderson and click on Chapter 3.

A recent college graduate, Todd has been investigating ways of applying a more chip-resistant paint to his employer's products, which are microwaves, refrigerators, and other household appliances. Today, Todd's boss told him two vice presidents have asked Todd to write a report describing his progress. "How should I write this report?" Todd asks himself. "What should I tell the vice presidents and how should I say it?"

To answer these questions, Todd must determine what his report must accomplish in order to be successful: He must define its objectives. Doing so will require some effort, but the result will guide him throughout the rest of his work on the report. When he plans and drafts, a carefully defined set of objectives will help him decide how long to make the report, what to say in it, what to present in prose and what in tables, charts, or drawings — how, in fact, to handle every aspect of his message. Similarly, when Todd revises his draft, his objectives will help him determine what needs improvement and how those improvements can best be made in order to meet the vice presidents' needs. This chapter presents ten guidelines that will enable Todd — and you — to develop expertise in defining objectives to make sound decisions about the content and design of your communications.

GUIDELINE 1 FOCUS ON WHAT YOU WANT TO HAPPEN WHILE YOUR READERS ARE READING
指导方针1：集中关注读者的阅读过程

To develop expertise in any intellectually or creatively challenging field, you must develop an expert's way of looking at the problems that the field addresses. Research shows that physicians who are highly skilled at diagnosis consider the same number of a patient's symptoms as do less skilled diagnosticians; however, the expert physicians are more skilled at focusing on the specific symptoms that point to the underlying disease (Patel & Groen, 1991). When shown a chessboard that represents the middle of a game, champion players (unlike less skilled ones) have the ability to focus on the configuration of the eight or so pieces that matter most when determining how to defend against an attack or launch one (Chase & Simon, 1973).

Similarly, expertise in defining the objectives of a workplace communication requires the ability to see communications in a certain way: from the reader-centered perspective described in Chapter 1. People who don't possess this expertise in defining objectives often describe the purpose of their communications by stating their topic: "I'm going to write about travel outside the solar system." Or they name the type of communication they are going to prepare: "I'm going to write a proposal" or "I'm going to create a website." To develop expertise in defining the objectives of your communication, you must focus not on your topic or communication type but on your *readers in the act of reading your message*.

Here's why. As explained in Chapter 1, when you write on the job, your goal will be to bring about change. You will be endeavoring to transform some aspect of the current situation — the way things are now — into a more desirable state.

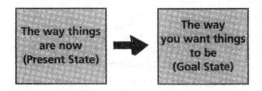

The desire for this change may originate from your boss, other persons in your employer's organization, clients, even you yourself. No matter where it originates, however, you will be able to achieve this change only through your communication's impact on your readers. After all, if you could make the change by yourself, you'd have no need to write.

Suppose you wish to obtain funding for a project. Your project will be funded only if your proposal persuades your boss to allocate the money you desire. Maybe you wish to help one of your employer's clients choose between two computers. The client will be able to select wisely only if your report enables readers to understand these alternatives fully and compare them meaningfully.

Consequently, the true objectives of your communication are to affect your readers in the ways necessary to bring about the desired change. And there's only one time when your communication has a direct impact on readers: while the readers are reading it. If all goes well then, your communication will succeed.

However, if things don't go well during your readers' reading moments, your communication won't be successful.

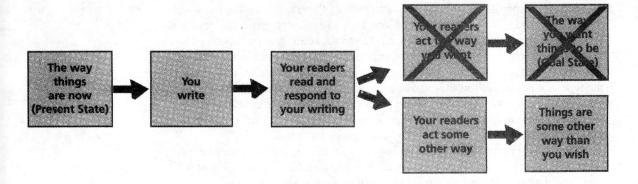

Because the success or failure of your writing depends on your readers' responses during this critical time, focus your objectives on what must happen while your readers are reading your message.

An excellent way to establish this focus is to follow a suggestion offered in Chapter 1: Create a mental portrait of your readers in the act of reading your communication. As your imaginary readers read each sentence or paragraph, watch their responses. If you see them reacting in the way you desire, great. If not, you've learned that you need to revise. Of course, your imaginary portrait can help you only if you know the facts about your readers that will enable you to accurately predict their reactions. The next four guidelines tell how to gather the information you need in order to make predictions that are as accurate as possible.

GUIDELINE 2 DEFINE YOUR USABILITY GOAL: ANALYZE YOUR READERS' READING TASKS

指导方针2：界定可用性目标：分析读者的阅读任务

Begin constructing your mental portrait of your readers by determining what will make your communication *usable* in their view.

As you learned in Chapter 1, usability is one of the two essential ingredients for success in a workplace communication. Usability is defined as the ease with which readers can use your communication to perform their tasks. The evolution of computer manuals provides an illustration. Years ago, most manuals were organized around the features of the software or hardware. For instance, they would describe the function each desktop icon, menu choice, or F-key enabled users to perform. This organization proved extremely frustrating to users, who didn't want to learn the functions of isolated icons or F-keys but rather the sequence of steps needed to complete their work. Computer manuals improved immensely once companies realized that they needed to study users' tasks and organize their manuals around them.

> Usability is the ease with which readers can use your communication to perform their tasks.

Similarly, to make *any* type of communication usable, you must first understand and support the tasks your readers wish to perform as they read what you've written for them. The following four-step procedure will enable you to do so.

> **IDENTIFYING YOUR READERS' TASKS**
> 1. Identify your readers' purpose for reading.
> 2. Identify the information your readers want from your communication.
> 3. Determine how your readers will look for this information.
> 4. Determine how they will use the information *while reading*.

Identifying Your Readers' Purpose for Reading

First, identify the specific purpose your readers will have in mind when they pick up and begin to read your communication. Almost certainly, they will be trying to gain information they can use in some practical way. A manager might read a report to gather information needed to make a decision. An engineer might consult a computer reference manual to solve a specific programming problem. To create a usable communication, you must design it in ways that enable your readers to easily locate and use the information they need in order to achieve their purpose.

Identifying the Information Your Readers Want from Your Communication

To assure that your communication includes the information your readers need, you must first determine what that information is. An excellent way to identify this information is to imagine the questions your readers will have in mind as they pick up your communication. Their questions, of course, are determined by their purpose in reading. For example, Todd has identified two reasons the vice presidents might have for requesting that he report on his progress in his investigation of new methods for applying chip-resistant paint. First, they might want to decide which method they want him to concentrate on in his future work. In this case, their questions are likely to be "Which alternatives appear to produce the best results?" "Which ones appear to be least costly?" and "How will our production line need to be altered if we employ each of the most promising alternatives?" Alternatively, the vice presidents may have asked Todd for a progress report because they are worried that he won't complete his work in time for the company to use his results on a new line of products it will begin manufacturing next year. In this instance, their questions will probably be "What work do you still have to do?" "How long will it take you?" and "If you can't be done by May 30 without extra help, how much help will you need?"

To write a report that helps the vice presidents achieve their purpose, Todd must pinpoint the specific questions they want his report to answer. If Todd's report answers one set of questions but the vice presidents are asking the other set, he will have failed to prepare a communication his readers find usable.

Determining How Your Readers Will Look for Information

Once you've identified the information your readers will seek, imagine the ways they will look for it. Here are three search strategies readers often use on the job, together with some strategies you can use to assist readers:

> **Learn More**
>
> For more information on graphics and page design, see Chapters 12 and 13.

THREE WAYS READERS SEARCH FOR INFORMATION

- **Thorough, sequential reading.** When you write to readers who will read each sentence and paragraph in turn, you can systematically build ideas from one sentence, paragraph, and section to the next.
- **Reading for key points only.** When you write to readers who will scan for the most important information, you can use lists, tables, boldface, and other strategies to make key points stand out.
- **Reference reading.** When you write to readers who will seek only specific pieces of information (as when troubleshooting a problem that has cropped up with a piece of equipment), you can use headings, tables of contents, indexes, and page design to guide your readers rapidly to the information they seek.

Determining How Your Readers Will Use the Information While Reading

Once readers find the information they are seeking, they want to use it. By learning how they will use your information *while they are reading*, you can determine the most helpful way to organize and present it. Here are three common ways people use information while reading at work, together with example writing strategies appropriate to each:

THREE WAYS PEOPLE USE INFORMATION AT WORK

- **To compare alternatives.** If the vice presidents will read Todd's report to identify the most promising painting process, he should organize in a way that will enable them to compare the alternatives easily on a point-by-point basis (cost of each, implementation time for each, etc.).
- **To determine how the information will affect them and their organization.** The engineer in charge of the production line in Todd's company might want to know how the new process would affect her responsibilities. To meet this engineer's needs, Todd would not write a progress report, but rather another kind of communication that focuses on the types of changes that might be involved, such as those in equipment and personnel.
- **To perform a procedure.** A technician might need directions for performing some part of the new process. Todd could most effectively assist this person by preparing step-by-step instructions in a numbered list.

Advice throughout the rest of this book describes ways to make your communications usable by employing your knowledge of the information your readers seek, the ways they will look for it, and the things they will do with it once they find it.

GUIDELINE 3 DEFINE YOUR PERSUASIVE GOAL: ANALYZE YOUR READERS' ATTITUDES
指导方针3：界定说服力目标：分析读者的态度

When creating your mental portrait of your readers, you should also tell how you want your communication to alter their attitudes. In doing so, you identify the persuasive goal of your communication. As you learned in Chapter 1, persuasiveness is the second of the two essential qualities of all on-the-job writing. Every communication you write at work must be persuasive, even ones you don't normally think of as persuasive. For example, the vice presidents will not rely on Todd's progress report as a basis for their decisions unless they are persuaded that it provides accurately all of the relevant information. Instructions cannot achieve their purposes if people are not persuaded to read and follow them.

Persuasion is all about influencing readers' attitudes. When their attitudes change, their actions will follow. When writing at work, focus on your readers' attitudes toward the following four objects:

Consumers assembling a product, executives making decisions, and supervisors managing factory production need much different things from the communications they read. To write effectively, you must identify and meet the needs of the particular persons to whom you are writing.

THINGS THAT YOUR READERS' ATTITUDES FOCUS ON

- **Your subject matter.** Many of the topics you write about will be ones your readers have thought about already and so have already formed attitudes about.
- **You.** As one recent college graduate observed, "As soon as I started my job, I realized that every time I communicate, people judge me based upon how well they think I write or speak." Even when you are merely answering factual questions, you will want your communication to inspire a favorable opinion of you as a person.

- **Your department or organization.** When you write to people outside your immediate working group, your communications will represent not only you but also your coworkers. Impressions your readers have of your department or company will shape their response to your message, so you will certainly want to influence your readers' attitude toward your organization.
- **The communication itself.** Readers can come to a communication with very high—or very low—motivation to read it. For example, many people are uninterested in reading instructions. When writing instructions, therefore, you will want to employ strategies that create the missing motivation.

A change in attitudes always involves a shift from the present attitude to the desired one. This means that when analyzing your audience you should not only specify what you want the readers' final attitude to be, but also determine what their present attitudes are. Often, you will need to *reverse* negative attitudes and also *reinforce* positive ones. You may also need to *shape* your readers' attitudes on topics they don't have opinions about at present.

The distinction among these three kinds of attitude change will be important to you because different kinds of change are best addressed by different persuasive strategies. To reinforce an attitude, you can build on the existing attitude and expect little resistance. Consequently, you can often present only positive points without trying to rebut arguments against your position. If you discuss negative points, it would be for the purpose of persuading readers that you have thoroughly investigated your topic. In contrast, if you want to reverse an attitude, you can expect your readers to be resistant. Consequently, you must not only cite positive points, but also address the counterarguments your readers will raise.

Figure 3.1 illustrates some ways you might want to alter your readers' attitudes in several typical communications.

FIGURE 3.1
Communications Alter Readers' Attitudes

WAYS COMMUNICATIONS CAN ALTER READERS' ATTITUDES

The Way Things Are Now	You Write	The Way You Want Them to Be
Your reader is a manager who wants to decide whether to purchase a certain piece of equipment.	You write a memo evaluating the equipment in terms of the benefits it will bring the company.	The manager decides to buy the equipment and feels confident that she made a good decision based on information you provided.
Your reader is the director of a plant that is using an outdated process.	You write a report on problems with the current process and the ways they can be overcome with various new processes.	After reading your report, the plant director feels that the process being used now may be faulty and that one of the new ones is worth investigating further.
Your readers are bank clerks who will use a new computer system. They fear it is more complicated than the present system.	You write a procedure manual that shows how easy the system is to use.	The bank clerks feel relaxed and self-confident after learning from your manual how to use the new system.

GUIDELINE 4 LEARN YOUR READERS' PERSONAL CHARACTERISTICS

指导方针 4：了解读者的个人特点

Different readers respond differently to the same writing strategies. Consequently, when you construct your mental portrait of your readers, you should incorporate those characteristics of your particular readers that will influence the way they respond to your communication. The following paragraphs discuss several reader characteristics that are especially important to consider.

Professional Specialty

People with different professional specialties ask different questions and use the answers differently. For instance, when reading a report on the industrial emissions from a factory, an environmental engineer working for the factory might ask, "How are these emissions produced, and what ideas does this report offer for reducing them?" whereas the corporate attorney might ask, "Do these emissions exceed standards set by the Environmental Protection Agency, and, if so, how can we limit our legal liability for these violations?"

The most obvious clues to your readers' specialties are their job titles: systems analyst, laboratory technician, bank cashier, director of public relations. However, don't settle for obtaining only a general sense of your readers' specialties. Determine as precisely as possible why each person will be reading your communication and exactly what information he or she will be looking for.

Organizational Role

Regardless of the particularities of their professional specialties, people at work usually play one of three organizational roles: decision maker, adviser, or implementer. Each role leads to a different set of questions.

Decision makers The decision makers' role is to say how the organization will act when it is confronted with a particular choice. Decision makers determine what the company should do in the future — next week, next month, next year. Consequently, decision makers usually ask questions shaped by their need to choose between alternative courses of action.

TYPICAL QUESTIONS ASKED BY DECISION MAKERS

- **What are your conclusions?** Decision makers want your conclusions, not the raw data you gathered or the details about your procedures. Conclusions can serve as the basis for decisions; details cannot.
- **What do you recommend?** Decision makers usually ask you about a topic because you have special knowledge of it. This knowledge makes your recommendation especially valuable to decision-making readers.
- **What will happen?** Decision makers want to know what will occur if they follow your recommendations—and what will happen if they don't. How much money will be saved? How much will production increase? How will customers react?

Advisers Advisers provide information and advice for decision makers to consider when deciding what the organization should do. Unlike decision makers, advisers are very interested in details. They need to analyze and evaluate the evidence supporting your general conclusions, recommendations, and projections.

Consequently, advisers ask questions that touch on the thoroughness, reliability, and impact of your work.

TYPICAL QUESTIONS ASKED BY ADVISERS

- Did you use a reasonable method to obtain your results?
- Do your data really support your conclusions?
- Have you overlooked anything important?
- If your recommendation is followed, what will be the effect on other departments?
- What kinds of problems are likely to arise?

Implementers Decisions, once made, must be carried out by someone. Implementers are these individuals. The most important questions asked by implementers are these.

TYPICAL QUESTIONS ASKED BY IMPLEMENTERS

- **What do you want me to do?** Whether you are writing step-by-step instructions, requests for information, or policies that others must follow, implementers want you to provide clear, exact, easy-to-follow directions.
- **Why do you want me to do it?** To produce satisfactory results, implementers often must know the reason for the policy or directive they are reading. Imagine, for instance, the situation of the managers of a factory who have been directed to cut by 15 percent the amount of energy used in production. They need to know whether they are to make long-term energy savings or compensate for a short-term shortage. If the latter, they might take temporary actions, such as altering work hours and curtailing certain operations. However, if the reduction is to be long-term, they might purchase new equipment and modify the factory building.
- **How much freedom do I have in deciding how to do this?** People often devise shortcuts or alternative ways of doing things. They need to know whether they have this freedom or whether they must do things exactly as stated.
- **What's the deadline?** To be able to adjust their schedules to include a new task along with their other responsibilities, implementers need to know when the new task must be completed.

Familiarity with Your Topic

Your readers' familiarity with your topic — company inventory levels, employee morale on the second shift, problems with new software — will determine how much background information you need to provide to make your communication understandable and useful to them. When you are writing about a topic they know well, you may not need to include any background at all. However, if you are treating a topic they don't know much about, you may have to explain the general situation before proceeding to the heart of your message. If your readers are unfamiliar with your topic, you may also need to explain how it relates to them so they can judge whether to bother reading about it.

Knowledge of Your Specialty

To use the information you provide, readers need to understand the terms and concepts you employ. Consider, for example, an instruction manual for a computer-controlled machine that directs the reader to "zero the tool along the Z-axis." Readers unfamiliar with this type of equipment might ask, "What is zeroing? What is the Z-axis?" If the instructions do not answer these questions, the readers will have to ask someone else for help, which defeats the purpose of the instructions. On the other hand, the instructions writer would not want to provide these definitions if all of his or her readers are already familiar with these terms. Coming upon such explanations, these readers would ask, "Why is this writer making me read about things I already know?"

Relationship with You

When you are having a conversation, you adjust your speech to your relationship with the other person. You talk with a friend more informally than you do with a college instructor you don't know well—and both your friend and your instructor might be startled if you didn't make such adjustments. Similarly, at work you should write in a way that reflects the relationships you have with your readers.

Personal Preferences

A variety of personal characteristics can also influence readers' responses to your writing. For example, you may be writing to an individual who detests the use of certain words or insists on particular ways of phrasing certain statements. Or you might be writing to someone who is keenly interested in information you would not have to supply to most people. Some readers favor brief messages, and some insist on more detail. It only makes sense to accommodate such personal preferences where feasible.

People's preferences are shaped by the customary practices employed where they work. This is important to keep in mind as you begin to work for a new company or department. When people say, "That's not the way we write here," they may be expressing preferences shared by many other people in the organization.

Special Considerations

This is a catchall category. It is a reminder that each reader is unique. You should always be on the lookout for reader characteristics you would not normally need to consider. For example, you may be addressing individuals with an especially high or low reading level, weak eyesight, or color blindness — and it will be essential for you to take these characteristics into consideration when writing.

It is also wise to consider the setting in which your readers will be reading, in case this factor suggests ways you can adapt your communication to make it more useful for them. For example, if you are writing a manual for a computer program, you might want to design it in a small format to help conserve desk space for your readers. If you are writing a repair manual for hydraulic pumps, you might print your manual on paper coated to resist the moisture, oil, and dirt that are unavoidable in that reading environment.

GUIDELINE 5 GLOBAL GUIDELINE: LEARN YOUR READERS' CULTURAL CHARACTERISTICS

整体指导方针5：了解读者的文化特点

International business is growing rapidly. Along with it, the likelihood that any college graduate will write to people in other cultures is also increasing. Every ten years since 1960, international trade for the United States has doubled, reaching over $2.5 trillion or more than fifty times the figure forty years ago (Lustig & Koester, 2003). In almost all countries, the number of companies with suppliers, buyers, and offices or other facilities in other countries continues to grow.

Also, the workplace in most countries is multicultural. At least 11 percent of United States residents were born in other countries (Census, 2000). At home, more than one in six speak a language other than English. Whether you are among the majority or the minority reflected in such statistics, you are likely to address persons from other cultural backgrounds even when writing to coworkers, clients, and others in your own country.

To succeed when writing to readers in another culture or with a cultural background different from your own, you may need to abandon or modify some of the writing strategies that bring you success in your own culture — including some of the strategies presented in this book. Why? Readers' responses to a communication depend not only on their individual characteristics discussed in Guideline 3, but also on values and expectations they share with others in their culture.

The influence of a culture on our readers' responses usually doesn't become evident to us until we write to persons in another culture. After all, when you are writing to people in your own culture, you are addressing people who share your sense of what makes a communication usable and persuasive. People in other cultures don't necessarily share these same assumptions. For example, many readers in the dominant business culture in the United States welcome blunt, brisk communications. When reading communications written in the indirect, leisurely style that is customary in Arab and Asian cultures, they may become impatient with the message and the messenger. Similarly, many Arab and Asian readers feel that the direct, forthright style common in the United States is rude and inconsiderate. Writers from each of these cultures can increase their chances of communicating successfully by learning about the other culture and adapting their writing accordingly.

Cultural Differences That Affect Communication

Because cultures differ from one another in so many ways, there is no magical set of cultural characteristics that will help you successfully adapt your writing in every case. However, the following seven characteristics are relevant in many situations.

- Amount of detail expected
- Distance between the top and bottom of organizational hierarchies
- Individual versus group orientation
- Preference for direct or indirect statements
- Basis of business decisions
- Behaviors in face-to-face communication
- Interpretation of images, gestures, and words

At the least, studying these seven will help you see how cultural characteristics influence reader responses. As you read them, remember that each contains a range of possibilities. Between the poles of low-context and high-context cultures are many gradations.

Amount of detail expected One of the pioneers in studying intercultural communication, Edward Hall (1976) distinguished among cultures on the basis of the amount of detail they provide in a communication. In countries such as Japan, communications provide a small amount of information because writers and readers both assume that readers will fill in the rest of the information through their knowledge of such things as the situation in which the communication is written, the topic, social customs, and so on. Hall called these high-context cultures because successful communication depends on the large amount of contextual information the readers bring to the message.

In contrast, in low-context cultures, such as the United States and much of Northern Europe, writers and readers both assume that readers are responsible for bringing very little contextual knowledge to a communication. Consequently, writers typically provide extensive detail, trying to cover thoroughly every aspect of their topic.

Knowledge of these differences and the ability to accommodate communications appropriately is important to you if you are writing from a high- or low-context culture to readers in the other kind of culture. Readers in a low-context culture can be offended if a writer includes more detail than they expect and need. The extra detail would seem to imply that they do not know the things they should know. Similarly, a low-context reader could feel that the writer who has provided a high-context amount of detail was not considering their needs because much of the expected information (even if not needed) wasn't provided.

Distance between the top and bottom of organizational hierarchies Through research that included the study of managers at IBM facilities in forty countries, Geert Hofstede (2001) distinguished cultures according to the distance they maintain

> **Learn More**
> For information on communicating between high-context and low-context cultures, see Chapter 4, page 109.

> **Learn More**
> For more information on communicating between cultures that have large and small distances from top to bottom of the organizational hierarchy, see Chapter 8, page 262.

between people at the bottom and the top of an organization's hierarchy. In the United States and in some European cultures, the distance is very great. In other cultures, such as the Japanese, the distance is much smaller. This information is helpful to writers because Hofstede also found that, in general, where the distance is greatest, communication styles are most formal whether the communications are written by people in lower ranks to people above them or vice versa.

Individual versus group orientation   Hofstede also distinguished cultures that focus on the individual from those that focus on the group. Individualistic cultures honor personal achievement and expect individuals to take care of themselves. The dominant cultures in the United States and northern Europe provide examples. In group-oriented cultures, success belongs to the group and people pursue group goals rather than individual ones. Many Asian cultures are group oriented.

Writers often can increase their effectiveness by adjusting to the individualistic or group orientation of their readers' culture. For example, in persuasive communications it can be helpful to highlight benefits to the individual, whereas an emphasis on benefits to the readers' organization can be more persuasive to readers in group-oriented cultures.

> **Learn More**
> For more information on communicating between individualistic and group-oriented cultures, see Chapter 5, page 142.

Preference for direct or indirect statements   Cultures also vary in the directness with which people typically make requests, decline requests, and express their opinions, particularly negative ones. For example, in U.S. and northern European cultures writers typically decline a request directly. They may apologize and offer an explanation for their decision. But they will state the denial explicitly. In contrast, Japanese and Korean cultures prefer an indirect style (Gudykunst & Ting-Toomey, 1998). Instead of declining a request explicitly, they might say that fulfilling it would be difficult or that they need time to think about how to reply. In this way, they save the requester the humiliation of being denied, while readers in those cultures know that the request will not be fulfilled.

Using one culture's style when writing to people in another culture can create troublesome misunderstandings. To many U.S. readers, an indirect refusal might be misinterpreted. Because they didn't hear the direct denial they expected, these U.S. readers could believe that the request could be fulfilled so they may persist in asking. On the other hand, readers in the Japanese and Korean cultures may interpret the direct U.S. style as rude and inconsiderate.

> **Learn More**
> For more information on communicating between cultures that have different preferences about direct and indirect statements, see Chapter 7, page 207.

Basis of business decisions   There are also differences among cultures in the ways business decisions are made. In the United States and many European cultures, organizations typically choose among alternatives on the basis of impersonal evaluations and data analyses. In Arab and other cultures, these same decisions are often made on the basis of relationships. For instance, whereas a U.S. company might choose a company to build a new plant or supply parts for its products by carefully studying detailed proposals from the competitors, an Arab company might select the company represented by a person with whom it would like to do business. These

> **Learn More**
> For more information on communicating between cultures that have different ways of making business decisions, see Chapter 5, page 142.

The distance people maintain between one another when talking varies considerably from one culture to another.

are differences that writers in either kind of culture would need to keep in mind when trying to win business, maintain business relationships, and even respond to complaints from organizations in the other kind of culture.

Behaviors in face-to-face communication   Cultures also differ with respect to a variety of behaviors in face-to-face encounters. For instance, in some cultures people stand much closer to one another when in conversation than in another. In some cultures people are expected to make eye contact when talking with another person. In other cultures they are expected not to. In some cultures people are usually expected to ask questions of superiors. In others, doing so would usually violate norms of acceptable behavior.

Being aware of these culturally formed differences can help you avoid misinterpreting behaviors of persons from other cultures in one-to-one conversations, team meetings, and oral presentations to a large or small group. And it can help you avoid engaging in behaviors that might be misinterpreted by them.

Interpretation of images, gestures, and words   An image, gesture, or word can elicit markedly different responses in different cultures. Even the same words have different meanings in different countries and cultures. Photographs, drawings, and other pictures sometimes depict relationships between people that seem ordinary in one culture but violate the cultural customs of another. Gestures likewise have different meanings in different cultures. When people in the United States signal "Okay" by joining a thumb and forefinger to form a circle, they are making a gesture

Learn More

To learn more about cultural differences in face-to-face communication, see Chapter 16, pages 454–455.

Learn More

Chapter 12 (page 346) has more information on the interpretation of images, and Chapter 8 (page 275) has more on the interpretation of words.

Guideline 5   **Learn Your Readers' Cultural Characteristics**

that is offensive in Germany and obscene in Brazil (Axtell, 1998). To avoid the risk of unintentionally offending others, some experts advise technical communicators to avoid showing hands in graphics that will be read by people in other cultures.

Applying Cultural Knowledge When You Write

As the preceding discussion indicates, gaining knowledge of your readers' culture can greatly increase your success in creating a communication that your readers will find useful and persuasive. It is intended to give you a sense of the kinds of variations that are possible and to help you see some of the ways these variations can impact readers' responses to what you write.

It is not, however, intended to suggest that gaining general knowledge about a culture can provide you with a recipe for adapting your communication strategies to the needs and expectations of your specific readers. As intercultural communication expert Ron Scollon (1999) says, "Cultures don't talk to each other. People do." When writing to people in other cultures, your reader-centered goal is the same as when addressing people in your own culture: to understand as fully as possible the relevant facts about the specific readers you are addressing.

In addition to the fact that every reader is an individual, a primary reason why you can't rely solely on general cultural information is that you are likely to be addressing your readers in their roles as employees of a company, government agency, or other organization. And organizations have cultures, too (Hofstede, 2002; Scollon & Scollon, 2001). In general, organizational cultures reflect the culture of the nation or region in which they are located. However, some organizational cultures have significant features that modify or run counter to the general culture in the region. For instance, in both the United States and Japan, most organizational cultures will mirror the features of the general culture of their nations. Nevertheless, some Japanese companies will have the relatively flat hierarchies and the accompanying informality that typifies U.S. culture. And some U.S. companies will have large distances between lower and higher ranks along with the associated formality that are typical of Japanese culture. Subsidiaries and branch facilities in any region of the world are likely to develop some — but not all — characteristics of the corporate headquarters, whether the headquarters are in Asia, the Middle East, or North America.

Researchers have also found that readers are influenced by the culture of their professions. Webb and Keene (1999) found that the worldwide culture of aeronautical engineering and science possesses characteristics that transcend geographical boundaries. Similarly, scientists, doctors, and teachers share many cultural traits with their counterparts around the globe.

Finally, when you are writing to individuals or organizations in another culture, there's a good chance that they have also made an effort to learn about your culture and to accommodate their communications to your cultural characteristics. Some researchers maintain that when people and organizations from two cultures communicate regularly, they create a third context as they develop their ways of understanding one another (Bolten, 1999; Steier, 1999).

These several factors all indicate that when writing to people in another culture, you should not rely solely on information about the communication-relevant features of that culture. As when you are writing to persons in your own culture, you should investigate as fully as possible the characteristics of specific individuals who will be your readers.

How To Gain Knowledge about Your Intercultural Readers

A variety of resources can help you learn about your readers' cultural characteristics. The most helpful are people — including your coworkers — who are familiar with your readers' regional and organizational culture. You may even be fortunate enough to be able to speak with coworkers who know the individuals to whom you are writing. If your organization has copies of successful communications that others have written to your readers, you will probably be able to learn a great deal from them.

You can also consult many helpful print and online sources that present broad descriptions of cultures around the world. Some of the information they provide concerns such topics as holidays, political systems, and wedding customs, so you may want to focus your attention on topics relevant to writing work-related communications. On the other hand, learning about these other topics can increase your general understanding of other cultures. Research has demonstrated a positive association between intercultural communication competence and awareness of the other culture (Wiseman, Hammer, & Nishida, 1989). To gain additional insight into the ways other cultures differ from yours, look at the information these sources provide people in other cultures about your own. Self-awareness is another characteristic that correlates intercultural competence (Gudykunst, Yang, & Nishida, 1987). Here are some sources you can consult:

- Cyborlink website: www.cyborlink.com
- David M. Kennedy Center for International Studies, Brigham Young University: www.culturegrams.com
- Global EDGE website: www.globaledge.msu.edu

You can also learn from the response you receive each time you write to readers in other cultures (Brownell, 1999). If the opportunity arises, ask your readers about their reactions to your communications. When preparing instructions or other communications that will be read by many people in another culture, conduct a user test (described in Chapter 15) with members of your target audience, if at all possible.

> For references and links to additional sources of information about cultures, go to **www.thomsonedu.com/english/anderson** and click on Chapter 3.

Importance of Your Attitudes

Having positive attitudes toward your readers is essential to success in creating reader-centered communications whether the readers are in your own culture or another one. However, your attitudes toward your readers and their cultures are especially important when you are writing to readers in other cultures. Research has shown that competence in intercultural communication has positive associations with open-mindedness (Adler, 1975), a nonjudgmental attitude (Ruben, 1976), empathy toward others (Chen & Tan, 1995; Ruben, 1976), and a positive attitude toward the other culture (Randolph, Landis, & Tzeng, 1977). On the other side, competence in intercultural communication has a negative association with ethnocentrism (Neuliep & McCroskey, 1997; Nishida, Hammer, & Wiseman, 1998). The more you focus on learning about your readers' cultures and the less you engage in judging them, the more successfully you will be able to write.

GUIDELINE 6 Study the Context in Which Your Readers Will Read

指导方针 6：研究读者的阅读语境

At work, people interpret what they read as a chapter in an ongoing story. Consequently, they respond to each message in light of prior events as well as their understanding of the people and groups involved. Fill out your mental portrait of your readers by imagining how the following circumstances might influence their response to your communication:

- **Recent events related to your topic.** Maybe you are going to announce the reorganization of a department that has just adjusted to another major organizational change. You'll need to make a special effort to present the newest change in a positive light. Or maybe you are requesting money to attend an important professional meeting. If your department has just been reprimanded for excessive travel expenses, you will have to make an especially strong case.

- **Interpersonal, interdepartmental, and intraorganizational relationships.** If you are requesting cooperation from a department that has long competed with yours for company resources, you will need to employ special diplomacy. Political conflicts between individuals and groups can also create delicate writing situations in which certain ways of expressing your message can appear to support one faction and weaken another even if you have no intention of doing so.

GUIDELINE 7 Ask Others to Help You Understand Your Readers and Their Context

指导方针 7：请他人帮助你了解读者和他们的语境

How can you learn all of the facts about your readers and their situation that are described in Guidelines 2 through 6? Experienced employees have often gained that knowledge through years of interacting with their readers. If you are a newcomer, you may have to ask others for help.

The best sources for most of the information are your actual readers. If possible, interview them as a first step in formulating your objectives. Better than anyone else, they can tell you about their needs, attitudes, preferences, and situations. Most readers will welcome the opportunity to tell you what they would find to be usable and persuasive in a communication you are writing for them.

If you cannot contact your readers, ask for help from your boss, coworkers, or anyone else who might have valuable insights about your readers and their circumstances. Like most activities of writing, defining objectives is one where you can benefit greatly from the assistance of other people.

GUIDELINE 8 LEARN WHO *ALL* YOUR READERS WILL BE
指导方针8：了解你所有的目标读者

So far, this chapter has assumed that you will know from the start just who your readers will be. That may not always be the case. Communications you prepare on the job may find their way to many people in many parts of your organization. Numerous memos and reports prepared at work are routed to one or two dozen people — and sometimes many more. Even a brief communication you write to one person may be copied or shown to others. To write effectively, you must learn who *all* your readers will be so you can keep them all in mind when you write. The following discussion will help you identify readers you might otherwise overlook.

Phantom Readers

The most important readers of a communication may be hidden from you. That's because at work, written communications addressed to one person are often used by others. Those real but unnamed readers are called *phantom readers*.

Phantom readers are likely to be present behind the scenes when you write communications that require some sort of decision. One clue to their presence is that the person you are addressing is not high enough in the organizational hierarchy to make the decision your communication requires. Perhaps the decision will affect more parts of the organization than are managed by the person addressed, or perhaps it involves more money than the person addressed is likely to control.

Much of what you write to your own boss may actually be used by phantom readers. Many managers accomplish their work by assigning it to assistants. Thus, your boss may sometimes check over your communications, then pass them along to his or her superiors.

After working at a job for a while, employees usually learn which communications will be passed up the organizational hierarchy. However, a new employee may be chagrined to discover that a hastily written memo has been read by executives at very high levels. To avoid such embarrassment, identify your phantom readers, then write in a way that meets their needs as well as the needs of the less influential person you are addressing.

Future Readers

Your communications may be put to use weeks, months, or even years after you imagined their useful life was over. Lawyers say that the memos, reports, and other documents that employees write today are evidence for court cases tomorrow. Most company documents can be subpoenaed for lawsuits concerning product liability, patent violation, breach of contract, and other issues. If you are writing a communication that could have such use, remember that lawyers and judges may be your future readers.

> For more information on the legal dimensions of on-the-job writing, go to **www.thomsonedu.com/english/anderson** and click on Chapter 3.

Your future readers also may be employees of your company who may retrieve your old communications for information or ideas. By thinking of their needs, you may be able to save them considerable labor. Even if you are asked to write something "just for the record," remember that the only reason to have a record is to provide some future readers with information they will need to use in some practical way that you should understand and support.

Complex Audiences

Writers sometimes overlook important members of their audience because they assume that all their readers have identical needs and concerns. Actually, audiences often consist of diverse groups with widely varying backgrounds and responsibilities.

That's partly because decisions and actions at work often impact many people and departments throughout the organization. For instance, a proposal to change a company's computer system will affect persons throughout the organization, and people in different areas will have different concerns: some with recordkeeping, some with data communication, some with security, and so on. People in each area will examine the proposal.

Even when only a few people are affected by a decision, many employers expect widespread consultation and advice on it. Each person consulted will have his or her own professional role and area of expertise, and each will play that role and apply that expertise when studying your communication.

When you address a group of people who will be reading from many perspectives, you are addressing a *complex audience*. To do that effectively, you need to write in a way that will meet each person's needs without reducing the effectiveness of your communication for the others. Sometimes you may have to make a tradeoff by focusing on the needs and concerns of the most influential members of your audience. In any case, the first step in writing effectively to a complex audience is to identify each of its members or groups.

Identifying Readers: An Example

The following example describes how one writer, Thomas McKay, identified a complex audience and then creatively addressed the needs of his various readers. McKay was writing on behalf of his employer, Midlands Research Incorporated, to request compensation from another company, Aerotest Corporation, which had sold Midlands faulty equipment for testing smokestack emissions. McKay addressed his letter to Robert Fulton, Aerotest's Vice President for Sales, but realized that Fulton would distribute copies to many others at Aerotest. To identify these other readers, McKay asked himself who at his own employer's company, Midlands, would be asked to read such a letter if it received one. Thinking about the people who would be consulted as Midlands decided how to respond, McKay identified the following phantom readers:

- Engineers in the department that designed and manufactured the faulty equipment, who would be asked to determine whether Aerotest's difficulties really resulted from flaws in the design.

- Aerotest's lawyers, who would be asked to determine the company's legal liability.
- Personnel in Aerotest's repair shop, who would be asked to examine the costs Midlands said it had incurred in repairing the equipment.

To meet the needs of the diverse readers in his complex audience, McKay created a letter with a modular design, a commonly used workplace strategy in which different, readily distinguishable parts of a communication each address a distinct group of readers. Modular designs are very common at websites, where home pages often have links for different kinds of users. For example, your college's home page may have separate links for current students, prospective students, faculty, and graduates. Figure 3.2 shows the modular design of the home page example from a company that makes surgical equipment. To create a modular design for his letter to Aerotest, McKay wrote a one-page letter that provided background information for all his readers (Figure 3.3). He also attached enclosures addressed to specific groups in his complex audience. Two enclosures contained detailed accounts of the problems Midlands encountered with the emissions testers. These enclosures answered this following question from Aerotest's engineers and lawyers: "Does McKay have good evidence that the problems encountered by Midlands were caused by poor work on

> **Learn More**
>
> For more information on modular designs, see Guideline 4 in Chapter 4 (page 106).

FIGURE 3.2
Modular Design of a Website

Guideline 8 Learn Who *All* Your Readers Will Be

FIGURE 3.3
Letter to a Complex Audience (Enclosures Not Shown)

In his letter requesting compensation for expenses caused by faulty equipment, McKay addresses one person (Robert Fulton) but designed his message for the complex audience he knows will read his letter.

In the first two paragraphs, McKay provides background information of interest to all members of his complex audience at Aerotest.

In the third paragraph, McKay discusses his three major points: the equipment failure resulted from faulty design and construction, repairs were costly for his company, and his company wants compensation.

McKay created a modular design by enclosing several items, each useful primarily to one part of his complex audience at Aerotest.
- For Aerotest's engineers and lawyers, two accounts of the problems that are intended to persuade that the difficulties really did arise from Aerotest's faulty equipment.

MIDLANDS RESEARCH INCORPORATED
2796 Buchanan Boulevard   Cincinnati, Ohio 45202

Mr. Robert Fulton   October 17, 2004
Vice President for Sales
Aerotest Corporation
485 Connie Avenue
Sea View, California 94024

Dear Mr. Fulton:

In August, Midlands Research Incorporated purchased a Model Bass 0070 sampling system from Aerotest. Our Environmental Monitoring Group has been using—or trying to use—that sampler to fulfill the conditions of a contract that MRI has with the Environmental Protection Agency to test for toxic substances in the effluent gases from thirteen industrial smokestacks in the Cincinnati area. However, the manager of our Environmental Monitoring Group reports that her employees have had considerable trouble with the sampler.

These difficulties have prevented MRI from fulfilling some of its contractual obligations on time. Thus, besides frustrating our Environmental Monitoring Group, particularly the field technicians, these problems have also troubled Mr. Bernard Gordon, who is our EPA contracting officer, and the EPA enforcement officials who have been awaiting data from us.

I am enclosing two detailed accounts of the problems we have had with the sampler. As you can see, these problems arise from serious design and construction flaws in the sampler itself. Because of the strict schedule contained in our contract with the EPA, we have not had time to return our sampler to you for repair. Therefore, we have had to correct the flaws ourselves, using our Equipment Support Shop, at a cost of approximately $15,000. Because we are incurring the additional expense only because of problems with the engineering and construction of your sampler, we hope that you will be willing to reimburse us, at least in part, by supplying without charge the replacement parts listed on the enclosed page. We will be able to use those parts in future work.

Thank you for your consideration in this matter.

Sincerely,

Thomas McKay
Thomas McKay
Vice President
Environmental Division

Enclosures: 2 Accounts of Problems
             1 Statement of Repair Expenses
             1 List of Replacement Parts

- For Aerotest's repair shop, a statement of the repair expenses intended to persuade that the costs he said his company incurred were reasonable.

- For Aerotest's shipping department, a list of replacement parts to use when sending the parts to McKay's company.

Aerotest's part?" McKay also attached a detailed statement of the repair expenses because he predicted that Aerotest's repair shop would be asked, "Do you think the repairs made by Midlands really cost $15,000?" Of course, neither McKay nor website designers could have developed a modular design if they had been unaware of the complexity their audiences. When defining your communication's objectives, take similar care to identify all of your readers.

GUIDELINE 9 IDENTIFY ANY CONSTRAINTS ON THE WAY YOU WRITE
指导方针9：找出写作方式的任何限制

So far, this chapter has focused your attention on developing a full understanding of your readers as you define your communication's objectives. As you gather the information that will form the basis for the way you craft your communication, you should also learn about any expectations, regulations, or other factors that may constrain what you can say and how you can say it. In the working world, expectations and regulations can affect any aspect of a communication — even tone, use of abbreviations, layout of tables, size of margins, and length (usually specifying a maximum length, not a minimum). It will be important for you to find out about these constraints and take them into account as you create your communication.

Some of these constraints come directly from the employer, reflecting such motives as the company's desire to cultivate a particular corporate image, to protect its legal interests (because any written document can be subpoenaed in a lawsuit), and to preserve its competitive edge (for example, by preventing employees from accidentally tipping off competitors about technological breakthroughs). In addition, most organizations develop writing customs — "the way we write things here." Writing constraints also can originate from outside the company — for instance, from government regulations that specify how patent applications, environmental impact reports, and many other types of documents are to be prepared. Similarly, scientific, technical, or other professional journals have strict rules about many aspects of the articles they publish.

Be sure to find out what these constraints are when you are defining your objectives so you can take them into account as you plan and draft your communication. Many companies publish style guides that set forth their regulations about writing. Ask if your employer has one. You can also learn about these constraints by asking coworkers and reading communications similar to yours that your coworkers have written in the past.

> To view sample style guides, go to www.thomsonedu.com/english/anderson and click on Chapter 3.

GUIDELINE 10 ETHICS GUIDELINE: IDENTIFY YOUR COMMUNICATION'S STAKEHOLDERS
道德指导方针10：明确交流过程中的参与者

There are many strategies for assuring that on-the-job writing is ethical. Some writers use an *alarm bell strategy*. They trust that if an ethical problem arises in their writing, an alarm bell will go off in their heads. Unless they hear that bell, however, they don't think about ethics. Other writers use a *checkpoint strategy*. At a single, predetermined point in the writing process, they review their work from an ethical perspective.

In contrast, this book teaches a more active and thorough *process strategy* for ethical writing. In it, you integrate an ethical perspective into *every* stage of your work on a communication. It's important to follow a process strategy because at every step of writing you make decisions that shape the way your communication will affect other people. Accordingly, at every step you should consider your decisions from the viewpoint of your personal ethical beliefs about the ways you should treat others.

Stakeholders

In a process approach to ethical writing, no step is more important than the first: defining objectives. When you are defining your communication's objectives, you are (in part) identifying the people you will keep in mind throughout the rest of your writing effort. When you follow the reader-centered approach to writing that is explained in this book, you begin by identifying your readers.

To write ethically, you must also identify another group of people: the individuals who will gain or lose because of your message. Collectively, these people are called *stakeholders* because they have a stake in what you are writing. Only by learning who these stakeholders are can you assure that you are treating them in accordance with your own ethical values.

How to Identify Stakeholders

Because communications written at work often have far-reaching effects, it's easy to overlook some stakeholders. If that happens, a writer risks causing accidental harm that could have been avoided if only the writer had thought through all the implications of his or her communications.

To identify the stakeholders in your communications, begin by listing the people who will be directly affected by what you say and how you say it. In addition to your readers, these individuals may include many other people. For instance, when Craig was preparing a report for his managers on the development of a new fertilizer, he realized that his stakeholders included not only the managers but also the farmers who would purchase the fertilizer and the factory workers who would handle the chemicals used to manufacture it.

Next, list people who will be affected indirectly. For example, because fertilizers run off the land into lakes and rivers, Craig realized that the stakeholders of his report included people who use these lakes and rivers for drinking water or recreation. Indeed, as is the case with many other communications, the list of indirect stakeholders could be extended to include other species (in this case, the aquatic life in the rivers and lakes) and the environment itself.

Finally, think of the people who may be remotely affected. These people may include individuals not yet born. For example, if Craig's fertilizer does not break down into harmless elements, the residue in the soil and water may affect future generations.

Additional Steps

As just explained, the reason for identifying stakeholders at the very beginning of your work on a communication is to enable you to take them into account throughout the rest of the writing process. The ethics guidelines in later chapters will explain how to do that. By following their advice, you will be able to identify and address the sometimes subtle ethical dimensions of your on-the-job writing, and you will be able to keep your stakeholders continuously in mind, just as you keep your readers continuously in mind, while you are writing.

EXPERTISE IN ACTION: AN EXAMPLE
实践中的技能：例子

To see how developing your expertise at defining the objectives of your communications can help you write successfully on the job, consider the following example.

Stephanie works for the Kansas City office of a nonprofit organization whose volunteers provide Braille translations for textbooks and other reading material requested by people who are blind. The office assigned all translations to the volunteers on a rotating basis. As a result, some urgently needed translations weren't completed on time because they were assigned to slow-working volunteers. Stephanie decided to write a memo to Ms. Land, her boss, to recommend that urgent translations be assigned to the fastest and most reliable volunteers rather than to the next persons on the list.

Stephanie began work on her memo by filling out a worksheet based on this chapter's nine guidelines. Her completed worksheet is shown in Figure 3.4 (page 90). A blank copy of the worksheet is provided in Figure 3.5 (page 92) for your use.

By completing each part of the worksheet, Stephanie gained important insights about the most effective way to draft her memo. For example, when responding to the questions about her reader's attitudes, Stephanie realized that Ms. Land would probably react defensively to any recommendation about the current system. Ms. Land had created the system and believed that it worked very well. Furthermore, she was the type of person who resists suggestions. By focusing on these characteristics of Ms. Land, Stephanie concluded that Ms. Land might even resist the suggestion that a problem existed. To write effectively, Stephanie would have to demonstrate that the current system could be improved — without seeming to criticize Ms. Land.

The worksheet also helped Stephanie focus on the fact that Ms. Land believed that Stephanie didn't understand all the issues involved with managing the agency. Therefore, Stephanie realized, Ms. Land would probably respond to her memo by looking for holes in Stephanie's reasoning. Consequently, as she filled out the worksheet's section about her memo's usability objectives, Stephanie concentrated on questions Ms. Land would ask as she searched for these possible holes. By identifying these questions, Stephanie pinpointed the information she would have to include in her memo in order to persuade Ms. Land that she had carefully considered all the organizational ramifications of her recommendation.

Similarly, when she filled out the situational analysis section of the worksheet, Stephanie noted that two months earlier Ms. Land had successfully resisted pressure

> To download a copy of the Worksheet for Defining Objectives that you can fill out, go to www.thomsonedu.com/english/anderson and click on Chapter 3.

FIGURE 3.4 Stephanie's Completed Worksheet for Defining Objectives

DEFINING OBJECTIVES

Overall Purpose

1. What are you writing?
   A proposal for a new method of assigning Braille translations in which the most urgent requests go to the quickest and most reliable volunteers.

2. What prompts you to write?
   I believe the new method will reduce the number of urgent translations not completed on time.

3. What outcome do you desire?
   I would like the new method to be put in effect, at least on a trial basis.

4. What outcome does your reader desire?
   Initially, at least, she'll prefer that the current system remain in place.

Reader Profile

1. Who is your primary reader?
   Ms. Land.

2. What is your reader's relationship to you?
   She is my boss and likes to maintain a formal superior-subordinate relationship.

3. What are your reader's job title and responsibilities?
   She is director of the Braille Division, responsible for recruiting and maintaining a large group of volunteer Braille translators, advertising translation services, and responding to requests for translations by assigning volunteers the work of making them.

4. Who else might read your communication?
   Rich Seybold and Mina Williams, Ms. Land's chief assistants.

5. How familiar is your reader with your subject?
   Ms. Land knows the present system of assigning Braille very well because she set it up and has run it for the past twelve years. She does not know that I am thinking of proposing an alternative but does know that some other offices of the Society for the Blind use systems similar to mine.

6. How familiar is your reader with your specialty?
   Very familiar.

7. Does your reader have any communication preferences you should take into account?
   She likes all communications to be "businesslike." She does not like informality.

8. Should you take into account any other things about your reader when writing?
   Ms. Land gives the impression of being very sure of herself but feels threatened by suggestions for change.

Situational Analysis

1. What events and circumstances influence the way you should write?
   Ms. Land was recently asked by three board members to retire. She successfully resisted.

FIGURE 3.4 (continued)

Usability Objectives (Reader's Tasks)
1. What are the key questions your reader will ask while reading?
   What makes you think anything is wrong with the present system?
   How, exactly, would your proposed system work?
   What would I have to do differently?
   How would the operations of the office be changed?
   How would we determine which translations deserve highest priority?
   How would we decide which translators are placed in our top group?
   What would it cost?

2. How will your reader search for the answer? (The reader may use more than one strategy.)
   - __X__ Sequential reading from beginning to end
   - __X__ Selective reading, as when using a reference book (what key terms will your reader look for?)
   - _____ Other (explain)

3. How will your reader use the information you provide?
   - __X__ Compare point by point (what will be the points of comparison?)
   - __X__ Attempt to determine how the information you provide will affect him or her
   - __X__ Attempt to determine how the information you provide will affect his or her organization
   - __X__ Follow instructions step by step
   - _____ Other (explain)
   She will compare her system with mine in terms of cost and speed of producing translations. Although she won't exactly look for instructions in my proposal, she will want to know in detail how it will work.

Persuasive Objectives (Reader's Attitudes)
1. What is your reader's attitude toward your subject? Why? What do you want it to be?
   Ms. Land thinks the present system runs as well as possible. I want her to see that a better system is possible.
2. What is your reader's attitude toward you? Why? What do you want it to be?
   Although I have worked for her for three years, Ms. Land still thinks of me as a newcomer who knows little and has impractical ideas. I want her to think that I am a helpful, knowledgeable, sensible person.

Stakeholders
1. Who, besides your readers, are stakeholders in your communication?
   The translators—including those who would be given priority assignments and those who wouldn't.
2. How will they be affected by it?
   I don't know. I'll have to investigate this.

Constraints
1. What expectations, regulations, or other factors limit the way you can write?
   None.

(continued)

FIGURE 3.5 Worksheet for Defining Objectives
To download a copy of this worksheet, go to Chapter 3 at www.thomsonedu.com/english/anderson.

DEFINING OBJECTIVES

Overall Purpose
1. What are you writing?
2. What prompts you to write?
3. What outcome do you desire?
4. What outcome does your reader desire?

Reader Profile
1. Who is your primary reader?
2. What is your reader's relationship to you?
3. What are your reader's job title and responsibilities?
4. Who else might read your communication?
5. How familiar is your reader with your subject?
6. How familiar is your reader with your specialty?
7. Does your reader have any communication preferences you should take into account?
8. Should you take into account any other things about your reader when writing?

Situational Analysis
1. What events and circumstances influence the way you should write?

Usability Objectives (Reader's Tasks)
1. What are the key questions your reader will ask while reading?
2. How will your reader search for the answer? (The reader may use more than one strategy.)
   _____ Sequential reading from beginning to end
   _____ Selective reading, as when using a reference book (what key terms will your reader look for?)
   _____ Other (explain)
3. How will your reader use the information you provide?
   _____ Compare point by point (what will be the points of comparison?)
   _____ Attempt to determine how the information you provide will affect him or her
   _____ Attempt to determine how the information you provide will affect his or her organization
   _____ Follow instructions step by step
   _____ Other (explain)

Persuasive Objectives (Reader's Attitudes)
1. What is your reader's attitude toward your subject? Why? What do you want it to be?
2. What is your reader's attitude toward you? Why? What do you want it to be?

Stakeholders
1. Who, besides your readers, are stakeholders in your communication?
2. How will they be affected by it?

Constraints
1. What expectations, regulations, or other factors limit the way you can write?

from several members of the agency's board of directors to force her to retire so that a younger person might take over. Stephanie realized that any reference to these board members or their wishes for streamlined operations would probably arouse a very hostile response from Ms. Land.

Finally, while trying to fill out the section concerning stakeholders, Stephanie discovered that she needed to talk with some of the translators to find out what they thought of her proposal. Through these interviews, she learned that those who might be judged less reliable and less speedy would be deeply offended. To avoid hurting their feelings, Stephanie modified her proposed plan in the following way: The agency would ask all the translators to tell how many pages they could commit to translating in a week. Urgent translations would go to those who made the largest commitments. Translators who failed to meet their original commitment would be invited to specify a lower commitment that would better suit their personal schedules.

Because of her expertise at defining objectives, Stephanie was able to write a detailed, diplomatic, 4-page memo. After several months of deliberation, Ms. Land accepted Stephanie's proposal.

CONCLUSION
总 结

As Stephanie's example illustrates, expertise at defining objectives is an indispensable element in the ability to write successfully at work. Without the insights she gained by defining the objectives of her memo to Ms. Land, Stephanie would have had a much smaller chance of persuading Ms. Land to alter the organization's procedures. By following this chapter's guidelines, you will be able to develop a similar level of expertise in this critical part of the reader-centered writing process.

Note, by the way, that you should follow these guidelines throughout your work on a communication, not just as your first step. As you plan, draft, evaluate, and revise, you will often refine your sense of what you want to accomplish and deepen your understanding of your readers. Make good use of what you learn. Let your new insights guide your future work, even when this means modifying your objectives and, therefore, changing a plan or draft you've already created.

EXERCISES 练 习

For additional exercises, go to www.thomsonedu.com/english/anderson. *Instructors:* The book's website includes suggestions for teaching the exercises.

EXPERTISE

1. Find an example of a communication you might write in your career. Following the guidelines in this chapter, define its objective. Be sure to identify each of the following items:

   The readers and their characteristics
   The stakeholders and the ways they might be affected by the communication
   The final result the writer desires
   The communication's usability goals
   The communication's persuasive goals

Then explain how the communication's features have been tailored to fit its objectives. If you can think of ways the communication might be improved, make recommendations.

2. Using the worksheet shown in Figure 3.5, define the objectives of an assignment you are preparing for your technical communication class. To download a copy of the worksheet, go to Chapter 3 at www.thomsonedu.com/english/anderson.

ONLINE

Find a web page that could be used as a resource for a person in the profession for which you are preparing. Describe the target readers, usability objectives, and persuasive objectives that the web page's creators might have had for it. Evaluate their success in achieving these objectives.

COLLABORATION

Working with another student, pick a technical or scientific topic that interests you both. Next, one of you should locate an article on the topic in a popular magazine such as *Time* or *Discover,* and the other should locate an article on the topic in a professional or specialized journal. Working individually, you should each study the ways your article has been written so that its target audience will find the article to be usable and persuasive. Consider such things as the way your article opens, the language used, the types of details provided, and the kind of visuals included. Next, meet together to compare the writing strategies used to meet the needs and interests of the two audiences. Present your results in the way your instructor requests.

ETHICS

A variety of websites present case studies that describe ethical issues that arise in business, engineering, science, and other fields. Locate, read, and respond to one such case. For links to ethics cases, go to Chapter 3 at www.thomsonedu.com/english/anderson.

CASE Announcing the Smoking Ban 宣布禁烟令

For additional cases, go to www.thomsonedu.com/english/anderson. Instructors: The book's website includes suggestions for teaching the cases.

As you sit in your office of the large, one-story building owned by your employer, you look up from the draft of an e-mail message that company president C. K. Mitchell sent you a few minutes ago. He asked you for your opinion of it.

The e-mail announces a new no-smoking policy for the company, which employs about 250 people. Smoking has been permitted in a smoking lounge located in your building between the manufacturing area, where most of the employees work, and the area that houses the offices for company managers and executives. The lounge is used by employees from both areas. There is also a smoking lounge in a nearby building that C. K. purchased a year ago to expand manufacturing capacity. C. K. recently announced that the continued growth of orders for the company's products necessitates closing the lounge in your building next month. The space is needed for additional manufacturing equipment.

Because this smoking lounge will be closed, the company must establish a new policy about smoking. C. K. has appointed a committee of top managers, including you, to make a recommendation to him. A vocal group of nonsmokers has long advocated a complete smoking ban inside your building. They complain that smoke escapes from the lounges and pollutes their work areas. Therefore, the committee has considered allowing people who work in your building to smoke only outside the door that leads from the manufacturing area to the parking lot. However, some nonsmokers complained that the constant opening of the door would enable smoke to invade their work area. Additionally, managers who smoked complained that this outdoor area is too far from their offices. In response to the managers' complaints, the committee almost recommended that C. K. allow people to smoke in their private offices, provided they shut the door and use an air purifier. However, Maryellen Rosenberg, Director of Personnel, observed that smokers who don't have private offices would complain that the policy discriminated against them. Smokers in both the manufacturing area and the office area also have objected to a total ban on smoking in your building, pointing out the unfairness of prohibiting them from smoking while employees in the newly acquired building could continue to use its smoking lounge.

In a meeting with C. K. yesterday, the committee recommended that C. K. ban smoking anywhere on company property. C. K. has accepted the recommendation. "What could be more appropriate," he asked, "for a company that tries to make people healthier?" Your company designs and markets exercise equipment for homes and fitness centers. After prompting from you and several others, C. K. decided to hire a consulting firm that offers a course to help employees stop smoking. The course will be offered to employees free of charge.

"C. K.'s e-mail announcing this policy had better be good," you think as you prepare to review his draft. Although the employees know that C. K. has been meeting with you and others to work out a policy, the committee's discussions have been kept secret. Nonetheless, feelings about the new policy have been running high. Some employees have talked of quitting if they can't smoke at work, and others have talked of quitting if smoking isn't prohibited. The controversies are harming morale, which is already low because C. K. recently reduced the company's contribution to the profit-sharing plan despite a steady rise in revenues. The money saved is being used to buy the building next door, a move that will save the company money in the long run. However, C. K.'s action is widely viewed as yet another example of his heavy-handed, insensitive style.

Your Assignment

First, to fashion a reasonable set of objectives for C. K.'s e-mail message, fill out a Worksheet for Defining Objectives (Figure 3.5; a downloadable copy is available at www.thomsonedu.com/english/anderson). Remember that the message must somehow satisfy all the employees. Second, evaluate C. K.'s draft (Figure 3.6) in light of the objectives you have established, and then revise the draft to make it more effective. Be prepared to explain your revisions to C. K.

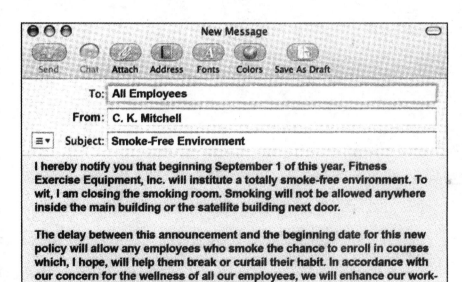

FIGURE 3.6
Draft E-mail for Use with Case

PART III PLANNING 计划

Chapter 4 Planning for Usability
Chapter 5 Planning Your Persuasive Strategies
Chapter 6 Conducting Reader-Centered Research

Planning for Usability
为可用性做出计划

4

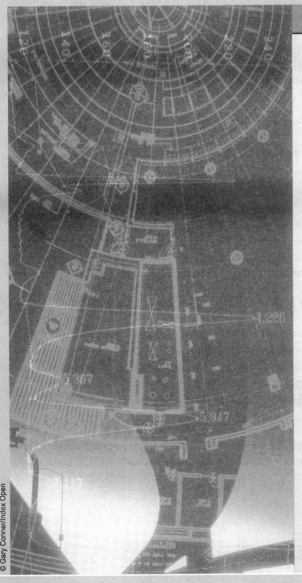

GUIDELINES

1. Identify the information your readers need *101*
2. Organize around your readers' tasks *101*
3. Identify ways to help readers quickly find what they want *106*
4. For a complex audience, plan a modular communication *106*
5. Look for a technical writing superstructure you can adapt *108*
6. Plan your graphics *108*
7. **Global Guideline:** Determine your readers' cultural expectations about what makes a communication usable *109*
8. Outline, if this would be helpful *111*
9. Check your plans with your readers *112*
10. **Ethics Guideline:** Investigate stakeholder impacts *112*

CHAPTER 4

Defining Objectives
Planning
Drafting
Revising

In the preceding chapter, you learned how to define the objectives of communications you write at work. This is the first of two chapters devoted to developing your expertise at translating your objectives into a successful plan of action.

Planning is an inevitable part of writing. Whenever you write to a friend, instructor, coworker, or client, you begin with at least *some* idea of what you will say and how you will say it. However, there is a great difference between expert planning and poor planning. By developing your expertise in planning, you increase your ability to identify the content, organization, style, graphics, and other features that are most likely to achieve the results you desire. In addition, by developing your planning expertise you become a more efficient writer, one who can avoid many of the false starts, inconsistencies, and other difficulties that would require rework before the communication could be sent to its readers.

This chapter and the next tell how take a reader-centered approach to planning. In this approach, you identify strategies for giving your on-the-job communications the two qualities that are indispensable for success: usability and persuasiveness *in your readers' eyes.*

> For additional information and links to relevant websites, go to **www.thomsonedu .com/english/anderson** and click on Chapter 4.

YOUR GOAL WHEN PLANNING FOR USABILITY
计划可用性的目标

As explained in Chapter 1, a usable communication enables its readers to find and use information easily as they perform some practical task. Their task might be purely mental, as when a manager at NASA compares alternative designs for a new component for the international space station, or it might mix mental and physical activities, as when an astronaut follows a set of instructions for installing the component in outer space.

Research indicates that readers find communications to be usable if they are:

Qualities of a usable communication

- **Complete — from your readers' perspective.** A usable communication contains all the information its readers require.
- **Task-oriented.** A usable communication is organized around its readers' tasks and supports the readers' performance of these tasks as fully as possible.
- **Accessible.** A usable communication enables its readers to locate quickly the information they want.

This chapter's first nine guidelines identify the key strategies and resources for planning complete, task-oriented, and accessible communications. The tenth guideline describes important steps for assuring that the communications you plan are ethical.

GUIDELINE 1 IDENTIFY THE INFORMATION YOUR READERS NEED
指导方针 1：明确读者所需的信息

Readers can't use what isn't there. Consequently, your first job when planning for usability is to ensure that your communication will be *complete*, that it will include all the information your readers need in order to perform their tasks.

Begin by listing the questions your readers will bring to your communication or ask while reading it. To make your communication usable to them, you will need to include the answers. You can identify many of these questions by imagining your readers' thoughts as they pick up and then use your communication. As you imagine your readers in the act of reading, consider their professional specialty, organizational role, cultural background, familiarity with your topic, and other characteristics that determine the amount and kinds of background information you must include to make your communication understandable and useful to them.

To identify all the information your *readers* will need, however, you must go beyond the questions you can predict that they will ask and the kinds of answers you believe will be most helpful to them. You may know important things that your readers don't realize they should ask about.

For example, Toni, a recently graduated computer engineer, has been asked to prepare a report comparing several software packages that her employer, a large civil engineering firm, plans to distribute to all of its professional employees. By imagining her readers in the act of reading her report, she has identified many questions that her complex audience will ask. She knows, for instance, that the managers of the four engineering departments will each ask, "How efficiently does each program handle the design functions performed by my department?" She knows that the head of the purchasing department will inquire, "What about leasing options?"

However, Toni has also learned that the company that makes one of the software programs is in financial trouble. If it goes out of business, Toni's company will be unable to obtain the assistance and upgrades it would expect to receive. Even though Toni's readers are not likely to ask, "Are any of the companies that make these programs on the verge of bankruptcy?" Toni should tell her readers about the company's financial problems.

On the other hand, Toni should avoid including information just because she finds it interesting or wants to demonstrate how much she knows. Such information only makes it more difficult for readers to locate and use the information they require. In a reader-centered communication, it's just as important to omit information your readers don't need as it is to provide all that they do.

> **Learn More**
>
> For detailed advice about identifying the information your readers need, see Chapter 3's Guidelines 2, 3, and 4 (pages 68–72).

GUIDELINE 2 ORGANIZE AROUND YOUR READERS' TASKS
指导方针 2：根据读者任务组织内容

Once identified, a communication's content must be organized. As explained in Chapter 1, reading involves a moment-by-moment interaction between reader and text. In this interaction, readers perform a sequence of mental tasks. In some cases, these mental tasks are mixed with physical tasks, as when people read instructions.

Your communications will be most usable if you organize them to mirror and support the readers' tasks.

We all intuitively employ a task-oriented organization when we tell someone how to walk or ride to a particular destination. We mentally trace the route they should follow, and we organize our directions in a way that mirrors their progress: "Go to the third stoplight, turn left and go for two blocks." In the same way, you can use a mental portrait of your readers (see Guideline 1 in Chapter 3) to create a task-oriented organization that guides them smoothly through a physical process or assists them in making a decision, planning future action, or performing other mental activities.

Imagine, for example, that you work in the dean's office of a small college. One of the computer's databases has been corrupted by a virus. You have been asked to compile a list with the names, home addresses, majors, and class standings (first-year, sophomore, junior, senior) of all students enrolled in a technical communication course. The instructors in this course have circulated sign-up sheets to their students.

> **Learn More**
>
> For more information on creating a mental portrait of your readers, see Chapter 1 (page 19) and Chapter 3's Guideline 1 (page 66).

Now, with the completed sheets in front of you, you must write a single list that includes all the information.

How will you organize the list? If you followed the usual advice about organizing, you would organize it "logically." However, there are many logical ways to organize the list: by major, class standing, hometown, and so on. Although any of these choices would be logical, they would not be equally usable. To make a truly usable list, you would need to identify the task for which the dean will use the list and then organize it to help her perform this specific task. If the dean wants to use your list to address letters sent to students who are seniors, another letter to those who are juniors, and so

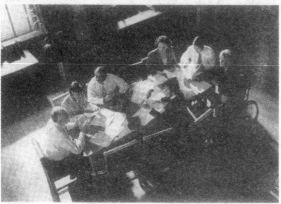

People use communications written at work to perform a wide variety of tasks.

on, you would organize the list according to class standings. If the dean will use your list to determine which departments send the most students to technical communication classes, you would arrange the list according to the students' majors. For other uses, still other organizational patterns would be effective in helping the dean perform the tasks she wants to accomplish while using your list.

Of course, readers' tasks vary greatly from situation to situation. Nevertheless, some tasks are common enough to make it possible to identify three strategies for organizing messages that almost always enhance usability:

- Organize hierarchically.
- Group together the items your readers will use together.
- Give the bottom line first.

These strategies are described in the following paragraphs.

Organize Hierarchically

When we read, we encounter small bits of information one at a time: First what we find in this sentence, then what we find in the next sentence, and so on. One of our major tasks is to build these small bits of information into larger structures of meaning that we can store and work with in our own minds. Represented on paper, these mental structures are hierarchical. They look like outlines (Figure 4.1, page 104) or tree diagrams (Figure 4.2, page 105), with the overall topic divided into subtopics and some or all of the subtopics broken down into still smaller units. For readers, building these hierarchies can be hard work, as we've all experienced when we've had to reread a passage because we can't figure out how its sentences fit together.

The easiest and surest way to help your readers build mental hierarchies is simply to present your information organized in that way. This doesn't mean that you need to start every writing project by making an outline (see Guideline 8). Often, you may be able to achieve a hierarchical organization without outlining. But you should always organize hierarchically.

Group Together the Items Your Readers Will Use Together

Creating a hierarchy involves *grouping* facts. You assemble individual facts into small groups and then gather these groups into larger ones. When grouping your facts, be sure to group together the information your readers will use together. As the example of creating a list of technical writing students illustrates, you increase your communication's usability when your grouping matches your readers' tasks. Daniel's situation provides another example.

Daniel is preparing a report that summarizes hundreds of research studies on the effects of sulfur dioxide (SO_2) emissions from automobiles and factories. Daniel could group his information in several ways. For instance, he could group together all the research published in a given year or span of years. Or he could discuss all the

FIGURE 4.1
Outline Showing the Hierarchical Organization of a Report

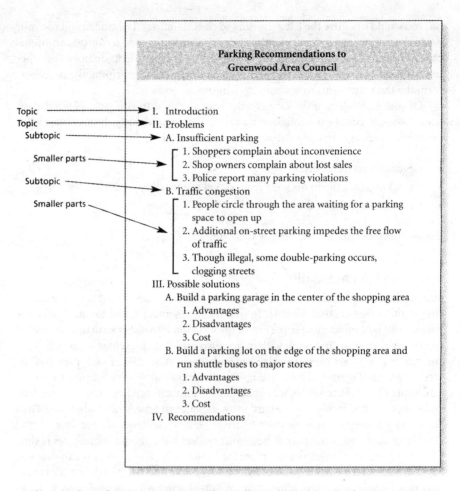

studies conducted in Europe in one place, all conducted in North America in another place, and so on. However, Daniel is employed by a federal task force. His report will be read by members of the U.S. Congress as they decide how to structure legislation on SO_2 emissions. Daniel knows that these readers will want to read about the impacts of SO_2 emissions on human health separately from the effects on the environment. Therefore, he organizes around kinds of impacts, not around the dates or locations of the studies.

Like Daniel, you can organize your communications in a usable, task-oriented manner by grouping together the information your readers will use together.

Give the Bottom Line First

Readers at work often say that their most urgent reading task is to find the writer's main point. The most obvious way to make it easy for them to find your main point is to put it first. Indeed, this strategy for task-oriented organization is the subject of

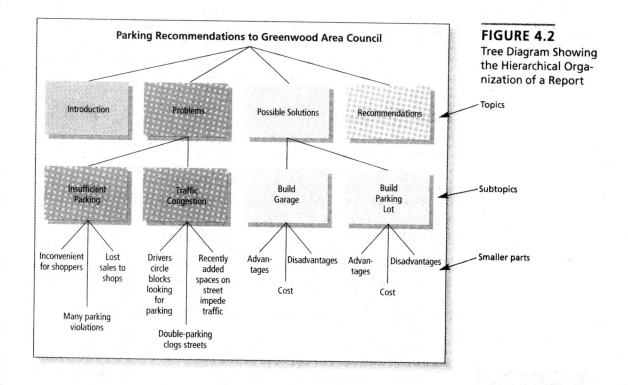

FIGURE 4.2
Tree Diagram Showing the Hierarchical Organization of a Report

one of the most common pieces of advice given in the workplace: "Put the bottom line first." The bottom line, of course, is the last line of a financial statement. Literally, the writers are being told, "Before you swamp me with details on expenditures and sources of income, tell me whether we made a profit or took a loss." However, this advice is applied figuratively to many kinds of communication prepared at work.

Of course, you don't always need to place your main point in the very first sentence, although this is sometimes the most helpful place for it. When appropriate, you can always provide relevant background information before stating your main point. But don't keep your readers in suspense. As soon as possible, get it out: Is the project on schedule, or must we take special action to meet the deadline? Will the proposed design for our product work, or must it be modified?

To some writers, it seems illogical to put the most important information first. They reason that the most important information is generally some conclusion they reached fairly late in their thinking about their subject. Consequently, they think, it is logical to describe the process by which they arrived at the conclusion before presenting the conclusion itself. However, such a view is writer-centered. It assumes that information should be presented in the order in which the writer acquired it. In most workplace situations such an organization runs counter to the sequence that readers would find most helpful.

Focus on use, not logic, when you organize.

There are, nevertheless, some situations in which it really is best to withhold the bottom line until later in a communication. You will find a discussion of such situations in the fifth guideline of Chapter 5. As a general rule, however, you can increase your readers' satisfaction and reading efficiency by creating a task-oriented organization in which you give the bottom line first.

GUIDELINE 3 IDENTIFY WAYS TO HELP READERS QUICKLY FIND WHAT THEY WANT

指导方针 3：确定帮助读者快速找到所需信息的方法

At work, readers often want to find a particular piece of information without reading the entire document that contains it. When you are planning, identify ways to make all information your readers might seek readily accessible to them. Along with completeness and task orientation, accessibility is one of the essential qualities of a usable communication.

To devise your accessibility strategies, turn once again to your mental portrait of your readers. Picture the various circumstances under which they would want to locate some particular subpart of your overall message. What will they be looking for? How will they search for it? With the answers to these two questions, you can plan the pathways that will guide your readers through your communication to the information they want.

For printed documents, you can construct these pathways with headings, topic sentences, tables of contents, and other devices.

For websites, you can use menus, links within the text, and clickable images and icons. In website design, accessibility also depends substantially on the *site map*, which describes the way the parts of the site are related to one another and defines the routes by which visitors gain access to the information they want. It's best to plan the site so that they can get there in three or four clicks rather than five or six.

All of these strategies for accessibility are discussed in detail elsewhere in this book. The important point now is that when planning your communication, even before you begin drafting, you should identify the ways you will make your communication accessible to your readers. Note, too, that all three of Guideline 2's strategies for organizing around your readers' tasks also increase the readers' ability to quickly access the information they are seeking when they want to use some — but not all — of your communication's content.

Learn More

For advice about creating site maps, see Chapter 18.

GUIDELINE 4 FOR A COMPLEX AUDIENCE, PLAN A MODULAR COMMUNICATION

指导方针 4：针对复杂的读者群，制订一个模块式交流

As explained in Chapter 3, at work you will sometimes need to write a single communication that must meet the needs of several readers or groups of readers, each with a different professional role, different background, and hence different set of questions. In the workplace, writers often meet the needs of these diverse audiences by creating modular communications in which different parts address different readers.

For example, many reports and proposals are written for both decision makers and advisers. Usually such reports have two parts: (1) a very brief summary—called an *executive summary* or *abstract*—at the beginning of the report, designed for decision makers who want only the key information; and (2) the body of the report, designed for advisers, who need the details. Typically, the executive summary is only a page or a few pages long, whereas the body may exceed a hundred pages. The body of the report might be divided into still other modules, one addressed to technical experts, one to accountants, and so on. Reports and proposals often include appendixes that present technical details.

Websites are often designed using a similar strategy, with different areas addressed to different groups of users. Figure 4.3 shows an example.

Learn More

For more on modular designs, turn to Chapter 3's Guideline 8 (page 85), including Figures 3.2 and 3.3.

To view other websites that illustrate good use of the guidelines in this chapter, go to **www.thomsonedu.com/english/anderson** and click on Chapter 4.

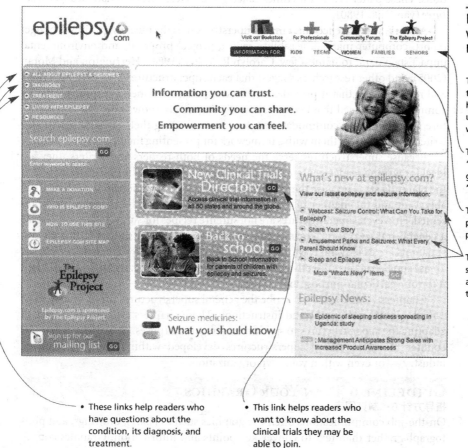

FIGURE 4.3
Website Showing Modular Design

To help each visitor find quickly the information most relevant to him or her, the Epilepsy Project used a modular design for its website.

The row of colored links provide "Information For" five different groups of readers, ranging from "kids" to "seniors."

There is also a separate link for professionals who work with persons who have epilepsy.

This very usable, reader-centered site also provides readers with access to answers to questions they may have.

- These links help readers who have questions about the condition, its diagnosis, and treatment.

- This link helps readers who want to know about the clinical trials they may be able to join.

Guideline 4 **For a Complex Audience, Plan a Modular Communication**

By creating a modular design, you make your communication accessible. Each reader can go directly to the section or sections that are most relevant to him or her. A modular design also allows you to treat each topic at the level that is appropriate for a specific group of readers. Doing this frees you from the difficulties of trying to discuss a topic at a sufficiently detailed level for technical readers while also making it simple enough for nonspecialists.

GUIDELINE 5 LOOK FOR A TECHNICAL WRITING SUPERSTRUCTURE YOU CAN ADAPT
指导方针 5：找到一个可供你改编的写作模式

At work, you will often write in a situation that closely resembles circumstances encountered by other people many times before. Like other people, you may need to report on a business trip, tell someone how to operate a piece of equipment, or request funds for a project you would like to conduct. For many of these recurring situations, writers employ conventional patterns for constructing their communications. These patterns are sometimes called *genres*. Here, they are named *superstructures* (van Dijk, 1980).

At work, you will encounter many superstructures: the business proposal, budget report, computer manual, feasibility report, project proposal, and environmental impact statement, to name a few. Carolyn R. Miller (1984), Herrington and Moran (2005), and other researchers suggest that each superstructure exists because writers and readers agree that it provides an effective pattern for meeting some particular communication need that occurs repeatedly. Figure 4.4 shows how the superstructure for proposals accommodates readers (by answering their questions) and also writers (by providing them with a framework for presenting their persuasive claims).

Because superstructures serve the needs of both readers and writers, they are ideal for writing reader-centered communications. They can be especially helpful at the planning stage because they suggest the kinds of information your readers probably want and the manner in which the information should be organized and presented. However, superstructures are not surefire recipes for success. Each represents a general framework for constructing messages in a typical situation. But no two situations are exactly alike. Moreover, for many situations no superstructure exists. To use superstructures effectively, look for an appropriate one; if you find one, adapt it to your particular purpose and readers.

Chapters 20 through 23 describe the general superstructures for letters, memos, e-mail, reports, proposals, and instructions. These chapters also describe ways of adapting the superstructures to specific readers and purposes. At work, you may encounter more specialized superstructures developed within your profession or industry — or even within your own organization.

GUIDELINE 6 PLAN YOUR GRAPHICS
指导方针 6：制订图表

On-the-job communications often use graphics such as charts, drawings, and photographs rather than text to convey key points and information. Graphics convey certain kinds of information more clearly, succinctly, and forcefully than words.

FIGURE 4.4
Superstructure for Proposal

SUPERSTRUCTURE FOR PROPOSALS		
TOPIC	READERS' QUESTION	WRITER'S PERSUASIVE POINT
Introduction	What is this communication about?	Briefly, I propose to do the following.
Problem	Why is the proposed project needed?	The proposed project addresses a problem, need, or goal that is important to you.
Objectives	What features will a solution to this problem need in order to be successful?	A successful solution can be achieved if it has these features.
Product or Outcome	How do you propose to do those things?	Here's what I plan to produce and how it has the features necessary for success.
Method	Are you going to be able to deliver what you describe here?	Yes, because I have a good plan of action (method), the necessary facilities, equipment, and other resources, a workable schedule, appropriate qualifications, and a sound management plan.
Costs	What will it cost?	The cost is reasonable.

Each topic in the superstructure for proposals answers a particular question by the reader in a way that readers will find persuasive.

When planning a communication, look for places where graphics provide the best way for you to show how something looks (in drawings or photographs), explain a process (flowcharts), make detailed information readily accessible (tables), or clarify the relationship among groups of data (graphs).

Chapter 12 provides detailed advice about where to use graphics and how to construct them effectively. However, don't wait until you read that chapter to begin planning ways to increase your communication's usability with graphics.

GUIDELINE 7 GLOBAL GUIDELINE: DETERMINE YOUR READERS' CULTURAL EXPECTATIONS ABOUT WHAT MAKES A COMMUNICATION USABLE

指导方针 7：确定不同文化背景的读者对于交流可用性的期待

Among cultures, there are many different assumptions about what makes a communication usable. As an example, consider differences in the amount of detail that readers in different cultures expect writers to provide. In some cultures, writers provide a large amount of detail to spell out fully the writers' meaning. Today, researchers follow Edward T. Hall (1976) in calling these *low-context* cultures. German, Scandinavian, and U.S. cultures are examples. Typical readers in low-context cultures expect a communication to provide plenty of detail. If they don't find that detail in a communication, these readers are likely to feel that the writer has ignored their need for a thorough discussion.

Learn More

For more information on writing to readers in other cultures, go to Chapter 3, page 76.

In other cultures, writers omit many details. They and their readers both expect the readers to supply the necessary details by drawing on their knowledge of the situation, the relevant facts and cultural conventions, and the history and nature of their relationship with the writer. These are *high-context* cultures. Arab and Asian cultures are examples. If a communication is filled with details that readers could supply on their own, the readers may feel insulted because the writer appears to assume that they lack the appropriate knowledge.

To illustrate the difference between technical communications written in high- and low-context cultures, researcher Daniel Ding (2003) compared Chinese and U.S. instructions for installing a water heater. The U.S. instructions meet the expectations of a low-context culture by telling the user how to perform each step and substep in the installation process. For instance, to explain how to connect the hot

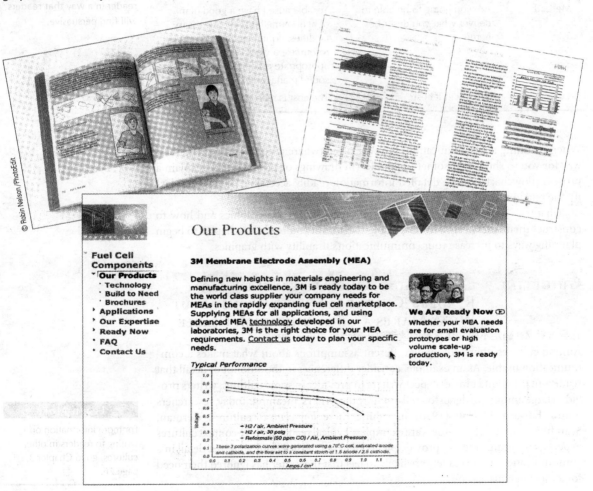

Reports, instructions, and web pages are among the many kinds of technical communications that use graphics extensively.

CHAPTER 4 **Planning for Usability**

and cold water pipes to the heater, the instructions say: "Put two or three turns of teflon tape or pipe joint compound around the threaded ends of the ¾" × 3" nipples and, using a pipe wrench, tighten the nipples into the 'HOT' and 'COLD' fittings of the water heater."

In contrast, the Chinese instructions meet the expectations of readers in a high-context culture by explaining the outcomes of each major step but not the actions needed to achieve the outcome. For instance, the Chinese instructions say that heater should be connected to the water pipes, but they don't describe actions necessary to connect them. There's no mention of turning the teflon tape three times, using pipe joint compound, or tightening with a pipe wrench. These details are considered to be part of the contextual knowledge the reader possesses.

When planning ways to make your communications usable to readers in other cultures, you should learn what these readers consider to be usable.

GUIDELINE 8 OUTLINE, IF THIS WOULD BE HELPFUL
指导方针 8：如果有帮助的话，可列提纲

When they talk about planning a communication, many people mention outlining and ask, "Is outlining worth the work it requires?" No single answer to this question is valid for all writers and all situations. The following general observations about outlining practices at work may help you determine when (and if) outlining might be worthwhile for you.

On the job, outlining is rarely used for short or routine messages. However, many writers outline longer, more complex communications, especially if they expect to have difficulties in organizing. They use outlining as a way of experimenting with alternative ways of structuring their message before they begin to invest time in drafting. Similarly, if they encounter problems when drafting, some writers will try to outline the troublesome passage.

Also, writers sometimes wish to — or are required to — share their organizational plans with a superior or coworker. Outlining provides them with a convenient way of explaining their plans to such individuals.

Finally, outlining can help writing teams negotiate the structure of a communication they must create together (see Chapter 16).

When you create an outline, remember that the kind of tidy structure shown in Figure 4.1 represents the product of the outlining process. Many writers begin organizing by making lists or diagrams, drawing arrows and pictures, and using many other techniques to think through possible ways of putting their information together for their readers.

Using Computers to Outline

Most desktop publishing programs include special tools for outlining. With these tools, you can, for instance, make an outline and then convert it immediately into the headings for your document. These tools will also allow you to convert from the normal view of your document to an outline view, so you can review the organizational

> For more on outlining, go to **www.thomsonedu.com/english/anderson** and click on Chapter 4.

structure that is evolving as you write. When you move material in the outline, the program automatically moves the corresponding parts of your full text, which can sometimes make for an extremely efficient way to revise a draft. Figure 4.5 shows some of the features of one widely used desktop publishing program's outlining tool.

GUIDELINE 9 CHECK YOUR PLANS WITH YOUR READERS
指导方针9：与读者核查计划

At the core of the guidelines you have just read is one common strategy: Focus on your readers as you plan. For that reason, the guidelines urged you to refer continuously to various sources of insight into what will make your communication usable in your readers' eyes. These include the understanding of your readers that you gained when defining your objectives and the superstructures that others have found successful in similar circumstances. Nevertheless, such planning involves guesswork about what will really work with your readers. Therefore, whenever you have the opportunity, bring your plans to your readers. Ask for their responses and requests. If it isn't feasible to check your plans with your readers, share them with someone who understands your readers well enough to help you find possible improvements. The better your plans, the better your final communication.

GUIDELINE 10 ETHICS GUIDELINE: INVESTIGATE STAKEHOLDER IMPACTS
道德指导方针10：调查参与者影响

As Chapter 3 explained, the first step in writing ethically is to identify your communication's stakeholders — the people who will be affected by what you say and how you say it. Next, learn how your communication will impact these people and how they feel about these potential effects.

Asking Stakeholders Directly

The best way to learn how your communication will affect its stakeholders is to talk to these individuals directly. In many organizations, such discussions are a regular step in the decision-making process that accompanies the writing of reports and proposals. When an action is considered, representatives of the various groups or divisions that might be affected meet together to discuss the action's potential impacts on each of them.

Similarly, government agencies often solicit the views of stakeholders. For example, the federal agencies that write environmental impact statements are required to share drafts of these documents with the public so that concerned citizens can express their reactions. The final draft must respond to the public's comments.

Even in situations that are traditionally viewed as one-way communications, many managers seek stakeholder inputs. For instance, when they conduct annual employee evaluations, some managers draft their evaluation, then discuss it with the employee before preparing the final version.

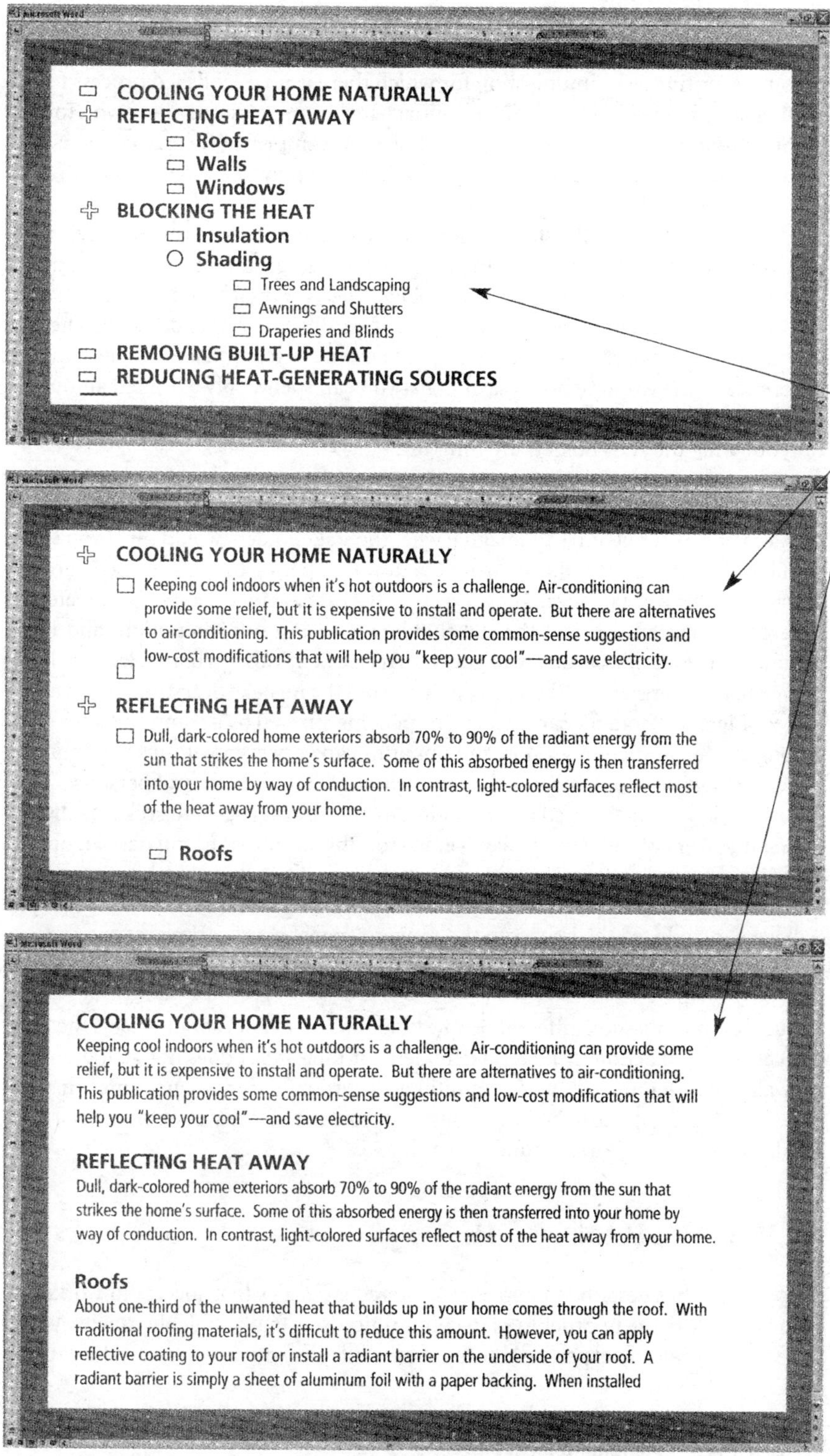

FIGURE 4.5
Outlining Functions of a Desktop Publishing Program

- ☐ **COOLING YOUR HOME NATURALLY**
- ✢ **REFLECTING HEAT AWAY**
  - ☐ **Roofs**
  - ☐ **Walls**
  - ☐ **Windows**
- ✢ **BLOCKING THE HEAT**
  - ☐ **Insulation**
  - ○ **Shading**
    - ☐ **Trees and Landscaping**
    - ☐ **Awnings and Shutters**
    - ☐ **Draperies and Blinds**
- ☐ **REMOVING BUILT-UP HEAT**
- ☐ **REDUCING HEAT-GENERATING SOURCES**

The outlining function of Microsoft Word enables you to:

- Create your outline.
- Add text under your headings.
- Shift instantly to a finished communication.

✢ **COOLING YOUR HOME NATURALLY**
  ☐ Keeping cool indoors when it's hot outdoors is a challenge. Air-conditioning can provide some relief, but it is expensive to install and operate. But there are alternatives to air-conditioning. This publication provides some common-sense suggestions and low-cost modifications that will help you "keep your cool"—and save electricity.
  ☐

✢ **REFLECTING HEAT AWAY**
  ☐ Dull, dark-colored home exteriors absorb 70% to 90% of the radiant energy from the sun that strikes the home's surface. Some of this absorbed energy is then transferred into your home by way of conduction. In contrast, light-colored surfaces reflect most of the heat away from your home.

  ☐ **Roofs**

You can easily switch between viewing the outline and the full text.

COOLING YOUR HOME NATURALLY
Keeping cool indoors when it's hot outdoors is a challenge. Air-conditioning can provide some relief, but it is expensive to install and operate. But there are alternatives to air-conditioning. This publication provides some common-sense suggestions and low-cost modifications that will help you "keep your cool"—and save electricity.

REFLECTING HEAT AWAY
Dull, dark-colored home exteriors absorb 70% to 90% of the radiant energy from the sun that strikes the home's surface. Some of this absorbed energy is then transferred into your home by way of conduction. In contrast, light-colored surfaces reflect most of the heat away from your home.

Roofs
About one-third of the unwanted heat that builds up in your home comes through the roof. With traditional roofing materials, it's difficult to reduce this amount. However, you can apply reflective coating to your roof or install a radiant barrier on the underside of your roof. A radiant barrier is simply a sheet of aluminum foil with a paper backing. When installed

You can reorganize your communication simply by moving a heading; the subheadings and text automatically move also.

Action You Can Take

If you are writing a communication for which there is no established process for soliciting stakeholders' views, you can initiate such a process on your own. To hear from stakeholders in your own organization, you can probably just visit or call. To contact stakeholders outside your organization, you may need to use more creativity and also consult with your coworkers.

If you already know the stakeholders well, you may be able to find out their views very quickly. At other times, an almost impossibly large amount of time would be needed to thoroughly investigate stakeholders' views. When that happens, the decision about how much time to spend can itself become an ethical decision. The crucial thing is to make as serious an attempt as circumstances will allow. There's all the difference in the world between saying that you can spend only a limited amount of time investigating stakeholders' views and saying that you just don't have *any* time to find out what the stakeholders are thinking.

Speaking for Others

To save time, you might try to imagine what the stakeholders would say if you spoke to them directly. Clearly this course of action is superior to ignoring stakeholders altogether. But you can never know exactly what others are thinking. The greater the difference between you and the stakeholders — in job title, education, and background — the less likely you are to guess correctly. So it's always best to let stakeholders speak for themselves. When you do this, avoid the mistake of assuming that all the stakeholders will hold the same view. The persons affected by a communication may belong to many different groups, and opinions can vary even within a single group. When letting stakeholders speak for themselves, seek out a variety of persons.

At work, you might need authorization from your managers to seek stakeholder views. If you encounter reluctance to grant you this permission, you have an opportunity to open a conversation with your managers about the ethical dimensions of the communication you are writing. Even if they aren't swayed this first time, you will have introduced the issue into the conversation at your workplace.

> **Learn More**
>
> For an additional discussion of ways to address an organization's reluctance to consider ethical issues, see the ethics guideline on page 294.

Seeking Stakeholder Views

In sum, on many issues, different people hold different views about what is the most ethical course of action. Asking stakeholders for their input does not guarantee that they all will be happy with what you ultimately write. But it does guarantee that you have heard their opinions. Without this step, you can scarcely attempt to take their needs and concerns into account.

CONCLUSION 总 结

This chapter has described the reader-centered strategies that successful workplace communicators use in order to plan communications that are highly usable. As you have seen, to develop expertise in using these strategies you must possess the detailed knowledge of your readers that you gained by following Chapter 3's reader-centered advice for defining your communication's objectives. The planning guide shown in Figure 4.6 summarizes this chapter's advice for using your knowledge of your readers to plan communications that are usable (complete, task-oriented, and accessible) as well as ethical.

FIGURE 4.6 Guide for Planning Your Usability Strategies

To download a copy of this planning guide, go to www.thomsonedu.com/english/anderson and click on Chapter 4.

PLANNING YOUR USABILITY STRATEGIES

Planning Content
1. What questions will your readers want your communication to answer?
2. What additional information do your readers need?
3. What information do you need to gather through research?

Organizing
1. What will be your readers' reading tasks?
2. If there is a technical writing superstructure you can adapt, which one is it?
3. What organization will best support your readers as they perform these tasks?
   - Group together the information your readers will use together
   - Create a hierarchical organization
   - Place the bottom line first
   - Use a modular design, if you have a variety of readers with different needs
   - Outline your organizational plan, if this will be helpful

Providing Quick Access to Information
1. What headings would help your readers find the information they want?
2. Would a table of contents help the readers?
3. If you are creating a website, sketch a reader-centered site map and identify the navigation aids you would provide
4. What other strategies will help your readers find information?

Planning Graphics
1. What tables, graphs, drawings, or other graphics increase the usability and persuasiveness of your communication?

Writing Ethically
1. Who, besides your readers, are the stakeholders in your report?
2. How might they be affected by it?
3. How can you assure that your readers and other stakeholders are treated ethically?

EXERCISES 练 习

EXPERTISE

Imagine that you are employed full-time and have decided to take a course at a local college. First, name a course you might like to take. Next, by following Guideline 1, list the information you would include in a memo in which you ask your employer to pay your tuition and permit you to leave work early two days a week to attend class.

ONLINE

Develop a list of questions that high school students might ask about studying in your major at your college. Then try to answer these questions by going to your college's website. How accessible are the answers? How complete are they from the viewpoint of high school students? How could the website be made more usable for these students?

COLLABORATION

Imagine that you have been hired to create a brochure or website that presents your college department in a favorable light to entering first-year students and students who are thinking of changing their majors. Working with another student and following the guidelines in this chapter, generate a list of things that you and your partner would want to say. How would the two of you group and order this information?

ETHICS

Think of a policy of your college or employer that you would like to change. Imagine that you are going to write a report recommending this change. After identifying all the stakeholders, tell how you could gain a complete understanding of the relevant concerns and values of each stakeholder or stakeholder group. Which stakeholders' concerns and values would be most difficult for your to learn about? Why? Would you have more difficulty listening sympathetically to some stakeholders than others? If so, who and why? How would you ensure that you treat these stakeholders ethically?

CASE: FILLING THE DISTANCE LEARNING CLASSROOM 参与远程学习

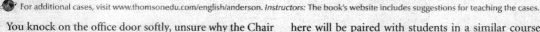
For additional cases, visit www.thomsonedu.com/english/anderson. *Instructors:* The book's website includes suggestions for teaching the cases.

You knock on the office door softly, unsure why the Chair of the English Department has asked to meet with you.

"Welcome," Professor Rivera says, immediately putting you at ease. "I'm glad you could come. Professor Baldwin suggested you might be able to help me with a sort of marketing project."

What a relief. At least you haven't done anything wrong.

"Have you heard about our new distance learning classroom?" Professor Rivera asks. You tell her you know that a large room in the English building is being redesigned as a computerized classroom.

"Well, in addition to computers, the room will have video cameras, projection equipment, special software, and a very large screen. By means of this equipment, it can be paired with a similar classroom elsewhere in the world so that students in both locations can become part of the same class.

"In fact, we're getting ready to conduct a few experimental sections of First-Year English in which students here will be paired with students in a similar course at a university in Brazil. A team of faculty from both schools has planned a common syllabus and paired sections here and in Brazil to meet at the same hours. When the Brazilian instructor or students speak, the students and instructor here will be able to see and hear them, and vice versa. Also, students in the two locations will exchange drafts via the Internet, and they will even be able to project a draft of a student's paper in both locations so that all the students can talk jointly about it."

"But isn't Portuguese the native language of Brazil?" you ask.

"Yes," Professor Rivera replies. "All of the Brazilian students will be studying English as a second language, although they will also have studied several years of it before attending their university. Of course, English is a second language for many students here at our own university as well."

"What an interesting project," you observe.

"Yes," Professor Rivera responds. "The faculty members involved think it will have several benefits for students. It's increasingly important for college graduates to be able to work in an international economic and intellectual environment. This course will help prepare them for such work. In addition, many businesses are now using exactly the kind of technology we have placed in the distance learning classroom to hold meetings that involve employees or clients located at various points around the globe. Students in the experimental classes will gain experience with such technology that could give them a tremendous boost in the job market."

"Sounds great," you say. "But what does it have to do with me? I've already completed that course."

"What we'd like you to do is to write a pamphlet we can send this summer to incoming students to entice some of them to sign up for the experimental distance learning sections of First-Year English."

"Sounds easy," you say.

"Well, there are some complications," Professor Rivera explains. "This is an experiment of sorts. Many tests will be run to determine the effects of the distance learning environment. The experiment is important because some faculty members are skeptical about the program, worried that it might focus on technology in ways that will detract from the quality of the writing instruction.

"Because this is an experiment, the faculty members who designed the program want the students in the distance learning sections to represent a cross section of students in First-Year English. It can't be populated with just students who have a high interest in technology or international studies. Therefore, they have asked the Admissions Office to generate a list of 240 randomly selected incoming students to whom the pamphlet will be sent. The aim of the pamphlet is to persuade at least half of the recipients to enroll in six special sections."

"In that case, writing the pamphlet will be a challenge," you agree.

"Will you accept the challenge?" Professor Rivera asks.
"Sure. Why not?"

YOUR ASSIGNMENT

Following the guidelines in Chapter 3, define the objectives for your pamphlet. Then, by following the guidelines in this chapter, list the things you would say in the pamphlet to the incoming students. Identify the things you would need to investigate further before writing.

5 Planning Your Persuasive Strategies
制订说服策略

GUIDELINES

1. Listen—and respond flexibly to what you hear *121*
2. Focus on your readers' goals and values *121*
3. Address—and learn from—your readers' concerns and counterarguments *125*
4. Reason soundly *127*
5. Organize to create a favorable response *132*
6. Build an effective relationship with your readers *134*
7. Determine whether to appeal to your readers' emotions *137*
8. **Global Guideline:** Adapt your persuasive strategies to your readers' cultural background *139*
9. **Ethics Guideline:** Employ ethical persuasive techniques *144*

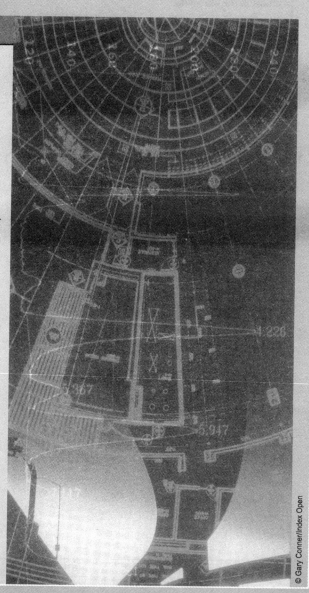

© Gary Conner/Index Open

As explained in Chapter 1, all on-the-job writing aims to persuade its readers in some way. At work, you will engage in two related but distinguishable kinds of persuasion, each with a distinctive goal.

> DEFINING OBJECTIVES
> PLANNING
> DRAFTING
> REVISING

CHAPTER 5

PERSUASION TO INFLUENCE ATTITUDES AND ACTION
说服力影响态度和行为

The goal of the first kind of persuasion is to *influence the attitudes and actions* of its readers. This is the goal that comes most readily to mind when we think of persuasion: to persuade readers to purchase our product or service, fund the project we are proposing, or adopt the policy we advocate. Persuasion aimed at influencing the readers' attitudes and actions is also a crucial element in many kinds of communication that we don't ordinarily think of as persuasive. For instance, instructions may seem to convey information only, without having any persuasive element. A report on a scientific or technical experiment may seem to convey facts only. However, if the report doesn't persuade that the writer used an appropriate research method, readers are likely to conclude that the results of the experiment are flawed. Even instructions have a persuasive element. If they don't persuade readers to follow their directions, the instructions' entire purpose is undermined.

> For additional information about persuasion, go to **www.thomsonedu.com/english/anderson** and click on Chapter 5.

PERSUASION TO HELP A TEAM DEVELOP KNOWLEDGE AND IDEAS COLLABORATIVELY
说服力帮助团队扩充知识和想出好点子

The second kind of persuasion is not as obvious as the first, but it is just as central as the first to your employer's success and your own. Rather than aiming to influence other people's actions, its goal is collaborative: *to help enable a group of people to work together to develop an idea or solution*. An example will explain how this second type of persuasion functions and how it is sometimes linked with the first.

Osage Incorporated was invited by a state transportation department to be one of five competing for a billion-dollar contract to build a high-speed transit system between two cities. To compete, Osage needed to write a proposal aimed at persuading state officials to award the transit-system contract to Osage rather than a competitor. Thus, the proposal's goal was to influence its readers' actions.

Before it could write the proposal, however, Osage needed to design the system it would build if it won the contract. As it did so, a team of engineers engaged in the second type of persuasion. Working together, these individuals all contributed to the group's effort by generating, exploring, evaluating, and building on ideas. The team's success depended on each engineer's skill at persuading where the goal is cooperation, not competition. If a team member had a good idea but couldn't present it persuasively, the team would fail to adopt the best alternative. Similarly, if a team member spotted a problem with an idea under consideration but couldn't persuade others that the problem was serious, the team might pursue a flawed plan.

This second type of persuasion is central to many types of workplace activities. It is required when scientists gather to discuss new data, when technicians team up to solve a technical problem, and when medical personnel confer about the best way to address the outbreak of an illness. It is also the type persuasion in which you engage when you work on a team project in your technical communication course or other classes.

HOW PERSUASION WORKS
说服力是怎样发挥作用的

Over twenty years ago, researchers Petty and Cacioppo (1986) explained the process by which we influence one another in both competitive and cooperative situations. The key, they demonstrated, is to concentrate on shaping our readers' attitudes.

At work, you will be concerned with your readers' attitudes toward a wide variety of subjects, such as products, policies, actions, and other people. As Chapter 3 explains, you may use your persuasive powers to change your readers' attitudes in any of the following ways:

Ways to change readers' attitudes

- **Reverse** an attitude you want your readers to abandon.
- **Reinforce** an attitude you want them to hold even more firmly.
- **Shape** their attitude on a subject about which they currently have no opinion.

What determines a person's attitude toward an idea, object, or action? Petty and Cacioppo (1981, 1986) have found that it isn't a single thought or argument, but the *sum* of the various thoughts a person associates with the idea, object, or action under consideration. Consider the following example.

Edward is thinking about purchasing a particular copy machine for his department. As he deliberates, a variety of thoughts cross his mind: the amount of money in his department's budget, the machine's special features (such as the ability to make copies directly from computer files), its appearance and repair record, his experience with another product made by the same company, and his impression of the manufacturer's marketing representative. Each of these thoughts will make Edward's attitude more positive or more negative. He may think his budget has enough money (positive) or too little (negative); he may like the salesperson (positive) or detest the salesperson (negative); and so forth.

Some of these thoughts will probably influence Edward's attitude more than others. For instance, Edward may like the machine's special features and color, but those two factors may be outweighed by reports that the machine's repair record is very poor. If the sum of Edward's thoughts associated with the machine is positive, he will have a favorable attitude toward it and may buy it. If the sum is negative, he will have an unfavorable attitude and probably not buy it.

THE SOURCES OF THIS CHAPTER'S ADVICE
本章建议的来源

Although we have learned a great deal about the ways attitudes are shaped in the past several decades, much of the best advice about how to write persuasively has been developed over a much longer period. After carefully observing the persuasive strategies used by citizens of ancient Greece more than 2400 years ago, Aristotle classified them into three main types: *logos* (appeals to logic), *pathos* (appeals to emotion), and *ethos* (for our purposes, roughly equivalent to credibility). Because of their effectiveness—and despite their age—Aristotle's concepts can serve you well in your workplace writing. Other highly effective persuasive strategies have developed since Aristotle's time, many of them through scientific studies conducted in the past 75 years. This chapter's nine reader-centered guidelines draw together some of the most helpful ideas gained over the long period from ancient Greece to our day.

GUIDELINE 1 LISTEN—AND RESPOND FLEXIBLY TO WHAT YOU HEAR
指导方针1：听——并灵活回应你所听到的

To communicate persuasively, you must listen well. Of course, the same might be said about any aspect of reader-centered writing. What you learn about your readers by listening to them and to people who tell you about them provides the basis for all your writing decisions. With respect to persuasion, however, listening makes an especially large contribution to your communication's success.

In competitive situations like the one described above, you will need to listen very carefully to the goals, needs, aims, and concerns of the readers who will decide whether to take the action you advocate. In collaborative persuasive situations you will need to listen carefully to what your team members are saying in order to contribute productively to the group's discussions.

Equally important to the way you listen will be the way you respond to what you hear. Be flexible. The things you hear may not only help you determine how to strengthen your communication but also suggest ways to improve the action or idea you are advocating.

The next two guidelines will help you determine what to listen for and how to make the most productive use of what you hear.

GUIDELINE 2 FOCUS ON YOUR READERS' GOALS AND VALUES
指导方针2：关注读者的目标和价值

A powerful way to prompt your readers to experience favorable thoughts about the ideas, actions, process, or product you advocate is to tell them how it will help them accomplish some goal they want to achieve. For instance, if Edward's goal is to be sure that his department produces polished copies, a writer could influence him to experience favorable thoughts toward a particular copier by pointing out that it prints high-quality images. If his goal is to keep costs low, a writer could influence him to view the copier favorably by emphasizing that it is inexpensive to purchase and run.

Similarly, at work you can increase the persuasiveness of communications on any topic by focusing on the goals that guide your readers' decisions and actions. Here is a three-step process for doing so:

Process for developing persuasive strategies based on your readers' goals

1. Identify your readers' goals.
2. Determine how the ideas or actions you are recommending can help your readers achieve their goals.
3. In your communication, focus on the ways your recommended actions and ideas can help your readers achieve their goals.

In cooperative situations, your readers' goals may be identical or similar to your own, though that is not always the case. In both cooperative and competitive situations, the best way to identify your readers' goals is to ask them — and listen carefully. It's also helpful to talk with coworkers who know your readers. You will also find it helpful to consider the ways that your readers' personal goals may be shaped by the following sources:

Sources of readers' goals

- Objectives of the organizations that employ your readers
- Values your readers derive from their organizations or from their personal lives
- Your readers' desires for achievement and growth

Organizational Goals

On the job, you will often write to coworkers and to employees in other organizations. Because they are hired to advance their employer's interests, employees usually adopt their employer's goals as their own. Consequently, one way to identify your readers' goals is to examine the goals of the organization for which they work.

In any organization, some goals are general and some specific. At a general level, many organizations share the same goals: to increase revenue, operate efficiently, keep employee morale high, and so on. However, each company also has its own unique goals. A company might be seeking to control 50 percent of its market, to have the best safety record in its industry, or to expand into ten states in the next five years. Moreover, each department within a company has specific objectives. Thus, the research department aims to develop new and improved products, the marketing department seeks to identify new markets, and the accounting department strives to manage financial resources prudently. When identifying goals to serve as the basis for persuasion, choose specific goals over general ones.

> To view additional communications that employ persuasive strategies described in this chapter, go to www.thomsonedu.com/english/anderson and click on Chapter 5.

Also, as you uncover an organization's various goals, focus on the ones that are most closely related to the specific idea, action, or process you are advocating. Then craft your communication to emphasize the ways that doing what you recommend will help your readers achieve the specific outcomes they desire.

Figure 5.1 shows a marketing brochure that uses organizational objectives to persuade its intended readers (purchasing managers for supermarkets and supermarket chains) to carry a certain product. Notice the boldface statements that proclaim how the product will build sales volume, stimulate impulse buying, and deliver profits.

FIGURE 5.1
Brochure That Stresses Organizational Objectives

Sparkling grape advantage.

Improved Sparkling Red and White Grape Juices will build your volume.
- Welch's is #1 brand of Sparkling Grape Juice.
- Welch's Sparkling Grape Juices comprise over 70% of Sparkling Grape Juice sales.
- Welch's has improved the taste of its already popular Sparkling Red and White Grape Juices to broaden consumer appeal.

Impactful product labels will help stimulate impulse purchases.
- Welch's labels scored the highest rating of any line ever tested by Perception Research Inc., the largest package design research firm in the U.S.
- These labels communicate key consumer benefits:
  - Non-Alcoholic
  - 100% Juice
  - No Sugar Added

Welch's Sparkling Juices will deliver incremental profits for your store.
- Welch's Sparkling Juices will generate on average $.64 per unit... many purchases are impulse/incremental.
- By stocking Welch's Sparkling Juices, your store can meet the growing consumer demand for high quality, non-alcoholic beverages.
- Strong Year-Round marketing support will generate trial and repurchase in your store.

The Sparkling profit advantage.

Case Cost ___
Allowance ___
Promoted Case Cost ___
Promoted Unit Cost ___
Suggested Retail ___
Profit Per Unit ___
Profit Per Case ___
Suggested Order ___
Total Profit ___
% Profit ___

Next Steps
1. Buy the complete line of Welch's Sparkling Non-Alcoholic Juices for immediate distribution.
2. Feature to support magazine coupons during November.
3. Display in multiple store locations during the holidays to generate impulse purchases of these unique, high margin products.

Values-Based Goals

Most companies have goals that involve social, ethical, and aesthetic values not directly related to profit and productivity. Some companies spell out these values in corporate credos; Figure 5.2 on page 124 is an example. Even in companies that do not have an official credo, broad human and social values may provide an effective foundation for persuasion, especially when you are advocating a course of action that seems contrary to narrow business interests. For example, by pointing to the benefits to be enjoyed by a nearby community, you might be able to persuade your employer to strengthen its water pollution controls beyond what is required by law.

In addition, individual employees bring to work personal values that can influence their decisions and actions. Especially when writing to only one or a few readers, learn whether they have personal values that are related to what you are recommending.

To see other corporate credos, go to www.thomsonedu.com/english/anderson and click on Chapter 5.

Achievement and Growth Goals

In studies of employee motivation that are still highly respected today, Abraham Maslow (1970) and Frederick Herzberg (1968) highlight another type of benefit you can use to persuade. Both researchers confirmed that, as everyone knew, employees are motivated by such considerations as pay and safe working conditions. However, the studies also found that after most people feel they have an adequate income

FIGURE 5.2
Corporate Credo that Includes Varied Objectives

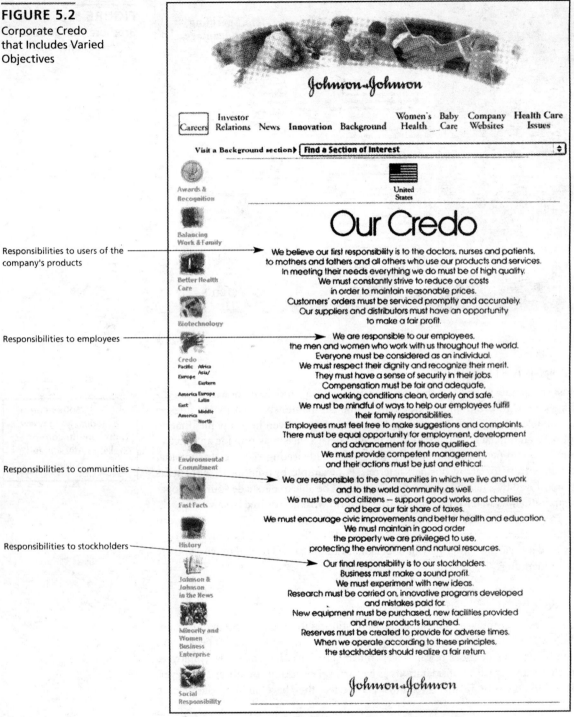

124 ■ CHAPTER 5 **Planning Your Persuasive Strategies**

and safe working conditions, they become less easily motivated by these factors. Consequently, such factors are called *deficiency needs:* they motivate principally when they are absent.

Once their deficiency needs are met — and even before — most people are motivated by so-called *growth needs,* including the desire for recognition, good relationships at work, a sense of achievement, personal development, and the enjoyment of work itself.

Many other studies have confirmed these findings. For instance, a study of supervisors showed that achievement, recognition, and personal relationships are much more powerful motivators than money (Munter, 1987). Another found that computer professionals are less motivated by salary or status symbols than by the opportunity to gain new skills and knowledge in their field (Warren, Roth, & Devanna, 1984).

These studies demonstrate that one powerful persuasive strategy is to show how the decisions or actions you are advocating will help your readers satisfy their desires for growth and achievement. When you request information or cooperation from a coworker, mention how much you value his or her assistance. When you evaluate a subordinate's performance, discuss accomplishments as well as shortcomings. When you ask someone to take on additional duties, emphasize the challenge and opportunities for achievement that lie ahead.

Figure 5.3 shows a recruiting brochure distributed by Procter & Gamble to attract new employees. Notice the many ways it appeals to college graduates by emphasizing the opportunities they would have with the company to assume responsibility, take on challenges, and grow professionally.

GUIDELINE 3   ADDRESS—AND LEARN FROM—YOUR READERS' CONCERNS AND COUNTERARGUMENTS

指导方针3：说——并从中了解读者的顾虑和反对观点

Although it is tempting to focus your attention on the reasons that your readers should agree with you, you can gain a great benefit from learning the reasons they may be reluctant to do so.

To begin, learning your readers' concerns and counterarguments can help you improve the project you are proposing or refine your ideas. That's because some of these concerns and counterarguments may be valid. By following Guideline 1's advice to remain flexible you can build on the insights of your readers.

When you are satisfied that your proposed idea or action is as sound as possible, use your insights into your readers' concerns and counterarguments to help you increase your communication's persuasiveness. Gaining additional insights into the nature of persuasion will help you do so.

Research shows that when people read, they not only pay attention to the writer's statements but also generate their own thoughts. Research further shows that whether readers' self-generated thoughts are favorable or unfavorable can have a greater influence on readers' attitudes than any point you make in the communication itself

FIGURE 5.3
Page from a Recruiting Website that Focuses on Growth Needs

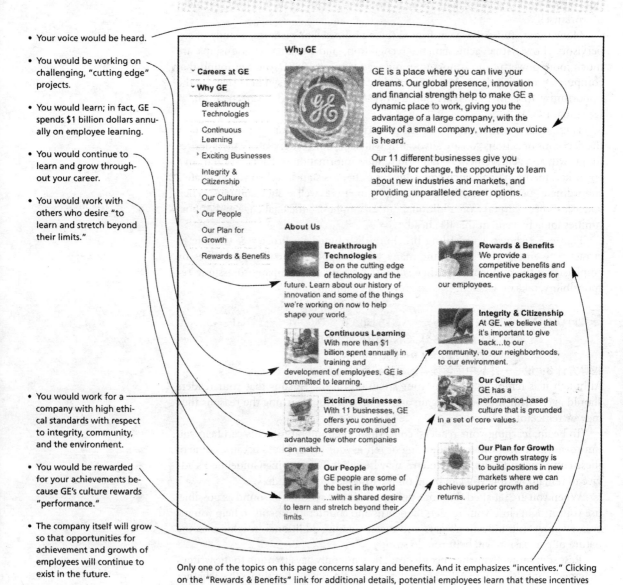

(Petty & Cacioppo, 1986). Consequently, when you are trying to persuade, avoid saying anything that might prompt negative thoughts.

One way to avoid arousing negative thoughts is to answer all the important questions your readers are likely to ask while reading your communication. Most of these questions will simply reflect the readers' efforts to understand your position or proposal thoroughly. "What are the costs of doing as you suggest?" "What do other people who have looked into this matter think?" "Do we have employees with the education, experience, or talent to do what you recommend?" If you answer such questions satisfactorily, they create no problem whatever. But if you ignore them, they may prompt the reader to think that you have overlooked some important consideration or ignored evidence that might weaken your position.

In addition to asking questions while reading, your readers may generate arguments against your position. For example, if you say there is a serious risk of injury to workers in a building used by your company, your readers may think to themselves that the building has been used for three years without an accident. If you say a new procedure will increase productivity by at least 10 percent, your readers may think to themselves that some of the data on which you are basing your estimate are inaccurate. Readers are especially likely to generate counterarguments when you attempt to reverse their attitudes. Research shows that people resist efforts to persuade them that their attitudes are incorrect (Petty & Cacioppo, 1986).

To deal effectively with counterarguments, you must offer a reason for relying on your position rather than on the opposing position. For example, imagine that you are proposing the purchase of a certain piece of equipment and that you predict your readers will object because it is more expensive than a competitor's product they believe to be its equal. You might explain that the competitor's product, though less expensive to purchase, is more expensive to operate and maintain.

One way to learn about the questions and counterarguments your readers might raise while reading is to ask them about their reasons for holding their present attitudes. Why do they do things the way they do? What arguments do they feel most strongly support their present position? You can also follow Chapter 3's advice for identifying your readers' questions, but focus specifically on questions that skeptical readers might pose.

Figure 5.4 shows a letter in which the marketing director of a radio station attempts to persuade an advertising agency to switch some of its ads to her station. Notice how she anticipates and addresses possible counterarguments.

GUIDELINE 4 REASON SOUNDLY
指导方针4：正确地推论

In today's workplace, as in ancient Greece, one of the most favorable thoughts your readers and listeners could possibly have is, "Yeah, that makes sense." One of the most unfavorable is, "Hey, there's a flaw in your reasoning."

Sound reasoning, the equivalent of Aristotle's *logos*, is especially important when you are trying to influence your readers' decisions and actions. In addition to identifying potential benefits that will appeal to your readers, you also must persuade

FIGURE 5.4
Letter that Addresses Counterarguments

WGWG
12741 Vienna Boulevard
Philadelphia, PA 19116

August 17, 2006

Mr. Roger L. Nordstrom
Llat Marketing, Inc.
1200 Langstroth Avenue
Philadelphia, Pennsylvania 19131

Dear Mr. Nordstrom:

What a lucky coincidence that we should have met at Shelby's last week. As I told you then, I believe you can improve the advertising service you provide many of your clients by switching to our station some of the radio advertising that you presently place for your clients with WSER and WFAC. Since we met, I have put together some figures.

The primary advantage of advertising with us is that you will extend the size of your audience considerably. As an example, consider the reach of the campaign you are now running for Fuller's Furniture Emporium. You currently buy 45 spots over four weeks on the other two stations. According to Arbitron market analysis, you thereby reach 63% of your target market—women in the 25–54 demographic group—an average of 16 times per week. However, there is a lot of overlap in the audiences of those two stations: many listeners switch back and forth between them.

In contrast, we serve a very distinct audience. By using only 30 spots on those two stations and giving 15 to us, you would increase your reach to 73% of the 25–54 group. It's true, of course, that this change would reduce from 16 to 13 the number of times the average listener hears your message. However, this is an increase of 8% in the portion of your target audience that you would reach.

But there's more. At the same time that you increase your audience, you would also decrease your costs. For example, if you switched the Fuller's Furniture Emporium spots in the way described, your costs would drop from $6,079 to $4,850. Our audience is smaller than the audiences on those stations, but our rates are only about half of theirs.

Writer states a counterargument that might occur to the reader.

Writer specifies a benefit to the reader that will outweigh the objection.

them that the decision or action you advocate will actually bring about these benefits—that the proposed new equipment really will reduce costs enough to pay for itself in just eighteen months or that the product modification you are recommending really will boost sales 10 percent in the first year.

Sound reasoning is also essential when you are describing conclusions you have reached after studying a group of facts, such as the results of a laboratory experiment or consumer survey. In such cases, you must persuade your readers that your conclusions are firmly based on the facts.

FIGURE 5.4
(continued)

Roger L. Nordstrom   —2—   August 17, 2006

As you consider these figures and others that might be given to you by other radio stations, be careful to evaluate them carefully. As we are all aware, anyone can manipulate statistics to their advantage. We recently discovered that one of our competitors was circulating data regarding the portion of the audiences of Philadelphia stations that are "unemployed." In that analysis, our station had a significantly higher portion of "unemployed" listeners than did either WSER or WFAC.

← *Writer states a counterargument the reader is likely to hear from competitors.*

However, after some investigation, we discovered that in those statistics, "unemployed" meant "unemployed outside the home." That meant that people "unemployed" are not necessarily breadwinners who are unable to provide an income for their families. They could be housewives with considerable power over family decisions about spending. In fact, surveys indicate that housewives are often the primary decision makers about such things as household furnishings—a point that is quite important with respect to your account with Fuller's Furniture Emporium.

← *Writer exposes faulty reasoning underlying the counterargument.*

I suggest that we get together soon so that we can sketch out the details of some radio advertising schedules that would include WGWG. I'll call you next week.

Cordially,

Ruth Anne Peterson

Ruth Anne Peterson
Marketing Director

Notice that in each of the situations just mentioned (as well as in any other you might encounter on the job), you must not only use sound reasoning, but also convince your readers that your reasoning is sound. The ability to do so is one of the most valuable writing skills you can develop.

Stephen Toulmin has developed a way of thinking about reasoning that will help you reason soundly and also show your readers that you do (Toulmin, Rieke, & Janik, 1984). You will also find Toulmin's concepts useful when you are analyzing and evaluating the reasoning in other people's communications.

How Reasoning Works

Sound reasoning involves your *claim*, your *evidence*, and your *line of reasoning*. The diagram illustrates the relationship among them.

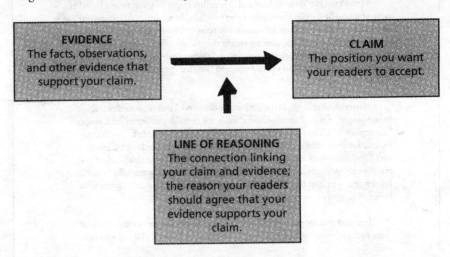

Imagine that you work for a company that manufactures cloth. You have found out that one of your employer's competitors recently increased its productivity by using newly developed computer programs to manage some of its manufacturing processes. If you were to recommend that your employer develop similar programs, your argument could be diagrammed as follows:

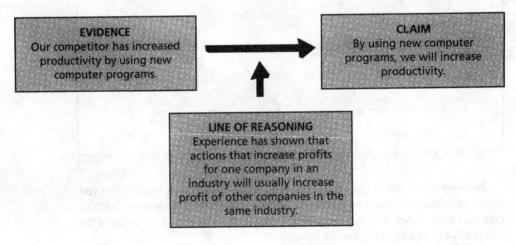

To accept your claim, readers must be willing to place their faith in both your evidence and your line of reasoning. The next two sections offer advice about how to persuade them to do so.

Present Sufficient and Reliable Evidence

First you must convince your readers that your evidence is both sufficient and reliable.

To provide *sufficient* evidence, you must furnish all the details your readers are likely to want. For instance, in the example of the textile mills, your readers would probably regard your evidence as skimpy if you produced only a vague report that the other company had somehow used computers and saved some money. They would want to know how the company had used computers, how much money had been saved, whether the savings had justified the cost of the equipment, and so forth.

To provide *reliable* evidence, you must produce the type of evidence your readers are likely to accept. The type of evidence varies greatly from field to field. For instance, in science and engineering, certain experimental procedures are widely accepted as reliable, whereas common wisdom and unsystematic observation usually are not. In contrast, in many business situations, personal observations and anecdotes provided by knowledgeable people often are accepted as reliable evidence. However, the following three types of evidence are widely accepted:

- **Data.** Readers typically respond very favorably to claims that are supported by numerical data.
- **Expert testimony.** People with advanced education, firsthand knowledge, or extensive experience related to a topic are often credited with special understanding and insight.
- **Examples.** Specific instances can effectively support general claims.

Explicitly Justify Your Line of Reasoning Where Necessary

To argue persuasively, you must not only present sufficient and reliable evidence, but also convince your readers that you are using a valid line of reasoning to link your evidence to your claim. Writers often omit any justification of their line of reasoning in the belief that the justification will be obvious to their readers. In fact, that is sometimes the case. In the construction industry, for example, people generally agree that if an engineer uses the appropriate formulas to analyze the size and shape of a bridge, the formulas will accurately predict whether or not the bridge will be strong enough to support the loads it must carry. The engineer doesn't need to justify the formulas themselves.

In many cases, however, readers search aggressively for a weak line of reasoning. In particular, they are wary of arguments based on false assumptions. For example, they may agree that if another textile mill like yours saved money by computerizing, then your mill would probably enjoy the same result; your readers, however, may question the assumption that the other mill is truly like yours. Maybe it makes a different kind of product or employs a different manufacturing process. If you think your readers will suspect that you are making a false assumption, offer whatever evidence or explanation you can to dispel their doubts.

> For a fuller explanation of Aristotle's thoughts on persuasion, go to www.thomsonedu.com/english/anderson and click on Chapter 5.

Readers also look for places where writers have overgeneralized by drawing broad conclusions from too few specific instances. If you think your readers will raise such an objection to your argument, mention additional cases. Or, narrow your conclusion to better match the evidence you have gathered. For example, instead of asserting that your claim applies to all textile companies in all situations, argue that it applies to specific companies or specific situations.

GUIDELINE 5 ORGANIZE TO CREATE A FAVORABLE RESPONSE

指导方针5：组织思路创造良好的回应

The way you organize a communication may have almost as much effect on its power to persuade as what you say in it. That point was demonstrated by researchers Sternthal, Dholakia, and Leavitt (1978), who presented two groups of people with different versions of a talk urging that a federal consumer protection agency be established. One version *began* by saying that the speaker was a highly credible source (a lawyer who graduated from Harvard and had extensive experience with consumer issues); the other version *ended* with that information.

Among people initially opposed to the speaker's recommendation, those who learned about his credentials at the beginning responded more favorably to his arguments than did those who learned about his credentials at the end. Why? This outcome can be explained in terms of two principles you learned in Chapter 1. First, people react to persuasive messages moment by moment. Second (and here's the key point), their reactions in one moment will affect their reactions in subsequent moments. In this experiment, those who learned of the speaker's credentials before hearing his arguments were relatively open to what he had to say. But those who learned of the speaker's credentials only at the end worked more vigorously at creating counterarguments as they heard each of his points. After those counterarguments had been recorded in memory, they could not be erased simply by adding information about the speaker's credibility.

Thus, it's not only the array of information that is critical in persuasion, but also the way readers process the information. The following sections suggest two strategies for organizing to elicit a favorable response: Choose carefully between direct and indirect organizational patterns, and create a tight fit among the parts of your communication.

Choose Carefully between Direct and Indirect Organizational Patterns

As you learned in Chapter 4, the most common organizational pattern at work begins by stating the bottom line — the writer's main point. Communications organized this way are said to use a *direct pattern* of organization because they go directly to the main point and only afterward present the evidence and other information related to it. For example, in a memo recommending the purchase of a new computer program, you might begin with the recommendation and then explain why you think the new program is desirable.

The alternative is to postpone presenting your main point until you have presented your evidence or other related information. This is called the *indirect pattern* of organization. For example, in a memo recommending the purchase of a new computer program, you might first explain the problems created by the current program, withholding until later your recommendation that a new one be purchased.

To choose between the direct and indirect organizational patterns, focus your attention on your readers' all-important initial response to your message. The direct pattern will start your readers off on the right foot when you have good news to convey: "You're hired," "I've figured out a solution to your problem," or something similar. By starting with the good news, you put your readers in a favorable frame of mind as they read the rest of your message.

The direct pattern also works well when you are offering an analysis or recommending a course of action that you expect your readers to view favorably — or at least objectively — from the start. Leah is about to write such a memo, in which she will recommend a new system for managing the warehouses for her employer, a company that manufactures hundreds of parts used to drill oil and gas wells. Leah has chosen to use the direct pattern shown in the left-hand column of Figure 5.5. This is an appropriate choice because her readers (upper management) have expressed dissatisfaction with the present warehousing system. Consequently, she can expect a favorable reaction to her initial announcement that she has designed a better system.

The direct pattern is less effective when you are conveying information your readers might view as bad, alarming, or threatening. Imagine, for example, that Leah's readers are the people who set up the present system and that they believe it

FIGURE 5.5 Comparison of Direct and Indirect Organizational Patterns for Organizing Leah's Memo

Direct Pattern	Indirect Pattern	
I. Leah presents her recommended strategy	I. Leah discusses the goals of the present system from the *reader's point of view*	The direct pattern presents the recommendation first.
II. Leah explains why her way of warehousing is superior to the present way	II. Leah discusses the ways in which the present system does and does not achieve the readers' goals	
III. Leah explains in detail how to implement her system	III. Leah presents her recommended strategy for achieving those goals more effectively, focusing on the ways her recommendation can overcome the shortcomings of the present system	The indirect pattern delays recommendation; it's for use where the reader may react unfavorably.
	IV. Leah explains in detail how to implement her system	

is working well. If Leah begins her memo by recommending a new system, she might put her readers immediately on the defensive because they might feel she is criticizing their competence. Then she would have little hope of receiving an open and objective reading of her supporting information. By using an indirect pattern, however, Leah can *prepare* her readers for her recommendation by first getting them to agree that it might be possible to improve on the present system. The right-hand column of Figure 5.5 shows an indirect pattern she might use.

You may wonder why you shouldn't simply use the indirect pattern all the time. It presents the same information as the direct organization (plus some more), and it avoids the risk of inciting a negative reaction at the outset. The trouble is that this pattern frustrates the readers' desire to learn the main point first.

In sum, the choice between direct and indirect patterns of organization can greatly affect the persuasiveness of your communications. To choose, you need to follow the basic strategy suggested throughout this book: Think about your readers' moment-by-moment reactions to your message.

Create a Tight Fit among the Parts of Your Communication

When you organize a communication, you can also strengthen its persuasiveness by ensuring that the parts fit together tightly. This advice applies particularly to longer communications, where the overall argument often consists of two or more subordinate arguments. The way to do this is to review side by side the claims made in the various parts of a communication.

For example, imagine that you are writing a proposal. In an early section, you describe a problem your proposed project will solve. Here, your persuasive points are that a problem exists and that the readers should view it as serious. In a later section, you describe the project you propose. Check to see whether this description tells how the project will address each aspect of the problem that you described. If it doesn't, either the discussion of the problem or the discussion of the project needs to be revised so the two match up. Similarly, your budget should include expenses that are clearly related to the project you describe, and your schedule should show when you will carry out each activity necessary to complete the project successfully.

Of course, the need for a tight fit applies not only to proposals but also to any communication whose various parts work together to affect your readers' attitudes. Whenever you write, think about ways to make the parts work harmoniously together in mutual support of your overall position.

GUIDELINE 6 BUILD AN EFFECTIVE RELATIONSHIP WITH YOUR READERS

指导方针6：与读者建立有效关系

One of the most important factors influencing the success of a persuasive communication is how your readers feel about you. You will remember from Chapter 1 that you should think of the communications you prepare at work as interpersonal interactions. If your readers feel well disposed toward you, they are likely to consider your points openly and without bias. If they feel irritated, angry, or otherwise unfriendly toward you, they may immediately raise counterarguments to every point you present, making it extremely unlikely that you will elicit a favorable reaction, even if all your points are clear, valid, and substantiated. Good points rarely win the day in the face of bad feelings.

The following sections describe two ways you can present yourself to obtain a fair — or even a favorable — hearing from your readers at work: Present yourself as a credible person, and present yourself as a friend, not a foe.

Present Yourself as a Credible Person

Your credibility is your readers' beliefs about whether or not you are a good source for information and ideas. If people believe you are credible, they will be relatively open to what you say. They may even accept your judgments and recommendations without inquiring very deeply into your reasons for making them. If people do not find you credible, they may refuse to give you a fair hearing no matter how soundly you state your case.

Because people's response to a message can depend so greatly on their views of the writer or speaker, Aristotle identified *ethos*, which corresponds roughly to credibility, as one of the three major elements of persuasion.

In a classic experiment, researchers H. C. Kelman and C. I. Hovland (1953) demonstrated how greatly your readers' perception of you can affect the way they respond to your message. They asked two groups to listen to a taped speech advocating lenient treatment of juvenile delinquents. Before playing their tape for one group, they identified the speaker as an ex-delinquent out on bail. They told another group that the speaker was a judge. Only 27 percent of those who heard the "delinquent's" talk responded favorably to it, while 73 percent of those who heard the "judge's" talk responded favorably.

Researchers have conducted many studies on the factors that affect an audience's impression of a person's credibility. In summarizing this research, Robert Bostrom (1981) has identified five key factors.

Several factors that influence credibility

STRATEGIES FOR BUILDING CREDIBILITY

1. **Expertise.** Expertise is the knowledge and experience that readers believe you possess that is relevant to the topic. *Strategies you can use:*
   - Mention your credentials.
   - Demonstrate a command of the facts.
   - Avoid oversimplifying.
   - Mention or quote experts so their expertise supports your position.
2. **Trustworthiness.** Trustworthiness depends largely on your readers' perceptions of your motives. If you seem to be acting from self-interest, your credibility is

low; if you seem to be acting objectively or for goals shared by your readers, your credibility is high. *Strategies you can use:*

- Stress values and objectives that are important to your readers.
- Avoid drawing attention to personal advantages to you.
- Demonstrate knowledge of the concerns and perspectives of others.

3. **Group membership.** You will gain credibility if you are a member of the readers' own group or a group admired by your readers. *Strategies you can use:*

- If you are associated with a group admired by your readers, allude to that relationship.
- If you are addressing members of your own organization, affirm that relationship by showing that you share the group's objectives, methods, and values.
- Use terms that are commonly employed in your organization.

4. **Dynamic appeal.** An energetic, enthusiastic person has much higher credibility than a passive, guarded one. *Strategies you can use:*

- State your message confidently and directly.
- Show enthusiasm for your ideas and subject.

5. **Power.** For example, simply by virtue of her position, a boss acquires some credibility with subordinates. *Strategies you can use:*

- If you are in a position of authority, identify your position if your readers don't know it.
- If you are not in a position of authority, associate yourself with a powerful person by quoting the person or saying that you consulted with him or her or were assigned the job by that individual.

Figure 5.6 shows a letter that puts many of these strategies into action. In it, the president of a biometric security company used these strategies to persuade the security chief of a chemical company to allow him to demonstrate a new security system. Figure 5.7 shows how the International Fund for Animal Welfare designed its website using similar strategies to persuade people to participate in and support its efforts.

Present Yourself as a Friend, Not a Foe

Psychologist Carl Rogers (1952) identified another important strategy in fostering open, unbiased communication: Reduce the sense of threat that people often feel when others are presenting ideas to them. According to Rogers, people are likely to feel threatened even when you make *helpful* suggestions. As a result, your readers may see you as an adversary even though you don't intend at all to be one.

Here are four methods, based on the work of Rogers, that you can use to present yourself as nonthreatening to your readers.

To see how to apply this advice, consider the following situation. Marjorie Lakwurtz is a regional manager for a company that employs nearly 1,000 students in

STRATEGIES FOR PRESENTING YOURSELF AS A FRIEND

1. **Praise your readers.**
   - When writing to an individual, mention one of his or her recent accomplishments.
   - When writing to another organization, mention something it prides itself on.
   - When praising, be sure to mention specifics. General praise sounds insincere.

2. **Present yourself as your readers' partner.**
   - Identify some personal or organizational goal of your readers that you will help them attain.
   - If you are already your readers' partner, mention that fact and emphasize the goals you share.

3. **Show that you understand your readers.**
   - Even if you disagree with your readers, state their case fairly.
   - Focus on areas of agreement.

4. **Maintain a positive and helpful stance.**
   - Present your suggestions as ways of helping your readers do an even better job.
   - Avoid criticizing or blaming.

---

many cities during the summer months to paint houses and other large structures. Each student is required to pay a $100 deposit, which is returned at the end of the summer. Students complain that the equipment they work with isn't worth anywhere near $100 so the deposit is unjustified. Furthermore, they believe that the company is simply requiring the deposit so it can invest the money during the summer. The company keeps all the interest on the deposits, not giving any to the students when it returns their deposits at the end of the summer.

Marjorie agrees that the students have a good case, so she wants to suggest a change. She could do that in a negative way by telling the company that it should be ashamed of its greedy plot to profit by investing other people's money. Or she could take a positive approach, presenting her suggested change as a way the company can better achieve its own goals. In the memo shown in Figure 5.8, she takes the latter course. Notice how skillfully she presents herself as her readers' partner.

GUIDELINE 7 DETERMINE WHETHER TO APPEAL TO YOUR READERS' EMOTIONS

指导方针 7：确定是否需要激发读者的情感

Of Aristotle's three types of persuasive strategies, the appeal to emotions (*pathos*) is used least in workplace communications. In many communications, it makes no appearance at all. In fact, readers would usually consider appeals to emotion in scientific research reports, test reports, and many other types of documents to be highly inappropriate.

FIGURE 5.6
Letter that Uses Several Strategies for Building Credibility

In this letter, Cameron Franks uses several strategies for building credibility.

Trustworthiness
He aligns his goal with his readers' goal: to improve security.

He reports that his product has been ordered by organizations whose security knowledge is assumed to be great.

Expertise
He indicates that his product is so technically innovative that it has won an award and a patent (third paragraph).

Group membership
He uses the word "us" to identify himself as a member of the same group as his reader: security professionals

Power
He indicates that he holds a powerful position in his own company

---

ABS Alpha Biometric Systems

17 Western Boulevard
Houston, TX 77002

November 12, 2007

Mr. Jeffrey Rajkumar, Security Chief
Antonio Chemicals
22898 Rockland Avenue
Dallas, TX 75226

Dear Mr. Rajkumar:

You can significantly improve security at Antonio Chemicals with our new biometric system, the Eye-C2. On the market for only six months, the Eye-C2 has already been ordered by several federal agencies and major corporations. It received a 2006 Innovation Award from the International Electronics Society.

Why this rapid success? As those of us in the security profession know, criminals have been gaining unauthorized access to high-security areas protected by biometric security systems that read fingerprints. After lifting an authorized person's fingerprint from a glass or other smooth surface, the criminals make a gelatin copy of it. When no one is around, they then have the fingerprint security system scan the gelatin copy, which the system cannot distinguish from a real fingerprint.

In contrast, our patented Eye-C2 scans the blood vessels in a person's retina. The blood vessels form a pattern that is unique to each person and inaccessible to criminals.

I am eager to demonstrate the Eye-C2 for you. Please let me know how I might arrange a meeting.

Sincerely,

Cameron Franks

Cameron Franks
President

---

138 ■ CHAPTER 5 **Planning Your Persuasive Strategies**

In others, appeals to emotion are important. For example, documents on either side of public policy often include them. Organizations that advocate opening new sections of federal land for oil and mineral exploration sometimes include photographs of animals in natural settings to emphasize the measures to be taken to protect them. Organizations opposed to opening the lands sometimes include photographs of damage accompanying such exploration in other areas.

Emotional appeals are also used widely by government agencies and private health providers as they advocate healthy lifestyles. Nonprofit foundations that support research for conditions such as arthritis, breast cancer, and AIDS use emotional appeals liberally. See Figure 5.9.

To recruit college graduates in engineering, science, and other specialized fields, employers often include photographs of happy employees to emphasize the pleasures of employment with them.

Base your decisions about whether — and how strongly — to appeal to your readers' emotions on your knowledge of your readers and their likely response. Situations in which you are using emotional appeals are ones in which it can be especially helpful to ask others to review your drafts.

> **Learn More**
> For more on having other people review your drafts, turn to page 407.

GUIDELINE 8 GLOBAL GUIDELINE: ADAPT YOUR PERSUASIVE STRATEGIES TO YOUR READERS' CULTURAL BACKGROUND

总体指导方针 8：调整说服策略使其适用于读者的文化背景

Whenever you are writing to readers in a culture other than your own, you will need to learn about the persuasive practices that succeed there. Like all other aspects of communication, every aspect of persuasion can differ from one culture to another.

Consider, for example, Guideline 2, which advises you to focus on your readers' goals and values. In different cultures, people's goals and values differ in ways that mean the benefits you highlight for readers in one culture are not necessarily those that would be appealing to readers in another culture. Marketing specialists are well aware of these differences. To appeal to car buyers, Volvo focuses on safety and durability in the United States, status and leisure in France, and performance in Germany (Ricks, 2000).

Cultural differences in goals and values influence persuasion in the workplace as well as in consumer marketing. For example, in Japan, where group membership is highly valued, the most effective way to influence attitudes of individual employees is to talk about the success the proposed action will bring to the group. In the United States, where individual achievement is highly valued, appeals to personal goals can be effective in ways they would not be in Japan.

Similarly, different cultures have different views of what counts as evidence that a particular action should be taken. Whereas many Western cultures base their arguments on facts, international communication experts Farid Elashmawi and

FIGURE 5.7
Website that Uses Several Strategies for Building Credibility

This website by the International Fund for Animal Welfare uses a variety of strategies for building credibility with readers it hopes to persuade to make donations and support the IFAW in other ways.

Trustworthiness. The row of flags not only enables readers from different countries to read the site in their own language, but also conveys the sense that the IFAW truly is "international."

Dynamic Appeal and Power. The flags also suggest that IFAW is so active and powerful that it is influential on several continents.

Trustworthiness. By showing two images that include both an animal and a human hand, the IFAW suggests that the donations they make will, in fact, be used for animals' direct care and protection.

Dynamic Appeal. By highlighting a rescue mission in its "Features" area, the IFAW indicates that it is involved in practical actions.

Expertise. The "Breaking News" section suggests that the IFAW is a knowledgeable and up-to-date organization.

Credibility and Dynamic Appeal. By announcing that its site has won one of the well-known Webby Awards, the IFAW provides an outside endorsement. By indicating that the award was for an "Activism" website, the IFAW builds its dynamic appeal.

Group Membership. By showing images of many animals, the IFAW indicates that it has the same commitment to animals and the environment that is shared by the readers most likely to provide support. (Note that this site does not attempt to persuade people that they should be commited to animals and the environment, but rather is designed to elicit support from people who already have this commitment.)

CHAPTER 5 **Planning Your Persuasive Strategies**

FIGURE 5.8
Memo in Which the Writer Establishes a Partnership with the Reader

---

PREMIUM PAINTING COMPANY

February 12, 2007

TO: Martin Sneed

FROM: Marjorie Lakwurtz   *ML*

RE: Improving Worker Morale

Now that I have completed my first year with the company, I have been thinking over my experiences here. I have enjoyed the challenges that this unique company offers, and I've been very favorably impressed with our ability to find nearly 1000 temporary workers who are willing to work so energetically and diligently for us. ◄——— *Marjorie opens by praising the reader.*

In fact, it's occurred to me that the good attitude of the students who work for us is one of the indispensable ingredients in our success. If they slack off or become careless, our profits could drop precipitously. If they become careless, splattering and spilling paint for instance, we would lose much of our profits in cleaning up the mess.

Because student morale is so crucial to us, I would like to suggest a way of raising it ◄——— *Marjorie presents herself as the reader's partner in the mutual goal of raising worker morale.*
even further—and of ensuring that it won't droop. From many different students in several cities, I have heard complaints about the $100 security deposit we require them to pay before they begin work. They feel that the equipment they work with is worth much less than that, so that the amount of this security deposit is very steep. Furthermore, there is a widespread belief that the company is actually cheating them by taking their money, investing it for the summer, and keeping the profits for itself.

Because the complaints are so widespread and because they can directly affect the ◄——— *Marjorie uses "we" to reinforce the sense of partnership.*
students' sense of obligation to the company, I think we should try to do something about the security deposit. First we could reduce the deposit. If you think that would be unwise, we could give the students the interest earned on their money when we return the deposits to them at the end of the summer.

FIGURE 5.8
(continued)

Marjorie shows that she understands the reader's perspective.

Marjorie counters a possible objection by making a positive suggestion.

Marjorie states and addresses another counterargument.

Marjorie closes on a positive note, reemphasizing her desire to work as her reader's partner.

Martin Sneed
February 12, 2007
Page 2

I realize that it would be difficult to calculate the precise amount of interest earned by each student. They begin work at different times in May and June, and they end at different times in August and September. However, we could establish a flat amount to be paid each student, perhaps basing it on the average interest earned by the deposits over a three-month period.

I'm sure that it has been somewhat beneficial for the company to have the extra income produced by the deposits. But the amount earned is still rather modest. The additional productivity we might enjoy from our students by removing this irritant to them is likely to increase our profits by much more than the interest paid.

If you would like to talk to me about this idea or about the feelings expressed by the students, I would be happy to meet with you.

FIGURE 5.9
Websites that Appeal to the Reader's Emotions

On its homepage, the National Cancer Institute (NCI) appeals to the emotions of cancer patients, their families, and friends.

In two ways, the site suggests the NCI understands these emotions and offers hope and relief.

1. The large photo portrays an individual overcome by emotions that many people feel when they visit the site. Another photo farther to the right shows three people on a beach, all apparently healthy and strong. Between these images are the NCI employees who will create this transformation: a researcher and a caregiver who looks directly at the reader.

2. The website identifies in words what many of its readers fear: "suffering and death due to cancer." It also promises to "eliminate" them.

In addition, the site also appeals to the readers' emotions by promising assistance to those who "need help." The NCI employees who will provide this help are represented by a smiling person who seems happy to hear from callers.

The site also uses several strategies for building credibility that are described on page 135.

Guideline 8 **Adapt Your Persuasive Strategies to Your Readers' Backgrounds**

Philip R. Harris (1998) report that in some Arab cultures people support their positions through emotions and personal relations.

You must adapt to your readers' culture even when following Guideline 1: Listen — and respond flexibly to what you hear. Imagine that you have sent an e-mail to members of your target audience to find out how they feel about an idea you are planning to propose. If your readers are in the United States, they are likely to tell you directly. However, in many Asian cultures, they are not likely respond in that way because they would not want you to lose face (Lustig & Koester, 1993). In this case, you may need to listen to their silence, which is an indirect way of indicating disagreement in many Asian cultures.

Guideline 9 Ethics Guideline: Employ Ethical Persuasive Techniques
道德指导方针9：采用符合道德规范的说服技巧

The ethical dimensions of on-the-job writing are never more evident than when you are trying to persuade other people to take a certain action or adopt a certain attitude. Here are four guidelines for ethical persuasion that you might want to keep in mind: Don't mislead, don't manipulate, open yourself to your readers' viewpoint, and argue from human values.

Don't Mislead

When you are writing persuasively, respect your readers' right to evaluate your arguments in an informed and independent way. If you mislead your readers by misstating facts, using intentionally ambiguous expressions, or arguing from false premises, you deprive your readers of their rights.

Don't Manipulate

The philosopher Immanuel Kant originated the enduring ethical principle that we should never use other people merely to get what we want. Whenever we try to influence our readers, the action we advocate should advance their goals as well as our own.

Under Kant's principle, for instance, it would be unethical to persuade readers to do something that would benefit us but harm them. High-pressure sales techniques are unethical because their purpose is to persuade consumers to purchase something they may not need or even want. Persuasion is ethical only if it will lead our readers to get something they truly desire.

Open Yourself to Your Readers' Viewpoint

To keep your readers' goals and interests in mind, you must be open to understanding their viewpoint. Instead of regarding their counterarguments as objections you must overcome, try to understand what lies behind their concerns. Consider ways of modifying your original ideas to take your readers' perspective into account.

In this way, rather than treat your readers as adversaries, accept them as partners in a search for a course of action acceptable to you all (Lauer, 1994). Management experts call this search for a "win-win" situation — a situation in which all parties benefit (Covey, 1989).

Argue from Human Values

Whenever you feel that human values are relevant, don't hesitate to introduce them when you are writing to persuade. Many organizations realize the need to consider these values when making decisions. In other organizations, human values are sometimes overlooked — or even considered to be inappropriate topics — because the employees focus too sharply on business objectives. However, even if your arguments based on human values do not prevail, you will have succeeded in introducing a consideration of these values into your working environment. Your action may even encourage others to follow your lead.

CONCLUSION 总 结

This chapter has focused on writing persuasively in both competitive and cooperative situations. As you can see, nearly every aspect of your communication affects your ability to influence your readers' attitudes and actions. Although the guidelines in this chapter will help you write persuasively, the most important persuasive strategy of all is to keep in mind your readers' needs, concerns, values, and preferences whenever you write.

Figure 5.10 provides a guide you can use when planning your persuasive strategies.

FIGURE 5.10 Guide for Planning Your Persuasive Strategies

To download a copy of this planning guide, go to www.thomsonedu.com/english/anderson and click on Chapter 5.

PLANNING YOUR PERSUASIVE STRATEGIES

Understanding Your Readers' Goals

1. What organizational goals affect your readers and are related to your topic?
2. What are your readers' values-based goals that are related to your topic?
3. What are your readers' achievement and growth goals?

Responding to Your Readers' Concerns and Counterarguments

1. What concerns or counterarguments might your readers raise?
2. How can you respond persuasively to these concerns and counterarguments?
3. Where do you need to be careful about inspiring negative thoughts?

Reasoning

1. What kinds of evidence will your readers consider to be reliable and persuasive support for your claims?
2. Where will you need to justify your line of reasoning?
3. Where do you need to be cautious about avoiding false assumptions and overgeneralizations?

Organizing

1. Would a direct or indirect organizational pattern be most effective?
2. What specific strategies can you use to create a tight fit among the parts?

Building a Relationship with Your Readers

1. What strategies can you use to present yourself as a credible person?
2. What strategies can you use to present yourself as a friend, not a foe?

Adapting to Your Readers' Cultural Background

1. Do you need to check your draft with people who share your readers' cultural background?

Persuading Ethically

1. Avoid misleading or manipulative statements.
2. Consider your readers' viewpoint openly.
3. Assure that the relevant human values are considered.

EXERCISES 练 习

EXPERTISE

1. Find a persuasive communication that contains at least 25 words of prose. It may be an advertisement, marketing letter, memo from school or work, or a web page. What persuasive strategies are used in the prose and any images that are included? Are the strategies effective for the intended audience? Are all of them ethical? What other strategies might have been used? Present your responses in the way requested by your instructor.
2. Do the "Unsolicited Recommendation" assignment given in Appendix B.

ONLINE

Study the website of a company or organization related to your major or career. What attitudes toward the organization and its products or services does the site promote? What persuasive strategies are used in the text and images in order to persuade readers to adopt the desired attitudes? How effective are these strategies? Are all of them ethical?

COLLABORATION

Working with one or two other students, analyze the letter shown in Figure 5.11 on page 148, identifying its strengths and weaknesses. Relate your points to the guidelines in this chapter. The following paragraphs describe the situation in which the writer, Scott Houck, is writing.

Before going to college, Scott worked for a few years at Thompson Textiles. In his letter, he addresses Thompson's Executive Vice President, Georgiana Stroh. He is writing because in college he learned many things that made him think Thompson would benefit if its managers were better educated in modern management techniques. Thompson Textiles could enjoy these benefits, Scott believes, if it would offer management courses to its employees and if it would fill job openings at the managerial level with college graduates. However, if Thompson were to follow Scott's recommendations, it would have to change its practices considerably. Thompson has never offered courses for its employees and has long sought to keep payroll expenses low by employing people without a college education, even in management positions. (In a rare exception to this practice, the company has guaranteed Scott a position after he graduates.)

To attempt to change the company's policies, Scott decided to write a letter to one of the most influential people on its staff, Ms. Stroh. Unfortunately for Scott, throughout the three decades that Stroh has served as an executive officer at Thompson, she has consistently opposed company-sponsored education and the hiring of college graduates. Consequently, she has an especially strong motive for rejecting Scott's advice: She is likely to feel that, if she agreed that Thompson's educational and hiring policies should be changed, she would be admitting that she had been wrong all along.

ETHICS

Find an online or print communication you feel is unethical. Identify the specific elements in the text images that you feel are untrue, misleading, or manipulative. Present your analysis in the way your instructor requests.

FIGURE 5.11
Letter for Exercise

616 S. College #84
Oxford, Ohio 45056
April 16, 2006

Georgiana Stroh
Executive Vice President
Thompson Textiles Incorporated
1010 Note Ave.
Cincinnati, Ohio 45014

Dear Ms. Stroh:

As my junior year draws to a close, I am more and more eager to return to our company, where I can apply my new knowledge and skills. Since our recent talk about the increasingly stiff competition in the textile industry, I have thought quite a bit about what I can do to help Thompson continue to prosper. I have been going over some notes I have made on the subject, and I am struck by how many of the ideas stemmed directly from the courses I have taken here at Miami University.

Almost all of the notes featured suggestions or thoughts I simply didn't have the knowledge to consider before I went to college! Before I enrolled, I, like many people, presumed that operating a business required only a certain measure of commonsense ability—that almost anyone could learn to guide a business down the right path with a little experience. However, I have come to realize that this belief is far from the truth. It is true that many decisions are common sense, but decisions often only appear to be simple because the entire scope of the problem or the full ramifications of a particular alternative are not well understood. A path is always chosen, but often is it the BEST path for the company as a whole?

In retrospect, I appreciate the year I spent supervising the Eaton Avenue Plant because the experience has been an impetus to actually learn from my classes instead of just receiving grades. But I look back in embarrassment upon some of the decisions I made and the methods I used then. I now see that my previous work in our factories and my military experience did not prepare me as well for that position as I thought they did. My mistakes were not so often a poor selection among known alternatives, but were more often sins of omission. For example, you may remember that we were constantly running low on packing cartons and that we sometimes ran completely out, causing the entire line to shut down. Now I know that instead of haphazardly placing orders for a different amount every time, we should have used a forecasting model to determine and establish a reorder point and a reorder quantity. But I was simply unaware of many of the sophisticated techniques available to me as a manager.

I respectfully submit that many of our supervisory personnel are in a similar situation. This is not to downplay the many contributions they have made to the company. Thompson can directly attribute its prominent position in the industry to the devotion and hard work of these people. But very few of them have more than a high school education or have read even a single text on management skills. We have always counted on our supervisors to pick up their

Georgiana Stroh   Page 2

management skills on the job without any additional training. Although I recognize that I owe my own opportunities to this approach, this comes too close to the commonsense theory I mentioned earlier.

The success of Thompson depends on the abilities of our managers relative to the abilities of our competition. In the past, EVERY company used this commonsense approach, and Thompson prospered because of the natural talent of people like you. But in the last decade, many new managerial techniques have been developed that are too complex for the average employee to just "figure out" on his or her own. For example, people had been doing business for several thousand years before developing the Linear Programming Model for transportation and resource allocation problem-solving. It is not reasonable to expect a high school graduate to recognize that his or her particular distribution problem could be solved by a mathematical model and then to develop the LP from scratch. But as our world grows more complex, competition will stiffen as others take advantage of these innovations. I fear that what has worked in the past will not necessarily work in the future: We may find out what our managers DON'T know CAN hurt us. Our managers must be made aware of advances in computer technology, management theory, and operations innovations, and they must be able to use them to transform our business as changing market conditions demand.

I would like to suggest that you consider the value of investing in an in-house training program dealing with relevant topics to augment the practical experience our employees are gaining. In addition, when management or other fast-track administrative positions must be filled, it may be worth the investment to hire college graduates whose coursework has prepared them to use state-of-the-art techniques to help us remain competitive. Of course, these programs will initially show up on the bottom line as increased expenses, but it is reasonable to expect that, in the not-so-long run, profits will be boosted by newfound efficiencies. Most important, we must recognize the danger of adopting a wait-and-see attitude. Our competitors are now making this same decision; hesitation on our part may leave us playing catch-up.

In conclusion, I believe I will be a valuable asset to the company, in large part because of the education I am now receiving. I hope you agree that a higher education level in our employees is a cause worthy of our most sincere efforts. I will contact your office next week to find out if you are interested in meeting to discuss questions you may have or to review possible implementation strategies.

Sincerely,

Scott Houck

FIGURE 5.11
(continued)

CASE: Debating a Company Drug-Testing Program 讨论一个公司的药物测试项目

For additional cases, go to www.thomsonedu.com/english/anderson. Instructors: The book's website includes suggestions for teaching the cases.

"Have you read your e-mail yet this afternoon?" Hal asks excitedly on the telephone. The two of you started working at Life Systems, Inc. in the same month and have become good friends even though you work in different departments. By now you've both risen to management positions.

"Not yet. What's up?"

"Wait 'til you hear this," Hal replies. "Tonti's sent us all a message announcing that she's thinking about starting a company drug-testing program." The person Hal calls "Tonti" is Maria Tonti, the company president, who has increased the company's profitability dramatically over the past five years by spurring employees to higher productivity while still giving them a feeling they are being treated fairly.

"A what?"

"Drug testing. Mandatory urine samples taken at unannounced times. She says that if she decides to go ahead with the program, any one of our employees could be tested, from the newest stockroom clerk to Tonti herself."

"You're kidding!" you exclaim as you swivel around and look out your window and across the shady lawn between your building and the highway.

"Nope. And she wants our opinion about whether she should start the program or not. In the e-mail she says she's asking all of her 'key managers' to submit their views in writing. She wants each of us to pick one side or the other and argue for it, so that she and her executive committee will know all the angles when they discuss the possibilities next week."

Hal pauses, waiting for your reaction. After a moment, you say, "Given the kinds of products we make, I suppose it was inevitable that Tonti would consider drug testing sooner or later." Life Support, Inc. manufactures highly specialized, very expensive medical machines, including some that keep patients alive during heart and lung transplant operations. The company has done extremely well in the past few years because of its advanced technology and — more important — its unsurpassed reputation for reliable machines.

You add, "Does she say what started her thinking about drug testing? Has there been some problem?"

"I guess not. In fact, she says she hasn't had a single report or any indication that any employee has used drugs. I wonder what kinds of response she'll get."

You speculate, "I bet she gets the full range of opinions — all the way from total support for the idea to complete rejection of it."

Just then someone knocks at your door. Looking over your shoulder, you see it's Scotty with some papers you asked him to get.

"I've got to go, Hal. Talk to you later."

"Before you hang up," Hal says, "tell me what you're going to say in your reply to Tonti."

"I don't know. I guess I'll have to think it over."

Your Assignment

Write a reply to Maria Tonti's e-mail message. Begin by deciding whether you want to argue for or against the drug-testing program. Then think of all the arguments you can to support your position. Next, think of the strongest counterarguments that might be raised against your position. In your memo, argue persuasively on behalf of your position, following the guidelines in Chapters 4 and 5. Remember to deal with the arguments on the other side.

Conducting Reader-Centered Research

进行以读者为中心的调研

6

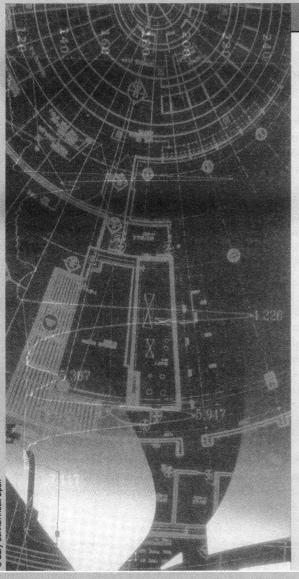

GUIDELINES

1. Define your research objectives *152*
2. Create an efficient and productive research plan *153*
3. Check each source for leads to other sources *155*
4. Carefully evaluate what you find *155*
5. Begin interpreting your research results even as you obtain them *156*
6. Take careful notes *157*
7. **Ethics Guideline:** Observe intellectual property law and document your sources *157*

CHAPTER 6

DEFINING OBJECTIVES
PLANNING
DRAFTING
REVISING

To succeed in the writing you do in your career, you must provide your readers with information and ideas they will find useful and persuasive. Sometimes, you will possess this knowledge before you begin to plan your communication. Often, however, you will need to conduct research to discover and develop your communication's content. This chapter will help you develop your expertise in conducting reader-centered research.

SPECIAL CHARACTERISTICS OF ON-THE-JOB RESEARCH
工作中研究的特点

The initial step in developing this expertise is understanding that research at work differs significantly from research in school. First, the *purposes* are very different. As explained in Chapter 1, your college instructors assign writing projects in order to advance your personal, intellectual, and professional development. Typically, your college research goal is to gain either a general overview or a comprehensive understanding of a topic that will be useful *to you* sometime *in the future*. In contrast, at work you will write for practical purposes, such as *helping others*—managers, coworkers, or clients—perform practical tasks and make good decisions on issues that confront them right now. Your research goal on the job will be to develop ideas, information, and arguments that *your readers* will find to be valuable *right now*.

Second, in the workplace it is much more important to be able to *conduct research efficiently*, without taking extra time to travel down avoidable dead ends or study material that will be irrelevant to your readers' current situation. You will need to produce your results quickly because your readers will have an immediate need for your results and because you will also have many other responsibilities and tasks to complete.

Third, in the workplace some (but not all) of the *ethical principles* concerning research differ from those that apply in school.

This chapter's first six guidelines will help you quickly and efficiently gather the information, ideas, and arguments your readers need from your communications. A seventh focuses on important ethical legal issues in workplace research. In addition, the Writer's Reference Guide that follows this chapter offers detailed advice for skillfully using five research methods often employed on the job.

> To read additional information and access links related to this chapter's guidelines, go to www.thomsonedu.com/english/anderson and click on Chapter 6.

GUIDELINE 1 DEFINE YOUR RESEARCH OBJECTIVES
指导方针1：确定研究目标

You can streamline your research by defining in advance what you want to find. After all, you are not trying to dig up everything that is known about your subject. You are seeking only information and ideas that will help you achieve your communication's objectives.

In fact, the most productive way to begin your research is by reviewing your communication's usability and persuasive goals (see Chapter 3). Your research objectives should be built squarely on them.

First, identify the information you need in order to write a communication your readers will find to be highly usable. Review the questions your readers will ask about your topic. The questions you can't answer immediately are the ones you need to research. Also review the kinds of answers your readers will want you to provide. For example, remind yourself whether they will want general information or specific details, introductory overviews or technical explanations. In addition, consider the point of view from which your readers will read your communication. Are they going to want it to meet their needs as engineers or accountants, consumers or producers? The answers to these questions will help you determine not only the kinds of information you must obtain but also where you should look for it.

Second, identify the kinds of information and arguments that will make your communication most persuasive in your readers' eyes. Given your readers' goals, values, and preferences, what kinds of information and arguments are most likely to influence their attitudes and actions? For example, are they primarily interested in efficiency or profitability, safety or consumer acceptance? Consider also the types of evidence and kinds of sources your readers will find most compelling. For instance, are they more likely to be swayed by quantitative data or by testimonials from leaders in their field?

Although you should define your research objectives at the outset, be prepared to revise them as you proceed. Research is all about learning. One thing you may learn along the way is that you need to investigate something you hadn't originally thought important—or even thought about at all.

> Base your research objectives on your communication's usability and persuasive goals.

GUIDELINE 2 CREATE AN EFFICIENT AND PRODUCTIVE RESEARCH PLAN
指导方针2：制定有效的研究计划

Many people conduct research haphazardly. They dash off to the library or log onto the Internet in the hopes of quickly finding just the right book or website. If the first source fails, they scoot off to another one. Such an approach can waste time and cause you to miss very helpful sources, including (perhaps) the one that includes exactly the information you need.

When planning, identify the sources that will be most persuasive to your readers. For instance, scientists are more likely to be persuaded by information you've gathered from an article in a research journal than by information from the Internet. Scientists reason that research journals assure that each article is scientifically sound before they publish it. No such evaluation exists for most items on the Internet.

You will conduct your research most efficiently and productively if you begin by making a plan. Here are key elements of a research plan.

Learn More

Guideline 4 (page 155) provides detailed advice about evaluating information you find in these and other sources.

Expertise in using research sources and methods is as important as expertise in any other writing activity.

MAKING A RESEARCH PLAN

- **Identify the sources and methods most likely to help you write an effective, reader-centered communication.** Consider the full range of information you must locate in order to assist and persuade your readers. Here are some strengths and weaknesses of several useful sources and methods:
    - **Books.** Broad coverage of established topics; often reviewed for accuracy in the publication process; quickly become out of date on rapidly developing topics.
    - **Research journals.** Up-to-date discussions that have been judged valid by specialists in the writer's field; often very sharply focused.
    - **Trade journals.** Solutions to practical problems encountered by many organizations in an industry or field; sometimes lack balance and depth.
    - **Popular periodicals.** General introductions to topics for nonspecialists; not generally considered authoritative on technical matters.
    - **Internet searches.** Very current information; quality can be difficult to assess.
    - **Interviews and surveys.** Opportunity to gather exactly the information you need in order to assist and persuade your readers; not suited to all topics.
    - **Specialized methods in your field.** Ideal for answering the questions you are learning to address through classes in your major.
    - **Your memory and creativity.** Invaluable resources; may need to be tested against other people's thoughts and experiences.
- **Consult general sources first.** By gaining a general view of your subject, you increase the ease with which you can locate, comprehend, and interpret the more detailed facts you are seeking. Useful general sources include encyclopedias, review articles that summarize research on a particular subject, and articles in popular magazines.
- **Conduct preliminary research when appropriate.** For example, before interviewing a technical specialist or upper-level manager, conduct the background research that will enable you to focus the interview exclusively on facts this person alone can supply. Similarly, before conducting a survey, determine what other surveys have learned and study the techniques they used.
- **Make a schedule.** Establish a deadline for completing all your research that leaves adequate time for you to draft and revise your communication. Then set dates for finishing the subparts of your research, remembering to complete general and preliminary research before proceeding with other sources and methods.
- **Study the research methods you are going to use.** In your schedule, include time to study research methods you haven't used before. Also, provide time to learn advanced techniques of methods, such as searching the Internet, whose basics you already know. The Writer's Reference Guide that follows this chapter provides detailed advice for skillfully using five research methods that are very helpful on the job.

While planning your research, you may find it helpful to use a planning guide like the one shown in Figure 6.1.

FIGURE 6.1 Planning Guide for Research

🌐 To download a copy of this planning guide, go to www.thomsonedu.com/english/anderson and click on Chapter 6.

Planning Guide for Research

Project Improved formula for antibacterial soap
Readers Vice Presidents for New Product Development and Marketing

Readers' Questions	Possible Sources	Assessment of Each Source	When to Consult
Are our competitors developing this same technology?	Trade journals	Probably reliable	Immediately
	Competitor reports to stockholders	Biased	Next week
When will our design be ready for production?	Kami Mason, Project Director	Objective, informed	Immediately
What will the manufacturing cost be?	Cost Engineering Department	Objective, but still working with estimates	Immediately; confirm close to completion of report

GUIDELINE 3 CHECK EACH SOURCE FOR LEADS TO OTHER SOURCES
指导方针3：检查每条资源，寻求更多线索

Conducting research is often like solving a crime. You don't know exactly what the outcome will be—or where to find the clues. Consequently, it makes sense to check each source for leads to other sources. Scrutinize the footnotes and bibliographies of every book, article, and report you consult. When you locate a book in the library stacks, browse through books nearby. When you interview people, ask them to suggest additional places to look and persons to contact. Be sure to schedule time to follow up on promising leads.

GUIDELINE 4 CAREFULLY EVALUATE WHAT YOU FIND
指导方针4：仔细评估你所找到的信息

You have no use for information that your readers won't find useful or persuasive or that you yourself don't believe to be credible. Consequently, you should evaluate continuously the facts and ideas you discover. If you discover that your readers will perceive a particular person to be biased, move on to someone with more credibility. If you find that a book or web page about your topic treats it at the wrong level or with the wrong focus, close it and move on to something else.

When evaluating sources, be as cautious about your own biases as you are about any biases your sources may possess. Don't dismiss a source simply because it contradicts your views or presents data that fail to support your conclusions. Your readers depend on your thoroughness and integrity.

The following questions can help you evaluate the sources you consult in your research.

> **Learn More**
>
> Special considerations for evaluating Internet sources are described on page 176.

QUESTIONS FOR EVALUATING A RESEARCH SOURCE

- Is it accurate?
- Is it up to date?
- Is it supported by evidence my readers will find compelling?
- Is it clearly relevant to my readers' situation?
- Is it complete?
- Is it unbiased?
- Does it conflict with other evidence?

GUIDELINE 5 Begin Interpreting Your Research Results Even as You Obtain Them

指导方针 5：得到研究成果即开始分析

Research involves more than just amassing information. To make your results truly useful and persuasive to your readers, you must also interpret them in light of your readers' desires, needs, and situation. For example, imagine that you have been asked to study two expensive pieces of equipment used for laboratory analyses needed by your employer. One piece, you discover, performs a certain function 9 percent more rapidly than the other. This fact alone would not be sufficient for a decision-making reader. You need to interpret the fact by telling the reader whether the greater speed would improve operations significantly enough to justify the added cost. And answering this secondary—but crucial—question may require additional research. The following questions will help you interpret your research results.

QUESTIONS FOR INTERPRETING RESEARCH RESULTS

- What do I conclude from these research results—and what might I need to learn in order to test my conclusions?
- Are other interpretations possible—and do I need to explore them?
- What does this mean my readers should do—and what information do I need to persuade them to do it?
- What must my readers do to carry out my recommendation—and what else must I learn so I can write a communication that will enable them to do that?
- What are the implications for stakeholders who are not my readers—and what else can I learn that will enable me to suggest ways to avoid undesirable consequences for them?

Guideline 6 Take Careful Notes
指导方针6：仔细作笔记

A simple but critical technique for conducting productive, efficient research is to take careful notes every step of the way. When recording the facts and opinions you discover, be sure to distinguish quotations from paraphrases so you can properly identify quoted statements in your communication. Also, clearly differentiate between ideas you obtain from your sources and your own ideas in response to what you find there.

In addition, make careful bibliographic notes about your sources. Include all the details you will need when documenting your sources (see Guideline 8). For books and articles, record the following details.

INFORMATION TO RECORD ABOUT YOUR SOURCES

BOOKS	ARTICLES
Author's or editor's full name	Author's or editor's full name
Exact title	Exact title
City of publication	Journal title
Year of publication	Volume (and issue unless pages are numbered consecutively throughout the volume)
Edition	Year of publication
Page numbers	Page numbers

For interviews, record the person's full name (verify the spelling!), title, and employer, if different from your own. Special considerations apply when your sources are on the Internet; they are described in Appendix A.

It is equally important for you to record the information you will need if you later find that you need to consult this source again. For instance, when you are working in a library, jot down the call number of each book; when interviewing someone, get the person's phone number or e-mail address; and when using a site on the World Wide Web, copy the universal resource locator (URL).

As you proceed, be sure to keep a list of sources that you checked but found useless. Otherwise, you may find a later reference to the same sources but be unable to remember that you have already examined them.

Guideline 7 Ethics Guideline: Observe Intellectual Property Law and Document Your Sources
道德指导方针7：遵守知识产权法并记录信息来源

Once you've completed your research and decided which resources you would like to use in your communication, you have two questions to answer:

- Do I need permission to use this material?
- Do I need to document this source in my communication?

The answers to these questions overlap, but they are not identical. To understand their relationship, you need to consider the laws concerning intellectual property as well as the ethical guidelines for acknowledging sources.

Intellectual Property Law

Broadly speaking, intellectual property law includes the following areas:

Three areas of intellectual property law

- **Patent law.** Governs such things as inventions and novel manufacturing processes.
- **Trademark law.** Pertains to such things as company and product names (Microsoft, Pentium), slogans ("We bring good things to life"), and symbols (the Nike "swoosh").
- **Copyright law.** Deals with such things as written works, images, performances, and computer software.

When you are writing at work, copyright law will probably be the most important to you. Copyright law was created to encourage creativity while also providing the public with an abundant source of information and ideas. To achieve these goals, copyright law enables the creators of a work to profit from it while also allowing others to use the work in limited ways without cost.

Any communication, such as a report, letter, e-mail, photograph, or diagram, is copyrighted as soon as it is created. If the creator generated the work on his or her own, that individual owns the copyright to it. If the creator made the work while employed by someone else, the copyright probably belongs to the employer. Whether the copyright owner is an individual or an organization, the owner has the legal right to prohibit others from copying the work, distributing it, displaying it in a public forum, or creating a derivative work based on it. When copyright owners grant others permission to do any of these things, they may charge a fee or make other contractual demands. The copyright owner has these rights even if the work does not include the copyright notation or the copyright symbol: ©.

The copyright law does, however, place limits on the copyright owner's rights. First, copyright expires after a certain number of years, which varies depending on the date of publication. Second, the law provides that other people, including you, may legally quote or reproduce parts of someone else's work without their permission if your use is consistent with the legal doctrine of *fair use*. Whether your use is "fair" depends primarily on the following four factors (Stanford University, 2005):

For more information about fair use, go to www.thomsonedu.com/english/anderson

- **Purpose of the use.** The law provides more liberal use for educational purposes than for commercial ones. Thus, copyright restrictions are generally stricter at work than in school.
- **Proportion of the work used.** Your quotation of a few hundred words from a long book is likely to be considered fair use, but quotation of the same number of words from a short pamphlet may not.
- **Publication status.** The law gives greater protection to works that a copyright owner has not published or distributed than to ones the owner has.

- **Economic impact.** If your use will diminish the creator's profits, it is unlikely that the law would consider it to be fair use.

It is also legal for you to use other people's work without their permission if the work is in the *public domain.* Such works include those created by or for the U.S. government and similar entities and works whose copyright has expired. Also, private individuals and organizations sometimes put their work in the public domain. The owners of websites that offer free use of clip art are an example.

Finally, you can generally use work that other people working for your employer created as part of their job responsibilities. In fact, in the workplace it is very common for employees to use substantial parts of communications created by other employees. For instance, when you are creating the final report on a project, you may incorporate portions of the proposal written to obtain the original authorization for the project as well as parts of progress reports written during the project.

The following guidelines on copyright coverage will help you observe intellectual property law.

> To learn more about the public domain, go to **www.thomsonedu.com/english/anderson** and click on Chapter 6.

OBSERVING COPYRIGHT

TEXT

Ask for permission except in the following circumstances:
- You created the source yourself.
- Someone else at your employer's created it.
- The source is in the public domain.
- The copyright owner explicitly includes a statement with the source that it may be used without permission.
- You are using the text for a course project that will not be published on paper or on the web.

Honor fair use restrictions. Don't use larger amounts of someone else's work than fair use allows.

When in doubt, ask someone. Intellectual property laws are complicated. If you are uncertain about what to do, consult your instructor, your employer's legal department, or the resources available at the website for this book, www.thomsonedu.com/english/anderson.

GRAPHICS

Note: Each graphic is separately copyrighted. Consequently, the principle of "fair use" does not apply. You always need permission to use a graphic, even if it is only a small part of a larger work.

Obtain permission for all graphics unless
- You created the graphic.
- Your employer is the copyright holder.
- The graphic is in the public domain.
- You are using the graphic for a course project that will not be published on paper or on the web.

WEBSITES

Note: Many people mistakenly believe that anything on the web is in the public domain. Actually, all web content is copyrighted by its creator.

Get permission to use web material unless
- The site belongs to your employer.
- The material you are going to use from the site is in the public domain.
- The site declares that its contents are available for free use.
- You are using the material for a course project that will not be published on paper or on the web.

Ethical Guidelines for Documenting Sources

On the job, as in college, you have an ethical obligation to credit the sources of your ideas and information by citing them in a reference list, footnotes, or bibliography. Failure to do so is considered plagiarism. However, standards for deciding exactly which sources need to be listed at work differ considerably from the standards that apply at school. By asking the questions listed below, you can usually determine whether you need to credit sources when writing on the job. Note, however, that ethical standards for citing sources differ from culture to culture. The questions below apply in the United States, Canada, and Europe. If you are working in another part of the world, ask your coworkers to help you understand the standards that apply where you are.

DETERMINING WHETHER YOU NEED TO DOCUMENT A SOURCE AT WORK

- **Did you obtain permission from the copyright owner?** If you obtained the copyright owner's permission, you must document the source.
- **Is the information I obtained from this source common knowledge?** Both in college and at work, you must indicate the source of ideas and information that (1) you have derived from someone else, and (2) are not common knowledge.
   However, what's considered common knowledge at work is different from what's considered common knowledge at school. At school, it's knowledge every person possesses without doing any special reading. Thus, you must document any material you find in print.
   At work, however, common knowledge is knowledge that is possessed by or readily available to people in your field. Thus, you do not need to acknowledge material you obtained through your college courses, your textbooks, standard reference works in your field, or similar sources.
- **Does my employer own it?** As explained above, employers own the writing done at work by their employees. Consequently, it is usually considered perfectly ethical to incorporate information from one proposal or report into another without acknowledging the source.

Learn More

You will find information about how to write bibliographic citations in Appendix A.

- **Am I taking credit for someone else's work?** On the other hand, you must be careful to avoid taking credit for ideas that aren't your own. In one case, an engineer was fired for unethical conduct because he pretended that he had devised a solution to a technical problem when he had actually copied the solution from a published article.
- **Am I writing for a research journal?** In articles to be published in scientific or scholarly journals, ethical standards for documentation are far more stringent than they are for on-the-job reports and proposals. In such articles, thorough documentation is required even for ideas based on a single sentence in another source. Thus, you must document any information you find in print or online. In research labs where employees customarily publish their results in scientific or scholarly journals, even information drawn from internal communications may need to be thoroughly documented.
- **Whom can I ask for advice?** Because expectations about documentation can vary from company to company and from situation to situation, the surest way to identify your ethical obligations is to determine what your readers and employer expect. Consult your boss and coworkers and examine communications similar to the one you are preparing. For clarification about what sources you need to document for your class, consult your instructor.

CONCLUSION 总 结

This chapter's seven reader-centered guidelines apply to all your research efforts regardless of the research method you employ. They are summarized in Figure 6.2. Following this chapter is a Writer's Reference Guide that provides additional advice for using five research techniques that are frequently employed in the workplace.

EXERCISES 练 习

EXPERTISE

1. Choose a concept, process, or procedure that is important in your field. Imagine that one of your instructors has asked you to explain it to first-year students in your major. (See the Writer's Reference Guide that follows this chapter for guidelines for using each of the following research methods.)
   a. Use brainstorming or freewriting to generate a list of things you might say in your talk.
   b. Use a flowchart, matrix, cluster sketch, or table to generate a list of things you might say.
   c. Compare your two lists. What inferences can you draw about the strengths and limitations of each technique?

2. Imagine that a friend wants to purchase some item about which you are knowledgeable (for example, a motorcycle, MP3 player, or sewing machine). The friend has asked your advice about which brand to buy. Design a matrix in which you list two or three brands and also at least six criteria you recommend your friend use to compare them. Fill in the matrix as completely as you can. Each box you can't fill indicates an area you must research. Describe the methods you would use to gather the additional information. (See the Writer's Reference Guide that follows this chapter for advice about using a matrix as a research tool.)

3. Imagine that you have been asked by the chair of your major department to study student satisfaction with its

FIGURE 6.2 Planning Guide for Conducting Reader-Centered Research

To download a copy of this planning guide, go to at www.thomsonedu.com/english/anderson and click on Chapter 6..

Reader-Centered Research

Review your communication's objectives.

1. Its usability objectives.
2. Its persuasive objectives.

Create an efficient plan for research.

1. Identify all sources and research methods that might be helpful.
2. Consult general sources first.
3. Conduct preliminary research when appropriate.
4. Master each of the research methods you are going to use.
5. Check each source for leads to other sources.
6. Evaluate the information for accuracy, completeness, currency, bias, agreement with other sources, and relevance to your readers' situation.
7. Interpret the information from the perspectives of your readers, your communication's stakeholders.

Take careful notes.

1. Facts and ideas your readers will find useful or persuasive.
2. Details about your sources.

Obtain permission from copyright holders, if necessary.

Document all sources you need to document in order to write ethically.

course offerings. Devise a set of six or more closed questions and four open-ended questions you could use in a survey or interviews. (For information about survey and interview questions, see pages 188–189 and 191–193 in the Writer's Reference Guide that follows this chapter.)

4. Create a research plan for a project you are preparing for your technical communication course.

ONLINE

1. Use two search engines and an Internet directory to look for websites on a topic related to your major. How many hits does each produce? Compare the first ten results from each search in terms of the quality of the sites and the amount and kind of information the search engine or Internet directory provides about each one. (For information about using search engines and Internet directories, see pages 172–179 in the Writer's Reference Guide that follows this chapter.)

2. Using a search engine and online library resources, identify three websites, two books, and two articles on a topic related to your field. Which would you find most interesting? Which would be most helpful if you were writing a paper on the topic for a class? Which would be most helpful if you were writing a report on the topic for your employer? (For information about using search engines and online library resources, see pages 180–185 in the Writer's Guide that follows this chapter.)

COLLABORATION

Working with another student, choose a topic that interests you both. Find five websites that provide substantial information on your topic. Which sites are most appealing to you initially? Following the advice on pages 176–177, evaluate each site, and then compare the results with your initial impression of it.

ETHICS

Create a bibliography of sources concerning an ethical issue related to your major or career. Include four websites, one book, and two journal articles that you believe would help you understand various approaches to this issue.

WRITER'S REFERENCE GUIDE: Using Five Reader-Centered Research Methods
写作者参考指南：使用五个以读者为中心的研究方法

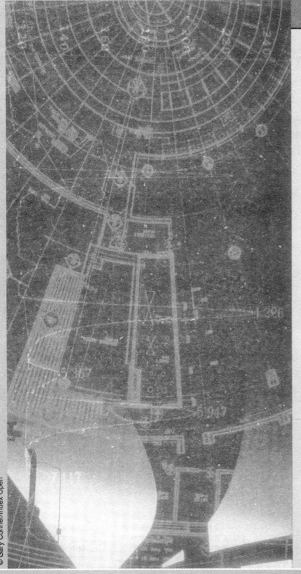

CONTENTS

- Exploring Your Own Memory and Creativity *166*
- Searching the Internet *172*
- Using the Library *180*
- Interviewing *185*
- Conducting a Survey *190*

> For additional information related to this reference guide, go to the section for this guide at **www.thomsonedu.com/english/anderson**.

This Guide tells how to use five research methods commonly employed on the job. Often, two or more of the methods are used in combination. Each method is discussed separately to create a reference source that gives you quick access to advice about the particular method you need to use.

No matter which method you use, be sure to follow Chapter 6's guidelines for conducting reader-centered research. They will help you work efficiently and produce information that establishes your credibility, meets your readers' needs, and persuades them to take the action you advocate.

In particular, keep Chapter 6's discussion of intellectual property, copyright, and plagiarism in mind (page 157). If you have any questions about how these guidelines apply to a project, ask your instructor or boss for advice.

EXPLORING YOUR OWN MEMORY AND CREATIVITY
开发自己的记忆力与创造力

Almost always, your best research aids will include your own memory and creativity. The following sections discuss four methods of exploiting the power of these mental resources. Each method can be useful at the beginning of your research and at many points along the way:

- Brainstorming
- Freewriting
- Drawing a picture of your topic
- Creating and studying a table or graph of your data

Brainstorming

When you brainstorm, you generate thoughts about your subject as rapidly as you can, through the spontaneous association of ideas, writing down whatever thoughts occur to you.

Brainstorming lets your thoughts run free.

Brainstorming's power arises from the way it unleashes your natural creativity. By freeing you from the confines imposed by outlines or other highly structured ways of organizing your ideas, brainstorming lets you follow your own creative lines of thought.

Brainstorming is especially effective at helping you focus on the core ideas you want to communicate to your readers, whether in an overall message or in one part of a longer message. It also works well in group writing projects: When the members brainstorm aloud, the ideas offered by one person often spark ideas for the others.

BRAINSTORMING PROCEDURE

1. Review your knowledge of your readers and your communication situation.
2. Ask yourself, "What do I know about my subject that might help me achieve my communication purpose?"
3. As ideas come, write them down as fast as you can, using single words or short phrases. As soon as you list one idea, move on to the next thought that comes to you.
4. When your stream of ideas runs dry, read back through your list to see if your previous entries suggest any new ideas.
5. When you no longer have any new ideas, gather related items in your list into groups to see if this activity inspires new thoughts.

The key to brainstorming is to record ideas quickly without evaluating any of the thoughts that come to mind. Record everything. If you shift your task from generating ideas to evaluating them, you will disrupt the free flow of associations on which brainstorming thrives.

Here's the first part of a brainstorming session by Nicole. She wanted to write to her boss about ways to improve the quality control procedures at her company, which makes machines that keep patients alive during organ transplant operations. Sitting at her computer, Nicole began by simply tapping out her initial thoughts on her subject.

Writing teams at work often brainstorm together to plan their communications.

Ideas for Quality Control Recommendations

Problem: Present system is unreliable
Everyone is "supposed" to be responsible for quality
No one has specific responsibilities
Workers feel rushed, sometimes ignore quality checks
People's lives are at stake
Near-fatal failure last year in Tucson
Need procedures to test critical components when they arrive from supplier
People follow their own shortcuts, using personal assembly techniques
Don't realize harm they could do
Product's overall record of performance is excellent

While she was brainstorming, Nicole sometimes moved from one idea to a related one. At other times, she jumped to a completely unrelated thought.

Exploring Your Own Memory and Creativity 167

After running out of ideas, Nicole grouped related items under common headings. Note how organizing her notes around her three main topics spurred her to develop additional thoughts.

Ideas for Quality Control Recommendations

Importance of Quality Control
- Lives depend on it (near-fatal failure in Tucson)
- Avoid product liability lawsuits ← *New ideas suggested by outlining*
- Keep sales up

Present System
- Overall record is excellent but could easily fail
- Everyone is supposed to be responsible for quality, but no one is
- Workers follow their own shortcuts and personal assembly techniques
- Workers feel rushed, sometimes ignore quality control checks
- Only consistent test is after the machine is built (some parts may cause the machine to fail due to flaws that are not detectable in the whole-machine test) ← *New idea*

Strategies for a Better System
- Test critical parts as they are delivered from the supplier
- Insist that standard assembly procedures be followed ← *New idea*
- Assign specific responsibilities—and rewards ← *New idea*

Freewriting

Freewriting is very much like brainstorming. Here, too, you tap your natural creativity, free from the confines of structured thought. You rapidly record your ideas as they pop into your mind. Only this time, you write prose rather than a list. The goal is to keep your ideas flowing.

FREEWRITING PROCEDURE

1. Review your knowledge of your readers and your communication situation.
2. Ask yourself, "What do I know about my subject that will help me achieve my communication purpose?"
3. As ideas come, write them down as sentences. Follow each line of thought until you come to the end of it, then immediately pick up the next line of thought that suggests itself.
4. Write rapidly without making corrections or refining your prose. If you think of a better way to say something, start the sentence anew.

5. Don't stop for gaps in your knowledge. If you discover that you need some information you don't possess, note that fact, then keep on writing.
6. When you finally do run out of ideas, read back through your material to select the ideas worth telling your readers. The rest you throw away.

Freewriting is especially helpful when you are trying to develop your main points. Use it when writing brief communications or parts of a long communication.

Below is a sample freewriting done by Miguel, an employee of a company that makes precision instruments. He had spent two weeks investigating technologies to be placed aboard airplanes for detecting microbursts and wind shear, two dangerous atmospheric conditions that have caused several crashes. Miguel wrote this freewriting draft when deciding what to say in the opening paragraph of his report.

Wind shear and microbursts have been blamed for several recent airline crashes (find out which ones—Dallas?). People are studying several technologies for detecting these conditions. Then pilots can fly around them. The technologies might be used on the ground or in planes. Onboard devices would be much more helpful to pilots. Several technologies are being studied. The equipment would need to be approved by the Federal Aviation Administration. It is eager for such devices to be developed. There would be a high demand for onboard devices from airlines. Many companies are working on them. The key point is we could make a lot of profit if we develop the right instrument first. We need to pick the most promising technology and develop it.	In Miguel's freewriting, ideas are jumbled together, but they are now recorded so he can sort through and organize them.

The following passage shows the paragraph Miguel wrote after freewriting. Note that it further develops some ideas from his freewriting, and it omits others. It is a fresh start—but one built on the ideas Miguel generated while freewriting.

We have a substantial opportunity to develop and successfully market instruments that can be placed aboard airplanes to detect dangerous wind conditions called wind shear and microbursts. These conditions have been blamed for several recent air crashes, including one of a Lockheed L-1011 that killed 133 people. Because of the increasing awareness of the danger of these wind conditions, the Federal Aviation Administration is encouraging research into a variety of technologies for detecting them. Most concern systems placed at airports or in large airplanes. We could establish a highly profitable niche by developing a system for use in small, private aircraft. In this report, I will review four major technologies, assessing the suitability of each for development by our company.	Freewriting produces ideas, not a draft. Through freewriting, Miguel realized that profitability was a key point and so placed it first in his subsequent draft. His ideas are now organized and clearly developed.

Drawing a Picture of Your Topic

Another effective strategy for exploiting your memory and creativity is to explore your topic visually. Here are four kinds of diagrams that writers at work have found to be useful.

Flowchart

When you are writing about a process or procedure, try drawing a flowchart of it. Leave lots of space around each box in the flowchart so you can write notes next to it. Here is a flowchart that Nicole used to generate ideas for a report recommending improved quality control procedures in the manufacture and delivery of the medical equipment sold by her employer.

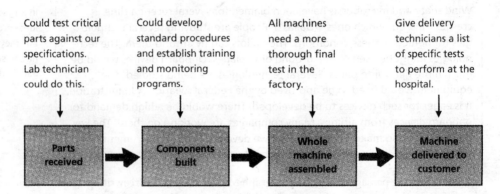

Above the flowchart, Nicole wrote the ideas that occurred to her as she studied the chart.

Matrix

A matrix is a table used to generate and organize ideas.

When you are comparing two or more alternatives in terms of a common set of criteria, drawing a matrix can aid you in systematically identifying the key features of each item being compared. Make a table in which you list the alternatives down the left-hand side and write the topics or issues to be covered across the top. Then, fill in each cell in the resulting table by brainstorming. Blank boxes indicate information you need to obtain. Miguel created the following matrix on his computer, but he could also have made it with pencil and paper.

	How It Works	Limitations	Potential Competition
Doppler radar	Detects rapidly rotating air masses, like those found in wind shear	Technology still being researched	General Dynamics Hughes
Infrared detector	Detects slight increases in temperature that often accompany wind shear	Temperature doesn't always rise	None—Federal Aviation Administration suspended testing
Laser sensor	Sudden wind shifts affect reflectivity of air that lasers can detect	Provides only 20-second warning for jets traveling at a typical speed	Walton Electronic Perhaps Sperry

Cluster Sketch

Creating a cluster sketch is a simple, powerful technique for exploring a topic visually. Write your overall topic in a circle at the center of a piece of paper, then add circles around the perimeter that identify the major issues or subtopics, joining them with lines to the main topic. Continue adding satellite notes, expanding outward as far as you find productive. Figure WG1.1 shows a cluster sketch created by Carol, an engineer who is leading a team assigned to help a small city locate places where it can drill new wells for its municipal water supply.

Your ideas radiate from the center of the page.

A variation of the cluster sketch is the idea tree, shown in Figure WG1.2. At the top of a sheet of paper, write your main topic. Then list the main subtopics or issues horizontally below, joining them to the main topic with lines. Continue this branching as long as it is fruitful.

Creating and Studying a Table or Graph of Your Data

Often at work you will need to write communications about data, such as the results of a test you have run, costs you have calculated, or production figures you have gathered. In such cases, many people find it helpful to begin their writing process by making the tables or graphs that they will include in their communication. Then they can begin to interpret the data arrayed before them, making notes about the data's meaning and significance to their readers.

FIGURE WG1.1
Cluster Sketch

Cluster sketches allow you to draw a map of your ideas.

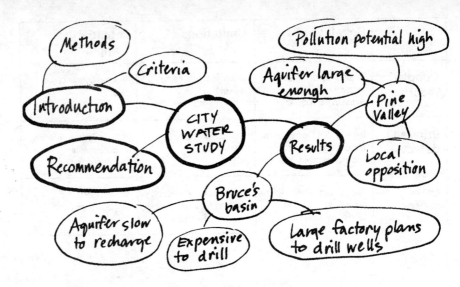

FIGURE WG1.2
Idea Tree

Idea trees help you develop the hierarchical structure of your communications.

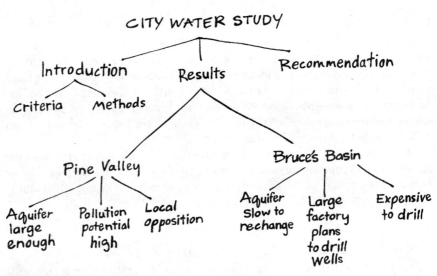

SEARCHING THE INTERNET
网上查询

The Internet has created a rich and continuously evolving aid to researchers. From your computer at home, school, or work, the Internet lets you read technical reports from companies such as IBM, download software, view pictures taken by NASA spacecraft in remote areas of the solar system, or join online discussions on an astonishing array of topics with people around the World. Figure WG1.3 lists just a few of the resources the Internet makes available to you.

Two types of tools can assist you in your Internet search. As a researcher, it's important that you understand the differences between the two.

- **Search Engines.** Search engines allow you to locate websites that include one or more words that you enter into the search engine. You can also use them to search for images, PowerPoint presentations, MP3s, and other types of files posted on the web. Although it might seem that a search engine is scouring the entire web each time you submit a request, the engine actually operates much

INTERNET RESOURCE	Examples
Corporate reports and information	IBM posts technical documents, Microsoft offers detailed information on its products, and the World Wildlife Fund reports on its environmental projects. Thousands of other profit and nonprofit organizations do the same.
	Examples IBM Research Papers on Networking http://www.research.ibm.com
	Microsoft product information and downloading http://www.microsoft.com
	World Wildlife Fund for Nature http://www.panda.org
Technical and scientific journals	Many technical and scientific journals are available online, though often only to people or through libraries that pay an online subscription fee.
	Examples Journal of Cell Biology http://www.jcb.org
	IEEE Transactions on Software Engineering http://www.computer.org/tse
Government agencies	Many government agencies have websites at which they provide reports, regulations, forms, and similar resources.
	Examples NASA http://www.nasa.gov National Institutes of Health http://www.nih.gov National Park Service http://www.nps.gov

FIGURE WG1.3
Some Major Internet Resources for Research

> For links to a variety of search engines and Internet directories, visit the section for this Writer's Reference Guide at www.thomsonedu.com/english/anderson.

differently. At regular intervals, perhaps every few days or weeks, the search engine uses a computer program called a spider to crawl across the web, extracting the words, Internet address, and other information from each location it visits. The spider delivers these results to a database, which indexes and stores the information. When you order a search, the search engine looks through its database.

- **Internet Directories.** Internet directories are created by people rather than computers. These people search the Internet for sites that are likely to be of interest to their users. Then they place each site in a highly structured framework that enables you to locate sites on a particular topic by browsing through a series of hierarchically organized menus. For instance, using Yahoo's popular directory to find information on basking sharks (the second largest of all sharks), you would first choose the category "Science," then "Biology," then "Zoology," then "Animals, Insects, and Pets," then "Fish," then "Saltwater," then "Marine and Anadromous Fish," then "Sharks," then "Basking Shark."

Yahoo, Google, and some other popular websites for Internet research include both a search engine and an Internet directory, although the directories are a little more difficult to locate.

Choosing the Search Tools to Use

> Advantages and disadvantages of search engines and Internet directories

Search engines and Internet directories provide distinctly different kinds of support for your research. Which is better? There's no absolute answer. Because a search engine's spider returns information about every site it visits, a search engine does not distinguish between sites created by experts and those created by second graders. Consequently, searching through the hundreds or thousands of sites identified by a search engine can be tedious and time consuming. An Internet directory can simplify your search because its database includes only a limited number of sites screened and selected by the people who created the directory. Thus they may return only a handful of good sites in response to a search. On the other hand, a directory may miss many sites that could be very useful to you. A search for "basking shark" with Yahoo's search engine produced about 199,000 sites, including some written by elementary school children, while Yahoo's Internet directory produced just 11 sites, missing some that are maintained by wildlife and scientific organizations.

> Different search engines work differently and produce different results. The same is true for Internet directories.

> For a comparison of various search engines, go to the section for this Writer's Guide at www.thomsonedu.com/english/anderson.

Even among search engines, there are substantial differences that affect the results they produce for you. For example, the spiders for different search engines follow different paths and therefore produce different results. As mentioned above, a search for "basking shark" with Yahoo produced about 199,000 sites. The same search with Google produced about one-fourth that number: 50,300. In addition to the number of sites identified, the differences between search engines affect such things as the types of site found, the types of information included with the search results, the order in which the sites are listed, and the freshness of the sites (how recently the spiders have updated the database). Internet directories also differ from one another. Because of such differences, it's often worthwhile to use more than one Internet search tool to ensure that you obtain a thorough, balanced understanding of the topic you are researching on your readers' behalf.

Using Keywords Effectively with Search Engines

When the search engines look for websites, they look for ones that use the words, called *keywords,* that you type into your computer. Your skill at playing what is essentially a word game can greatly increase the efficiency and effectiveness of your search. Choose your keywords carefully and creatively. Your goal is to use the words that match the words used in the sites that will be most valuable to you. For example, if you search for "genetic engineering" you will undoubtedly find a multitude of websites. That's fine, except that many of the sites that are the most valuable for research on this topic use the term "gene splicing" instead. Because you can't predict in advance what terms others might use, you need to use your own vocabulary flexibly and creatively. If you don't locate exactly what you need with the first words you enter, brainstorm. Think of synonyms for the words you've listed, scan through an encyclopedia or reference book to see what terms it uses, or ask a reference librarian (reference librarians know a great deal about electronic resources as well as about printed ones).

Google uses thousands of PCs to store and search information about websites visited by its spider.

Search engines often pose one of two challenges for researchers: too many results or too few. You can use *Boolean operators* to narrow, expand, or shape your search results. If you enter two or more words, most search engines will automatically look for all sites that have *any* of these words. With Boolean operators, however, you can define other relationships among your keywords.

USING BOOLEAN OPERATORS	
WHEN YOU USE THESE WORDS...	THE COMPUTER SEARCHES FOR...
laser AND surgery	only sites that contain both words
laser OR surgery	all sites that contain either word
surgery NOT laser	only sites that contain the first word but not the second

Searching the Internet

MANY SEARCH TOOLS ALSO INCLUDE OTHER OPERATORS	
"laser surgery"	only sites with this exact phrase: these words next to one another in this order
laser NEAR surgery	all sites that contain the terms within a certain number of words of one another (e.g., ten words or fifteen words)
surg* (a wildcard)	all sites that contain the root word within another word (e.g., *surgeon, surgery, surgical*)

Different search engines and Internet directories use different sets of operators, and some use different symbols for the same operators. For instance, some use the plus sign (+) instead of AND, and the minus sign (−) instead of NOT. With some, you can click on a link for advanced search functions that are equivalent to the Boolean operators, plus other features for sharpening your search, such as searching only for sites written in a certain language or only ones that include images or a movie. An especially helpful feature of some search tools allows you to search only certain domains.

For a brief tutorial on conducting efficient web searches, go to page 178.

Evaluating Your Search Results

Evaluating the usefulness and credibility of your search results is relatively easy if you are using an Internet directory. The people constructing a directory also write a brief description of each site they include.

In contrast, search engines display pieces of information from the site itself, typically including the size of the web page and up to three brief sets of words (not sentences) from the text. The first step in evaluating search results is to examine this information to determine whether it would be worthwhile to link to the site.

The site's domain can be especially helpful because, on the Internet, different types of organizations are assigned to different domains, which are included in the URL (address) of the sites created by those organizations. For instance, in the following URL, the three-letters "edu" identify the "education" domain, meaning that the site belongs to an educational institution, in this case the University of Florida ("ufl").

http://www.flmnh.ufl.edu/fish/Gallery/Descript/baskingshark/baskingshark.html — Location of a site's domain in its address

Other domains often used by researchers include:

.com   Commercial (sites for businesses)
.gov   Government (sites for local, state, and federal governments)
.org   Not-for-profit organizations

Depending on what you are looking for, sites in any of these domains may be good sources or bad ones. For example, a .com site may provide useful details about the features of its products but biased information about product quality or lawsuits against the corporation.

When reviewing a site's URL, look also for a tilde (~), which often indicates that the site is a personal site. For instance, an official website created for Miami University (Ohio) is:

www.muohio.edu/aboutmiami

In contrast, all files created as part of personal sites by faculty, staff, and students include a tilde:

www.muohio.edu/~filename

Finally, if you decide to visit a site, evaluate its contents critically. In addition to applying the evaluative criteria described in Chapter 6 (page 155), determine whether the site identifies the person or organization that created it, whether you can contact the creator, and when the site was last modified (how up to date it is).

Keeping Records

Finally, when conducting Internet research, keep careful records of the sites you find valuable. It's easy to lose your way when searching the Internet, which can make it difficult to relocate a site you need to visit again. Most browsers provide a bookmark feature that lets you add any page you are visiting to a personalized menu of sites you can return to with a single click. Even so, it's best to write down the URL of any site whose information you believe you will provide to your readers.

Be sure to record the date you visit each site. Sites can change and even disappear suddenly, so this date is a crucial part of your bibliographic citation, as Appendix A explains.

Bookmark valuable sites and write down their URLs.

Writer's Tutorial
Three ways to Search Efficiently on the Internet

写作者指南：
三种网上查询的有效方式

By narrowing your search to specific parts of the Internet, you can increase the efficiency of your research and also focus your energy on websites your readers will find credible. The directions below show how to narrow a search with Google. Other search engines have similar options.

USE AN ADVANCED SEARCH

Save time by using an advanced search to limit the kinds of web pages a search engine looks for. You'll receive more limited, more sharply focused search results.

1. Choose **Advanced Search.**
2. Activate the Boolean operators (see page 175).
3. Limit the search to web pages that are:
   - Written in a certain language
   - Created in a certain file format (e.g., doc, xls)
   - Updated in the last 3 months, 6 months, etc.
   - Located in a certain domain (e.g., edu, org, com)

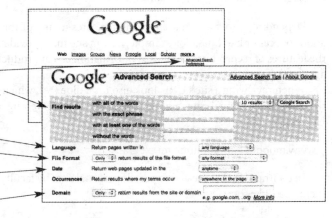

USE A FOCUSED SEARCH

Save time by telling the search engine to look only for a certain type of source.

You can also gain credibility by focusing the search on types of sites your readers respect.

For example, Google's Scholar search looks only at sites refereed by experts in their subjects.

1. Click on **more** on the home page.
2. Click on **Scholar.**
3. If you wish, add advanced search options that are customized for a Scholar search.

Note: A Google Scholar search includes books and journals that are not on the web. You can follow up with a library search.

178 ■ Writer's Reference Guide **Using Five Reader-Centered Research Methods**

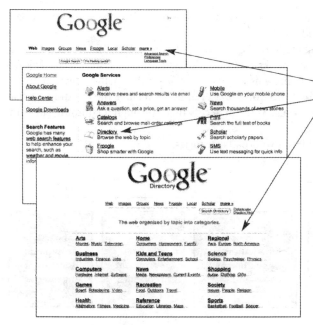

Use a Directory Search

Save time by using an Internet directory to search only through sites that human reviewers have judged to be good sources.

In Google, do the following:
1. Click on **more** on the home page.
2. Click on **Directory**.
3. Choose the major category in which you will find useful information.
4. As each new screen appears, choose the most appropriate subcategory until you find the list of sites indexed for your search topic.

Save Page for Future Reference

Save time by saving web pages you may want to visit again later in your research. Here are two ways to save a page.

- Create a bookmark in your browser.
- Use your browser's SAVE option. Record the date to include in your documentation.

NOTE: Copyright law protects Information and images at websites. You must ask permission to reproduce an entire site or any image in it unless the site fits an exception in intellectual property law (page 157).

Learn More at the Website
For more advice about Internet research, go to www.thomsonedu.com/english/anderson.

USING THE LIBRARY
利用图书馆

When you are preparing to write many communications, the library will be your best source of information and ideas.

Libraries are as much online as on the shelf.

The first step in using the library effectively is to discard the old image of it as a place that primarily houses books and periodicals. Although libraries still feature these publications, most are now as much online as on the shelf. In fact, many libraries are so computerized that you don't even need to enter the buildings to use many of their resources because you can access them through a computer in your classroom, home, or office.

Library resources fall into two broad categories.

Major library resources

Research Aids
- Reference librarians
- Catalogs, indexes, etc.

Information Sources
- Printed books, periodicals, government documents, etc.
- Electronic books, periodicals, government documents, etc.
- Connections to external sources via the Internet

Generally, your excursions in library research will begin with one of the research aids, which can guide you to the most productive information sources. The following sections will help you use the research aids productively and also introduce some of the information sources with which you may not be familiar.

Reference Librarians

You will rarely find any research aid more helpful than reference librarians. They can tell you about specialized resources that you may not be aware of, and they can explain how to use the time-saving features of these resources.

Tell the reference librarian your communication's objectives.

Reference librarians will be able to give you the best help if you indicate very specifically what you want. In addition to stating your topic, describe what the purpose of your communication is, who your readers are, and how your readers will use your communication.

Library Catalog

The library catalog lists the complete holdings of a library, including books, periodicals, pamphlets, recordings, videotapes, and other materials. In most libraries, the catalog is computerized so you can search for items in several ways. If you are looking for a particular book whose title you know or for work written or edited by a person whose name you know, library catalogs are very simple to use. However, when you begin by looking for information about a particular topic, your success may depend on your ingenuity and knowledge of how to use the computerized catalog that most libraries have.

To search for a specific topic, you have two choices:

- **Subject search.** To aid researchers, librarians include subject headings in the record for each library item. When you indicate that you want to do a subject search, the computer will prompt you to enter the words that identify the subject you are looking for. The computer will search through all items that have been tagged with the exact words you entered.
- **Word search.** When you indicate that you wish to conduct a word search, you will also be prompted to enter the words that identify your subject. This time, however, the computer will search the entire contents of all its records, including the title, author, and subject lines as well as tables of contents and other information that particular records might have.

Many employers have their own libraries that include resources directly related to their specialties.

Conducting Subject and Word Searches

Subject and word searches in computerized library catalogs are very similar to keyword searches on the Internet. Therefore, all the advice given on page 175 applies. However, there is also one very important difference: When identifying the words used to describe the subject of a book, librarians use a formal and restricted set of terms that are defined in a large volume entitled the *Library of Congress Subject Headings List.* In the discussion about keyword searches on the Internet, you learned that some websites might use the term "gene splicing" and others might use "genetic engineering." In library subject headings, only "genetic engineering" is used. Consequently, while "gene splicing" will produce some results in an Internet search, it won't produce any in a subject search in a library. For help in determining the correct terms for subject searches, you have three resources:

- Many computerized library catalogs will tell you the correct term if you use an incorrect one that it recognizes as a synonym.

- The *Library of Congress Subject Headings List* is available at any library.
- Reference librarians are most willing to assist you.

Many computerized library catalogs will let you choose between abbreviated and extended displays of your search results. Extended displays are usually more helpful because they give you more information to consider as you decide whether or not to look at the entry for a particular item.

Refining and Extending Your Search

If your initial effort produces too few results, an overwhelming number of them, or an inadequate quality or range of them, there are several ways to refine and extend your search:

- **Look in the catalog entries of books you find for leads to other books.** Catalog entries not only name the subject headings under which a book is cataloged, but they also provide links to lists of other works that also have those subject headings.
- **Use Boolean operators and similar aids.** If you receive too many results, you may narrow the search in many of the ways described in the discussion of Internet searches (see page 175).
- **Use other resources.** Don't limit yourself only to resources you locate through the library catalog. Your best source of information may be a corporate publication or other item not listed there. A reference librarian can help you identify other aids to use.
- **When you go to the library shelves, browse.** Sometimes books that will assist you are located right next to books you found through the library catalog. Don't miss the opportunity to discover them. Browse the shelves.

Indexes

Indexes are research aids that focus on specific topics or specific types of publications. Most catalog the contents of periodicals, but some include television programs, films, and similar items. Many are available online.

To use indexes well, you need to select ones that cover the topic you are researching:

- **General periodical indexes.** They index the contents of publications directed to a general audience. The familiar *Reader's Guide to Periodical Literature* is an example.

- **Specialized periodical indexes.** Almost every field has at least one. Examples are *Applied Science and Technology Index, Biological and Agricultural Index, Business Periodicals Index,* and *Engineering Index.*
- **Newspaper indexes.**

Some indexes not only list articles, but also provide an abstract (or summary) of each one. Figure WG1.4 shows an index entry that includes an abstract. By scanning through an abstract, you can usually tell whether reading the entire article would be worthwhile.

Some indexes include abstracts.

Whether you are using a printed or a computerized index, you can often speed your search by looking at the index's thesaurus. Different indexes use different sets of terms. Most publish this list in a thesaurus that can be accessed through a menu selection in the online version or found in the front or back of the printed version.

Find out what indexing terms are used.

Computerized indexes work the same way that library catalogs do. You can search by the same variables: author, title, words. Searches can also be limited in similar fashion, although different indexes do this in different ways, so you should look at the "Help" feature for instructions.

Use "Help" to customize a search.

Reference Works

When you hear the term *reference works*, you probably think immediately (and quite correctly) of encyclopedias, dictionaries, and similar storehouses of knowledge, thousands of pages long. What you may not realize is that many of these resources, such as the *Encyclopedia Americana,* are now available online or on CD-ROM, so that finding information in them can be very quick and easy.

In addition to such familiar reference works as the *Encyclopedia Britannica,* thousands of specialized reference works exist. Some surely relate to your specialty. For example, there are the *Encyclopedia of the Biological Sciences, McGraw-Hill Encyclopedia of Science and Technology* (20 volumes), *Elsevier's Medical Dictionary, Harper's Dictionary of Music,* and the *Petroleum Dictionary.*

Government Documents

Every year, the U.S. Government Printing Office distributes millions of copies of its publications, ranging from pamphlets and brochures to periodicals, reports, and books. Some are addressed to the general public, while others are addressed to specialists in various fields. Sample titles include: *Acid Rain, Chinese Herbal Medicine, Poisonous Snakes of the World,* and *A Report on the U.S. Semiconductor Industry.*

FIGURE WG1.4
Abstract from an Abstracting Index

This abstract illustrates the research help you can receive when using online databases and indexes.

Full citation. In addition to using this information to locate this item, you can copy and paste the citation into your notes for possible inclusion in your references.

Links to other works by the author. These links can help you find other publications that may also relate to your research.

Abstract. This summary helps you decide whether it would be worthwhile to read the entire publication article.

Subject codes. This list identifies the keywords used to index this article. You can use it to link to other publications that were coded with these words.

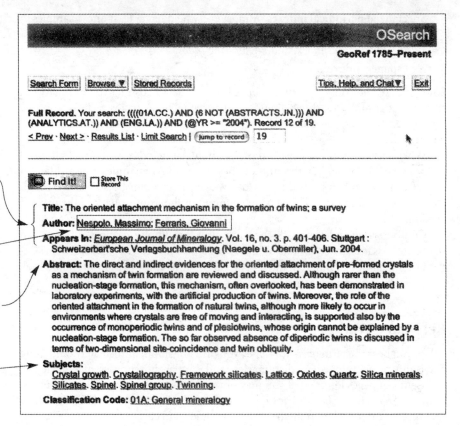

Government publications that may be especially useful to you are reports on research projects undertaken by government agencies or supported by government grants and contracts. Annually, the National Technical Information Service acquires more than 150,000 new reports on topics ranging from nuclear physics to the sociology of Peruvian squatter settlements. Chances are great that some relate to your subject.

The following indexes are especially helpful. A reference librarian can help you find many others.

> **INDEXES TO U.S. GOVERNMENT PUBLICATIONS**
>
> - Monthly Catalog of U.S. Government Publications
>   Publications handled by the Government Printing Office
>   http://www.access.gpo.gov/su_docs/dpos/adpos400.html
> - Government Reports Announcements and Index (GRAI)
>   Technical and research reports handled by the National Technical Information
>   Service http://www.ntis.gov/search.htm
> - Lists of Publications by Specific Agencies
>   EPA http://www.epa.gov/ncepihom/
>   NASA http://techreport.larc.nasa.gov/cgi-bin/NTRS
>   National Institutes of Health http://www.nih.gov>>

Computerized Full-Text Sources

Many libraries also offer computer access to the full text of various sources. These include standard reference works, such as the *Encyclopedia Britannica*, and specialized publications such as scientific journals. These utilities allow you to search for topics in the same sorts of ways described in the discussion of the library catalog. When you locate an article of interest, you can read the text on your computer screen, download it to your computer's memory, or print a copy of it.

You can download full texts.

INTERVIEWING
采 访

At work, your best source of information will often be another person. In fact, people will sometimes be your only source of information because you'll be researching situations unique to your organization or its clients and customers. Or you may be asking an expert for information that is not yet available in print or from an online source.

The following advice focuses on face-to-face interviews, but it applies also to telephone interviews, which are quite common in the workplace.

Preparing for an Interview

Preparing for an interview involves three major activities:

- **Choose the right person to interview.** Approach this selection from your readers' perspective. Pick someone you feel confident can answer the questions your readers are likely to ask in a way that your readers will find useful and

Take a reader-centered approach to selecting your interviewee.

Writer's Tutorial
Conducting Efficient Library Research

写作者指南：
利用图书馆进行有效的研究

By wisely using various features of online library catalogs and indexes, you can increase your research efficiency.

FINDING BOOKS

Online library catalogs typically show an opening page that invites you to search by one of four topics: keywords, author, title, and subject.

However, you can often research more efficiently by using an advanced search to sharpen your focus.

1. Activate Boolean operators between your keywords (see page 175). Each "and" can be changed to "or" or "not."
2. Limit the search to sources that are:
   - Written in a certain language.
   - A certain type of resource (e.g., book, periodical).
   - Published before or after a certain date.
3. Examine the search results to determine which items are worth clicking on for more details.

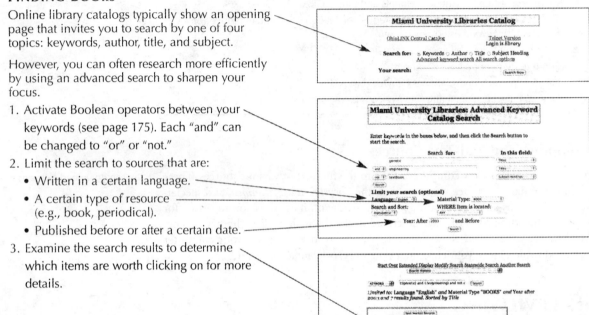

FOLLOWING LEADS TO OTHER SOURCES

Use the detailed description of a source to find other helpful items.

1. Click on the author's name to see other items written by this person.
2. Note whether the item has a bibliography you can review for leads to other sources.
3. Click on the relevant subject headings to see other items indexed the same way (see page 181).

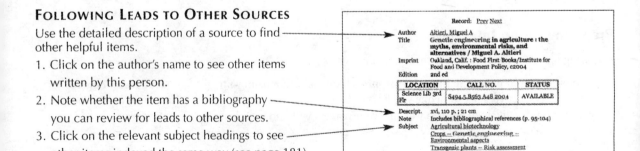

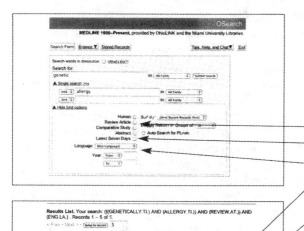

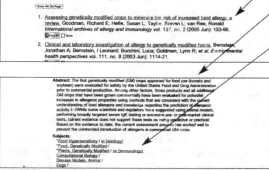

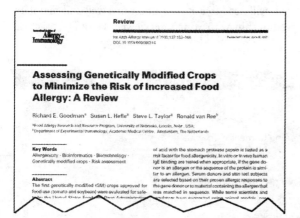

FINDING PERIODICAL SOURCES

Save time using online indexes.

1. Ask a librarian to help you choose the best index or indexes for your topic.
2. Use the advanced search functions to search for items that are:
   - A certain type (e.g., a review article).
   - Published before or after a certain date.
   - Written in a certain language.
3. Click on items in the search results list that look as though they might be useful (see page 155).
4. Read the abstract to decide whether it would be worthwhile to get the full item.
5. Click on the subject terms that are relevant to your research in order to view other articles indexed the same way (see page 181).

Some let you read sources instantly on screen.

Learn More at the Website
For more advice about library research, go to www.thomsonedu.com/english/anderson.

A well-planned interview can be productive and enjoyable for both interviewer and interviewee.

credible. If you are seeking someone to interview who is outside your own organization, the directories of professional societies may help you identify an appropriate person.

- **Make arrangements.** Contact the person in advance to make an appointment. Let the person know the purpose of the interview. This will enable him or her to start thinking about how to assist you before you arrive. Be sure to say how long you think the interview will take. This will enable your interviewee to carve out time for you. If you would like to record the interview, ask permission in advance.
- **Plan the agenda.** As the interviewer, you will be the person who must identify the topics that need to be discussed. Often, it's best simply to generate a list of topics to inquire about. But if there are specific facts you need to obtain, identify them as well. To protect against forgetting something during the interview, bring a written list of your topics and specific questions. For advice on phrasing questions, see the section on surveys (pages 190–196).

Conducting the Interview

Do only 10 percent to 20 percent of the talking.

Unless you are seeking a simple list of facts, your goal in an interview should be to engage the other person in a conversation, not a question-and-answer session. In this conversation, your goal should be to have the other person do 80 percent to 90 percent of the talking—and to have him or her focus on the information you need. To achieve these goals, you will need to ask your questions well and maintain a productive interpersonal relationship with your interviewee. Here are practical steps that you can take.

CONDUCTING A PRODUCTIVE INTERVIEW

Establish rapport.
- Arrive on time.
- Thank the person for agreeing to meet with you.

Explain your goal.
- Tell what you are writing and who your readers will be.
- Explain the use your readers will make of your communication.
- Describe the outcome you desire.

Ask questions that encourage discussion.

- Use questions that ask the interviewee to explain, describe, and discuss. They can elicit valuable information that you might not have thought to ask for. Avoid closed questions that request a yes/no or either/or response.

  Closed question: Does the present policy create any problems?
  Open question: What are your views of the present policy?

- Use neutral, unbiased questions.

  Biased question: Don't you think we could improve operations by making this change?
  Neutral question: If we made this change, what effect would it have on operations?

- Begin with general questions, supplemented by more specific follow-up questions that seek additional details important to you.

  General question: Please tell me the history of this policy.
  Follow-up question: What role did the labor union play in formulating the policy?

Show that you are attentive and appreciative.

- Maintain eye contact and lean forward.
- Respond with an occasional "uh-huh" or "I see."
- Comment favorably on the interviewee's statements.

  Examples: "That's helpful." "I hadn't thought of that." "This will be useful to my readers."

Give your interviewee room to help you.

- If the interviewee pauses, be patient. Don't jump in with another question. Assume that he or she is thinking of some additional point. Look at him or her in order to convey that you are waiting to hear whatever he or she will add.
- If the interviewee begins to offer information out of the order you anticipated, adjust your expectations.

Keep the conversation on track.

- If the interviewee strays seriously from the topic, find a moment to interrupt politely in order to ask another question. You might preface the question by saying something like this: "My readers will be very interested to know . . ."

> **Be sure you understand and remember.**
> - If anything is unclear, ask for further explanation.
> - On complicated points, paraphrase what your interviewee has said and then ask, "Have I understood correctly?"
> - Take notes. Jot down key points. Don't try to write down everything because that would be distracting and would slow down the conversation.
> - Double-check the spelling of names, people's titles, and specific figures.

It's especially important that you assume leadership for guiding the interview. You are the person who knows what information you need to obtain on your readers' behalf. Consequently, you may need to courteously redirect the conversation to your topics.

Concluding the Interview

During the interview, keep your eye on the clock so that you don't take more of your interviewee's time than you requested. As the time limit approaches, do the following:

- **Check your list.** Make sure that all your key questions have been answered.
- **Invite a final thought.** One of the most productive questions that you can ask near the end of an interview is, "Can you think of anything else I should know?"
- **Open the door for follow-up.** Ask something like this: "If I find that I need to know a little more about something we've discussed, would it be okay if I called you?"
- **Thank your interviewee.** If appropriate, send a brief thank-you note by letter, memo, or e-mail.

CONDUCTING A SURVEY
开展问卷调查

While an interview enables you to gather information from one person, a survey enables you to gather information from *groups* of people.

Surveys support practical decision making.

On the job, surveys are almost always used as the basis for practical decision making. Manufacturers survey consumers when deciding how to market a new product, and employers survey employees when deciding how to modify personnel policies or benefit packages. Some surveys, such as those used to predict the outcomes of state and national elections, require the use of specialized techniques that are beyond the scope of this book. However, in many situations, you will be able to conduct surveys that provide a solid basis for on-the-job decision making if you follow the suggestions given in the following sections.

Writing the Questions

The first step in writing survey questions is to decide exactly what you want to learn. Begin by focusing on the decisions your readers must make. This will help you determine what sorts of information your survey must yield.

For example, Roger identified many questions his survey needed to ask by thinking in detail about the decisions his reader would need to make. Roger worked for a small restaurant chain that asked him to study the feasibility of opening a doughnut shop next to a college campus. He already had investigated possible sites and looked into licensing, insurance, wholesale suppliers, and related matters. Next he needed to find out if there would be enough business to make the shop profitable. As he thought about the decisions that would be based on his report, he realized that his employer would be interested not only in predicting the amount of sales but also in learning what kinds of doughnuts, pastries, coffee, and other products to offer; what prices to charge; and even what the opening and closing hours should be. Consequently, Roger designed questions on each of these topics.

Formulate survey questions based on the factors your readers will consider when making their decision.

The following suggestions will help you create an effective questionnaire that provides useful information and elicits the cooperation of the people you ask to fill it out.

- **Mix closed and open questions.** *Closed questions* allow only a limited number of possible responses. They provide answers that are easy to tabulate. *Open questions* allow the respondent freedom in devising the answer. They provide respondents an opportunity to react to your subject matter in their own terms. See Figure WG1.5.

  You may want to follow each of your closed questions with an open one that simply asks respondents to comment. A good way to conclude a survey is to invite additional comments.

- **Ask reliable questions.** A *reliable* question is one that every respondent will understand and interpret in the same way. For instance, if Roger asked, "Do you like high-quality pastries?" different readers might interpret the term "high-quality" in different ways. Roger might instead ask how much the respondents would be willing to pay for pastries or what kinds of snacks they like to eat with their coffee.

FIGURE WG1.5
Closed and Open Questions

	Closed Questions
Forced Choice	▪ Respondents must select one of two choices (yes/no, either/or). Example Would you buy doughnuts at a shop near campus, yes or no?
Multiple Choice	▪ Respondents select from several predefined alternatives. How many times a month would you visit the shop? ____ 1 to 2 ____ 3 to 4 ____ 5 or more
Ranking	▪ Respondents indicate an order of preference. Example Please rank the following types of doughnuts, using a 1 for your favorite, and so on.
Rating	▪ Respondents pick a number on a scale. Example Please circle the number on the following scale that best describes the importance of the following features of a doughnut shop: Music Unimportant 1 2 3 4 5 Important Tables Unimportant 1 2 3 4 5 Important
	Open Questions
Fill in the Blank	▪ Respondents complete a statement. Example When deciding where to eat a late-night snack, I usually base my choice on _____.
Essay	▪ Respondents can frame responses in any way they choose. Example Please suggest ways we could make a doughnut shop that would be appealing to you.

- **Ask valid questions.** A *valid* question is one that produces the information you are seeking. For example, to determine how much business the doughnut shop might attract, Roger could ask either of these two questions:

Invalid
- How much do you like doughnuts?

Valid
- How many times a month would you visit a doughnut shop located within three blocks of campus?

The first question is invalid because the fact that students like doughnuts does not necessarily mean that they would patronize a doughnut shop. The second question is valid because it can help Roger estimate how many customers the shop would have.

- **Avoid biased questions.** Don't phrase your questions in ways that seem to guide your respondents to give a particular response.

    | • Wouldn't it be good to have a coffee shop near campus? | Biased |
    | • How much would you like to have a coffee shop near campus? | Unbiased |

- **Place your most interesting questions first.** Save questions about the respondent's age or similar characteristics until the end.
- **Limit the number of questions.** If your questionnaire is lengthy, people may not complete it. Decide what you really need to know and ask only about that.
- **Test your questionnaire.** Even small changes in wording may have a substantial effect on the way people respond. Questions that seem perfectly clear to you may appear puzzling or ambiguous to others. Before completing your survey, try out your questions with a few people from your target group.

Contacting Respondents

There are three methods for presenting your survey to your respondents:

- **Face-to-face.** In this method, you read your questions aloud to each respondent and record his or her answers on a form. It's an effective method of contacting respondents because people are more willing to cooperate when someone asks for their help in person than they are when asked to fill out a printed questionnaire. The only risk is that your intonation, facial expressions, or body language may signal that you are hoping for a certain answer. Research shows that respondents tend to give answers that will please the questioner.

In face-to-face interviews, the interviewer carefully avoids facial expressions, comments, or other indications that he or she wants a particular response to a question.

- **Telephone.** Telephone surveys are convenient for the writer. However, it can sometimes be difficult to use a phone book to identify people who represent the group of people being studied.
- **Mail or handout.** Mailing or handing your survey forms to people you hope will respond is less time consuming than conducting a survey face to face or by telephone. Generally, however, only a small portion of the people who receive

survey forms in these ways actually fill them out and return them. Even professional survey specialists typically receive responses from only about 20 percent of the people they contact.

Selecting Your Respondents

At work, writers sometimes present their survey questions to every person who belongs to the group whose attitudes or practices they want to learn about. For example, an employee assigned to learn what others in her company feel about a proposed change in health care benefits or a switch to flextime scheduling might send a survey questionnaire to every employee.

Your sample should reflect the composition of the overall group.

However, surveys are often designed to permit the writers to generalize about a large group of people (called a *population*) by surveying only a small portion of individuals in the group (called a *sample*). To ensure that the sample is truly representative of the population, you must select the sample carefully. Here are four types of samples you can use:

- **Simple random sample.** Here, every member of the population has an equal chance of being chosen for the sample. If the population is small, you could put the name of every person into a hat, then draw out the names to be included in your sample. If the population is large—all the students at a major university, for example—the creation of a simple random sample can be difficult.

- **Systematic random sample.** To create a systematic random sample, you start with a list that includes every person in the population—perhaps by using a phone book or student directory. Then you devise some pattern or rule for choosing the people who will make up your sample. For instance, you might choose the fourteenth name on each page of the list.

Convenience samples can give unreliable results.

- **Convenience sample.** To set up a convenience sample, you select people who are handy and who resemble in some way the population you want to survey. For example, if your population is the student body, you might knock on every fifth door in your dormitory, or stop every fifth student who walks into the library. The weakness of such samples is obvious: From the point of view of the attitudes or behaviors you want to learn about, the students who live with their parents or in apartments may be significantly different from those who live in dorms, just as those who don't go to the library may differ in substantial ways from those who do.

- **Stratified sample.** Creating a stratified sample is one way to partially overcome the shortcomings of a convenience sample. For instance, if you know that 15 percent of the students in your population live at home, 25 percent live in apartments, and 60 percent live in dormitories, you would find enough representatives of each group so that they constituted 15 percent, 25 percent, and 60 percent of your sample. Even if you can't choose the people in each group randomly, you would have made some progress toward creating a sample that accurately represents your population.

When creating your sample, you must determine how many people to include. On one hand, you want a manageable number; on the other hand, however, you also want enough people to form the basis for valid generalizations. Statisticians use formulas to decide on the appropriate sample size, but in many on-the-job situations, writers rely on their common sense. One good way to decide is to ask what number of people your readers would consider to be sufficient.

> Use enough respondents to persuade your readers.

Interpreting Survey Results

When you've collected the completed surveys, how should you interpret the data you've gathered? Start by thinking about the decisions your readers hoped you would help them make. For example, Roger might look in several ways at the data he obtained through his survey about the feasibility of opening a doughnut shop near campus.

- **Focus on percentages, not raw numbers.** When reading Roger's report, his boss will be more interested in the *percentage* of respondents who gave one answer, rather than the number who did. Percentages are his focus because he will use the results from the sample he surveyed in order to make estimates about the responses he would receive from the entire population (that is, the entire student body). If 10 percent of his 100 respondents said they would purchase doughnuts once a week, he would estimate that 10 percent, or 500, of the school's 5,000 students would do the same.
- **Extend the interpretation far enough to answer the readers' key questions.** Of course, Roger's boss wants more than percentages. The boss's core question is whether the store would be profitable. To determine profitability, Roger will have to use other data to determine the likely amount that each customer will spend at the shop every week or every month. Multiplying that number by the estimated 500 customers would provide an estimate of monthly revenue. Of course, his boss will want additional data as well: What is Roger's estimate of the number of students who would purchase doughnuts every other week or every other day? And how many doughnuts and other products does Roger estimate the customers would buy?
- **Look at responses from subgroups.** Roger can help his boss make a good decision by also studying the data from various subgroups of respondents. For example, Roger's boss would probably want to know whether men would

frequent the shop more often than women (or vice versa). This information might assist in making decisions about the advertising and decor for the shop. Similarly, by determining whether students who live on campus are more likely than those who live off campus to patronize the shop, Roger could help his boss choose the most profitable location.

- **Evaluate the importance of differences.** It is beyond the goal of this Guide to discuss statistical analyses of data. Even without using statistics, however, Roger's boss will want him to make judgments about the importance of any differences he found. Is the percentage of customers who are women a little greater or less than the percentage who are men? If the difference is small, it is likely not a sound basis for making a big decision. If it is large, it would be unwise to ignore the fact. When judging differences, remember to think of proportions. If 10 percent of the women and 5 percent of the men will make a purchase once a week, Roger would make a mistake to say that the difference is only 5 percent. In fact, twice as many women as men would be putting money into the shop's till.

Reporting Survey Results

When reporting survey data, you will serve your readers and maintain your credibility if you guard against overstating your conclusions. Often, there are other ways to look at the same data. Also, surveys always produce estimates, not certainties. Draw reasonable conclusions, state them clearly. But do not attribute more certainty to your results than the data justify.

You will be most likely to meet your readers' needs and to persuade them that your interpretations are reasonable if you give them specific data rather than generalizations. Avoid terms like *many* (how many?) and *majority* (51 percent or 99 percent?).

Finally, remember that the interpretation of data is one of the places where critical thinking is most valuable. As you draw your conclusions, consider alternatives as well. If the alternatives are significant, address them in the communication you give to your readers. In reader-centered writing (and research), your goal is not to be right but to provide your readers with the information they need as they make their decisions.

PART IV DRAFTING PROSE ELEMENTS
草拟文本

Chapter 7 Drafting Paragraphs, Sections, and Chapters

Writer's Reference Guide to Using Seven Reader-Centered Organizational Patterns

Chapter 8 Developing an Effective Style

Chapter 9 Beginning a Communication

Chapter 10 Ending a Communication

Chapter 11 Writing Reader-Centered Front and Back Matter

Drafting Paragraphs, Sections, and Chapters
起草段落、节和章

GUIDELINES

1. Begin by announcing your topic *201*
2. Present your generalizations before your details *204*
3. Move from most important to least important *206*
4. Consult conventional strategies when having difficulties organizing *206*
5. **Global Guideline:** Consider your readers' cultural background when organizing *207*
6. Reveal your communication's organization *208*
7. Smooth the flow of thought from sentence to sentence *219*
8. **Ethics Guideline:** Examine the human consequences of what you're drafting *222*

CHAPTER 7

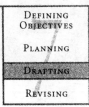

Defining Objectives
Planning
Drafting
Revising

This chapter marks a major transition in your study of on-the-job writing. In the preceding four chapters, you learned how to define the objectives of a communication in a reader-centered way and then plan reader-centered strategies for achieving these objectives. This chapter is the first of seven that will help you develop your expertise in transforming these plans into action as you draft the communication's prose, graphics, and graphic design.

DRAFTING USABLE, PERSUASIVE PROSE
起草可用的、有说服力的文章

> To read additional information, see more examples, and access links related to this chapter's guidelines, go to **www.thomsonedu.com/english/anderson** and click on Chapter 7.

This chapter's reader-centered guidelines apply to paragraphs, to the groups of paragraphs that make up the sections and chapters of longer communications, and even to whole communications in their entirety. For convenience's sake, this chapter uses the word *segments* to designate these variously sized prose units.

How can the same guidelines apply with equal validity to segments that range in size from a few sentences to an entire communication that may be tens or hundreds of pages long? There are two reasons, one related to each of the two indispensable qualities of an effective workplace communication: Usability and Persuasiveness.

- **Usability: Regardless of a segment's size, readers must perform the same mental tasks in order to understand and use its content.** You may have heard a paragraph defined as a group of sentences about the same subject. With only slight variation, that definition applies equally well to larger segments: A section or chapter is a group of paragraphs on the same subject, and an entire communication is a group of sections or chapters on the same topic.

  To understand and use any segment, whether a short paragraph or an entire communication, readers do the same things:
  1. Determine what its topic is.
  2. Figure out how its various parts (words, sentences, paragraphs, etc.) fit together to form a cohesive whole.

  Because all segments make the same mental demands on readers, you can increase the usability of every segment you write by using the same strategies.

- **Persuasiveness: Regardless of a segment's size, readers mentally process its persuasive claims and evidence in the same way.** As Chapter 5 explains, readers perform a consistent set of mental activities when reading persuasive arguments. For instance, they look for benefits to their organizations and themselves, and they spontaneously raise counterarguments. Because these reading activities remain constant, you can enhance the persuasiveness of every segment you write by employing the same strategies.

This chapter's first seven guidelines will help you draft highly usable, highly persuasive segments of all sizes. An eighth guideline discusses the ethical importance of remembering the human consequences of what you are drafting.

GUIDELINE 1 BEGIN BY ANNOUNCING YOUR TOPIC
指导方针1：从主题入手

You have undoubtedly heard that you should begin your paragraphs with topic sentences. This guideline extends that advice to all your segments, large and small: To make your communications easier to understand and use, begin every segment with a topic statement that tells what the segment is about.

How Topic Statements Increase Usability

How do topic statements increase usability? A key element in usability is the ease with which readers can understand your message. As mentioned above, to understand a paragraph, readers must establish in their own minds meaningful relationships among the sentences from which it is built. The same goes for larger segments. To understand a section, chapter, or entire communication, they must understand how its parts fit together to construct its larger meaning.

Researchers have discovered that as people try to discern the relationships among the parts of a paragraph or longer segment, they engage in two kinds of mental processing:

- **Bottom-up processing.** In bottom-up processing, readers proceed in much the same way as people who are working a jigsaw puzzle *without* having seen a picture that tells them whether the finished puzzle will show a garden, city street, or three cats. As they read, they try to guess how the small bits of information they gather from each sentence fit together with the information from the other sentences to form the segment's general meaning.
- **Top-down processing.** In top-down processing, readers proceed like people who have seen a picture of the finished jigsaw puzzle *before* they begin. Because they know the communication's overall structure in advance, they know immediately how the information they obtain from each sentence fits into the larger meaning of the segment.

Although readers engage continuously in both processes, the more top-down processing they can perform, the more easily they can understand and remember the message. You can help your readers do more top-down processing by telling them explicitly what each segment is about.

Moreover, the topic statements you provide will be especially helpful if you place them at the *beginning* of your segments. In a classic experiment, researchers John D. Bransford and Marcia K. Johnson (1972) demonstrated how much this placement

Topic statements are especially helpful to readers when placed at the beginning of a segment.

helps readers understand and remember a message. They asked people to listen to the following passage being read aloud.

Passage used in an experiment that demonstrated the importance of top-down processing

> The procedure is actually quite simple. First you arrange things into different groups. Of course, one pile may be sufficient depending on how much there is to do. If you have to go somewhere else due to lack of facilities, that is the next step; otherwise you are pretty well set. It is important not to overdo things. That is, it is better to do too few things at once than too many. In the short run this may not seem important but complications can easily arise. A mistake can be expensive as well. At first the whole procedure will seem complicated. Soon, however, it will become just another facet of life. . . . After the procedure is completed, one arranges the materials into different groups again. Then they can be put into their appropriate places. Eventually they will be used once more and the whole cycle will then have to be repeated. However, that is part of life.

The researchers told one group the topic of this passage in advance; they told the other group afterwards. Then they asked both groups to write down everything they remembered from what they had heard. People who had been told the topic (washing clothes) before hearing the passage remembered many more details than those who were told afterwards.

As Bransford and Johnson's study suggests, by stating the topic at the beginning of your segments you increase the usability of your prose for readers who want to understand your communication thoroughly and remember what you said. You also increase your communication's usability for readers who are skimming for particular facts. The first sentence of each segment tells them whether the segment is likely to contain the information they are seeking.

Here are three of the most common and effective ways to provide topic statements at the beginning of your segments.

INDICATING THE TOPIC OF A SEGMENT

- **Use a sentence.** An example is the sentence that introduced this list of strategies ("Here are three of the most common ways to make these helpful statements").
- **Use a single word.** The word "First" that begins the second paragraph on page 69 tells the reader, "You are now going to read a segment that explains the 'four-step' procedure for identifying your readers' tasks that was just mentioned."
- **Use a question.** The question ("How do topic statements increase usability?") that begins the second paragraph of the discussion of this guideline told you that you were about to read a segment explaining the ways topic statements contribute to usability.

When you state explicitly the topic of each segment, small and large, you create a hierarchy of topic statements. Figure 7.1 shows the interlocking, hierarchically organized topic statements from a report in which an engineering firm is seeking to persuade a financially troubled zoo that it can overcome its difficulties by hiring the firm for several construction projects that will attract more visitors. The topic statements correspond to the following major points from one section of the report's outline.

II. Problem: Budget Crisis
  A. History of the Crisis
  B. Cause of the Crisis
    1. Rising costs are *not* the cause
    2. Declining revenues are the cause

Outline corresponding to the page shown in Figure 7.1

FIGURE 7.1 Interlocking Topic Statements (see above for the outline of this passage)

Chapter 2
PROBLEM: BUDGET CRISIS

The Metropolitan Zoo faces a severe budget crisis. The crisis first surfaced last August, when the zoo discovered that operating expenses for the year were going to exceed income by $247,000. Emergency measures, including a reduction in working hours for some employees, lowered the actual loss by December 31 to $121,000. However, the zoo faces similar difficulties again this year—and in future years—unless effective measures are taken.

Causes of the Budget Crisis

What is causing this budget crisis, which first appeared in a year when the zoo thought it would enjoy a large profit? The crisis is *not* caused by rising costs. In fact, the zoo actually reduced operating costs by 3% last year. The greatest savings were related to energy expenses. The new power plant began operation, reducing fuel consumption by 15%. Also, design changes in the three largest animal houses conserved enough heat to reduce their heating expenses by 9%. Finally, a new method of ordering and paying for supplies lowered expenses enough to offset inflation.

The budget crisis is caused instead by declining revenues. During the past year income from admission fees, concession sales, and donations has dropped. Because of the decline in paid admissions, overall income from this source was $57,344 less last year than the year before. [This discussion of falling revenue continues for two pages.]

The writer has created an interlocking set of topic statements that correspond to the outline shown above.

She announces the topic for the entire chapter in its first sentence (budget crisis).

In the second sentence, she provides the topic statement for the first section for the chapter (history of the crisis). Note that a topic statement does not need to be the first sentence of a paragraph.

The writer provides the topic statement for the second section of the chapter (cause of the budget crisis). Here, she places the topic statement in the first sentence of the entire section.

She provides the topic statement for the second subtopic (falling revenue is the cause).

She provides the topic statement for the first subtopic (rising revenue is the cause).

Guideline 1 **Begin by Announcing Your Topic**

GUIDELINE 2 PRESENT YOUR GENERALIZATIONS BEFORE YOUR DETAILS

指导方针2：在考虑细节前先考虑总体框架

In many of the segments you write at work, you will be presenting detailed facts about your topic in order to explain or support a general point you want your readers to understand or accept. You can increase both the usability and the persuasiveness of most of your on-the-job writing not only by stating your topic at the beginning of each segment (Guideline 1), but also by stating your general point about your topic *before* you present your details.

How Initial Generalizations Make Writing Easier to Understand and Use

When you present your generalizations first, you save your readers the work of trying to figure out what your general point is. Imagine, for instance, that you are a manager who finds the following sentences in a report:

Details without an initial generalization

> Using the sampling technique just described, we passed a gas sample containing 500 micrograms of VCM through the tube in a test chamber set at 25°C. Afterwards, we divided the charcoal in the sampling tube into two equal parts. The front half of the tube contained approximately 2.3 of the charcoal while the back half contained the rest. Analysis of the back half of the tube revealed no VCM; the front half contained the entire 500 micrograms.

As you read these details, you probably find yourself asking, "What does the writer want me to get from this?" You would have been saved that labor if the writer had begun the segment with the following statement:

> We have conducted a test that demonstrates the ability of our sampling tube to absorb the necessary amount of VCM under the conditions specified.

By placing the generalization at the head of the paragraph, the writer would also help you use the segment more efficiently as you performed the managerial task of determining whether the writer's conclusion is valid. Because you would already know the writer's generalization, you could immediately assess whether each detail does, indeed, provide adequate support for the conclusion that the sample tube absorbs the necessary amount of VCM. In contrast, if the writer waited to reveal his or her conclusion after presenting his or her details, you would have to recall each detail from memory—or even reread the passage—in order to assess the strength of its support for the writer's conclusion.

How Initial Generalizations Make Writing More Persuasive

Left to themselves, readers are capable of deriving all sorts of generalizations from a passage. Consider the following sentences:

- Richard moved the gas chromatograph to the adjacent lab.
- He also moved the electronic balance.
- And he moved the experimental laser.

One reader might note that everything Richard moved is a piece of laboratory equipment and consequently might generalize that "Richard moved some laboratory equipment from one place to another." Another reader might observe that everything Richard moved was heavy and therefore might generalize that "Richard is strong." A member of a labor union in Richard's organization might generalize that "Richard was doing work that should have been done by a union member, not by a manager" and might file a grievance. Different generalizations lead to different outcomes.

A key point is that readers naturally formulate generalizations even if none are provided. Of course, when you are writing persuasively you will want your readers to draw one particular conclusion—and not other possible ones. You can increase your chances of succeeding by stating your desired generalization explicitly and by placing that generalization ahead of your supporting details so that your readers encounter it before forming a different generalization on their own.

Present your generalization before your readers begin to formulate contradictory ones.

Sometimes You Shouldn't Present Your Generalizations First

Although you can usually strengthen your segments by stating your generalizations before your details, watch for situations where you need to follow a different strategy. As explained in Chapter 5, if you launch a segment with a generalization that is likely to provoke a negative reaction from your readers, you may decrease your communication's persuasiveness. In such cases, you can usually increase your communication's persuasiveness by postponing your general points until *after* you've laid the relevant groundwork with your details by using the indirect organizational pattern (described in Chapter 5).

How Guideline 2 Relates to Guideline 1

Taken together, Guidelines 1 and 2 advise you to announce your topic and state your main point about it at the beginning of each segment. Often, you can make your writing more concise and forceful by doing both in a single sentence. Consider the opening for a two-page discussion of an engineer's experimental results.

> We conducted tests to determine whether the plastic resins can be used to replace metal in the manufacture of the CV-200 housing. The tests showed that there are three shortcomings in plastic resins that make them unsuitable as a replacement for the metal.

Separate sentences state the topic and the writer's generalization.

The first sentence announces the topic of the segment (the tests), and the second states the writer's generalization about the topic (the resins are not a good substitute for metal). By combining both the topic and generalization into a single sentence, the engineer saved many words.

Topic and generalization are combined in one sentence.

> Our tests showed three shortcomings in plastic resins that make them unsuitable as a replacement for metal in the manufacture of the CV-200 housing.

GUIDELINE 3 MOVE FROM MOST IMPORTANT TO LEAST IMPORTANT

指导方针 3：从最重要到最不重要

Guidelines 1 and 2 discussed the way you begin your segments. Guideline 3 focuses, instead on the way you order the material that follows your opening sentence or sentences. It applies particularly to passages in which you present parallel pieces of information, such as a list of five recommendations or an explanation of three causes of a problem. Whether you present each item in a single sentence or in several paragraphs, put the most important item first and then proceed in descending order of importance.

By putting the most important information first, you increase your communication's usability by making it easier for readers who scan to locate your key points without reading your entire communication. Placing your most important information first also increases your communication's persuasiveness by presenting the strongest support for your arguments in the most prominent spot.

To identify the most important information, consider your communication from your readers' viewpoint. What information will they be most interested in or find most persuasive? For example, in the segment on the three shortcomings of plastic resins, readers will certainly be more interested in the major shortcoming than the minor ones. Similarly, if the readers must be persuaded that plastic resins are not a good substitute for metal, they are sure to find the major shortcoming more compelling than minor ones.

Occasionally, you may encounter situations where you must ignore this guideline in order to present your overall message clearly and economically. For instance, to explain clearly the multiple causes of a flooding along a river, you may need to describe events chronologically even though the event that occurred first was not the one with the greatest impact. In general, though, presenting the most important information first will be most helpful and persuasive to your readers.

GUIDELINE 4 CONSULT CONVENTIONAL STRATEGIES WHEN HAVING DIFFICULTIES ORGANIZING

指导方针 4：组织文章出现困难时借鉴常用策略

Every writer occasionally gets stumped when trying to organize a particular paragraph, section, or chapter. Often the problem is one that many others have faced, such as how to describe a certain process or how to explain the causes of a particular event. For many commonly encountered organizational problems there are conventional strategies for arranging material in ways that will be understandable and useful to readers. By consulting these strategies, you will often find a quick and effective solution to your own problem.

The Writer's Reference Guide following this chapter tells how to use seven of these strategies that are especially useful on the job. As you study the strategies, remember to use them only as guides. To make them work in your particular context, you will need to adapt them to your purpose and the needs of your readers.

GUIDELINE 5 GLOBAL GUIDELINE: CONSIDER YOUR READERS' CULTURAL BACKGROUND WHEN ORGANIZING

指导方针5：组织文章时考虑读者的文化背景

The advice you have read so far in this chapter is based on the customs of readers in the United States and other Western countries where readers expect and value what might be called a *linear* organization. In this organizational pattern, writers express their main ideas explicitly and develop each one separately, carefully leading readers from one to another. As international communication experts Myron W. Lustig and Jolene Koester explain, this pattern can be visualized as "a series of steps or progressions that move in a straight line toward a particular goal or idea" (1993, p. 218).

In other cultures, writers and readers are accustomed to different patterns. For example, the Japanese use a nonlinear pattern that many researchers call a *gyre* (Connor, 1996). The writer approaches a topic by indirection and implication because in Japanese culture it's rude and inappropriate to tell the reader the specific point being conveyed. Communication specialist Kazuo Nishiyama (1983) gives an example: When a Japanese manager says, "I'd like you to reflect on your proposal for a while," the manager can mean, "You are dead wrong, and you'd better come up with a better idea very soon. But I don't say this to you directly because you should be able to understand what I'm saying without my being so rude." Similarly, in Hindi (one of the major languages of India), paragraphs do not stick to one unified idea or thought, as they do in the United States and many other Western nations. Linguist Jamuna Kachru (1988) explains that in the preferred Hindi style, the writer may digress and introduce material related to many different ideas.

Because of these cultural differences, serious misunderstandings can arise when your readers are employed by other companies in another country, work for your own company in another country, or even work in your own building but were raised observing the customs of another culture. Such misunderstandings cannot be avoided simply by translating the words of your communication: The whole message must be structured to suit the customs of your readers' culture.

GUIDELINE 6 REVEAL YOUR COMMUNICATION'S ORGANIZATION

指导方针6：展示交流的组织模式

Combined with strategies described in Chapters 4 and 5, the advice given in this chapter's first five guidelines enable you to organize communications in reader-centered ways that are highly usable and persuasive. To realize the full benefit of your organizing efforts, however, you must also "reveal" a communication's organization by drawing a map of it for your readers.

A well-drawn map can increase your communication's usability for the two most common types of readers. For readers hoping to find a specific piece of information without reading other material, your map provides quick access to their destination. For readers who are reading the entire communication sequentially, the map explains how the parts fit together, thereby making your communication easier to understand. Even in the most carefully organized communication, the relationships among the parts may not be evident to readers unless the writer explicitly indicates them. That's because information about organization can be quite distinct from information about subject matter, as this diagram indicates:

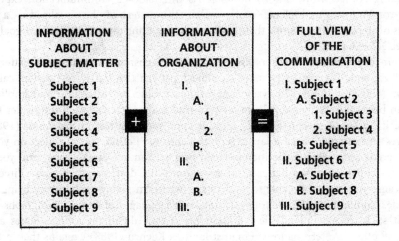

As another way to appreciate the distinction between information about subject matter and information about organization, look at Figure 7.2. Unless you can read Japanese, the text will be incomprehensible to you, but the organization of information is clear, thanks to the skillful use of several techniques described later in this chapter.

By providing a map that reveals the way your communication is organized, you also increase the communication's persuasiveness. The map allows your readers to expend less attention unraveling the communication's organization so they can de-

FIGURE 7.2
Page Printed in Japanese

— The blue block gives primary emphasis to the page's title.

— Large, bold type shows where major sections begin.

— Indention signals subordination.

— A table provides another way of using visual design to signal the organization of information.

vote more attention to the data and other evidence that support your claims. By reducing the effort required to understand your communication, your map also increases the likelihood that readers will study your entire argument with care rather than skimming or stopping reading altogether.

Guideline 6 **Reveal Your Communication's Organization**   209

The following sections discuss four techniques for revealing organization:

- Forecasting statements
- Transitions
- Headings
- Visual arrangement of your text on the page

Forecasting Statements

Forecasting statements tell the reader the organization of what lies ahead. Often, they appear along with a topic sentence, which they supplement. For instance, here is the topic sentence for a section of a brochure published by a large chain of garden nurseries:

Topic sentence | Our first topic is the trees found in the American Southwest.

Although this topic sentence tells what the section is about, it gives no hint of the way the section has been organized. The section might discuss evergreen trees first and then deciduous trees. It might discuss healthy trees and then diseased ones, or it might be organized in some other way. Readers would have no way of knowing. A forecasting statement resolves that uncertainty.

Forecasting statement | Our first topic is the trees found in the American Southwest. <u>Some of the trees are native, some imported.</u>

Forecasting and topic statements are often combined in one sentence:

Forecasting statement | Our first topic is the trees—<u>both native and imported</u>—found in the American Southwest.

Forecasting statements may vary greatly in the amount of detail they provide. The sample sentences above provide both the number and the names of the categories to be discussed. A more general preview is given in the next example, which tells its readers to expect a list of actions but not what these actions are or how many will be discussed:

Forecasting statement | To solve this problem, the department must take <u>the following actions.</u>

When you are deciding how much detail to include in a forecasting statement, there are three main points to consider.

WRITING FORECASTING STATEMENTS

- **Say something about the segment's arrangement that readers will find helpful.**
  Usually, the more complex the relationship among the parts, the greater the amount of detail that is needed.

- **Say only as much as readers can easily remember.** A forecasting statement should help readers, not test their memories. When forecasting a segment that will discuss a three-step process, you could name all the steps. If the process has eight steps, state the number without naming them.
- **Forecast only one level at a time.** Don't list all the contents of a communication at its outset. That will only confuse your readers. Tick off only the major divisions of a particular section. If those divisions are themselves divided, provide each of them with its own forecasting statement.

Transitions

When you organize a communication, you understand the connections between adjacent parts—how one topic leads to the second and the second follows from the first. To make your communication as usable and persuasive as possible, you need to ensure that your readers see these relationships as they progress through it. If they miss a connection along the way, they will miss part of your meaning.

Forecasting statements, as helpful as they are, usually don't provide this information. They tell the sequence in which upcoming topics will appear, but not the connections that link them together. Positioned between topics, transitions add the needed explanation.

Transitions include three elements: a reference to the preceding topic, the topic (or topic statement) that is beginning, and the link between the two.

| This large increase in contributions will enable us to expand our free health care program in several ways. | Transition based on cause and effect |

This sentence begins with the preceding topic (the increase in contributions) and ends with the next topic (the ways the free health care program might be expanded). The link between the two is that the contributions have created the opportunity for the expansion.

| Having finally reached Dingham Point, the expedition spent the next three days building rafts to cross the river. | Transition based on sequence of events |

Here, the link between the last topic (about the journey to Dingham Point) and the next one (building the raft) is that one followed the other.

Sometimes you can signal transitions without using any words at all. For example, in a report that presents three brief recommendations, you might arrange the recommendations in a numbered list. The numbers themselves would provide the transition from one recommendation to the next. Similarly, in a memo covering several separate topics, the transition from one to the next might be provided by giving each topic a heading (see the discussion of headings that follows).

Headings

A third technique for revealing organization is to use headings. They serve as signposts that tell readers what the successive parts of a communication are about. At work, writers use headings not only in long documents, such as reports and manuals, but also in short ones, such as letters and memos. To see how effectively the insertion of headings can reveal organization, look at Figure 7.3, which shows two versions of the same memo, one without headings and one with them. Figure 7.4 highlights the use of headings at a website.

Provide headings wherever there is a major shift in topic. In much on-the-job writing, such a shift occurs every few paragraphs. Avoid giving every paragraph its own heading, which would give your prose a disjointed appearance rather than helping readers see how things fit together. An exception occurs in communications designed to provide readers quick access to specific pieces of information, as in a warranty, troubleshooting guide, reference manual, or fact sheet. In these documents, headings may even label sentence fragments or brief bits of data, turning the communication into something very much like a table of facts.

To be helpful, each heading must unambiguously indicate the kind of information that is included in the passage it labels.

CREATING TEXT FOR HEADINGS

- **Ask the question that the segment will answer for your readers.** Headings that ask questions such as "What happens if I miss a payment on my loan?" or "Can I pay off my loan early?" are especially useful in communications designed to help readers decide what to do.
- **State the main idea of the segment.** This strategy is often used in documents that offer advice or guidance. A brochure on bicycling safety uses headings such as "Ride with the Traffic," "Use Hand Signals," and "Ride Single File."
- **Use a key word or phrase.** This type of heading is especially effective when a full question or statement would be unnecessarily wordy. For instance, in a request for a high-end multimedia production system, the section that discusses prices might have a heading that reads, "How Much Will the System Cost?" However, the single word "Cost" would serve the same purpose.

Often, however, parallel headings make a communication's content easier to access and understand. For instance, when you are describing a series of steps in a process, parallel phrasing cues readers that the segments being labeled are logically parallel: "Opening the Computer Program," "Entering Data," and so on. However, in some situations, a mix of heading types will tell readers more directly what each section is about. Figure 7.5 shows the table of contents from a booklet titled *Getting the Bugs Out* that uses all three types of headings. Notice where they are parallel—and where they are not.

FIGURE 7.3
The Same Memo with and without Headings

Garibaldi Corporation
INTEROFFICE MEMORANDUM

June 15, 2006

TO   Vice Presidents and Department Managers
FROM   Davis M. Pritchard, President
RE   PURCHASES OF COMPUTER AND FAX EQUIPMENT

Three months ago, I appointed a task force to develop corporate-wide policies for the purchase of computers and fax equipment. Based on the advice of the task force, I am establishing the following policies.

Objectives of Policies
The task force was to balance two possibly conflicting objectives: (1) to ensure that each department purchases the equipment that best serves its special needs and (2) to ensure compatibility among the equipment purchased so the company can create an efficient electronic network for all our computer and fax equipment.

Computer Purchases
I am designating one "preferred" vendor of computers and two "secondary" vendors.

   Preferred Vendor: The preferred vendor, YYY, is the vendor from which all purchases should be made unless there is a compelling reason for selecting other equipment. To encourage purchases from the preferred vendor, a special corporate fund will cover 30% of the purchase price so that individual departments need fund only 70%.

   Secondary Vendor: Two other vendors, AAA and MMM, offer computers already widely used in Garibaldi; both computers are compatible with our plans to establish a computer network. Therefore, the special corporate fund will support 10% of the purchase price of these machines.

Fax Purchases
We will select one preferred vendor and no secondary vendor for fax equipment. The task force will choose between two candidates: FFF and TTT. I will notify you when the choice is made early next month.

David Pritchard's first version lacked visual cues to the memo's organization.

By adding headings, he helped readers see how his memo is organized. The bold headings tell readers that these are the main parts of the memo.

With indenting, he indicates that these are the two parts of the computer policy.

Guideline 6   **Reveal Your Communication's Organization**

FIGURE 7.4
Website with Headings

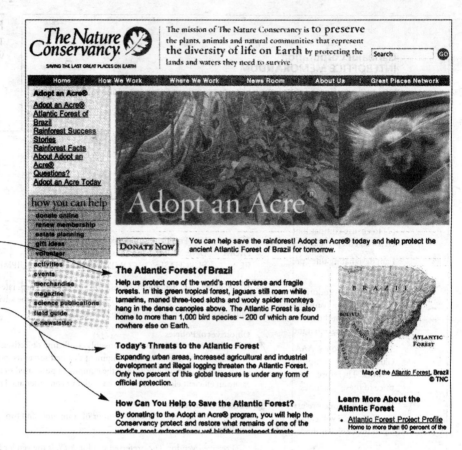

Headings are as helpful to readers on web pages as they are in printed communications.

This page's title is in bold and larger type.

The headings, which are also in bold, use a type that is smaller than the heading's but larger than the text's.

The visual appearance of headings is important to readers. To be useful, headings must stand out. If more than one level of heading is used, each must communicate its hierarchical relationship visually.

DESIGNING HEADINGS VISUALLY

1. **Make headings stand out from the text, perhaps using these strategies.**
   - Use bold.
   - Use a different color than is used for the text.
   - Place headings at the left-hand margin or center them.
2. **Make major headings more prominent than minor ones. Here are some strategies to consider.**
   - Make major headings larger.
   - Center the major headings and tuck the others against the left-hand margin.

CHAPTER 7 **Drafting Paragraphs, Sections, and Chapters**

- Use all capital letters for the major headings and initial capital letters for the others.
- Give the major headings a line of their own and put the others on the same line as the text that follows them.

3. **Give the same visual treatment to headings at the same level in the hierarchy.**

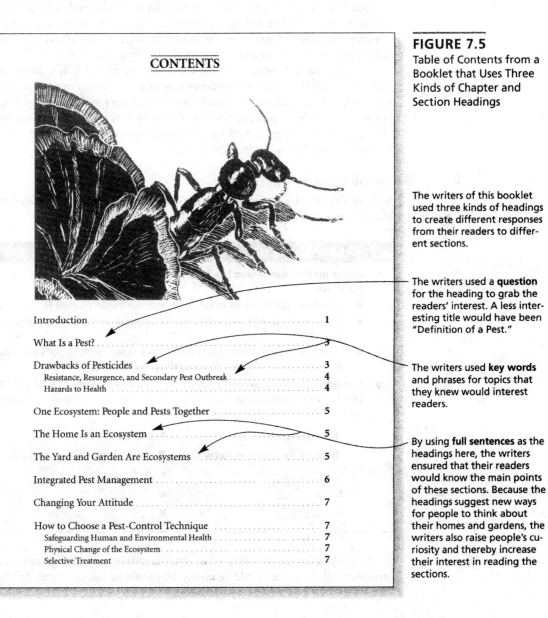

FIGURE 7.5
Table of Contents from a Booklet that Uses Three Kinds of Chapter and Section Headings

The writers of this booklet used three kinds of headings to create different responses from their readers to different sections.

The writers used a **question** for the heading to grab the readers' interest. A less interesting title would have been "Definition of a Pest."

The writers used **key words** and phrases for topics that they knew would interest readers.

By using **full sentences** as the headings here, the writers ensured that their readers would know the main points of these sections. Because the headings suggest new ways for people to think about their homes and gardens, the writers also raise people's curiosity and thereby increase their interest in reading the sections.

Usually, you can use two or more of these techniques together so that they reinforce one another. By doing so, you can readily create two or three easily distinguishable levels of headings that instantly convey the organizational hierarchy of your communication. Figure 7.6 shows an example.

If you feel that additional levels are needed, try making the most important sections into separate chapters, with the chapter titles serving as the highest level of heading (see Figure 7.6). Alternatively, you can reinforce the headings with letters and numbers in outline fashion, as shown in Figure 7.7. In most circumstances, however, the numbers and letters of an outline diminish the effectiveness of headings by distracting the readers' eyes from the headings' key words.

By convention, headings and the topic statements that follow them reinforce each other, with the topic statement repeating one or more key words from the heading. Topic statements do not contain pronouns that refer to the headings. For example, the heading "Research Method" would not be followed by a sentence that says, "Designing this was a great challenge." Instead, the sentence would read, "Designing the research method was a great challenge."

Visual Arrangement of Text

You can also reveal your communication's organization through the visual arrangement of your text on the page.

ARRANGING TEXT VISUALLY TO REVEAL ORGANIZATION

- **Adjust the location of your blocks of type.** Here are three adjustments you can make:
  - Indent paragraphs lower in the organizational hierarchy. (See Figure 7.7.)
  - Leave extra space between the end of one major section and the beginning of the next.
  - In long communications, begin each new chapter or major section on its own page, regardless of where the preceding chapter or section ended.
- **Use lists.** By placing items in a list, you signal readers that items hold a parallel place in your organizational hierarchy. Usually, numbers are used for sequential steps. Bullets are often used where a specific order isn't required.

Number List	**Bullet List**
The three steps we should take are:	Three features of the product are:
1. _____	■ _____
2. _____	■ _____
3. _____	■ _____

When you are constructing a list, give the entries a parallel grammatical construction: All the items should be nouns, all should be full sentences, or all should

FIGURE 7.6
Headings that Indicate Organizational Hierarchy

Section 1
INTRODUCTION ← Section heading

Southwestern Senior Services, Inc., is requesting support to develop an innovative behavior-management approach for nursing home residents who wander. The approach will be tested at Locust Knoll Village, a comprehensive philanthropic retirement community in the Chicago area.

"Wandering" Defined ← A-level heading

Wandering is one of several deviant behaviors associated with the aging process. The term refers to disoriented and aimless movement toward undefinable objectives and unattainable goals. Snyder et al. (1998) describe the wanderer as moving about and traversing locations 32.5% of waking hours, as opposed to 4.2% for nonwanderers. Wanderers differ significantly from nonwanderers on a number of psychological variables and, overall, have more psychological problems, as assessed by the Human Development Inventory (Pyrek and Snyder, 1997).

Causes ← A-level heading

The limited research on wandering has focused on organic and psychosocial factors.

Organic Factors. Early research typically attributed wandering behaviors to damage to the brain as a result of disease, rather than to cognitive impairment. More recently geropsychologists and gerontologists are beginning to believe that organic pathologies do not explain functional disorders or disruptive behavior (Monsour and Robb, 1992). The main reason for this shift in thinking is the research by Busse (1997) and Verwoerdt (1976), who found no consistent relationship between impairment and organic changes in the brain vessels. ← B-level heading

Psychosocial Factors. Monsour and Robb (1992) and Snyder et al. (1998) suggest that the following three psychosocial factors are associated with wandering: ← B-level heading

1. Lifelong patterns of coping with stress. Wanderers, as opposed to nonwanderers, typically respond to dramatic changes in routine or environment through motoric responses. Releases from tension developed early in life may have been brisk walks or long strolls.

2. Previous work roles. High rates of physical activity required by jobs held early in life may permanently influence behaviors, so that, for example, a mail carrier who delivered on foot may experience a compulsion to walk long after retirement.

3. Search for security. Some wanderers call out to dead parents or spouses, indicating that they are searching for security.

FIGURE 7.7
Indentation of Text Used to Indicate Organizational Hierarchy

Subordinate material is indented.

To emphasize this caution, the writer uses an icon and moves the text margin farther left.

A second level of indentation signals a second level of subordination.

Managing Disk Partitions

Use extreme caution when navigating through this next portion of Setup. You can easily create, destroy, and reformat entire disk partitions with a couple of keystrokes. Keep in mind that you're running a cousin of the powerful and potentially destructive DOS FDISK utility.

12. Setup lists hard disks, partitions, and unpartitioned areas on your computer. It then asks you where to install NT 4.0. Use the UP and DOWN ARROW keys to scroll through the list and highlight a partition. Go to step 12a.

    You'll need to find a destination partition with at least 115MB of free space on which to install Windows NT Server.

    In the list, all non-SCSI drives are displayed as "IDE/ESDI Disk." A SCSI drive is displayed as "Disk # at id # on bus # on" followed by the name of the SCSI adapter driver. The ID number is the SCSI ID assigned to the drive.

    Areas of your disks that contain no partition are displayed as "Unpartitioned space." Partitions that have been created but not yet formatted are displayed as "New (Unformatted)" or as "Unformatted or Damaged." Don't worry about the latter. This is just NT's generic way of saying that it doesn't recognize a partition as formatted.

    If you're installing Windows NT Server on a computer that contains a previous version of Windows NT and you were using disk stripes, mirrors, or volume sets, these partitions are shown as "Windows NT Fault Tolerance" partitions. Don't delete any of these partitions. See the section entitled "Migrating Fault Tolerance from Windows NT 3.x" in Chapter 19 for details on using existing fault-tolerance partitions.

    If you don't see all of your partitions listed, you may just need to use the UP and DOWN ARROW keys to scroll and display them. Only hard disks are included in this list.

    Don't panic if the drive letter assignments seem out of whack. They probably don't match the drive letters that you see under DOS or even under another version of NT. Once you've got NT up and running, you'll be able to change drive letter assignments very easily.

    12a. If you're ready to select a partition on which NT 4.0 will be installed, highlight that partition, press ENTER, and go to step 13. If you're not, go to step 12b to delete an existing partition or step 12c to create a new partition.

        You can select an unformatted partition or an existing formatted FAT or NTFS partition. Unpartitioned space isn't a valid destination for NT installation. You need to partition it first, in step 12c.

        If the partition that you select isn't large enough, Setup will complain and send you back to step 12.

be questions, and so on. Mixing grammatical constructions distracts readers and sometimes indicates a shift in point of view that breaks the tight relationship that should exist among the items.

WITHOUT PARALLELISM	WITH PARALLELISM	
Benefits	Benefits	
• Increased sales	• Increased sales	
• Decreased production costs	• Decreased production costs	
• ⟦Morale that is higher⟧ ◄──	• Higher morale	── Not Parallel
Recommendations	Recommendations	
1. Sell our Tallahassee plant.	1. Sell our Tallahassee plant.	
2. Place the two Baton Rouge plants under a single manager.	2. Place the two Baton Rouge plants under a single manager.	
3. ⟦We should also seek a better location for our Columbia warehouse.⟧ ◄──	3. Seek a better location for our Columbia warehouse.	── Not Parallel

GUIDELINE 7 SMOOTH THE FLOW OF THOUGHT FROM SENTENCE TO SENTENCE

指导方针7：逐句调整理顺思路

As people read through the chapters, sections, and paragraphs discussed in Guideline 6, they are continuously determining how the sentence they are now reading relates to the sentence they just completed. This connection-making process occurs so rapidly that readers aren't even aware of it until they hit a sentence that doesn't seem to fit. Then, they either stop to figure out the relationship or they push ahead, missing some of the writer's meaning. To avoid these undesirable results, smooth the flow of thought from sentence to sentence, using the following strategies.

- Use transitional words and phrases
- Use echo words
- Keep a steady focus from sentence to sentence

Use Transitional Words and Phrases

Transitional words and phrases can serve as links that tie one sentence to the next. Here are some of the most commonly used transitional words:

Links in time	after, before, during, until, while	Transitional words and phrases
Links in space	above, below, inside	
Links of cause and effect	as a result, because, since	
Links of similarity	as, furthermore, likewise, similarly	
Links of contrast	although, however, nevertheless, on the other hand	

These and many more are undoubtedly familiar to you. The important point is to remember to use them when they will help your readers follow the flow of thought through your communication. When using them, put them where they will help your readers most: at the beginning of sentences. In that position, they immediately signal the relationship between that sentence and the preceding one.

Use Echo Words

Another way to guide your readers from one sentence to the next is to use *echo words*. An echo word is a word or phrase that recalls to the readers' minds some information they've already encountered. For example:

> The word echoed is "cured."
> The echo word is "cure."

> Inflation can be cured. The cure appears to require that consumers change their basic attitudes toward consumption.

In this example, the noun *cure* at the beginning of the second sentence echoes the verb in the first. It tells readers that what follows in the second sentence will discuss the curing they have just read about in the first.

There are many other kinds of echo words.

- **Pronouns**

  > In the second sentence, "It" echoes "copier" in the first sentence.

  > We had to return the copier. Its frequent breakdowns were disrupting work.

- **Another word from the same "word family" as the word being echoed**

  > In the second sentence, "Oscilloscope" echoes "lab equipment" in the first sentence.

  > I went to my locker to get my lab equipment. My oscilloscope was missing.

- **A word or phrase that recalls some idea or theme expressed but not explicitly stated in the preceding sentence**

  > In the second sentence, the words "these transactions" echo the purchase and retiring of shares described in the first sentence.

  > The company also purchased and retired 17,399 shares of its $2.90 convertible, preferred stock at $5.70 a share. These transactions reduce the number of outstanding convertible shares to 635,200.

Like transitional words and phrases, echo words help readers most when they appear at the beginning of a sentence.

Note that if you use *this* or *that* as an echo word at the beginning of a sentence, you should follow it with a noun. If used alone at the beginning of a sentence, you can leave your readers uncertain about what *this* is.

> Original

> Our client rejected the R37 compound because it softened at temperatures about 500°C. This is what our engineers feared.

In this example, the reader would be unsure whether "This" refers to the client's dissatisfaction or the softening of the R37. The addition of a noun after "This" clears up the ambiguity.

> Revised

> Our client rejected the R37 compound because it softened at temperatures about 500°C. This softening is what our engineers feared.

Keep a Steady Focus from Sentence to Sentence

The preceding strategies for guiding readers from sentence to sentence involve situations where the two sentences have different topics. In some cases, the topic can remain the same. In these situations, keep a steady focus on that topic. To do so, you need only keep that topic in the subject position of both sentences. You can repeat the same word, use a synonym, or use an echo word (see the discussion of echo words above).

| The links of the drive chain must fit together firmly. They are too loose if you can easily wiggle two links from side to side more than ten degrees. | These sentences have the same focus because they both have the same subject. |

Because *They* in the second sentence is an echo word for *The links* in the first sentence, both sentences have the same subject.

Maintaining a steady focus requires that you consider alternative ways of writing a sentence. For example, you could fashion a sentence in either of the following ways.

| The system has saved thousands of dollars this month alone. | Version A |
| Thousands of dollars have been saved by the system this month alone. | Version B |

Both versions contain the same information. To decide between them, you could look at the preceding sentence to see which will keep a steady focus. If the preceding sentence had said, "Our company's new inventory system reduces our costs considerably," then Version A would maintain the steady focus because it has the same subject (the system) as the preceding sentence.

| Our company's new inventory system reduces costs considerably. The system saved thousands of dollars this month alone. | Both sentences have the same subject. |

In order to keep a steady focus, you may sometimes need to use a sentence that has the passive voice. As Chapter 8 explains, it is usually desirable to use the active voice, not the passive. However, the chapter also explains that sometimes the passive is more appropriate, even preferable, to the active. One such time occurs when the passive voice enables you to avoid a needless shift in the topic of two adjacent sentences. Consider the following paragraph from an accident report.

Learn More

For more on the active and passive voice, see Chapter 8, page 266.

| After lunch on Tuesday, Tom took a shortcut back to his workstation. Fifteen yards above the factory floor, a can of paint slipped off a scaffold and hit him on the left foot. Consequently, he missed seventeen days of work. | The focus shifts from the first sentence to the second. |

The subject of the first and third sentences is the same: "Tom" and "he." However, the second sentence shifts the topic from Tom to the can of paint. Furthermore, because the second sentence shifts, the third does also in bringing the focus back to Tom. The writer could avoid these two shifts by rewriting the second sentence in the passive voice, making Tom its subject, not the can of paint.

| He was hit on the left foot by a can of paint that slipped off a scaffold fifteen yards above the factory floor. | Better second sentence |

GUIDELINE 8 ETHICS GUIDELINE: EXAMINE THE HUMAN CONSEQUENCES OF WHAT YOU'RE DRAFTING
道德指导方针 8：在起草文章时考虑读者感受

When drafting their communications, employees sometimes become so engrossed in the technical aspects of their subject that they forget the human consequences of what they're writing. When this happens, they write communications in which their stakeholders are overlooked. Depending on the situation, the consequences can be quite harmful or relatively mild—but they can always lead to the unethical treatment of other people.

Mining Accidents

An example is provided by Beverly A. Sauer (2003), who has studied the reports written by the federal employees who investigate mining accidents in which miners are killed. In their reports, Sauer points out, the investigators typically focus on technical information about the accidents without paying sufficient attention to the human tragedies caused by the accidents. In one report, for example, the investigators describe the path of an underground explosion as it traveled through an intricate web of mineshafts and flamed out of various mine entrances. At one entrance, investigators write, "Debris blown by the explosion's forces damaged a jeep automobile parked near the drift openings." The investigators don't mention in this passage that in addition to damaging the jeep, the explosion killed sixteen miners who were in the mineshafts.

In addition to overlooking the victims of the disasters, the investigators' reports often fail to identify the human beings who created the conditions that caused the accidents. One report says, "The accident and resultant fatality occurred when the victim proceeded into an area of known loose roof before the roof was supported or taken down." This suggests that the miner was crushed to death by a falling mine roof because he was careless. Sauer's research showed, however, that in the same mines ten fatalities had occurred in five years—and seven resulted from falling roofs. Managers of the mines were not following safety regulations, and mine safety inspectors were not enforcing the law.

Writing with Awareness of Human Consequences

Of course, there's nothing the inspectors' reports can do on behalf of the deceased miners or their families. However, the stakeholders in the inspectors' reports include other miners who continue to work in what is the most dangerous profession in the United States. As Sauer points out, the investigators' readers include the federal officials responsible for overseeing the nation's mining industry. If the inspectors wrote in ways that made these readers more aware of the human consequences of mining accidents—and of the human failings that often bring them about—the federal officials might be more willing to pass stricter laws and insist that existing regulations be strictly enforced.

In Europe, where government regulation of mining is much stronger, the death and injury of miners are much rarer events than in the United States. The high accident rate that makes mining so dangerous in the United States, she argues, results in part from the way mining investigators write their reports.

Of course, most people aren't in professions where lives are at stake. In any profession, however, it's possible to become so focused on your technical subject matter that you forget the human consequences of your writing.

To avoid accidentally treating others unethically, you can take the following steps.

Miners in the United States would be safer if the persons who prepare mining accident reports paid more attention to the human consequences of their writing, Dr. Beverly Sauer argues.

AVOIDING ACCIDENTALLY TREATING OTHERS UNETHICALLY

- **When beginning work on a communication, identify its stakeholders** (page 87). Certainly, the stakeholders of the mining disaster reports include miners whose lives are endangered if government officials don't enact and enforce life-saving safety measures.
- **Determine how the stakeholders will be affected by your communication** (page 112).
- **Draft your communication in a way that reflects proper care for these individuals.** Be sure that all your decisions about what to say, what *not* to say, and how to present your message are consistent with your personal beliefs about how you should treat other people.

CONCLUSION 总 结

This chapter has suggested that you can increase the usability and persuasiveness of your communications if you begin your segments with topic statements; present generalizations before details; organize from most important to least important; reveal your communication's organization with headings, forecasting statements, and similar devices; and consider your readers' cultural background.

Remember that the first seven guidelines in this chapter are suggestions, not rules. The only "rule" for writing segments is to be sure your readers know what you are talking about and how your various points relate to one another. Sometimes you will be able to do this without thinking consciously about your techniques. At other times, you will be able to increase the clarity and persuasiveness of your segments by drawing on this chapter's advice.

To assure that you are always drafting ethically, the eighth guideline is something you *should* treat as a rule: Remember the human consequences of what you are writing.

EXERCISES 练 习

EXPERTISE

1. Circle the various parts and subparts of the passage in Figure 7.8 to show how the smaller segments are contained within larger ones.

2. Identify the topic statements in Figure 7.8 by putting an asterisk before the first word of each sentence that indicates the topic of a segment.

FIGURE 7.8
Passage Containing Several Levels of Segments

Importing Insects

By importing insects from other parts of the world, nations can sometimes increase the productivity of their agricultural sector, but they also risk hurting themselves. By importing insects, Australia controlled the infestation of its continent by the prickly pear, a cactus native to North and South America. The problem began when this plant, which has an edible fruit, was brought to Australia by early explorers. Because the explorers did not also bring its natural enemies, the prickly pear grew uncontrolled, eventually rendering large areas useless as grazing land, thereby harming the nation's farm economy. The problem was solved when scientists in Argentina found a small moth, Cactoblastis cactorum, whose larvae feed upon the prickly pear. The moth was imported to Australia, where its larvae, by eating the cactus, reopened thousands of acres of land.

In contrast, the importation of another insect, the Africanized bee, could threaten the well-being of the United States. It once appeared that the importation of this insect might bring tremendous benefits to North and South America. The Africanized bee produces about twice as much honey as do the bees native to the Americas.

However, the U.S. Department of Agriculture now speculates that the introduction of the Africanized honey bee into the U.S. would create serious problems. The problems arise from the peculiar way the Africanized honey bee swarms. When the honey bees native to the United States swarm, about half the bees leave the hive with the queen, moving a small distance. The rest remain, choosing a new queen. In contrast, when the Africanized honey bee swarms, the entire colony moves, sometimes up to fifty miles. If Africanized bees intermix with the domestic bee population, they might introduce these swarming traits. Beekeepers could be abandoned by their bees, and large areas of cropland could be left without the services of this pollinating insect. Unfortunately, the Africanized honey bee is moving slowly northward to the United States from Sao Paulo, Brazil, where several years ago a researcher accidentally released 27 swarms of the bee from an experiment.

Thus, while the importation of insects can sometimes benefit a nation, imported insects can also alter the nation's ecological system, thereby harming its agricultural business.

3. Circle all the forecasting statements in Figure 7.6 (page 217). For those segments that lack explicit forecasting statements, explain how readers might figure out the way in which they are organized.

NOTE: Additional exercises are provided at the end of the Writer's Reference Guide that follows this chapter. See page 255.

ONLINE

Examine the ways that this chapter's guidelines are applied by a website that explains technical or scientific topics. For example, study the explanation of a medical topic at the National Cancer Institute (www.nci.nih.gov), the National Institute on Drug Abuse (www.nida.nih.gov), or WebMD (www.WebMD.com). Present your analysis in the way your instructor requests.

COLLABORATION

1. Figure 7.9 shows an e-mail whose contents have been scrambled. Each statement has been assigned a number. Working with one or two other students, do the following.

   a. Write the numbers of the statements in the order in which the statements would appear if the e-mail were written in accordance with the guidelines in this chapter. Place an asterisk before each statement that would

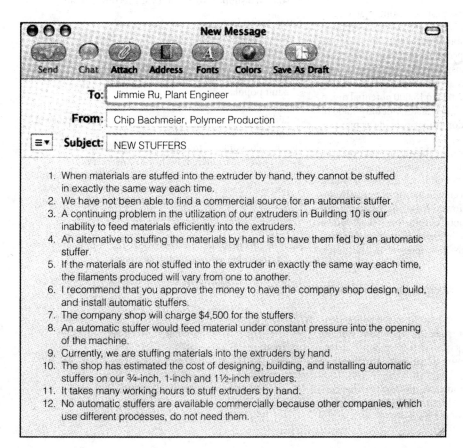

FIGURE 7.9
Memo for Collaboration Exercise

begin a segment. (When you order the statements, ignore their particular phrasing. Order them according to the information they provide the reader.)

b. Using the list you just made, rewrite the e-mail by rephrasing the sentences so that the finished message conforms with all the guidelines in this chapter.

ETHICS

Using the Internet or a library, find the ethics codes for three corporations. Examine the ways this chapter's guidelines would help these corporations write codes that clearly convey their ethical commitments.

CASE: INCREASING ORGAN DONATIONS 增加器官捐赠活动

For additional cases, visit www.thomsonedu.com/english/anderson. Instructors: The book's website includes suggestions for teaching cases.

Case created by Gail S. Bartlett

You've been working for the past six months at Organ Replacement Gives a New Start (ORGANS), a regional clearinghouse for information about organ donation. At any given moment, 30,000 people in the United States are on a waiting list for organ transplants. Seven of them will die today, and every 20 minutes another will join the waiting list. It is believed that from 12,000 to 15,000 potential organ donors die each year in the United States, but only 4,500 of them actually donate. One donor may provide as many as six organs for transplant.

To discover ways of increasing the number of potential organ donors in the area, Eleanor Gaworski, executive director of ORGANS, asked staff member Aaron Nicholson to study and report on a recent Gallup survey of attitudes toward organ donation. However, Aaron suddenly left ORGANS to take another job. Eleanor has asked you to prepare the report using the information he has collected. The information includes the following tables and notes.

YOUR ASSIGNMENT

According to your instructor's directions, do one of the following:

A. For one of the tables, or for a group of the tables identified by your instructor, state the important conclusion or conclusions that you draw, explain the evidence that supports your conclusion, and make a recommendation.

B. Using all the tables or a group identified by your instructor, write a full report to Eleanor. Include an introduction; a brief explanation of the survey method used; the key conclusions you draw, together with the specific results that support them; and your recommendation.

Notes Aaron Left

Largest survey ever conducted on attitudes about organ donation

National survey—6,127 people interviewed

Procedures used make results representative of the U.S. adult population

Telephone survey

In tables, not all percentages total 100 percent because of rounding

Organs taken only from people who are brain-dead

Brain-dead means there is no hope of recovery

Younger people have more organs to donate; as people get older, fewer of their organs are suitable for donation

People do not need to sign an organ donor card or to indicate on their driver's license their desire to donate organs

Next of kin's permission is always needed even if a person has indicated a desire to donate organs

1. Do you support or oppose the donation of organs for transplants?

	Support	Oppose	Don't Know
Total	85%	6%	9%
Age 18–24	81%	10%	9%
25–34	85	7	8
35–44	91	4	5
45–54	86	4	9
55+	81	7	11

2. How likely are you to want to have your organs donated after your death?

	Very Likely	Somewhat Likely	Not Very/ Not at All Likely	Don't Know
Total	37%	32%	25%	6%
Age 18–24	33%	41%	22%	5%
25–34	38	40	17	5
35–44	50	28	17	5
45–54	41	36	18	5
55+	27	26	38	9

3. Is there a particular reason you are not likely to want to have your organs donated upon your death? What might that reason be? (Asked of persons who reported they are not likely to want to have their organs donated)

Response Mentioned	% of Times
Medical reasons	13%
Believe I'm too old	10
Don't want body cut up/Want to be buried as a whole person	9
Don't feel right about it	6
Against religion	5
Other	10
No reason/Don't know/ Haven't given much thought	47

4. Have you made a personal decision about whether or not you would want your or your family members' organs donated in the event of your or their deaths?

Percent Who Have Made Decision about:

	Own Organs	Family Members' Organs
Total	42%	25%
Age 18–24	40%	23%
25–34	43	26
35–44	49	32
45–54	46	33
55+	36	17

Attitude Toward Organ Donation

Support	45%	27%
Oppose	39	25

5. Have you told some member of your family about your wish to donate your organs after your death? (Asked of respondents who reported themselves likely to wish to become organ donors)

	Yes
Total	52%
Age 18–24	39%
25–34	52
35–44	58
45–54	51
55+	52

6. How willing are you to discuss your wishes about organ donation with your family? Would you say very willing, somewhat willing, not very willing, or not at all willing? (Asked of those who have not discussed wishes with family)

Response	Likely to Donate	Not Likely to Donate
Very willing	36%	23%
Somewhat willing	53	35
Not very willing	7	13
Not at all willing	3	23
Don't know	2	4

7. If you had *not discussed* organ donation with a family member, how likely would you be to donate his or her organs upon death?

	Very/ Somewhat Likely	Not Very/ Not at All Likely	Don't Know
Total	47%	45%	7%
Age 18–24	44%	52%	4%
25–34	51	44	5
35–44	54	42	4
45–54	51	43	6
55+	38	49	13

Attitude Toward Organ Donation

	Very/ Somewhat Likely	Not Very/ Not at All Likely	Don't Know
Support	52%	41%	7%
Oppose	11	84	5

8. If a family member *had requested* that his or her organs be donated upon death, how likely would you be to donate the organs upon death?

	Very/ Somewhat Likely	Not Very/ Not at All Likely	Don't Know
Total	93%	5%	2%
Age 18–24	94%	5%	1%
25–34	94	5	2
35–44	97	2	1
45–54	96	3	1
55+	87	8	3
Attitude Toward Organ Donation			
Support	95%	3%	1%
Oppose	69	24	6

9. Most of the people who need an organ transplant receive a transplant.

	Strongly Agree/Agree	Disagree/ Strongly Disagree	Don't Know
Total	20%	68%	12%
Age 18–24	32%	54%	14%
25–34	19	72	9
35–44	14	74	12
45–54	12	75	13
55+	24	63	13
Attitude Toward Organ Donation			
Support	19%	70%	11%
Oppose	32	55	14

10. It is possible for a brain-dead person to recover from his or her injuries.

	Strongly Agree/Agree	Disagree/ Strongly Disagree	Don't Know
Total	21%	63%	16%
Age 18–24	28%	52%	19%
25–34	25	60	15
35–44	20	65	15
45–54	16	71	13
55+	18	64	17

Attitude Toward Organ Donation
Support	20%	65%	15%
Oppose	33	51	15

11. I am going to read you a couple of statements. For each one, please tell me if that statement must be true or not true before an individual can donate his or her organs.

Statement	True	False	Don't Know
The person must carry a signed donor card giving permission.	79%	15%	5%
The person's next of kin must give his or her permission.	58%	34%	8%

12. In the past year, have you read, seen, or heard any information about organ donation?

	Yes
Total	58%
Age 18–24	36%
25–34	47
35–44	61
45–54	65
55+	68
Attitude Toward Organ Donation	
Support	61%
Oppose	38

Survey results are from the Gallup Organization, Inc., *The American Public's Attitudes toward Organ Donation and Transplantation*, conducted for The Partnership for Organ Donations, Boston, MA, February 1993. Used with permission.

WRITER'S REFERENCE GUIDE:
Using Seven Reader-Centered Organizational Patterns
写作者参考指南：使用七个以读者为中心的组织模式

This guide provides detailed, reader-centered advice for using seven patterns for organizing information and arguments. In some brief communications, you may use only one of these patterns, but in most cases, you will weave them together, as described on page 254.

- Formal Classification (Grouping Facts)   *230*
- Informal Classification (Grouping Facts)   *233*
- Comparison   *236*
- Description of an Object (Partitioning)   *240*
- Description of a Process (Segmenting)   *242*
- Cause and Effect   *246*
- Problem and Solution   *251*
- Combinations of Patterns   *254*

Formal Classification (Grouping Facts)

正式分类（事实归类）

On the job, you will sometimes have to write about what seems to be a miscellaneous set of facts. To organize these facts, you can use a strategy called classification. In *classification*, you arrange your material into groups of related items that satisfy the following criteria:

- Every item has a place. In one group or another, every item fits.
- Every item has only one place. If there are two logical places for an item, you must describe it in both locations, thereby creating redundancy. Or you will have to describe it in only one location, thereby requiring your readers to guess where to find the information. Neither alternative is desirable from your readers' perspective.
- The groupings are useful to your readers. Items that readers will use together should be grouped together.

There are two types of classification: formal classification, which is discussed below, and informal classification, which is described on pages 233–235.

How Formal Classification Works

In formal classification, you group items according to a principle of classification—that is, according to some observable characteristic that every item possesses. Usually, you will have several to choose from. While writing a marketing brochure about sixty adhesives manufactured by her employer, a chemical company, Esther could use any characteristic possessed by all the adhesives, such as price, color, and application (that is, whether it is used to bond wood, metal, or ceramic). To choose among these potential principles of classification, she thought about the way consumers would use her brochure. Realizing that they would look for the adhesive best suited to the particular job they were doing, Esther organized around the type of material each adhesive was designed to bond.

In classification, large groups can be organized into subgroups. Within her sections on adhesives for wood, metal, and ceramic, Esther subdivided the adhesives according to strength of the bond created by each one.

Learn More

The formal classification pattern is often combined with other patterns. See page 254.

GUIDELINES FOR FORMAL CLASSIFICATION

1. **Choose a principle of classification that is suited to your readers and your purpose.** Consider the way your readers will use the information you provide.
2. **Use only one principle of classification.** To create a hierarchical organization that has only one place for each item, you must use only one principle of classification at a time. For example, you might classify the cars owned by a large corporation as follows:

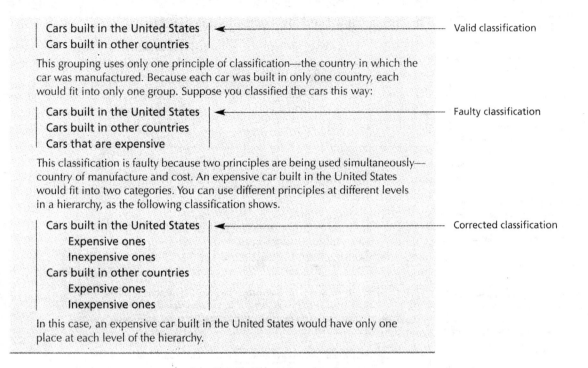

| Cars built in the United States | ← Valid classification |
| Cars built in other countries | |

This grouping uses only one principle of classification—the country in which the car was manufactured. Because each car was built in only one country, each would fit into only one group. Suppose you classified the cars this way:

Cars built in the United States	← Faulty classification
Cars built in other countries	
Cars that are expensive	

This classification is faulty because two principles are being used simultaneously—country of manufacture and cost. An expensive car built in the United States would fit into two categories. You can use different principles at different levels in a hierarchy, as the following classification shows.

Cars built in the United States	← Corrected classification
Expensive ones	
Inexpensive ones	
Cars built in other countries	
Expensive ones	
Inexpensive ones	

In this case, an expensive car built in the United States would have only one place at each level of the hierarchy.

Classification in Graphics

Tables and graphs often accompany passages organized by formal classification. In the chart below, the principle of classification is the country that owned a successfully launched spacecraft, even if it paid another country to lift the craft into space.

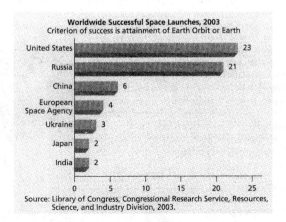

Learn More

For advice about constructing graphics, go to Chapter 12 (page 325) and the Writer's Reference Guide: Creating 13 Types of Graphics (page 351).

Formal Classification (continued)

> To see other communications that use formal classification, go to Writer's Reference Guide: Using Seven Organizational Patterns at www.thomsonedu.com/english/anderson.

Passage Organized by Formal Classification

In the following passage, the writer uses formal classification to organize his discussion of various methods for detecting coronary heart disease. For his principle of classification, he uses the extent to which each method requires physicians to introduce something into the patient's body. The writer selected this principle of classification because he wants to focus on a new method for which nothing needs to be placed in the patient's body.

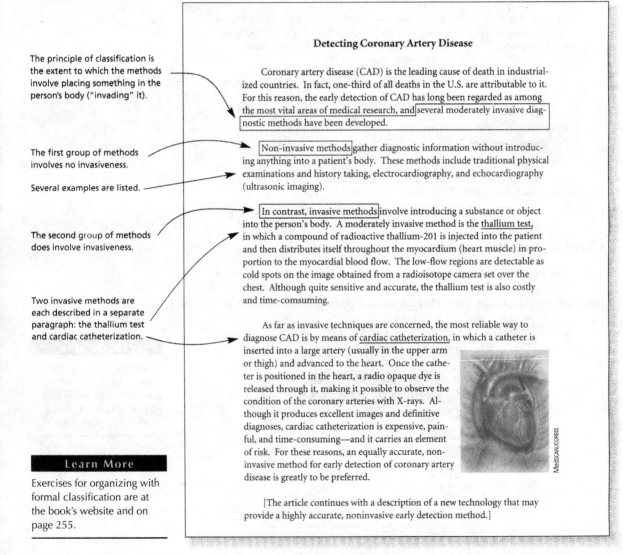

Detecting Coronary Artery Disease

Coronary artery disease (CAD) is the leading cause of death in industrialized countries. In fact, one-third of all deaths in the U.S. are attributable to it. For this reason, the early detection of CAD has long been regarded as among the most vital areas of medical research, and several moderately invasive diagnostic methods have been developed.

Non-invasive methods gather diagnostic information without introducing anything into a patient's body. These methods include traditional physical examinations and history taking, electrocardiography, and echocardiography (ultrasonic imaging).

In contrast, invasive methods involve introducing a substance or object into the person's body. A moderately invasive method is the thallium test, in which a compound of radioactive thallium-201 is injected into the patient and then distributes itself throughout the myocardium (heart muscle) in proportion to the myocardial blood flow. The low-flow regions are detectable as cold spots on the image obtained from a radioisotope camera set over the chest. Although quite sensitive and accurate, the thallium test is also costly and time-comsuming.

As far as invasive techniques are concerned, the most reliable way to diagnose CAD is by means of cardiac catheterization, in which a catheter is inserted into a large artery (usually in the upper arm or thigh) and advanced to the heart. Once the catheter is positioned in the heart, a radio opaque dye is released through it, making it possible to observe the condition of the coronary arteries with X-rays. Although it produces excellent images and definitive diagnoses, cardiac catheterization is expensive, painful, and time-consuming—and it carries an element of risk. For these reasons, an equally accurate, non-invasive method for early detection of coronary artery disease is greatly to be preferred.

[The article continues with a description of a new technology that may provide a highly accurate, noninvasive early detection method.]

Annotations:
- The principle of classification is the extent to which the methods involve placing something in the person's body ("invading" it).
- The first group of methods involves no invasiveness.
- Several examples are listed.
- The second group of methods does involve invasiveness.
- Two invasive methods are each described in a separate paragraph: the thallium test and cardiac catheterization.

Learn More
Exercises for organizing with formal classification are at the book's website and on page 255.

Informal Classification (Grouping Facts)

非正式分类（事实归类）

Informal classification can help you create a reader-centered communication when you need to organize information about a large number of items but find it impossible or undesirable to classify them according to the kind of objective characteristic that is necessary for formal classification.

For example, Calvin needed to organize his analysis, requested by his employer, of advertisements in three trade journals for the heavy equipment industry. Calvin could have created a formal classification by grouping the ads according to an objective characteristic, such as their size or number of words used in them. Instead, however, he classified them according to the type of advertising appeal they made. Obviously, "type of advertising appeal" is not an objective characteristic. Defining an ad's appeal requires subjective interpretation and judgment. Calvin used this informal classification because it best matched his reader's goal, which was to plan the advertising strategies he would use later in the year when he began placing ads in the three journals.

Like formal classification, informal classification enables you to organize communications in a way that achieves the following goals (page 230).

- Every item has a place.
- Every item has only one place.
- The groupings are useful to your readers.

GUIDELINES FOR INFORMAL CLASSIFICATION

1. **Group your items in a way that is suited to your readers and your purpose.** Calvin organized his analysis around "type of advertising appeal" because he knew his employer was looking for advice about the design of ads.

2. **Create logically parallel groups.** For instance, if you were classifying advertisements, you wouldn't organize into groups like this:

   Focus on price
   Focus on established reputation
   Focus on advantages over a competitor's product
   Focus on one of the product's key features
   Focus on several of the product's key features

   The last two categories are at a lower hierarchical level than the other three. To make the categories parallel, you could combine them in the following way:

   Focus on price
   Focus on established reputation
   Focus on advantages over a competitor's product
   Focus on the product's key features
       Focus on one key feature
       Focus on several key features

Learn More

The informal classification pattern is often combined with other patterns. See page 254.

Informal Classification (continued)

3. **Avoid overlap among groups.** Even when you cannot use strict logic in classifying items, strive to provide one and only one place for each item. To do this, you must avoid overlap among categories. For example, in the following list the last item overlaps the others because photographs can be used in any of the other types of advertisements listed.

> Focus on price
> Focus on established reputation
> Focus on advantages over a competitor's product
> Focus on the product's key features
> Use of photographs

Table Organized Using Informal Classification

In the following table, the writer used informal classification to organize advice about preventing identity theft.

The types of identity theft described in this table are organized using informal classification.

- There is not a consistent principle of classification. Most of the categories describe what is stolen (e.g., your social security number). The last two describe the means used to steal.

- There is overlap among some of the categories. For example, a thief can use a stolen social security number to open a credit card account in your name.

Remember that informal classification is not a flaw. Communications organized by informal classification can be very useful.

PROTECT YOURSELF FROM IDENTITY THEFT		
Type of Theft	**What Thieves Do**	**Protection**
Social Security Number	■ Open credit card accounts in your name ■ Obtain loans in your name	■ Give your number only to businesses you know and trust ■ Ask to give an alternative identifier when your SS number is requested
Credit Cards	■ Steal your wallet or purse ■ Intercept information when you are buying online ■ Create fraudulent online businesses ■ Steal preapproved credit card offers mailed to you	■ Check companies with the Better Business Bureau before buying online ■ Use a secure web browser to buy online
Checks	■ Steal your checks or checking account number from your home or office	■ Notify your bank immediately if your checks are stolen
Cellular Telephone Service	■ Open telephone service in your name ■ Use your calling card and PIN to make calls	■ If this occurs, immediately ask your service provider to close your account, and establish another one with a new PIN.
Internet Account Updates	■ Send phony e-mail requesting your credit card information to update or verify a company's records	■ Check with your Internet Service Provider before responding to such a request
Phony Identity Theft Protections Services	■ Request personal information in order to "protect" you	■ Check out the company with the Better Business Bureau before giving personal information

Based on Chicago Better Business Bureau, www.chicago.bbb.org/idtheft/typesof.html.

Outline of Report Organized Using Informal Classification

The outline below shows how three writers used informal classification to organize their report on the ways to identify water plants that might be cultivated, harvested, and dried to serve as fuel for power generators. They organized each section around topics that would be most important to the specialists who would read that section.

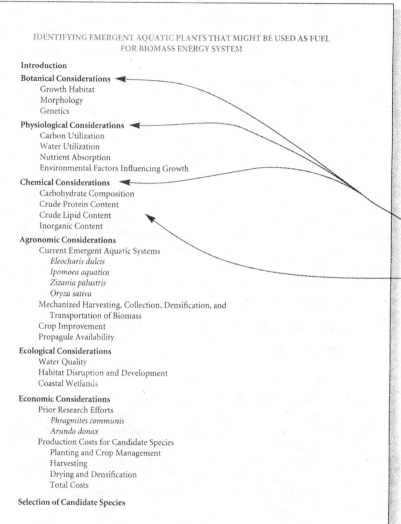

IDENTIFYING EMERGENT AQUATIC PLANTS THAT MIGHT BE USED AS FUEL FOR BIOMASS ENERGY SYSTEM

Introduction
Botanical Considerations
    Growth Habitat
    Morphology
    Genetics
Physiological Considerations
    Carbon Utilization
    Water Utilization
    Nutrient Absorption
    Environmental Factors Influencing Growth
Chemical Considerations
    Carbohydrate Composition
    Crude Protein Content
    Crude Lipid Content
    Inorganic Content
Agronomic Considerations
    Current Emergent Aquatic Systems
        Eleocharis dulcis
        Ipomoea aquatica
        Zizania palustris
        Oryza sativa
    Mechanized Harvesting, Collection, Densification, and Transportation of Biomass
    Crop Improvement
    Propagule Availability
Ecological Considerations
    Water Quality
    Habitat Disruption and Development
    Coastal Wetlands
Economic Considerations
    Prior Research Efforts
        Phragmites communis
        Arundo donax
    Production Costs for Candidate Species
        Planting and Crop Management
        Harvesting
        Drying and Densification
        Total Costs
Selection of Candidate Species

To see other communications that use informal classification, go to Writer's Reference Guide: Using Seven Organizational Patterns at **www.thomsonedu.com/english/anderson.**

The writers used informal classification to organize the report outlined here. In each section, they included information relevant to one specialty area: botanists, physiologists, chemists, and so on. The writers also used informal classification to organize the subsections.

Learn More

Exercises for organizing with informal classification are at the book's website and on page 255.

Comparison

对 比

At work, people write comparisons often, usually for one of the following reasons:

- **To help readers make a decision.** The workplace is a world of choices. People are constantly choosing among courses of action, competing products, alternative strategies. To help them choose, employees often compare the options in writing.
- **To help readers understand research findings.** Much workplace research focuses on differences and similarities between two or more items or groups—of people, animals, climates, chemicals, and so on. To explain the findings of this kind of research, researchers organize their results as comparisons.

Two Patterns for Organizing Comparisons

In some ways, comparison is like classification (page 230). You begin with a large set of facts about the things you are comparing, and you group the facts around points of comparison that enable your readers to see how the things are like and unlike one another. In comparisons written to support decision-making, points of comparison are called criteria.

When writing a comparison, you can choose either of two organizational patterns. Both include the same contents but arrange the contents differently.

Consider, for example, Lorraine's situation. Lorraine's employer has decided to replace the aging machines it uses to stamp out metal parts for the bodies of large trucks. Lorraine has been assigned to investigate the two machines the company is considering. Having amassed hundreds of pages of information, she must now decide how to organize her report to the company's executives. For organizing her comparison, Lorraine can choose the divided pattern or the alternating pattern.

> **Learn More**
>
> A point of comparison is very much like a principle of classification. See the section on "Formal Classification," page 230.

DIVIDED PATTERN	ALTERNATING PATTERN
Machine A	**Cost**
Cost	Machine A
Efficiency	Machine B
Construction Time	**Efficiency**
Air Pollution	Machine A
Et cetera	Machine B
Machine B	**Construction Time**
Cost	Machine A
Efficiency	Machine B
Construction Time	**Air Pollution**
Air Pollution	Machine A
Et cetera	Machine B
	Et Cetera
	Machine A
	Machine B

When To Use Each Pattern

To make a reader-centered choice between the alternating and divided patterns, consider the way your readers will use your information. Because the alternating pattern is organized around the criteria, it is ideal when readers want to make point-by-point comparisons among alternatives. Lorraine should select this pattern so her readers can find the information about the costs, capabilities, and other characteristics of both stamping machines in one place. The divided pattern would separate the information about each machine into different sections, requiring her readers to flip back and forth to compare the machines in detail.

The divided pattern is well suited to situations where readers want to read all the information about each alternative in one place. Typically, this occurs when both the general nature and the details of each alternative can be described in a short space—say, one page or so. An acoustical engineer used the divided pattern to provide a restaurant manager with information about three sound systems for her business. He described each system in a single page.

Whether you use the alternating or divided pattern, you can usually assist your readers by incorporating two kinds of preliminary information:

- **Description of the criteria.** This information lets your readers know from the start what the relevant points of comparison are.
- **Overview of the alternatives.** This information provides your readers with a general sense of what each alternative entails before they focus on the details you provide.

In both patterns, the statement of criteria would precede the presentation of details.

Taking these additional elements into account, the general structure of the two patterns is as follows:

DIVIDED PATTERN	ALTERNATING PATTERN
Statement of Criteria	Statement of Criteria
Overview of Alternatives	Overview of Alternatives
Evaluation of Alternatives	Evaluation of Alternatives
Alternative A	Criterion 1
Criterion 1	Alternative A
Criterion 2	Alternative B
Alternative B	Criterion 2
Criterion 1	Alternative A
Criterion 2	Alternative B
Conclusion	Conclusion

Comparison (continued)

Learn More

The comparison pattern is often combined with other patterns. See page 254.

Learn More

For advice about constructing graphics, go to Chapter 12 (page 325) and the Writer's Reference Guide: Creating Eleven Types of Graphics (page 351.).

GUIDELINES FOR USING COMPARISONS

1. **Choose points of comparison suited to your readers and purpose.** When helping readers understand something, focus on major points, not minor ones. When helping readers make a decision, choose criteria that truly make a difference.

2. **Discuss each alternative in terms of all your criteria or points of comparison.** If no information is available concerning some aspect of one alternative, tell your readers. Otherwise, they may assume that you didn't try to obtain it.

3. **Arrange the parts in an order your readers will find helpful.** Often, you can help most by discussing the most significant differences first. Sometimes, it's best to briefly mention criteria on which the alternatives are very similar so that readers can then focus on the criteria that make a difference. In comparisons designed to aid understanding, it's usually best to begin with what's familiar to your readers and then lead them to the less familiar.

4. **Include graphics if they will help your readers understand and use your communication.** Tables, graphs, diagrams, and drawings can be especially helpful.

Graphics in Comparisons

Writers often use tables and graphs to help readers compare alternatives and make decisions. The website below helps vacationers pick a campground in New South Wales, Australia.

In this table, the points of comparison are

- fees
- facilities
- types of camping available

By using icons rather than words, the writers help their readers read this table quickly.

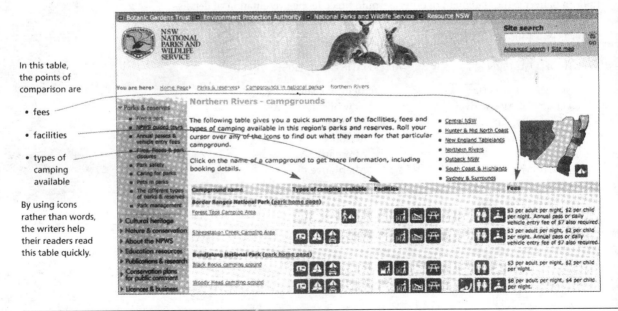

238   Writer's Reference Guide   **Using Seven Reader-Centered Organizational Patterns**

Research Findings Organized By Comparison

In the following memo, the writer uses the alternating pattern of comparison to help a decision-maker choose among three alternatives.

> To see other communications that explain about comparison relationships, go to Writer's Reference Guide: Using Seven Organizational Patterns at www.thomsonedu.com/english/anderson.

AdvanceTech
Memorandum

To   Mehash Mehta
From   Kenneth Abney
Date   September 10, 2006

Subject   **Recommendations for Smart Phone Purchase**

Last week, Marisol de Silva asked me to provide you with a comparison of the top "smart" phones (cell phones that also serve as hand-held computers). He explained that AdvancedTech might purchase smart phones for all 27 sales representatives and all 140 installation and service technicians.

I have studied product capabilities and published reviews for the three smart phones that received the highest ratings by *PCWorld* magazine: PalmOne Treo 600; T-Mobile Sidekick, and BlackBerry 7210/7230.

— Kenneth explains his research method, including the method by which he chose the smart-phones to compare.

All three provide high quality phone service and comparable computing capabilities. The key criteria for selection are ease of use and the ability to meet potential needs created by possible future expansion of our business. Here are my recommendations:

— Kenneth begins his comparison by explaining what all three alternatives have in common.

- If we continue to do business in North America only, the PalmOne Treo is our best choice. Offering both a stylus and thumb keyboards along with a brilliant screen and speakerphone, it is the easiest to use. It is the only one that provides an expansion slot, so that it can be adapted to additional uses. These features offset its high price.

— Kenneth makes two recommendations, one for each of two possible situations.

- If we will soon open offices outside North America, the BlackBerrry 7230 would be preferable. It supports the Global System for Mobile Communication (GSM) used elsewhere in the world.

The following table compares the phones in detail. If you want more information, please let me know.

	RAM	Input	Resolution	Expansion	Speakerphone	GSM	Price
PalmOne Treo 600	24 MB	Stylus Thumb keyboard	160 x 160	SD Slot	Yes	No	$600
T-Mobile Sidekick	32 MB	Thumb keyboard	240 x 460	No	No	No	$250
BlackBerry 7230	16 MB	Thumb keyboard	240 x 160	No	No	Yes	$400

— He provides his reader with additional detail in an easy-to-read table.

Learn More

Exercises for writing comparisons are at the book's website and on page 255.

Comparison   239

Description of an Object (Partitioning)

描述一个物体（分割）

In your career, you will have many occasions to describe a physical object for your readers. If you write about an experiment, you may need to describe your equipment. If you write instructions, you may need to describe the machines your readers will be using. If you propose a new purchase, you may need to describe the object you want to buy.

To organize descriptions, use a strategy called partitioning. Partitioning uses the same basic procedure as does classifying (page 230). Think of the object as a collection of parts. Then identify a principle of classification for organizing the parts into groups of related parts. At work, the principle most useful to your readers will usually be location or function.

> **Learn More**
>
> For more on principles of classification, see the section on "Formal Classification," page 230.

Example: Partitioning a Car

Consider, for instance, how you could use location and function to organize a discussion of the parts of a car.

To organize by location, you might talk about the car's interior (passenger compartment, trunk), exterior (front, back, sides, and top), engine compartment, and underside (wheels, transmission, and muffler).

To organize by function, you might focus on parts that provide power and ones that guide the car. The power-producing parts are in several locations: The gas pedal is in the passenger compartment, the engine is under the hood, and the transmission and axle are on the underside. Nevertheless, you would discuss them together because they are related by function.

Of course, other principles of classification are possible.

> **Learn More**
>
> The partitioning pattern is often combined with other patterns. See page 254.

GUIDELINES FOR DESCRIBING AN OBJECT

1. **Choose a principle of classification suited to your readers and purpose.** For instance, when describing a car for new owners who want to learn about the vehicle they've purchased, you might organize according to location. Your readers would learn about the conveniences in the passenger compartment, trunk, and so on. In contrast, when describing the car for auto repair specialists, you could organize according to function or the kinds of problems they might encounter.

2. **Use only one basis for partitioning at a time.** To assure that you have one place and only one place for each part you describe, use only one basis for partitioning at a time, just as you use only one principle of classification at a time (see page 230).

3. **Arrange the parts of your description in a way your readers will find useful.** When partitioning by location, you might move systematically from left to right, front to back, or outside to inside. When partitioning by function, you might trace the order in which the parts interact during a process that interests your readers.

> **Learn More**
>
> Exercises for organizing with partitioning are at the book's website and on page 255.

4. **When describing each part, provide details that your readers will find useful.** For instance, when describing a car tire to a consumer, you might describe the air pressure the tires should have. When describing the same tire to an engineer, you might provide a technical description of the steel belts in the tire's core.
5. **Include graphics if they will help your readers understand and use your information about the object.** Graphics that are especially helpful to readers of a description of an object include drawings, diagrams, and photographs.

> **Learn More**
>
> For advice about constructing graphics, go to Chapter 12 (page 325) and the Writer's Reference Guide: Creating 13 Types of Graphics (page 351).

Description Organized by Partitioning

This description of new technologies for airplanes is organized by partitioning.

ADAPTIVE AIRCRAFT WINGS

In an effort to increase fuel efficiency, scientists at Daimler-Chrysler and the German Aerospace Research Center are experimenting with an "adaptive wing" that can change its geometry automatically during flight. The wing has four major components.

> To see other communications that use partitioning, go to Writer's Reference Guide: Seven Organizational Patterns at **www.thomsonedu.com/english/anderson.**

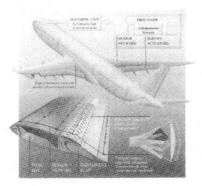

This description is partitioned according to function.

- The sensors gather information.

- **Sensor Network** Dozens of sensors located at widely differing points under the wing skin monitor airflow, laminar flow length, and pressure distribution.

- **Processor** Using information from the sensors, a special computer processor calculates the ideal geometry for the wing, taking into account the plane's speed, altitude, and weight.

- The processor analyzes the information.

- **Intelligent Flap** Located at the rear of a wing, the intelligent flap extends to the length calculated by the processor. Also, the flap's trailing edge can be changed to "tune" the flap to meet the demands of specific flight conditions. These adjustments to the flap enable the wings to provide maximum lift with minimum drag in all flight situations.

- The processor sends instructions to the intelligent flap and the adjustable contour region.

- **Adjustable Contour Region** Responding to signals from the processor, actuators in a region of the wing's upper surface can thicken or smooth the wing's surface. These adjustments can increase the wing's aerodynamic efficiency by weakening the effect of the "compression wave" that exerts drag when it forms at the leading edge of the wing.

Description of a Process (Segmenting)

描述一个过程（分段）

A description of a process explains the relationship of events over time. You may have either of two purposes in describing a process:

- To enable your readers to perform the process. For example, you may be writing instructions that will enable your readers to analyze the chemicals present in a sample of liver tissue, make a photovoltaic cell, apply for a loan, or run a computer program.
- To enable your readers to understand the process. For example, you might want your readers to understand the following:
    - How something is done. For instance, how coal is transformed into synthetic diamonds.
    - How something works. For instance, how the lungs provide oxygen to the bloodstream.
    - How something happened. For instance, how the United States developed the space programs that eventually landed astronauts on the moon.

In either case, you need to help your readers understand the overall structure of the process. To do this, you segment the process. Imagine the entire process as a long line or string of steps. Divide the process (or cut the string) into segments at points where one major group of related steps ends and another begins. If some or all of the major groups are large, you may divide them into subgroups, thereby creating an organizational hierarchy. The outline on the right shows how you might segment the steps in the process for building a cabinet.

> **Making a Cabinet**
> Obtaining Materials
> Preparing the Pieces
>   Cutting the wood
>   Routing the wood
> Assembling the Cabinet
>   Building the base
>   Mounting the doors
> Finishing the Cabinet
>   Sanding
>   Applying the stain
>   Applying the sealant

Principles of Classification for Segmenting

To determine where to segment the process, you need a principle of classification. Commonly used principles include the time when the steps are performed (first day, second day; spring, summer, fall), the purpose of the steps (to prepare the equipment, to examine the results), and the tools used to perform the steps (for example, table saw, drill press, and so on).

Processes can be segmented by a variety of classification principles. Pick the principle that best supports your readers' goals. For instance, if you were writing a history of the process by which the United States placed a person on the moon, you would segment the process according to the passage of various laws and appropriation bills if your readers were members of the US Congress. If your readers are scientists and engineers, however, you might focus on efforts to overcome various technical problems.

Learn More

For more on principles of classification, see the section on "Formal Classification," page 230.

GUIDELINES FOR SEGMENTING

1. **Choose a principle for segmenting suited to your readers and your purpose.** If you are writing instructions, group the steps in ways that support an efficient or comfortable rhythm of work. If you want to help your readers understand a process, organize around concerns that are of interest or use to them.
2. **Make your smallest groupings manageable.** If your smallest groupings include too many steps or too few, your readers will not see the process as a structured hierarchy of activities or events but rather as a long, unstructured list of steps—first one, then the next, and so on.
3. **Describe clearly the relationships among the steps and groups of steps.** To understand and remember the process, readers need to understand how the parts fit together. Where the relationships among the groups of steps will be obvious to your readers, simply provide informative headings. At other times, you will need to explain the relationships in introductory statements, transitions between groups of steps, and, perhaps, in a summary at the end.
4. **Provide enough detail about each step to meet your readers' needs.** Use your understanding of your readers and the ways they will use your communication to determine the appropriate level of detail.
5. **Include graphics if they will help your readers understand and use your information about the process.** Graphics that are especially helpful to readers of a description of a process are diagrams, drawings, photographs, and flowcharts.

Learn More
The segmenting pattern is often combined with other patterns. See page 254.

Learn More
For advice about constructing graphics, go to Chapter 12 (page 325) and the Writer's Reference Guide: Creating 13 Types of Graphics (page 351.).

A Graphic Organized by Segmenting a Process

In the flowchart below, writers at Lawrence Livermore National Laboratory explained the five-step process by which lasers are used to create nuclear fission.

Three hundred million watts of laser energy is projected into a small container that holds a spherical fusion-fuel capsule.	Reflecting from the container's specially coated walls, the laser beams are converted to x-rays that create a 3-million-degree oven.	The heat energy implodes the fusion-fuel cell to 20 times the density of lead.	The fuel core ignites at 100 million kelvins.	A thermonuclear burn spreads through the fuel, creating gain equivalent to the power of miniature star lasting less than a billionth of a second.

The text explains the steps in the process.

The drawings illustrate each step.

Description of a Process (Segmenting) 243

Description of a Process (continued)

Instructions Organized by Segmenting a Process

The pages shown below are from instructions for using a computerized telescope that automatically points to a star or constellation specified by the operator. They are segmented according to the major groups of steps in the process: setting it up, activating the computer, entering the date and location, and so on. See more examples of instructions organized by segmenting on pages 661 and 666.

To see other communications that use segmenting, go to Writer's Reference Guide: Using Seven Organizational Patterns at **www.thomsonedu.com/english/anderson.**

As the headings on these pages indicate, the writers have organized this instruction manual by segmenting the overall process of setting up and using the telescope.

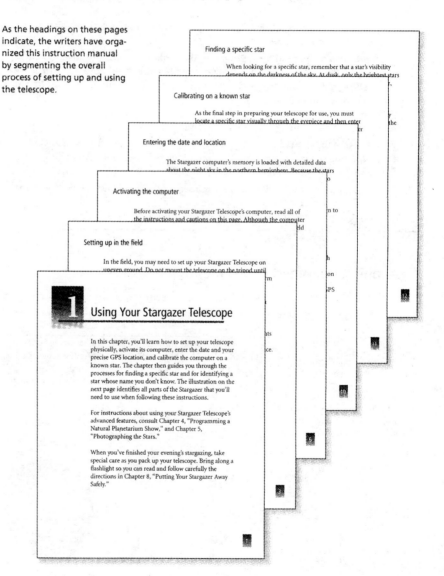

244   Writer's Reference Guide   **Using Seven Reader-Centered Organizational Patterns**

Explanation Organized by Segmenting a Process

In the following passage, the writer describes one theory about the way planets were formed. Notice how the writer uses headings to signal the major phases of the process.

How Planets Are Formed

Theoretical astrophysicists have developed an elaborate model describing the formation of stars like our Sun. In this theory, planet formation is a natural and almost necessary result of the process of star formation. *— The topic is introduced.*

A Proto-Star Is Born
These astrophysicists believe that the process of star formation begins when a dense region of gas and dust in an interstellar cloud becomes gravitationally unstable. The cloud begins a slow, quasistatic contraction as both its internal turbulent and magnetic support are gradually lost through cooling and the outward diffusion of the magnetic field. The core of this cloud condenses to form a proto-star. *— First stage is described.*

If there is sufficient angular momentum, the collapsing cloud may fragment into two or more smaller pieces, thus leading to the formation of a binary or multiple star. *— Alternative outcomes are identified.*

A Rotating Disc Forms
The remaining gas and dust from the cloud continue to fall inwards. Because this material must conserve the initial angular momentum of the cloud, it forms into a rotating disc around the proto-star in accordance with Kepler's laws, with the inner portion of the disc rotating more rapidly than the outer region. *— Second stage is described. Headings help to distinguish the stages.*

Planets Are Created
The process of planet formation occurs within this rotating disc. Dust grains collide and stick together, forming larger particles. This collisional growth continues over millions of years and eventually results in the creation of rocky bodies a few kilometers in diameter, known as "planetesimals." At this point the gravitational attraction of the planetesimals begins to dominate their random velocities, increasing their growth rate to the point where planetary cores about a thousand kilometers across can form rapidly. *— Third stage is described in two parts, with separate paragraphs devoted to planetesimals and to planets.*

As the proto-planetary disc continues to evolve, the planetary cores in the inner portion of the disc collide, merge and grow to become terrestrial planets such as Earth and Mars. In the outer disc, the cores grow to larger masses. Once the planetary core reaches about 10 Earth masses, its gravity is sufficient to capture gaseous hydrogen and helium from the disc, forming a gas-giant planet such as Jupiter or Saturn. This rapid-growth phase removes most of the material near the orbit of the growing planet, forming a gap in the disc and effectively shutting off the growth process.

Thus, scientists think that planets are built from their cores outward by accretion processes in the disc of gas and dust that surrounds a star during its creation. *— A concluding sentence summarizes the overall process.*

Learn More
Exercises for writing about segmenting are at the book's website and on page 255.

Description of a Process (Segmenting)

Cause and Effect

原因和结果

Questions about cause and effect are very common in the workplace. Profits slumped or skyrocketed. What caused the change? The number of children diagnosed with autism is increasing. How come? If we clear underbrush from forest floors, how will our action affect animal habitats and the severity of forest fires??

At work, you are likely to write about cause and effect for one of two distinct purposes.

- to help your readers understand a cause-and-effect relationship.
- to persuade your readers that a certain cause-and-effect relationship exists.

The strategies for organizing for these two purposes are somewhat different.

Helping Readers Understand a Cause-and-Effect Relationship

Some cause-and-effect relationships are accepted by people knowledgeable about the topic but need to be explained to those who are not.

For instance, geologists agree about what causes the Old Faithful geyser in the United States' Yellowstone National Park to erupt so regularly. However, many park visitors do not know. Consequently, the park publishes brochures that explain the cause.

Depending on your profession, you may need to explain cause-and-effect relationships to members of the general public; to employees in your own organization, such as coworkers or executives outside your specialty; or to other readers. The following reader-centered guidelines will help you do so effectively in any situation.

> **Learn More**
>
> The cause-and-effect pattern is often combined with other patterns. See page 254.

> **Learn More**
>
> For advice about constructing graphics, go to Chapter 12 (page 325) and the Writer's Reference Guide: Creating Eleven Types of Graphics (page 351).

GUIDELINES FOR EXPLAINING A CAUSE-AND-EFFECT RELATIONSHIP

1. **Begin by identifying the cause or effect that you are going to explain.** Let your readers know from the beginning exactly what you are going to explain. This advance notice will help them better understand what follows.
2. **Carefully explain the links that join the cause and effect that you are describing.** Remember that you are not simply listing the steps in a process. You want your readers to understand how each step leads to the next one.
3. **If you are dealing with several causes or effects, group them into categories.** Categories help readers to understand a complex set of factors.
4. **Include graphics if they will help your readers understand the relationship you are explaining.** Among the many kinds of graphics that assist readers in visualizing cause-and-effect relationships are those used to describe processes, including flowcharts, diagrams, and drawings.

Sample Explanation of Cause and Effect

The following passage uses a cause-and-effect relationship to explain how CD's work.

How Light Makes Music

When you listen to your favorite songs on a CD, you are enjoying the music that light makes.

Your CD has three layers. On the bottom is a stiff, protective layer of acrylic. Next is a thin layer of reflective aluminum, which is coated with a clear plastic layer that is 1.2 mm thick. Your CD player projects a shaft of light, in the form of a laser beam, at a tiny spot on the reflective aluminum. As your CD spins, the player reads the variations in the intensity of the light that is reflected from the aluminum.

What causes the intensity of the reflected light to vary? Although a CD seems smooth, its ability to make music depends on millions of pits in the clear plastic layer. Only about 0.5 microns deep and several microns long, they are burned into the aluminum side of the clear plastic layer when the CD is manufactured. Despite being "clear," the plastic layer absorbs some light. It absorbs less where the pits are because the plastic is thinner there. As a CD spins, areas with and without pits pass rapidly under the CD player's laser beam. By reading the variations in the intensity of the reflected light, the CD player makes music.

A Laser Puts Music on a CD by Creating Pits in the
Aluminum Side of the Clear Plastic Layer

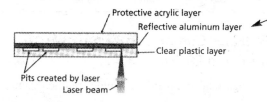

This passage explains how a CD player reads music from a CD. The same technology is used for DVDs.

This paragraph provides background that helps readers understand the cause-and-effect explanation given in the next paragraph.

In this explanation, the effect (variations in the intensity of light) is described first. The explanation follows. In other cause-and-effect passages, the order is reversed.

Many kinds of graphics are used with explanations of cause and effect. In this case, the author uses a diagram to provide a visual description of the process by which pits that "make" the music are created on a CD.

Persuading Readers that a Cause-and-Effect Relationship Exists

About many events, people disagree. They may disagree about past events, such as what caused damage to a jet engine's turbine blade or what caused the disappearance of the Inca civilization in Central America. Alternatively, they may disagree about the future. Examples include disagreements about the effects of growing genetically modified crops or the effect on sales that a proposed price reduction would have on company profits.

Whether you are writing about causes of a past event or the effects of a future action, your goal is to persuade your readers to accept your explanation. The guidelines on the next page will help you argue persuasively, as will the guidelines in Chapter 5, "Planning Your Persuasive Strategies."

Cause and Effect (continued)

> **GUIDELINES FOR PERSUADING READERS TO ACCEPT YOUR VIEW OF CAUSE AND EFFECT**
>
> 1. **State your claim at the beginning of your passage.** By letting them know your claim in advance, you will help them see—and evaluate—the way your evidence supports the claim.
> 2. **Choose evidence your readers will find credible.** As explained in Chapter 5, different kinds of evidence are credible in different situations and industries. You will have to understand your readers in order to determine whether data, expert testimony, or some other form of evidence will be most persuasive for them.
> 3. **Explain your line of reasoning.** The heart of your explanation is the links you draw between the cause or effect you are discussing. Explain them thoroughly.
> 4. **Avoid faulty logic.** If your readers find your logic to be faulty, they will reject your explanation. See below for descriptions of two logical fallacies that are common in arguments concerning cause and effect.
> 5. **Address counterarguments.** To persuade readers to accept your account of a cause-and-effect relationship, you must persuade them to reject alternative explanations. Therefore, you need to identify the other explanations they might consider and explain why yours is better.
> 6. **Include graphics if they will help your readers understand the relationship you are discussing.** Graphics used to describe processes, such as flowcharts, diagrams, and drawings, can be very helpful.

Learn More
For more advice about persuading readers, see Chapter 5, "Planning Your Persuasive Strategies," page 118.

Learn More
For advice about constructing graphics, go to Chapter 12 (page 325) and the Writer's Reference Guide: Creating Eleven Types of Graphics (page 351).

Logical Fallacies Common in Arguments about Cause and Effect

The following logical fallacies can undermine arguments about cause and effect.

- **Post hoc, ergo propter hoc fallacy.** This fallacy occurs when a writer argues that because an event occurred after another event, it was caused by that event. For example, in an attempt to persuade his employer, a furniture company, to switch to computerized machinery, Samuel argued that a competitor's profits had risen substantially after making that switch. Samuel's boss pointed out that the competitor's sales increase may have been caused by other changes made at the same time, such as creation of new designs or reconfiguration of sales districts. Samuel's commission of this fallacy didn't mean he was incorrect. However, to persuade his boss that computerization had caused the sales increase, Samuel needed to do more than simply state that it had preceded the increase.
- **Overgeneralization.** Writers overgeneralize when they draw conclusions on insufficient evidence. For instance, writers overgeneralize if they draw a conclusion about the causes of a manufacturing error after examining only 2 percent of the faulty products.

Sample Passage Persuading about a Cause-and-Effect Relationship

In the following passage about the death of the dinosaurs, the writer applies the guidelines for persuading about cause and effect.

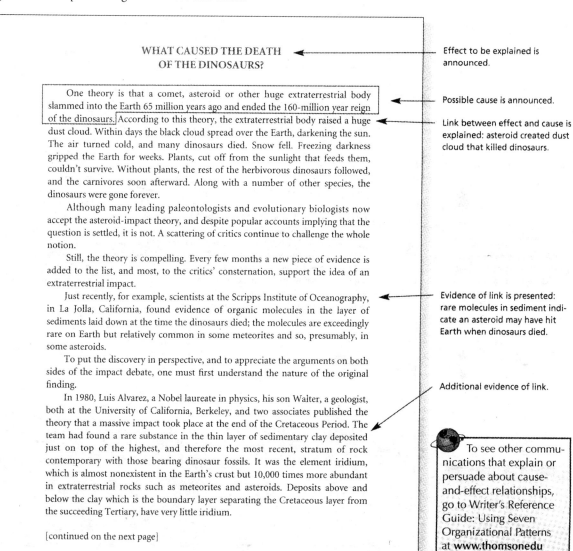

WHAT CAUSED THE DEATH OF THE DINOSAURS?

— Effect to be explained is announced.

One theory is that a comet, asteroid or other huge extraterrestrial body slammed into the Earth 65 million years ago and ended the 160-million year reign of the dinosaurs. According to this theory, the extraterrestrial body raised a huge dust cloud. Within days the black cloud spread over the Earth, darkening the sun. The air turned cold, and many dinosaurs died. Snow fell. Freezing darkness gripped the Earth for weeks. Plants, cut off from the sunlight that feeds them, couldn't survive. Without plants, the rest of the herbivorous dinosaurs followed, and the carnivores soon afterward. Along with a number of other species, the dinosaurs were gone forever.

— Possible cause is announced.

— Link between effect and cause is explained: asteroid created dust cloud that killed dinosaurs.

Although many leading paleontologists and evolutionary biologists now accept the asteroid-impact theory, and despite popular accounts implying that the question is settled, it is not. A scattering of critics continue to challenge the whole notion.

Still, the theory is compelling. Every few months a new piece of evidence is added to the list, and most, to the critics' consternation, support the idea of an extraterrestrial impact.

Just recently, for example, scientists at the Scripps Institute of Oceanography, in La Jolla, California, found evidence of organic molecules in the layer of sediments laid down at the time the dinosaurs died; the molecules are exceedingly rare on Earth but relatively common in some meteorites and so, presumably, in some asteroids.

— Evidence of link is presented: rare molecules in sediment indicate an asteroid may have hit Earth when dinosaurs died.

To put the discovery in perspective, and to appreciate the arguments on both sides of the impact debate, one must first understand the nature of the original finding.

— Additional evidence of link.

In 1980, Luis Alvarez, a Nobel laureate in physics, his son Walter, a geologist, both at the University of California, Berkeley, and two associates published the theory that a massive impact took place at the end of the Cretaceous Period. The team had found a rare substance in the thin layer of sedimentary clay deposited just on top of the highest, and therefore the most recent, stratum of rock contemporary with those bearing dinosaur fossils. It was the element iridium, which is almost nonexistent in the Earth's crust but 10,000 times more abundant in extraterrestrial rocks such as meteorites and asteroids. Deposits above and below the clay which is the boundary layer separating the Cretaceous layer from the succeeding Tertiary, have very little iridium.

[continued on the next page]

To see other communications that explain or persuade about cause-and-effect relationships, go to Writer's Reference Guide: Using Seven Organizational Patterns at www.thomsonedu.com/english/anderson.

Cause and Effect (continued)

Sample Passage Persuading about a Cause-and-Effect Relationship (continued)

Additional evidence continued. → Because the same iridium anomaly appeared in two other parts of the world, in clay of exactly the same age, the Alvarez team proposed that the element had come from an asteroid that hit the Earth with enough force to vaporize, scattering iridium atoms in the atmosphere worldwide. When the iridium settled to the ground, it was incorporated in sediment laid down at the time.

Link is restated. → More startling was the team's proposal that the impact blasted so much dust into the atmosphere that it blocked the sunlight and prevented photosynthesis (others suggested that a global freeze would also have resulted). They calculated that the object would have had to be about six miles in diameter.

Additional evidence of link. → Since 1980, iridium anomalies have been found in more than 80 places around the world, including deep-sea cores, all in layers of sediment that formed at the same time.

Challenge to link is explained: molecules perhaps from volcano, not asteroid. → One of the most serious challenges to the extraterrestrial theory came up very quickly. Critics said that the iridium could have come from volcanic eruptions, which are known to bring up iridium from deep within the Earth and feed it into the atmosphere. Traces of iridium have been detected in gases escaping from Hawaii's Kilauea volcano, for example.

Challenge is refuted by new evidence: other molecules couldn't have come from volcano. → The new finding from Scripps appears to rule out that explanation, though, as a source for iridium in the Cretaceous–Tertiary (K–T) boundary layer. Chemists Jeffrey Bada and Nancy Lee have found that the same layer also contains a form of amino acid that is virtually nonexistent on Earth—certainly entirely absent from volcanoes—but abundant, along with many other organic compounds, in a type of meteor called a carbonaceous chondrite.

Learn More

Exercises for writing about cause and effect are at the book's website and on page 256.

Problem and Solution

问题和解决方法

Problems and their solutions will be one of the most frequent topics of your on-the-job writing. The problems you discuss may arise from dissatisfaction with some strategy, product, process, or policy. Alternatively, they may arise from an aspiration to achieve a new goal, such as greater efficiency, or take advantage of a new opportunity, such as the potential to do business in another country. In either case, you will usually be writing proposals for future actions or reports on completed ones.

Proposing Future Action

In proposals to readers outside your organization, you will probably be seeking contracts worth thousands or even millions of dollars. Often, other individuals or organizations will be competing for the same contract. When writing proposals to readers inside your own organization, you might be urging support for a large research or development project or simply suggesting a small alteration in policy or procedure. Always, your goal will be to obtain support or approval for the problem-solving project you propose.

> **Learn More**
>
> Chapter 22 on "Writing Reader-Centered Proposals" provides additional information on organizing with the problem-and-solution pattern, which provides the overall structure for proposals.

GUIDELINES FOR PERSUADING READERS TO ACCEPT YOUR PROPOSED SOLUTION

1. **Describe the problem in a way that makes it seem significant to your readers.** Remember that your aim is to persuade them to take the action you recommend. They will not be very interested in taking action to solve a problem they regard as insignificant.
2. **Describe your method.** Readers want enough detail to feel confident that it is practical and technically sound. Depending on your reader and the situation, this might require a great deal of information or relatively little.
3. **When describing your method, explain how it will solve the problem.** Provide the evidence and reasoning needed to persuade your readers that your method will, in fact, solve their problem.
4. **Anticipate and respond to objections.** As when reading any persuasive segment, your readers may object to your evidence or your line of reasoning. Devote special attention to determining what those objections are so you can respond to them.
5. **Specify the benefit.** With as much specificity as will interest them, describe the benefits they and their organization will enjoy if they support or fund your proposed action.
6. **Include graphics if they will help your readers understand and approve your proposed solution.** Review opportunities to use graphics that can help your readers understand the problem and your proposed solution and that can highlight the benefits to your readers of supporting the action you propose. Among the graphics often used in problems and their solutions are tables, flowcharts, drawings, photographs, and diagrams.

> **Learn More**
>
> The problem-and-solution pattern is often combined with other patterns. See page 254.

Problem and Solution (continued)

Memo Proposing the Solution to a Problem

In the following memo, the writer uses the problem-and-solution strategy to recommend that her employer investigate the Kohle Reduktion method of steelmaking. Proposals for further study are common in the workplace.

🔍 To see other communications that explain or persuade about problem-and-solution relationships, go to Writer's Reference Guide: Using Seven Organizational Patterns at **www.thomsonedu.com/english/anderson.**

MANUFACTURING PROCESSES INSTITUTE
Interoffice Memorandum   June 21, 2006

To   Cliff Leibowitz
From   Candace Olin
RE   Suggestion to Investigate Kohle Reduktion Process for Steelmaking

As we have often discussed, it may be worthwhile to set up a project investigating steelmaking processes that could help the American industry compete more effectively with the more modern foreign mills. I suggest we begin with an investigation of the Kohle Reduktion method, which I learned about in the April 2005 issue of *High Technology*.

Problem is identified. → A major problem for American steelmakers is the process they use to make the molten iron ("hot metal") that is processed into steel. Relying on a technique

Problem is explained. → developed on a commercial scale over 100 years ago by Sir Henry Bessemer, they make the hot metal by mixing iron ore, limestone, and coke in blast furnaces. To make the coke, they pyrolize coal in huge ovens in plants that cost over $100 million and create enormous amounts of air pollution.

Solution is announced. → In the Kohle Reduktion method, developed by Korf Engineering in West Germany, the hot metal is made without coke. Coal, limestone, and oxygen are mixed in a gasification unit at 2500°. The gas rises in a shaft furnace above the

Solution is explained. → gasification unit, chemically reducing the iron ore to "sponge iron." The sponge iron then drops into the gasification unit, where it is melted and the contaminants are removed by reaction of the limestone. Finally, the hot metal drains out of the bottom of the gasifier.

Link between problem and solution is explained. → The Kohle method, if developed satisfactorily, will have several advantages. It will eliminate the air pollution problem of coke plants, it can be built (according to Korf estimates) for 25% less than conventional furnaces, and it may cut the cost of producing hot metal by 15%.

This technology appears to offer a dramatic solution to the problems with our nation's steel industry: I recommend that we investigate it further. If the method proves feasible and if we develop an expertise in it, we will surely attract many clients for our consulting services.

Learn More
Exercises for writing about problems and their solutions are at the book's website and on page 256.

Reporting on a Past Problem-Solving Project

Reports on past problem-solving projects are often used to teach other employees how to approach similar challenges. They are also used to demonstrate a company's capabilities in proposals.

GUIDELINES FOR DESCRIBING PROBLEMS AND THEIR SOLUTIONS

1. **Begin by identifying the problem.** Make the problem seem significant to your readers. Emphasize the aspects of the problem most directly affected by your solution.
2. **Describe your method.** Provide the details needed by your readers.
3. **Describe the results.** Enumerate the benefits produced. Tell what was learned.
4. **Include graphics that will help your readers understand and use your communication.**

Learn More

For advice about constructing graphics, go to Chapter 12 (page 325) and the Writer's Reference Guide: Creating 13 Types of Graphics (page 351).

Passage Reporting on a Past Problem-Solving Project

In the passage below, Rashid uses the problem-solution pattern of organization.

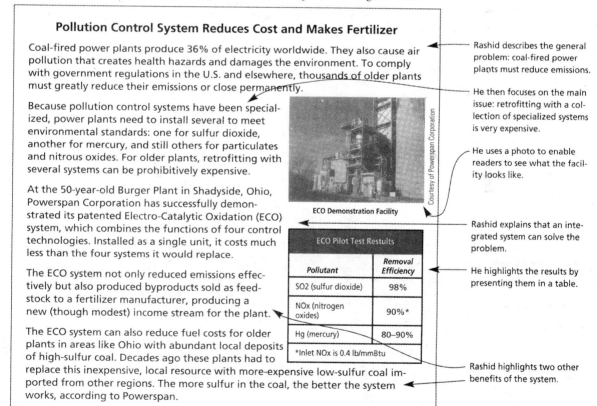

Pollution Control System Reduces Cost and Makes Fertilizer

Coal-fired power plants produce 36% of electricity worldwide. They also cause air pollution that creates health hazards and damages the environment. To comply with government regulations in the U.S. and elsewhere, thousands of older plants must greatly reduce their emissions or close permanently.

Because pollution control systems have been specialized, power plants need to install several to meet environmental standards: one for sulfur dioxide, another for mercury, and still others for particulates and nitrous oxides. For older plants, retrofitting with several systems can be prohibitively expensive.

At the 50-year-old Burger Plant in Shadyside, Ohio, Powerspan Corporation has successfully demonstrated its patented Electro-Catalytic Oxidation (ECO) system, which combines the functions of four control technologies. Installed as a single unit, it costs much less than the four systems it would replace.

The ECO system not only reduced emissions effectively but also produced byproducts sold as feedstock to a fertilizer manufacturer, producing a new (though modest) income stream for the plant.

The ECO system can also reduce fuel costs for older plants in areas like Ohio with abundant local deposits of high-sulfur coal. Decades ago these plants had to replace this inexpensive, local resource with more-expensive low-sulfur coal imported from other regions. The more sulfur in the coal, the better the system works, according to Powerspan.

ECO Demonstration Facility
Courtesy of Powerspan Corporation

ECO Pilot Test Results

Pollutant	Removal Efficiency
SO2 (sulfur dioxide)	98%
NOx (nitrogen oxides)	90%*
Hg (mercury)	80–90%

*Inlet NOx is 0.4 lb/mmBtu

- Rashid describes the general problem: coal-fired power plants must reduce emissions.
- He then focuses on the main issue: retrofitting with a collection of specialized systems is very expensive.
- He uses a photo to enable readers to see what the facility looks like.
- Rashid explains that an integrated system can solve the problem.
- He highlights the results by presenting them in a table.
- Rashid highlights two other benefits of the system.

Combinations of Patterns

模式合并

To see other communications that use combinations of patterns, go to Writer's Reference Guide: Using Seven Organizational Patterns at www.thomsonedu.com/english/anderson.

This Writer's Reference Guide describes seven organizational patterns in isolation from one another. In practice, you will almost always need to weave two or more together. In a short memo, for instance, you might describe a problem in two sentences, identify its causes in three more, briefly compare alternative solutions, and finally recommend one.

The outline below shows how six patterns were integrated in a 25-page feasibility report.

Like many technical communications, this report interweaves six organizational patterns.

To organize this part, the writers **classified** the companies according to their location.

They organized Chapter II around a **problem** and its possible **solution**.

When explaining why the solar cells collect heat, the writers organized by **cause and effect**.

The writers organized each of these subsections by **partitioning** the component into its major subparts.

They organized their discussion of the construction schedule by gathering the steps into related groups of steps (**segmenting** the process).

The writers used the divided pattern for **comparisons** in their section on cost.

Solar Roofs for New Restaurants
A Feasibility Report for the Brendon's Restaurant Chain

I. Introduction
   A. The Brendon's Restaurant commissioned us to determine the feasibility of covering its restaurant roofs with photovoltaic cells (solar cells) that generate electricity
   B. Background
      1. Brendon's builds 30 new restaurants a year
      2. Brendon's is committed to environmental responsibility
      3. Federal government has goal of one million solar roofs in the U.S. by 2010
      4. Experiences of other companies
         a. Europe
         b. Asia
         c. United States

II. Technical Assessment
   A. Problems
      1. Solar cells do not generate enough electricity to pay for themselves (though this technology is advancing rapidly)
      2. Solar cells collect heat, so additional power would be needed to cool the building
      3. Putting solar cells on top of the regular roof would add 15% to construction time
   B. Potential Solutions (Used by Applebee's Restaurant in Salisbury, North Carolina)
      1. Use the collected heat to preheat the large amount of water used by the restaurant
         a. Collect the heat under the solar cells (instead of venting it)
         b. Use electricity from the solar cells to power fans that blow hot air to the preheating system
      2. Use large solar panels that can serve as the roof itself

III. Components of System
   A. Structure of the Solar Panels
   B. Structure of the Heat Ducts
   C. Structure of the Water Heating System

IV. Construction Schedule

V. Cost Comparison

VI. Conclusion

EXERCISES 练 习

EXPERTISE

1. To choose the appropriate principle of classification for organizing a group of items, you need to consider your readers and your purpose. Here are three topics for classification, each with two possible readers. First, identify a purpose that each reader might have for consulting a communication on that topic. Then identify a principle of classification that would be appropriate for each reader and purpose.
   a. *Types of instruments or equipment used in your field*
      Student majoring in your field
      Director of purchasing in your future employer's organization
   b. *Intramural sports*
      Director of intramural sports at your college
      Student
   c. *Flowers*
      Florist
      Owner of a greenhouse that sells garden plants

2. Use a principle of classification to create a hierarchy having at least two levels. Some topics are suggested below. After you have selected a topic, identify a reader and a purpose for your classification. Depending on your instructor's request, show your hierarchy in an outline or use it to write a brief discussion of your topic. In either case, state your principle of classification.
   Have you created a hierarchy that, at each level, has one and only one place for every item?
   Boats   Computers
   Cameras   Physicians
   The skills you will need on the job
   Tools, instruments, or equipment you will use on the job
   Some groups of items used in your field (for example, rocks if you are a geologist, or power sources if you are an electrical engineer)

3. Partition an object in a way that will be helpful to someone who wants to use it. Some objects are suggested below. Whichever one you choose, describe a specific instance of it. For example, describe a particular brand and model of food processor rather than a generic food processor. Be sure that your hierarchy has at least two levels, and state the basis of partitioning you use at each level. Depending on your instructor's request, show your hierarchy in an outline or use it to write a brief discussion of your topic.

   Aqualung   Microwave oven
   Graphing calculator   Bicycle
   Some instrument or piece of equipment used in your field that has at least a dozen parts

4. Segment a procedure to create a hierarchy you could use in a set of instructions. Give it at least two levels. Some topics are listed below. Show the resulting hierarchy in an outline. Be sure to identify your readers and purpose. If your instructor requests, use the outline to write a set of instructions.
   Changing an automobile tire
   Making homemade yogurt
   Starting an aquarium
   Rigging a sailboat
   Developing a roll of film
   Some procedure used in your field that involves at least a dozen steps
   Some other procedure of interest to you that includes at least a dozen steps

5. Segment a procedure to create a hierarchy you could use in a general description of a process. Give it at least two levels. Some suggested topics are listed below. Show the resulting hierarchy in an outline. Be sure to identify your readers and purpose. If your instructor requests, use the outline to write a general description of the process addressed to someone unfamiliar with it.
   How the human body takes oxygen from the air and delivers it to the parts of the body where it is used
   How television signals from a program originating in New York or Los Angeles reach television sets in other parts of the country
   How aluminum is made
   Some process used in your field that involves at least a dozen steps
   Some other process of interest to you that includes at least a dozen steps

6. One of your friends is thinking about making a major purchase. Some possible items are listed below. Create an outline with at least two levels that compares two or more good alternatives. If your instructor requests, use that outline to write your friend a letter.
   Stereo   Computer
   Binoculars   Bicycle
   CD player
   Some other type of product for which you can make a meaningful comparison on at least three important points

7. Think of some way in which things might be done better in a club, business, or some other organization. Imagine that you are going to write a letter to the person who can bring about the change you are recommending. Create an outline with at least two levels in which you compare the way you think things should be done and the way they are being done now.

8. A friend has asked you to explain the causes of a particular event. Some events are suggested below. Write your friend a brief letter explaining the causes.
   Static on radios and televisions
   Immunization from a disease
   Freezer burn in foods
   Yellowing of paper

9. Think of a problem you feel should be corrected. The problem might be noise in your college library, shoplifting from a particular store, or the shortage of parking space on campus. Briefly describe the problem and list the actions you would take to solve it. Next, explain how each action will contribute to solving the problem. If your instructor requests, use your outline to write a brief memo explaining the problem and your proposed solution to a person who could take the actions you suggest.

Developing an Effective Style
形成有效的风格

8

GUIDELINES

GUIDELINES FOR CREATING YOUR VOICE
1. Find out what's expected *258*
2. Consider the roles your voice creates for your readers and you *260*
3. Consider how your attitude toward your subject will affect your readers *261*
4. Say things in your own words *261*
5. **Global Guideline:** Adapt your voice to your readers' cultural background *262*
6. **Ethics Guideline:** Avoid stereotypes *262*

GUIDELINES FOR CONSTRUCTING SENTENCES
1. Simplify your sentences *264*
2. Put the action in your verbs *265*
3. Use the active voice unless you have a good reason to use the passive voice *266*
4. Emphasize what's most important *267*
5. Vary your sentence length and structure *268*
6. **Global Guideline:** Adapt your sentences for readers who are not fluent in your language *269*

GUIDELINES FOR SELECTING WORDS
1. Use concrete, specific words *270*
2. Use specialized terms when—and only when—your readers will understand them *271*
3. Use words accurately *272*
4. Choose plain words over fancy ones *273*
5. Choose words with appropriate associations *274*
6. **Global Guideline:** Consider your readers' cultural background when choosing words *275*
7. **Ethics Guideline:** Use inclusive language *276*

CHAPTER 8

Defining Objectives
Planning
Drafting
Revising

When we talk about "writing style," we can mean any one of many things. For example, when we speak of Shakespeare's style or Jane Austen's style, we mean the features that make that person's writing unique. In contrast, when we speak of legal style or scientific style, we are referring to writing characteristics shared by certain groups of professional people, such as lawyers or scientists. We also use the word *style* to talk about a communication's readability and impact, saying that a communication is written in a clear or muddy style, an inspiring or boring style. We even use the word *style* to express judgments about the writer, not the writing, as when we say that a style is friendly or stuffy, relaxed or stiff, helpful or condescending.

At work, you must juggle all these dimensions of style at once, striving simultaneously to express your individuality, observe the stylistic conventions of your profession and your employer's organization, make reading easy for your readers, and create the impact you desire. The task isn't easy. These goals sometimes conflict. Furthermore, one style won't suit all occasions.

As you balance these various considerations, take the same reader-centered approach that you apply to every other aspect of your writing: Consider your options in light of the way they will affect your readers' view of your communication's usability and persuasiveness. By following this chapter's three sets of guidelines, you can develop expertise in making reader-centered decisions about the three major building blocks of writing style: voice, sentence structure, and word choice.

> To read additional information, see more examples, and access links related to this chapter's guidelines, go to Chapter 8 at www.thomsonedu.com/english/anderson.

CREATING YOUR VOICE
有自己的想法和见解

While reading something you've written, your readers "hear" your voice. Based on what they hear, they draw conclusions about you and your attitudes that can greatly enhance — or detract from — the persuasiveness of your communications. Consequently, the ability to craft and control your voice is an area of expertise essential to your success at writing on the job.

GUIDELINE 1 FIND OUT WHAT'S EXPECTED
指导方针1：确定读者期待看到的成果

To a large extent, an effective voice is one that matches your readers' sense of what's appropriate. When successful employees are asked to identify the major weaknesses in the writing of new employees, they often cite the inability to use a tone and style that are appropriate to their readers.

Here are three questions to ask yourself when determining how to match your voice to your readers' expectations:

Questions for determining what your readers expect

- **How formal do my readers think my writing should be?** An informal style sounds like conversation. You use contractions (*can't*, *won't*), short words, and colloquial words and phrasing. A formal style sounds more like a lecture or speech, with longer sentences, formal phrasing, and no contractions.

- **How subjective or objective do my readers believe my writing should be?** In a subjective style, you would introduce yourself into your writing by saying such things as "I believe . . ." and "I observed . . . ." In an objective style, you would mask your presence by stating your beliefs as facts ("It is true that . . .") and by reporting about your own actions in the third person ("The researcher observed . . .") or the passive voice ("It was observed that . . .").
- **How much "distance" do my readers expect me to establish between them and me?** In a personal style, you appear very close to your readers because you do such things as use personal pronouns (*I, we*) and address your readers directly. In an impersonal style, you distance yourself from your readers — for instance, by avoiding personal pronouns and by talking about yourself and your readers in the third person ("The company agrees to deliver a fully operable model to the customer by October 1").

Here are some major factors that may influence your readers' expectations about style:

- Your professional relationship with your readers (customers? supervisors? subordinates?)
- Your purpose (requesting something? apologizing? advising? ordering?)
- Your subject (routine matter? urgent problem?)
- Type of communication (e-mail? letter? formal report?)
- Your personality
- Your readers' personalities
- Customs in your employer's organization
- Customs in your field, profession, or discipline

To learn what style your readers expect, follow the advice in Chapter 3: Ask people who know (including even your readers) and look for communications similar to the one you are writing.

What If the Expected Style Is Ineffective?

Note that sometimes the expected style may be less effective than another style you could use. For example, in some organizations the customary and expected style is a widely (and justly) condemned style called *bureaucratese*. Bureaucratese is characterized by wordiness that buries significant ideas and information, by weak verbs that disguise action, and by abstract vocabulary that detaches meaning from the practical world of people, activities, and objects. Often, such writing features an inflated vocabulary and a general pomposity that slows or completely blocks comprehension. Here's an example:

According to optimal quality-control practices in manufacturing any product, it is important that every component part that is constituent of the product be examined and checked individually after being received from its supplier or other source but before the final, finished product is assembled. (45 words)	Bureaucratese

The writer simply means this:

Plain English | Effective quality control requires that every component be checked individually before the final product is assembled. (16 words)

Here is another pair of examples:

Bureaucratese | Over the most recent monthly period, there has been a large increase in the number of complaints that customers have made about service that has been slow. (27 words)

Plain English | Last month, many more customers complained about slow service. (9 words)

> For more information on plain English laws and other efforts to eliminate bureaucratese, go to Chapter 8 at www.thomsonedu.com/english/anderson.

Bureaucratese is such a serious barrier to understanding that many states in the United States have passed laws *requiring* plain English in government publications and other documents, such as insurance policies. This chapter's guidelines will help you avoid bureaucratese. However, some managers and organizations want employees to use that puffed-up style, thinking it sounds impressive. If you are asked to write in bureaucratese, try to explain why a straightforward style is more effective, perhaps sharing this book. If you fail to persuade, be prudent. Use the style that is required. Even within the confines of a generally bureaucratic style, you can probably make improvements. For instance, if your employer expects a wordy, abstract style, you may still be able to use a less inflated vocabulary.

GUIDELINE 2 CONSIDER THE ROLES YOUR VOICE CREATES FOR YOUR READERS AND YOU

指导方针2：考虑文章语气为你和读者确立的角色

When you choose the voice with which you will address your readers, you define a role for yourself. As manager of a department, for instance, you could adopt the voice of a stern taskmaster or an open-minded leader. The voice you choose also implies a role for your readers. And their response to the role given to them can significantly influence your communication's overall effectiveness. If you choose the voice of a leader who respects your readers, they will probably accept their implied role as valued colleagues. If you choose the voice of a superior, unerring authority, they may resent their implied role as error-prone inferiors — and resist the substance of your message.

By changing your voice in even a single sentence, you can increase your ability to elicit the attitudes and actions you want to inspire. Consider the following statement drafted by a divisional vice president.

In this draft, the vice president uses a domineering voice. | I have scheduled an hour for you to meet with me to discuss your department's failure to meet its production targets last month.

In this sentence, the vice president has chosen the voice of a powerful person who considers the reader to be someone who can be blamed and bossed around, a role the reader probably does not find agreeable. By revising the sentence, the vice president creates a much different pair of roles for herself and her readers.

> Let's meet tomorrow to see if we can figure out why your department had difficulty meeting last month's production targets.

In this revision, she creates a supportive voice.

The vice president transformed her voice into that of a supportive person. The reader became someone interested in working with the writer to solve a problem that stumps them both. As a result of these changes in voice and roles, the meeting is likely to be much more productive.

GUIDELINE 3 CONSIDER HOW YOUR ATTITUDE TOWARD YOUR SUBJECT WILL AFFECT YOUR READERS
指导方针3：考虑你对主题的态度将如何影响读者

In addition to communicating attitudes about yourself and your readers, your voice communicates an attitude toward your subject. Feelings are contagious. If you write about your subject enthusiastically, your readers may catch your enthusiasm. If you seem indifferent, they may adopt the same attitude.

E-mail presents a special temptation to be careless about voice because it encourages spontaneity. As Laura B. Smith (1993) says, "Staring at e-mail can make users feel dangerously bold; they sometimes blast off with emotions that they probably would not use in a face-to-face meeting." Your risk of regretting an e-mail you've written is increased by the ease with which e-mails can be forwarded to readers you didn't intend to see your message. Never include anything in an e-mail that you wouldn't be prepared for a large audience to read. Check carefully for statements that your readers might interpret as having a different tone of voice than the one you intend.

GUIDELINE 4 SAY THINGS IN YOUR OWN WORDS
指导方针4：用自己的话阐述

No matter what style you choose, be sure to retain your own voice in your writing. You can do that even in your formal writing — for instance, in a scientific or engineering report. James Watson (1968), winner of the Nobel Prize for his role in discovering the structure of DNA, praised Linus Pauling, three-time winner of the same prize, for his distinctive writing style in highly technical papers. When you are using a formal style, the objective is not to silence your own voice; it's to let your style sound like *you*, writing in a formal situation.

To check whether you are using your own voice, try reading your drafts aloud. Where the phrasing seems awkward or the words are difficult for you to speak, you may have adopted someone else's voice — or slipped into bureaucratese, which reflects no one's voice. Reading your drafts aloud can also help you spot other problems with voice — such as sarcasm or condescension.

Despite the advice given in this guideline, it will sometimes be appropriate for you to suppress your own voice. For example, when a report, proposal, or other document is written by several people, the contributors usually strive to achieve a uniform voice so that all the sections will fit together stylistically. Similarly, certain kinds of official documents, such as an organization's policy statements, are usually written in the employer's style, not the individual writer's style. Except in such situations, however, let your own voice speak in your writing.

Sometimes it's appropriate to suppress your own voice.

GUIDELINE 5 GLOBAL GUIDELINE: ADAPT YOUR VOICE TO YOUR READERS' CULTURAL BACKGROUND

整体指导方针 5：根据读者的文化背景调整语气

From one culture to another, general expectations about the voice vary considerably. Understanding the differences between the expectations of your culture and those of your readers in another culture can be especially important because, as Guideline 2 explains, the voice you use tells your readers about the relationship you believe you have with them.

> **Learn More**
>
> For more advice about adapting communications to your readers' cultural background, go to Chapter 3, page 76.

Consider, for instance, the difficulties that may arise if employees in the United States and in Japan write to one another without considering differences in the expectations about voice that are most common in each culture. In the United States and Europe, employees often use an informal voice and address their readers by their first names. In Japan, writers commonly use a formal style and address their readers by their titles and last names. If a U.S. writer used a familiar, informal voice in a letter, memo, or e-mail to Japanese readers, these readers might feel that the writer has not properly respected them. On the other hand, Japanese writers may seem distant and difficult to relate to if they use the formality that is common in their own cultures when writing to U.S. readers. In either case, even if the readers are aware that a writer's voice results from his or her own culture's practices, the readers may judge that the writer hasn't taken the trouble to learn about or doesn't care about the readers' culture — which would not form a good basis for a productive relationship.

Directness is another aspect of voice. The Japanese write in a more personal voice than do people from the United States, whose direct, blunt style the Japanese find abrupt (Ruch, 1984). Like businesspeople in the United States, the Dutch also use a straightforward voice that causes the French to regard writers from both countries as rude (Mathes & Stevenson, 1991). When writing to people in other cultures, try to learn and to use the voice that is customary there. Library and Internet research provide helpful information about many cultures. You can also learn about the voice used in your readers' culture by studying communications they have written. If possible, ask for advice from people who are from your readers' culture or who are knowledgeable about it.

GUIDELINE 6 ETHICS GUIDELINE: AVOID STEREOTYPES

道德指导方针 6：避免成见

Let's begin with a story. A man and a boy are riding together in a car. As they approach a railroad crossing, the boy shouts, "Father, watch out!" But it is too late. The car is hit by a train. The man dies, and the boy is rushed to a hospital. When the boy is wheeled into the operating room, the surgeon looks down at the child and says, "I can't operate on him. He's my son."

When asked to explain why the boy would call the deceased driver "Father" and the living surgeon would say "He's my son," people offer many guesses. Perhaps the driver is a priest or the boy's stepfather or someone who kidnapped the boy as a baby. Few guess that the surgeon must be the boy's mother. Why? Our culture's stereotypes about the roles men and women play are so strong that when people think of a surgeon, many automatically imagine a man.

Stereotypes, Voice, and Ethics

What do stereotypes have to do with voice and ethics? Stereotypes are very deeply embedded in a culture. Most of us are prone to use them occasionally especially when conversing informally. As a result, when we use more colloquial and conversational language to develop our distinctive voice for our workplace writing, we may inadvertently employ stereotypes. Unfortunately, even inadvertent uses of stereotypes have serious consequences for individuals and groups. People who are viewed in terms of stereotypes lose their ability to be treated as individual human beings.

Further, if they belong to a group that is unfavorably stereotyped, they may find it nearly impossible to get others to take their talents, ideas, and feelings seriously. The range of groups disadvantaged by stereotyping is quite extensive. People are stereotyped on the basis of their race, religion, age, gender, sexual orientation, weight, physical handicap, and ethnicity. In some workplaces, manual laborers, union members, clerical workers, and others are the victims of stereotyping by people in white-collar positions.

The following suggestions will help you avoid stereotypes.

> **Learn More**
>
> For a discussion of stereotypes and word choice, see page 276.

AVOIDING STEREOTYPES

- **Avoid describing people in terms of stereotypes.** In your reports, sales presentations, policy statements, and other communications, avoid giving examples that rely upon or reinforce stereotypes. For example, don't make all the decision makers men and all the clerical workers women.
- **Mention a person's gender, race, or other characteristic only when it is relevant.** To determine whether it's relevant to describe someone as a member of a minority group, ask yourself if you would make a parallel statement about a member of the majority group. If you wouldn't say, "This improvement was suggested by Jane, a person without any physical disability," don't say, "This improvement was suggested by Margaret, a person with a handicap." If you wouldn't say, "The Phoenix office is managed by Brent, a hard-working white person," don't say, "The Phoenix office is managed by Terry, a hard-working Mexican-American."
- **Avoid humor that relies on stereotypes.** Humor that relies on a stereotype reinforces the stereotype. Refrain from such humor not only when members of the stereotyped group are present, but at all times.

CONSTRUCTING SENTENCES
造 句

Researchers who have studied the ways our minds process information have provided us with many valuable insights about ways to write reader-centered sentences. Based primarily on these research findings, the following six guidelines explain ways to construct highly usable, highly persuasive sentences.

GUIDELINE 1 SIMPLIFY YOUR SENTENCES
指导方针1：简化句子

The easiest way to increase usability is to simplify your sentences. Reading is *work*. Psychologists say that much of the work is done by short-term memory. It must figure out how the words in each sentence fit together to create a specific meaning. Fewer words mean less work. In addition, research shows that when you express your message concisely, you make it more forceful, memorable, and persuasive (F. Smith, 2004).

SIMPLIFYING SENTENCES

1. **Eliminate unnecessary words.** Look for places where you can convey your meaning more directly. Consider this sentence:

    Wordy
    > The <u>physical size</u> of the workroom is too small <u>to accommodate</u> this equipment.

    With unnecessary words removed in two places, the sentence is just as clear and more emphatic:

    Unnecessary words deleted
    > The workroom is too small for this equipment.

    Unnecessary words can also be found in many common phrases. "Due to the fact that" can be shortened to "Because." Similarly, "They do not pay attention to our complaints" can be abbreviated to "They ignore our complaints." "At this point in time" is "Now."

2. **Place modifiers next to the words they modify.** Short-term memory relies on word order to indicate meaning. If you don't keep related words together, your sentence may say something different from what you mean.

    > A large number of undeposited checks were found in the file cabinets, which were worth over $41,000.

    According to the way the English language works, this sentence says that the file cabinets were worth over $41,000. Yet, the author meant that the checks were worth that amount. Of course, readers would probably figure out what the writer meant because it is more likely that the checks were worth that much money than that the file cabinets were. But readers arrive at the correct meaning only after performing work they would have been saved if the writer had kept related words together—in this example, by putting *which were worth over $41,000* after *checks*, rather than after *file cabinets*.

3. **Combine short sentences.** Often, combining two or more short sentences makes reading easier because doing so both reduces the total number of words and helps the reader see the relationships among the points presented.

    Separate
    > Water quality in Hawk River declined in March. This decline occurred because of the heavy rainfall that month. All the extra water overloaded Tomlin County's water treatment plant.

    Combined
    > Water quality in Hawk River declined in March because heavy rainfalls overloaded Tomlin County's water treatment plant.

CHAPTER 8 Developing an Effective Style

GUIDELINE 2 PUT THE ACTION IN YOUR VERBS
指导方针2：运用动词

Most sentences are about action. Sales rise, equipment fails, engineers design, managers approve. Clients praise or complain, and technicians advise. Yet, many people bury the action in nouns, adjectives, and other parts of speech. Consider the following sentence:

| Our department accomplished the conversion to the new machinery in two months. | Original |

It could be energized by putting the action (*converting*) into the verb:

| Our department converted to the new machinery in two months. | Revised |

Not only is the revised version briefer, it is also more emphatic and lively. Furthermore, according to researchers E. B. Coleman and Keith Raynor (1964), when you put the action in your verbs, you can make your prose up to 25 percent easier to read.

To create sentences that focus on action, do the following:

FOCUSING SENTENCES ON ACTION

- **Avoid sentences that use the verb *to be* or its variations (*is, was, will be*, etc.).** The verb *to be* often tells what something is, not what it does.

| The sterilization procedure is a protection against reinfection. | Original |
| The sterilization procedure protects against reinfection. | Revised |

- **Avoid sentences that begin with *It is* or *There are*.**

It is because the cost of raw materials has soared that the price of finished goods is rising.	Original
Because the cost of raw materials has soared, the price of finished goods is rising.	Revised
There are several factors causing the engineers to question the dam's strength.	Original
Several factors cause the engineers to question the dam's strength.	Revised

- **Avoid sentences where the action is frozen in a word that ends with one of the following suffixes: *-tion, -ment, -ing, -ion, -ance*.** These words petrify the action that should be in verbs by converting them into nouns.

| Consequently, I would like to make a recommendation that the department hire two additional programmers. | Original |
| Consequently, I recommend that the department hire two additional programmers. | Revised |

Although most sentences are about action, some aren't. For example, topic and forecasting statements often introduce lists or describe the organization of the discussion that follows.

| Topic sentence for which the verb *to be* is appropriate | There are three main reasons the company should invest money to improve communication between corporate headquarters and the out-of-state plants. |

GUIDELINE 3 USE THE ACTIVE VOICE UNLESS YOU HAVE A GOOD REASON TO USE THE PASSIVE VOICE
指导方针 3：尽量使用主动语态

Another way to focus your sentences on action and actors is to use the *active voice* rather than the *passive voice*. To write in the active voice, place the actor — the person or thing performing the action — in the subject position. Your verb will then describe the actor's action.

| Active voice | 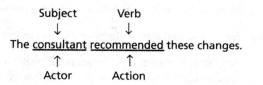 |

In the passive voice, the subject of the sentence and the actor are different. The subject is *acted upon* by the actor.

| Passive voice | 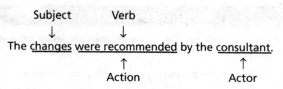 |

Here are some additional examples:

| Passive voice | The Korean ore was purchased by us. |
| Active voice | We purchased the Korean ore. |

Research shows that readers comprehend active sentences more rapidly than passive ones (Layton & Simpson, 1975). Also, the active voice eliminates the vagueness and ambiguity that often characterize the passive voice. In the passive voice, a sentence can describe an action without telling who did it. For example, "The ball was hit" is a grammatically correct sentence but doesn't tell who or what hit the ball. With the active voice, the writer identifies the actor: "Linda hit the ball."

The following sentence illustrates the importance of ensuring that readers understand who the actor is.

| Passive voice | The operating temperatures must be checked daily to protect the motor from damage. |

Will the supervisor of the third shift know that he is the person responsible for checking temperatures? In the passive voice, this sentence certainly allows him to imagine that someone else, perhaps a supervisor on another shift, is responsible.

| There are some places where the passive voice is appropriate. | Although the passive voice generally reduces readability, it has some good uses. One occurs when you don't want to identify the actor. The following sentence is from |

CHAPTER 8 *Developing an Effective Style*

a memorandum in which the writer urges all employees to work harder at saving energy but avoids causing embarrassment and resentment by naming the guilty parties.

> The lights on the third floor have been left on all night for the past week, despite the efforts of most employees to help us reduce our energy bills.

Passive voice

Also, consider this sentence:

> I have been told that you may be using the company telephone for an excessive number of personal calls.

Passive voice

Perhaps the person who told the writer about the breach of corporate telephone policy did so in confidence. If the writer decided that it would be ethically acceptable to communicate this news to the reader without naming the person who made the report, then she has used the passive voice effectively. (Be careful, however, to avoid using the passive voice to hide an actor's identity when it is unethical to do so — for instance, when trying to avoid accepting responsibility for your employer's actions.)

Another good reason for using the passive voice is discussed in Chapter 7, Guideline 7, page 221.

GUIDELINE 4 EMPHASIZE WHAT'S MOST IMPORTANT
指导方针 4：强调重点

Another way to write clear, forceful sentences is to direct your readers' attention to the most important information you are conveying.

EMPHASIZING WHAT'S MOST IMPORTANT

1. **Place the key information at the end of the sentence.** As linguist Joseph Williams (2005) points out, you can demonstrate to yourself that the end of the sentence is a place of emphasis by listening to yourself speak. Read the following sentences aloud:

   > Her powers of concentration are extraordinary.
   >
   > Last month, he topped his sales quota even though he was sick for an entire week.

   As you read these sentences aloud, notice how you naturally stress the final words *extraordinary* and *entire week*.

   To position the key information at the end of a sentence, you may sometimes need to rearrange your first draft.

The department's performance has been superb in all areas.	Original
In all areas, the department's performance has been superb.	Revised
The <u>bright exterior design</u> is one of the product's most appealing features to college-age customers.	Original
One of the product's most appealing features to college-age customers is its <u>bright exterior design</u>.	Revised

2. **Place the key information in the main clause.** If your sentence has more than one clause, use the main clause for the information you want to emphasize. Compare the following versions of the same statement.

> Although our productivity was down, our profits were up.
>
> Although our profits were up, our productivity was down.

In the first version, the emphasis is on profits because *profits* is the subject of the main clause. The second version emphasizes productivity because *productivity* is the subject of the main clause. (Notice that in each of these sentences, the emphasized information is not only in the main clause but also at the end of the sentence.)

3. **Emphasize key information typographically.** Use boldface and italics. Be careful, however, to use typographical highlighting sparingly. When many things are emphasized, none stands out.

4. **Tell readers explicitly what the key information is.** You can also emphasize key information by announcing its importance to your readers.

> Economists pointed to three important causes of the stock market's decline: uncertainty about the outcome of last month's election, a rise in inventories of durable goods, and —*most important*— signs of rising inflation.

GUIDELINE 5 VARY YOUR SENTENCE LENGTH AND STRUCTURE

指导方针5：句子长度和结构不应一成不变

If all the sentences in a sentence group have the same structure, two problems arise: Monotony sets in, and (because all the sentences are basically alike) you lose the ability to emphasize major points and deemphasize minor ones.

You can avoid such monotony and loss of emphasis in two ways:

- **Vary your sentence length.** Longer sentences can be used to show the relationships among ideas. Shorter sentences provide emphasis in the context of longer sentences.

> In April, many amateur investors believed that another rally was about to begin. Because exports were increasing rapidly, they predicted that the dollar would strengthen in global monetary markets, bringing foreign investors back to Wall Street. Also, unemployment dropped sharply, which they interpreted as an encouraging sign for the economy. **They were wrong on both counts.** Wall Street interpreted rising exports to mean that goods would cost more at home, and it predicted that falling unemployment would mean a shortage of workers, hence higher prices for labor. **Where amateur investors saw growth, Wall Street saw inflation.**

This short sentence receives emphasis because it comes after longer ones.

The final sentence is also emphasized because it is much shorter than the preceding one.

- **Vary your sentence structure.** For example, the grammatical subject of the sentence does not have to be the sentence's first word. In fact, if it did, the

English language would lose much of its power to emphasize more important information and to deemphasize less important information.

One alternative to beginning a sentence with its grammatical subject is to begin with a clause that indicates a logical relationship.

| <u>After we complete our survey,</u> we will know for sure whether the proposed site for our new factory was once a Native American camping ground. | Introductory clause |

| <u>Because we have thoroughly investigated all the alternatives,</u> we feel confident that a pneumatic drive will work best and provide the most reliable service. | Introductory clause |

GUIDELINE 6   GLOBAL GUIDELINE: ADAPT YOUR SENTENCES FOR READERS WHO ARE NOT FLUENT IN YOUR LANGUAGE

整体指导方针 6：为不熟悉你的语言的读者调整语句

The decisions you make about the structure of your sentences can affect the ease with which people who are not fluent in English can understand your message. Companies in several industries, including oil and computers, have developed simplified versions of English for use in communications for readers in other cultures. In addition to limited vocabularies, simplified English has special grammar rules that guide writers to using sentences that will be easy for their readers to understand. Because many readers may not need this degree of simplification, be sure to learn as much as possible about your specific readers. Also, remember that simplifying your sentence structure should not involve simplifying your thought.

GUIDELINES FOR CREATING SENTENCES FOR READERS WHO ARE NOT FLUENT IN ENGLISH

- **Use simple sentence structures.** The more complex your sentences, the more difficult they will be for readers to understand.
- **Keep sentences short.** A long sentence can be hard to follow, even if its structure is simple. Set twenty words as a limit.
- **Use the active voice.** Readers who are not fluent in English can understand the active voice much more easily than they can understand the passive.

Learn More

For more advice on adapting communications to your readers' cultural background, go to Chapter 3, page 76 and the other Global Guidelines throughout this book.

For more on simplified versions of English, go to www.thomsonedu.com/english/anderson, Chapter 8.

SELECTING WORDS
选　词

When selecting words, your first goal should be to increase the usability of your writing by enabling your readers to grasp your meaning quickly and accurately. At the same time, you need to keep in mind that your word choices affect your readers' attitudes toward you and your subject matter. Therefore you also need to choose words that will increase your communication's persuasiveness.

GUIDELINE 1 USE CONCRETE, SPECIFIC WORDS
指导方针1：使用具体的词

Almost anything can be described either in relatively abstract, general words or in relatively concrete, specific ones. You may say that you are writing on a piece of *electronic equipment* or that you are writing on *a laptop computer connected to a color laser printer.* You may say that your employer produces *consumer goods* or that it makes *cell phones.*

When groups of words are ranked according to degree of abstraction, they form *hierarchies.* Figure 8.1 shows such a hierarchy in which the most specific terms identify concrete items that we can perceive with our senses; Figure 8.2 shows a hierarchy in which all the terms are abstract but some are more specific than others.

You can increase the clarity, and therefore the usability, of your writing by using concrete, specific words rather than abstract, general ones. Concrete words help your readers understand precisely what you mean. If you say that your company produces television shows for a *younger demographic segment,* they won't know whether you mean *teenagers* or *toddlers.* If you say that you study *natural phenomena,* your readers won't know whether you mean *volcanic eruptions* or the *migration of monarch butterflies.*

Such vagueness can hinder readers from getting the information they need in order to make decisions and take action. Consider the following sentence from a memo addressed to an upper-level manager who wanted to know why production costs were up:

Original | The cost of one material has risen recently. |

This sentence doesn't give the manager the information she needs to take remedial action. In contrast, the following sentence, using specific words, tells precisely what

FIGURE 8.1
Hierarchy of Related Words That Move from Abstract to Concrete

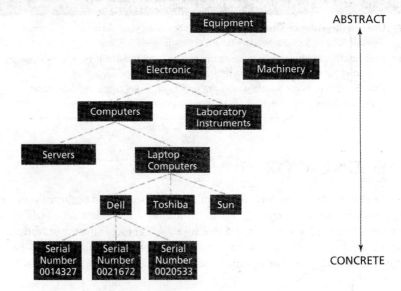

CHAPTER 8 **Developing an Effective Style**

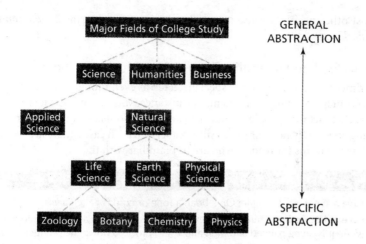

FIGURE 8.2
Hierarchy of Related Words That Move from a General to a Specific Abstraction

the material is, how much the price has risen, and the period in which the increase took place.

| The cost of the bonding agent has tripled in the past six months. | Revised

Of course, abstract and general terms do have important uses. For example, in scientific, technical, and other specialized fields, writers often need to make general points, describe the general features of a situation, or provide general guidance for action. Your objective when choosing words is not to avoid abstract, general words altogether, but rather to avoid using them when your readers will want more specific ones.

GUIDELINE 2 USE SPECIALIZED TERMS WHEN—AND ONLY WHEN—YOUR READERS WILL UNDERSTAND THEM

指导方针2：使用专业术语——当且仅当读者能够理解时

You can increase the usability and persuasiveness of your writing by using wisely the specialized terms of your own profession.

In some situations, specialized terms help you communicate effectively:

- **They convey precise, technical meanings economically.** Many terms have no exact equivalent in everyday speech.
- **They help you establish credibility.** By using the special terms of your field accurately, you show your fellow specialists that you are adept in it.

However, you should avoid using technical terms your readers won't understand. Consider the following sentence:

| The major benefits of this method are smaller in-gate connections, reduced breakage, and minimum knock-out—all leading to great savings. |

Although this sentence would be perfectly clear to any manager who works in a foundry that manufactures parts for automobile engines, it would be unintelligible to most other people because it includes the specialized terms *in-gate connections* and *knock-out*.

How to Explain Unfamiliar Terms If You Must Use Them

Sometimes you may need to use specialized terms even though some people in your audience may not understand them. For instance, you may be writing to a group of readers that includes people in your field and others outside of it, or you may be explaining an entirely new subject to your readers. In such cases, there are several ways to define the terms for readers who are not familiar with them.

DEFINING TERMS YOUR READERS DON'T KNOW

1. **Give a synonym.** Example: On a boat, a rope or cord is called a *line*.
2. **Give a description.** Example: The *exit gate* consists of two arms that hold a jug while it is being painted and then allow it to proceed down the production line.
3. **Make an analogy.** Example: An atom is like a miniature solar system in which the nucleus is the sun and the electrons are the planets that revolve around it.
4. **Give a classical definition.** In a classical definition, you define the term by naming some familiar group of things to which it belongs and then identifying the key distinction between the object being defined and the other members of the group. Examples:

WORD	GROUP	DISTINGUISHING CHARACTERISTIC
A crystal is a	solid	in which the atoms or molecules are arranged in a regularly repeated pattern.
A burrow is a	hole in the ground	dug by an animal for shelter or habitation.

GUIDELINE 3 USE WORDS ACCURATELY
指导方针 3：使用精确的词

Whether you use specialized terms or everyday ones and whether you use abstract, general terms or concrete, specific ones, you must use all your words accurately. This point may seem obvious, but inaccurate word choice is all too common in on-the-job writing. For example, people often confuse *imply* (meaning to *suggest* or *hint*, as in "He implied that the operator had been careless") with *infer* (meaning to draw a *conclusion based upon evidence*, as in "We infer from your report that you do not expect to meet the deadline"). It's critical that you avoid such errors. They distract your readers from your message by drawing their attention to your problems with word choice, and they may lead your readers to believe that you are not skillful or precise in other areas — such as laboratory techniques or analytical skills.

How can you ensure that you use words accurately? There's no easy way. Consult a dictionary whenever you are uncertain. Be especially careful when using words that are not yet part of your usual vocabulary. Pay attention as well to the way words are used by other people.

GUIDELINE 4   CHOOSE PLAIN WORDS OVER FANCY ONES
指导方针 4：选择平实的语言而不是华丽的辞藻

You can also make your writing easy to understand by avoiding using fancy words where plain ones will do. At work, some writers do just the opposite, perhaps thinking that fancy words sound more official or make them sound more knowledgeable. The following list identifies some commonly used fancy words; it includes only verbs but might have included nouns and adjectives as well.

FANCY VERBS	COMMON VERBS
ascertain	find out
commence	begin
compensate	pay
constitute	make up
endeavor	try
expend	spend
fabricate	build
facilitate	make easier
initiate	begin
prioritize	rank
proceed	go
terminate	end
transmit	send
utilize	use

There are two important reasons for preferring plain words over fancy ones:

- **Plain words promote efficient reading.** Research has shown that even if your readers know both the plain word and its fancy synonym, they will still comprehend the plain word more rapidly (Smith, 2004).
- **Plain words reduce your risk of creating a bad impression.** If you use words that make for slow, inefficient reading, you may annoy your readers or cause them to conclude that you are behaving pompously, showing off, or trying to hide a lack of ideas and information behind a fog of fancy terms. Consider, for instance, the effect of the following sentence in a job application letter:

| I am transmitting the enclosed résumé to facilitate your efforts to determine the pertinence of my work experience to your opening. | Pompous word choices |

Don't misunderstand this guideline. It doesn't suggest that you should use only simple language at work. When addressing people with vocabularies comparable to your own, use all the words at your command, provided that you use them accurately and appropriately. This guideline merely cautions you against using needlessly inflated words that bloat your prose and open you to criticism from your readers.

GUIDELINE 5   CHOOSE WORDS WITH APPROPRIATE ASSOCIATIONS
指导方针5：选用含义恰当的词

The three previous guidelines for choosing words relate to the literal or dictionary meaning of words. At work, you must also consider the associations your words have for your readers. In particular, be especially sensitive to your words' *connotation* and *register*.

Connotation

Connotation is the extended or suggested meaning that a word has beyond its literal meaning. For example, according to the dictionary, *flatfoot* and *police detective* are synonyms, but they connote very different things: *flatfoot* suggests a plodding, perhaps not very bright cop, while *police detective* suggests a trained professional.

Verbs, too, have connotations. For instance, to *suggest* that someone has overlooked a key fact is not the same as to *insinuate* that she has. To *devote* your time to working on a client's project is not the same as to *spend* your time on it.

Research on the impact of connotation

The connotations of your words can shape your audience's perceptions of your subject matter. Researchers Raymond W. Kulhavy and Neil H. Schwartz (1981) demonstrated those effects in a classic experiment for which they created two descriptions of a company that differed in only seven out of 246 words. In one, the seven words suggested stiffness, such as *required* and *must*. In the other, those seven words were replaced by ones that suggested flexibility, such as *asked* and *should*. None of the substitutions changed the facts of the overall passage. Here's a sentence from the first version:

First version
> Our sales team is constantly trying to locate new markets for our various product lines.

In the second version of this sentence, the researchers replaced the flexible word *trying* with the stiff word *driving*.

Second version
> Our sales team is constantly driving to locate new markets for our various product lines.

The researchers found that people who read the flexible version believed that the company would actively commit itself to the welfare and concerns of its employees, voluntarily participate in affirmative action programs for women and minorities, receive relatively few labor grievances, and pay its employees well. People who read that version also said they would recommend the company to a friend as a place to work. People who read the stiff version reported opposite impressions of the company. That readers' impressions of the company could be affected so dramatically by just seven nonsubstantive words highlights the great importance of paying attention to the connotations of the words you use.

Register

Linguists use the term *register* to identify a second characteristic exhibited by words: their association with certain kinds of communication situations or context. For example, in an ad for a restaurant we might expect to see the claim that it offers *amazingly* delicious food. However, we would not expect to see a research company boast in a proposal for a government contract that it is capable of conducting *amazingly* good studies. The word *amazingly* is in the register of consumer advertising but not in the register of research proposals.

If you inadvertently choose words with the wrong register, your readers may infer that you don't fully grasp how business is conducted in your field, and your credibility can be lost.

GUIDELINE 6 GLOBAL GUIDELINE: CONSIDER YOUR READERS' CULTURAL BACKGROUND WHEN CHOOSING WORDS

整体指导方针6：选词时考虑读者的文化背景

Take special care in your choice of words when writing to readers in other cultures. Some words whose meaning is obvious in your own culture can be misunderstood or completely mystifying to readers from other cultures. This is true whether your communication will go to your readers in English or whether it will be translated for them. In fact, misunderstanding can even occur when you are writing to readers in other cultures where the native language is English. In the United States, people play football with an oblong object which they try to carry over a goal line or kick through uprights. In England, India, and many other parts of the world, football is played with a round object that people are forbidden to carry and attempt to kick into a net.

The following guidelines will help you choose words your readers will understand in the way you intend. Of course, different readers in other cultures have different levels of facility with English, so follow the guidelines only to the extent that your readers require.

> **Learn More**
>
> For more advice on adapting communications to your readers' cultural background, go to Chapter 3, page 76 and the other Global Guidelines throughout this book.

GUIDELINES FOR CHOOSING WORDS FOR INTERCULTURAL COMMUNICATIONS

- **Use simple words.** The more complex your vocabulary, the more difficult it will be for readers not fluent in English to understand you.
- **Use the same word each time you refer to the same thing.** For instance, in instructions, don't use both "dial" and "control" for the part of a test instrument. In context, those two terms may be synonyms in your language, but they will each be translated into a different word in the other language, where the translated words may not be synonyms.
- **Avoid acronyms your readers won't understand.** Most acronyms that are familiar to you will be based on words in *your* language: AI for Artificial Intelligence; ACL for Anterior Cruciate Ligament.
- **Avoid slang words and idioms.** Most will have no meaning for people in other cultures. Instead of "We want a level playing field," say "We want the decision to be made fairly." Instead of saying "We want to run an idea past you," say "We'd like your opinion of our idea."

At work, even small departments often include a rich diversity of employees.

Even if you follow these guidelines, it's best always to ask someone familiar with that culture to review the words you've chosen. Doing so can also help you avoid another type of problem caused by words in your language that sound like words in another language but can have a completely different meaning. Only after Chevrolet introduced its Nova car to Latin America did the car maker realize that in Spanish *No va* means "It doesn't go." Sales were slight until the name was changed (Grosse & Kujawa, 1988). In the 1920s, when Coca-Cola introduced its beverage in China, the company selected for its logo a series of Chinese characters that, when pronounced, sounded like the name of the beverage: *Ke Kou Ke La*. Later, they learned that the characters mean "Bite the wax tadpole." The characters used on Chinese Coke bottles today mean "Happiness in the mouth" (Ricks, 1983).

GUIDELINE 7   ETHICS GUIDELINE: USE INCLUSIVE LANGUAGE

道德指导方针7：使用总括性的语言

When constructing your voice, use language that includes all persons instead of excluding some. For example, avoid sexist language because it supports negative stereotypes. Usually, these stereotypes are about women, but they can also adversely affect men in certain professions, such as nursing. By supporting negative stereotypes, sexist language can blind readers to the abilities, accomplishments, and potential of very capable people. The same is true of language that insensitively describes people with disabilities, illnesses, or other limitations.

Learn More

For another discussion of stereotypes and ethics, see page 263.

For additional suggestions about ways to avoid sexist and discriminatory language, go to Chapter 8 at www.thomsonedu.com/english/anderson.

USING INCLUSIVE LANGUAGE

1. Use nouns and pronouns that are gender-neutral rather than ones containing the word *man*.

   Instead of: businessman, workman, mailman, salesman

   Use: businessperson, manager, *or* executive; worker; mail carrier; salesperson

   Instead of: manmade, man hours, man-sized job

   Use: synthetic, working hours, large job

2. Use plural pronouns or *he or she* instead of sex-linked pronouns when referring to people in general.

   Instead of: "Our home electronics cater to the affluent shopper. She looks for premium products and appreciates a stylish design."

   Use the plural: "Our home electronics cater to affluent shoppers. They look for premium products and appreciate a stylish design."

   Instead of: "Before the owner of a new business files the first year's tax returns, he might be wise to seek advice from a certified public accountant."

   Use *he or she*: "Before the owner of a new business files the first year's tax returns, he or she might be wise to seek advice from a certified public accountant."

3. Refer to individual men and women in a parallel manner.
   Instead of: "Mr. Sundquist and Anna represented us at the trade fair."
   Use: "Mr. Sundquist and Ms. Tokagawa represented us at the trade fair" or "Christopher and Anna represented us at the trade fair."
4. Revise salutations that imply the reader of a letter is a man.
   Instead of: Dear Sir, Gentlemen
   Use: The title of the department or company or the job title of the person you are addressing: Dear Personnel Department, Dear Switzer Plastics Corporation, Dear Director of Research
5. When writing about people with disabilities, refer to the person first, then the disability.
   Instead of: the disabled, mentally retarded people
   Use: people with disabilities, people with mental retardation

What about *Miss, Mrs.,* and *Ms.*?

People are sometimes unsure whether to use the traditional terms *Miss* or *Mrs.* or the newer term *Ms.* On one hand, people charge that using the older terms suggests that a woman's marital status is somehow relevant to her ability to perform her job. After all, they point out, all men, whether married or single, are addressed as *Mr.* On the other hand, some women prefer to be addressed as either *Mrs.* or *Miss.* If you know an individual's preference, follow it. If you don't know the individual's preference, use *Ms.*, which has been accepted as the nonsexist term in the workplace.

CONCLUSION 总 结

Your writing style can make a great deal of difference to the success of your writing. The voice you use, the sentence structures you employ, and the words you select affect both your readers' attitudes toward you and your subject matter and also the readability and impact of your writing. This chapter has suggested many things you can do to develop a highly usable, highly persuasive style. Underlying all these suggestions is the advice that you take the reader-centered approach of considering all your stylistic choices from your readers' point of view.

EXERCISES 练 习

You can download Expertise Exercises 2 through 5 from Chapter 8 at www.thomsonedu.com/english/anderson.

EXPERTISE

1. Imagine that you are the head of the Public Safety department at your college. Faculty and staff have been parking illegally, sometimes where there aren't parking spots. Sometimes individuals without handicaps are parking in spots reserved for those with handicaps. Write two memos to all college employees announcing that beginning next week, the Public Safety department will strictly enforce parking rules — something it hasn't been doing. Write the first memo in a friendly voice and the second in a stern voice. Then compare the specific differences in

organization, sentence structure, word choice, and other features of writing to create each voice. (Thanks to Don Cunningham, Auburn University, for the idea for this exercise.)

2. Without altering the meaning of the following sentences, reduce the number of words in them.
   a. After having completed work on the data-entry problem, we turned our thinking toward our next task, which was the processing problem.
   b. Those who plan federal and state programs for the elderly should take into account the changing demographic characteristics in terms of size and average income of the composition of the elderly population.
   c. Would you please figure out what we should do and advise us?
   d. The result of this study will be to make total whitewater recycling an economical strategy for meeting federal regulations.

3. Rewrite the following sentences in a way that will keep the related words together.
   a. This stamping machine, if you fail to clean it twice per shift and add oil of the proper weight, will cease to operate efficiently.
   b. The plant manager said that he hopes all employees would seek ways to cut waste at the supervisory meeting yesterday.
   c. About 80 percent of our clients, which include over fifteen hundred companies throughout North and South America and a few from Africa, where we've built alliances with local distributors, find the help provided at our website to be equivalent in most cases to the assistance supplied by telephone calls to our service centers.
   d. Once they wilt, most garden sprays are unable to save vegetable plants from complete collapse.

4. Rewrite the following sentences to put the action in the verb.
   a. The experience itself will be an inspirational factor leading the participants to a greater dedication to productivity.
   b. The system realizes important savings in time for the clerical staff.
   c. The implementation of the work plan will be the responsibility of a team of three engineers experienced in these procedures.
   d. Both pulp and lumber were in strong demand, even though rising interest rates caused the drying up of funds for housing.

5. Rewrite the following sentences in the active voice.
   a. Periodically, the shipping log should be reconciled with the daily billings by the Accounting Department.
   b. Fast, accurate data from each operating area in the foundry should be given to us by the new computerized system.
   c. Since his own accident, safety regulations have been enforced much more conscientiously by the shop foreman.
   d. No one has been designated by the manager to make emergency decisions when she is gone.

6. Create a one-sentence, classical definition for a word used in your field that is not familiar to people in other fields. The word might be one that people in other fields have heard of but cannot define precisely in the way specialists in your field do. Underline the word you are defining. Then circle and label the part of your definition that describes the familiar group of items that the defined word belongs to. Finally, circle and label the part of your definition that identifies the key distinction between the defined word and the other items in the group. (Note that not every word is best defined by means of a classical definition, so it may take you a few minutes to think of an appropriate word for this exercise.)

7. Create an analogy to explain a word used in your field that is unfamiliar to most readers. (Note that not every word is best defined by means of an analogy, so it may take you a few minutes to think of an appropriate word for this exercise.)

ONLINE

Using your desktop publishing program, examine the readability statistics for two communications. These might be two projects you're preparing for courses, or they might be a course project and a letter or e-mail to a friend or family member. What differences, if any, do you notice in the statistics? What accounts for the differences? Are the statistics helpful to you in understanding and constructing an effective writing style in either case? Read the explanations of the scores that are provided with your desktop publishing program; these may be provided in the program's Help feature. Do the interpretations of your scores agree with your own assessment of your communications? If not, which do you think is more valid? (To learn how to obtain the readability statistics with your program, use its Help feature.)

COLLABORATION

Working with another student, examine the memo shown in Figure 8.3. Identify places where the writer has ignored the guidelines given in this chapter. You may find it helpful to use

FIGURE 8.3
Memo for Collaboration Exercise

MEMO

July 5, 2006

TO: Gavin MacIntyre, Vice President, Midwest Region

FROM: Nat Willard, Branch Manager, Milwaukee Area Offices

The ensuing memo is in reference to provisions for the cleaning of the six offices and two workrooms in the High Street building in Milwaukee. This morning, I absolved Thomas's Janitor Company of its responsibility for cleansing the subject premises when I discovered that two of Thomas's employees had surreptitiously been making unauthorized long-distance calls on our telephones.

Because of your concern with the costs of running the Milwaukee area offices, I want your imprimatur before proceeding further in making a determination about procuring cleaning services for this building. One possibility is to assign the janitor from the Greenwood Boulevard building to clean the High Street building also. However, this alternative is judged impractical because it cannot be implemented without circumventing the reality of time constraints. While the Greenwood janitor could perform routine cleaning operations at the High Street establishment in one hour, it would take him another ninety minutes to drive to and fro between the two sites. This is more time than he could spare and still be able to fulfill his responsibilities at the High Street building.

Another alternative would be to hire a full-time or part-time employee precisely for the High Street building. However, that building can be cleaned so expeditiously, it would be irrational to do so.

The third alternative is to search for another janitorial service. I have now released two of these enterprises from our employ in Milwaukee. However, our experiences with such services should be viewed as bad luck and not affect our decision, except to make us more aware that making the optimal selection among companies will require great care. Furthermore, there seems to be no reasonable alternative to hiring another janitorial service.

Accordingly, I recommend that we hire another janitorial service. If you agree, I can commence searching for this service as soon as I receive a missive from you. In the meantime I have asked the employees who work in the High Street building to do some tidying up themselves and to be patient.

---

a dictionary. Then write an improved version of the memo by following the guidelines in this chapter.

ETHICS

1. Find a communication that fails to use inclusive language and revise several of the passages to make them inclusive.

2. The images in advertising often rely on stereotypes. Find one advertisement that perpetuates one or more stereotypes and one that calls attention to itself by using an image that defies a stereotype. Evaluate the ethical impact of each image. Present your results in the way your instructor requests.

9 Beginning a Communication
开始交流

GUIDELINES

1. Give your readers a reason to pay attention *281*
2. State your main point *285*
3. Tell your readers what to expect *286*
4. Encourage openness to your message *287*
5. Provide necessary background information *289*
6. Include a summary unless your communication is very short *290*
7. Adjust the length of your beginning to your readers' needs *291*
8. **Global Guideline:** Adapt your beginning to your readers' cultural background *294*
9. **Ethics Guideline:** Begin to address unethical practices promptly—and strategically *294*

As you learned in Chapter 1, reading is a dynamic interaction between your readers and your words and graphics. Your readers' response to one sentence or paragraph can influence their reactions to all the sentences and paragraphs that follow. Consequently, the opening sentence or section takes on special importance: It helps to establish the frame of mind readers bring to all the sentences and sections that follow.

CHAPTER 9

DEFINING OBJECTIVES

PLANNING

DRAFTING

REVISING

To read additional information, see more examples, and access links related to this chapter's guidelines, go to Chapter 9 at **www.thomsonedu.com/english/anderson.**

In this chapter, you will learn eight reader-centered strategies for beginning your communications in highly usable and highly persuasive ways. Rarely, if ever, will you use all eight at once. To decide which one or combination to use in a particular circumstance, you will need to build on the knowledge of your readers that you gained while defining your communication's objectives (Chapter 3). The chapter's ninth guideline discusses ethical approaches to situations in which people at work sometimes wonder whether they should begin to try communicating at all.

INTRODUCTION TO GUIDELINES 1 THROUGH 3
介绍指导方针 1 至 3

The first three guidelines echo strategies described in Chapter 7 for beginning paragraphs, sections, and chapters: Announce the topic, state the main point, and forecast your communication's organization. These helpful strategies from Chapter 7 are incorporated into this chapter's Guidelines 1 through 3 so you can see how to apply them when beginning your entire communication.

GUIDELINE 1 GIVE YOUR READERS A REASON TO PAY ATTENTION
指导方针 1：给读者一个关注的理由

The most important function of a beginning is to persuade your readers to devote their full attention to your message rather than skimming it or—worse yet—setting it aside unfinished or dropping it in the trash. This is not an easy task. At work, people complain that they receive too many e-mails, memos, and reports. As they look at each communication, they ask, "Why should I read this?" Your goal is to convince them not only to pay *some* attention to your message, but also to pay *close* attention. Doing so will be especially important when your communication is primarily persuasive. Research has shown that the more deeply people think about a message while reading or listening to it, the more likely they are to hold the attitudes it advocates, the more likely they are to resist attempts to reverse those attitudes, and the more likely they are to act upon those attitudes (Petty & Cacioppo, 1986).

People are more likely to be persuaded by messages they think deeply about.

To grab your readers' attention, you must do two things at the outset:

- Announce your topic.
- Tell your readers how they will benefit from the information you are providing.

Be sure to do *both* things. Don't assume that your readers will automatically see the value of your information after you have stated your topic. Benefits that appear obvious to you may not be obvious to them. Compare the following sets of statements:

STATEMENTS OF TOPIC ONLY (AVOID THEM)	STATEMENTS OF TOPIC AND BENEFIT (USE THEM)
This memo tells about the new technology for reducing carbon dioxide emissions.	This memo answers each of the five questions you asked me last week about the new technology reducing carbon dioxide emissions.
This report discusses step-up pumps.	Step-up pumps can save us money and increase our productivity.
This manual concerns the Cadmore Industrial Robot 2000.	This manual tells how to prepare the Cadmore Industrial Robot 2000 for difficult welding tasks.

Importance of Subject Lines in E-mails

E-mails present a special challenge. They have, in effect, two beginnings: the first sentences and the subject line. No matter how skillfully you craft the opening sentences, they won't be read unless your subject line persuades your intended readers to open your message. Name your topic precisely and indicate that what you have to say about it will benefit your readers. Do the same in the subject lines that memos usually include and letters sometimes do.

> **Learn More**
>
> For more on subject lines in e-mail, memos, and letters, go to Chapter 20, pages 527, 533, and 537.

This subject line indicates only the writer's topic. → Subject: Springer Valves

The revised subject line also indicates that the reader will benefit by finding recommendations. → Subject: Recommendation for Improving Springer Valves

This subject line is vague about the topic (what data?). → Subject: Data

This is more precise: It tells what kind of data and also indicates the reader will benefit by finding an analysis of the data. → Subject: Analysis of Probe Data

Two Ways to Highlight Reader Benefits

Two strategies are particularly effective at persuading people that they will benefit from reading your communication.

Refer to Your Reader's Request At work, you will often write because a coworker, manager, or client has asked you for a recommendation or information. To establish the reader benefit of your reply, simply refer to the request.

| As you requested, I am enclosing a list of the steps we have taken in the past six months to tighten security in the Information Technology Department. | References to the readers' request |

| Thank you for your inquiry about the capabilities of our Model 1770 color laser printer. | |

Offer to Help Your Readers Solve a Problem The second strategy for highlighting reader benefits at the beginning of a communication is to tell your readers that your communication will help them solve a problem they are confronting. Most employees think of themselves as problem-solvers. Whether the problem involves technical, organizational, or ethical issues, they welcome communications that help them find a solution.

Communication experts J. C. Mathes and Dwight W. Stevenson (1991) have suggested an especially powerful approach to writing beginnings that builds on readers' concerns with problem-solving. First, list problems that are important to the people you are going to address in your communication. From the list, pick one that the information and ideas you will provide can help them solve. When you've done that, you have begun to think of yourself and your readers as partners in a joint problem-solving effort in which your communication plays a critical role. The following diagram illustrates this relationship.

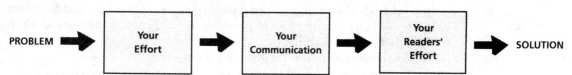

| Once you have determined how to describe a problem-solving partnership between you and your readers, draft the beginning of your communication using the following strategy: | Writer and readers are problem-solving partners. |

ESTABLISHING A PROBLEM-SOLVING PARTNERSHIP WITH YOUR READERS

| 1. **Tell your readers the problem you will help them solve.** Be sure to identify a problem your readers deem important.
2. **Tell your readers what you have done toward solving the problem.** Review the steps you have taken as a specialist in your own field, such as developing a new feature for one of your employer's products or investigating products offered by competitors. Focus on activities that will be significant to your readers rather than listing everything you've done.
3. **Tell your readers how your communication will help them as they perform their part of your joint problem-solving effort.** For example, you might say that it will help them compare competing products, understand a new policy for handling purchase orders, or develop a new marketing plan. | To establish a problem-solving partnership, tell your readers these three things. |

Guideline 1 **Give Your Readers a Reason to Pay Attention**

The following diagram shows the relationships among the three elements in this type of reader-centered beginning.

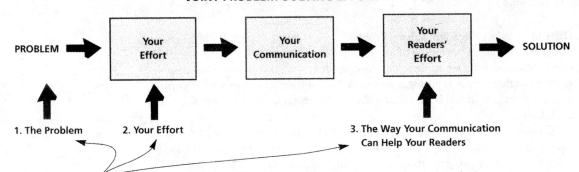

The three elements of a beginning that describes a problem-solving situation

Carla, a computer consultant, used this strategy when she wrote the beginning of a report about her trip to Houston, where she studied the billing system at a hotel her employer recently purchased. First, she identified the problem that her communication would help her readers solve: The Houston hotel was making little money, perhaps because its billing system was faulty. Next she reviewed what she had done in Houston to help her readers solve this problem: She evaluated the billing system and formulated possible improvements. Finally, she determined how her report would help her readers perform their own problem-solving activities: It would help them choose the best course of action by providing data and recommendations on which they could base their decision.

Here is how Carla wrote the beginning of her report:

Carla names the problem her report will help solve.

Carla describes her work toward solving the problem.

Carla tells how her report will help her readers do their part toward solving the problem.

> Last year, our Houston hotel posted a profit of only 4 percent, even though it is almost always 78 percent filled. A preliminary examination of the hotel's operations suggests that its billing system may generate bills too slowly and it may be needlessly ineffective in collecting overdue payments. After examining the hotel's billing cycle and collection procedures, I identified four ways to improve them. To aid in the evaluation of my recommendations, this report discusses the costs and benefits of each one.

Must You Always Provide All This Information? Beginnings that use this strategy may be shorter or longer than Carla's. Just make sure your readers understand all three elements of the problem-solving situation. If one or more of the elements will be obvious to them, there's no benefit in discussing them in detail. For example, if the only persons who would read Carla's report were thoroughly familiar with the details of the problem in Houston and the work she did there, Carla could have written a very brief beginning:

> In this report, I evaluate the billing system in our Houston hotel and recommend ways of improving it.

She included more explanation because she knew her report would also be read by people who were hearing about her trip for the first time.

Here are some situations in which a full description of the problem-solving situation usually is desirable:

- **Your communication will be read by people outside your immediate working group.** The more distant some or all of your readers are, the less likely that all of them will be familiar with your message's context.
- **Your communication will have a binding and a cover.** Bound documents are usually intended for large groups of current readers and they are often filed for consultation by future readers. Both groups are likely to include at least some readers who will have no idea of the problem-solving situation you are addressing.
- **Your communication will be used to make a decision involving a significant amount of money.** Such decisions are often made by high-level managers who need to be told about the organizational context of the reports they read.

Circumstances in which you may need to describe the problem-solving situation in detail

Defining the Problem in Unsolicited Communications In your career, you will have many occasions to make a request or recommendation without being asked to do so. When writing these unsolicited communications, you may need to persuade your readers that a problem even exists. This can require some creative, reader-centered thinking.

Consider the way Roberto accomplished this goal. He works for a company that markets computer programs used to control manufacturing processes. One program contained bugs that Roberto wanted to fix because he sympathized with the customers who called for help in overcoming problems caused by the bugs. However, Roberto knew that his boss did not want to assign computer engineers to this task. Instead, she wanted the engineers to spend all their time on her top priority, which was to develop new products rapidly. Consequently, Roberto wrote his boss a memo that opened by discussing the difficulty the company had been having in releasing new products on time. He then showed how much time the computer engineers needed to spend helping customers overcome problems caused by the bugs rather than working on new products. By tying his request to a problem that his reader found significant (rather than to the problems that actually prompted him to write), Roberto succeeded in being assigned to fix the two most serious bugs.

GUIDELINE 2 STATE YOUR MAIN POINT
指导方针2：说出主要观点

You can usually boost your communication's usability and persuasiveness by stating your main point in your beginning. In earlier chapters, you learned three major reasons for doing so:

- You help your readers find what they most want or need.
- You increase the likelihood that your readers will actually read your main point instead of putting your communication aside before they get to it.

Reasons for stating your main point at the beginning

- You provide your readers with a context for viewing the details that follow.

Choose Your Main Point Thoughtfully

Choose the main point of your communication in the same way you choose the main point of each segment. If you are responding to a request, your main point will be the answer to the question your reader asked. If you are writing on your own initiative, your main point might be what you want your readers to think or do after reading your communication.

Here are some sample statements:

From the beginning of a memo written in a manufacturing company:

> We should immediately suspend all purchases from Cleves Manufacturing until it can guarantee us that the parts it supplies will meet our specifications.

Each of these beginnings states the writer's main point.

From the beginning of a memo written to a department head in a food services company:

> I request $1,200 in travel funds to send one of our account executives to the client's Atlanta headquarters.

From a research report:

> The test results show that the walls of the submersible room will not be strong enough to withstand the high pressures of a deep dive.

GUIDELINE 3 TELL YOUR READERS WHAT TO EXPECT
指导方针3：向读者介绍结构及内容

Unless your communication is very short, its beginning should tell readers what to expect in the segments that follow. This guideline echoes the advice given in Chapter 7: "Use forecasting statements." A forecasting statement positioned at the beginning of a communication should focus its organization and scope.

Learn More

For more on forecasting statements, turn to page 210.

Tell about Your Communication's Organization

By telling your readers about your communication's organization in your beginning, you provide them with a framework for understanding the connections among the various pieces of information you convey. This framework substantially increases your communication's usability by helping your readers to see immediately how each new point you make relates to the points they have already read. It also helps skimming readers to navigate quickly to the information they are seeking.

You can tell your readers about the organization of your communication in various ways:

The writers use sentences to forecast the organization of their report.

> In this report, we state the objectives of the project, compare the three major technical alternatives, and present our recommendation. The final sections include a budget and a proposed project schedule.

This booklet covers the following topics:	These writers use a list to forecast their booklet's organization.
• Principles of Sound Reproduction • Types of Speakers • Choosing the Speakers That Are Right for You • Installing the Speakers	

Tell about Your Communication's Scope

Readers want to know from the beginning what a communication does and does not contain. Even if they are persuaded that you are addressing a subject relevant to them, they may still wonder whether you will discuss the specific aspects of the subject they want to know about.

Often, you will tell your readers about the scope of your communication when you tell them about its organization: When you list the topics it addresses, you indicate its scope.

There will be times, however, when you will need to include additional information. That happens when you want your readers to understand that you are not addressing your subject comprehensively or that you are addressing it from a particular point of view. For instance, you may be writing a troubleshooting manual to help factory workers solve a certain set of problems that often arise with the manufacturing robots they monitor. Other problems — ones your manual doesn't address — might require the assistance of someone else. In that case, you should tell your readers explicitly about the scope of your manual:

This manual treats problems you can correct by using tools and equipment normally available to you. It does not cover problems that require work by computer programmers or electrical engineers.	In the first sentence, the writer describes the manual's contents. To avoid possible misunderstanding, the writer adds the second sentence to tell what it does not contain.

GUIDELINE 4 ENCOURAGE OPENNESS TO YOUR MESSAGE
指导方针 4：鼓励对信息的开放性

Other chapters in this book have emphasized that readers can respond in a variety of ways as they read a communication. For example, when they read a set of recommendations you are making, they can try to understand your arguments or search for flaws. When they read a set of instructions you have prepared, they can follow your directions in every detail or attempt the procedure on their own, consulting your instructions only if they get stumped.

Because the way you begin a communication has a strong effect on your readers' response, you should always pay attention to the persuasive dimension of your beginnings. Always begin in a way that encourages your readers to be open and receptive to the rest of your communication.

Readers' Initial Reactions Can Vary

Ordinarily, you will have no trouble eliciting a receptive response because you will be communicating with fellow employees, customers, and others who want the information you are providing. In certain circumstances, however, your readers may have a more negative attitude toward your message. In such situations, you will need to take special care in drafting the beginning of your communication if you are to win a fair hearing for your message.

Your readers' initial attitude toward your message will be negative if the answer to any of the following questions is "yes." If that is the case, try to pinpoint the attitudes that are likely to shape your readers' reactions to your communication, and then devise your beginning accordingly.

Questions for determining whether readers might resist your message

- Does your message contain bad news for your readers?
- Does your message contain ideas or recommendations that will be unwelcome to your readers?
- Do your readers feel distrust, resentment, or competitiveness toward you, your department, or your company?
- Are your readers likely to be skeptical of your knowledge of your subject or situation?
- Are your readers likely to be suspicious of your motives?

The strategy that is most likely to promote a positive initial reaction or to counteract a negative one differs from situation to situation. However, here are three strategies that often work.

STRATEGIES FOR ENCOURAGING OPENNESS

- **Present yourself as a partner, not as a critic or a competitor.** Suggest that you are working with your readers to help solve a problem they want to solve or to achieve a goal they want to achieve. (See Guideline 1.)
- **Delay the presentation of your main point.** An initial negative reaction may prompt your readers to aggressively devise counterarguments to each point that follows. Therefore, if you believe that your readers may react negatively to your main point, consider making an exception to Guideline 2, which tells you to state your main point in your beginning. If you delay the presentation of your main point, your readers may consider at least some of your other points objectively before discovering your main point and reacting against it.
- **Establish your credibility.** As Chapter 5 suggests, people are more likely to respond favorably to a message if they have confidence in the person delivering it. Consequently, you can promote openness to your message if you begin by convincing your readers that you are an expert in your subject and knowledgeable about the situation. This does not mean, however, that you should announce your credentials in the beginning of *every* communication. If you needlessly present your credentials, you merely burden your readers with unnecessary information. Avoid discussing your qualifications when writing to people, such as your coworkers, who have already formed a favorable opinion of your expertise.

Learn More
See also Chapter 5's discussion of the indirect pattern of organization (page 132).

Learn More
See also Chapter 5's suggestions for building credibility (page 135).

Tell Yourself a Story

Although the strategies suggested above will often encourage openness, don't employ them mechanically. Always keep in mind the particular attitudes, experiences, and expectations of your readers as you craft the beginning of a communication.

You might do this by telling yourself a story about your readers. The central figure in your story should be your reader — an individual if you are writing to one person, or a typical member of your audience if you are writing to a group. Begin your story a few minutes before this person picks up your communication and continue it until the moment he or she reads your first words. Although you would not actually include the story in your communication, creating it can help you decide how to begin.

Here is a sample story, written by Jolene, a manager in an insurance company. Jolene wrote it to help herself understand the readers of an instruction manual she is preparing that will teach new insurance agents how to use the company's computer system.

It's Monday afternoon. After half a day of orientation meetings and tours, Bob, the new trainee, sits down at the computer terminal for the first time to try to learn this system. He was a French major who has never used a data entry program. Now, in two hours, he is supposed to work his way through this manual and then enter some sample policy information. He feels rushed, confused, and quite nervous. He knows that the information is critical, and he does not want to make an error. Despite his insecurity, Bob will not ask questions of the experienced agent in the next office because (being new to the company) he doesn't want to make a bad impression by asking dumb questions. Bob picks up the instruction manual for the SPRR program that I am writing; he hopes it will tell him quickly what he needs to know. He wants it to help him learn the system in the time allotted without his making any mistakes and without his having to ask embarrassing questions.	Jolene predicts her readers' attitudes by imagining a story about one of them.

This story helped Jolene to focus on several important facts: The reader will be anxious, hurried, and uncertain. Those insights helped her write an effective opening for her manual:

This manual tells you how to enter policy information into our SPRR system. It covers the steps for opening a file for a new policy, entering the relevant information, revising the file, and printing a paper copy for your permanent records.	Jolene adopts a helpful tone.
By following these instructions carefully, you can avoid making time-consuming errors. In addition, the SPRR system is designed to detect and flag possible errors so you can double-check them.	Jolene reassures her readers.

By identifying her readers' probable feelings, Jolene was able to reduce their anxiety and encourage them to be more open to her instructions.

GUIDELINE 5 PROVIDE NECESSARY BACKGROUND INFORMATION
指导方针5：提供必要的背景知识

As you draft the beginning of a communication, ask yourself whether your readers will need any background information to understand what you are going to tell them.

Here are some examples of situations that might require such information at the beginning:

Signs that your readers need background information

- **Your readers need to grasp certain general principles in order to understand your specific points.** For instance, your discussion of the feasibility of locating a new plant in a particular city may depend on a particular analytical technique that you will need to explain to your readers.
- **Your readers are unfamiliar with technical terms you will be using.** For example, as a specialist in international trade, you may need to explain certain technical terms to the board of directors before you present your strategies for opening up foreign markets.
- **Your readers are unfamiliar with the situation you are discussing.** For example, imagine that you are reporting to the executive directors of a large corporation about labor problems at one of the plants it recently acquired in a takeover. To understand and weigh the choices that face them, the directors will need an introduction to the plant and its labor history.

Not all background information belongs at the beginning of your communication. Information that pertains only to certain segments should appear at the beginning of those segments. In the beginning of your communication, include only background information that will help your readers understand your overall message.

GUIDELINE 6 INCLUDE A SUMMARY UNLESS YOUR COMMUNICATION IS VERY SHORT

指导方针6：要有总结——除非篇幅很短

At work, it's quite common for communications as short as a page or two to start with a brief summary of the entire message. These summaries help busy managers learn the main points without reading the entire document, and they give these readers an overview of the communication's content and organization.

In short communications, such as memos and letters, opening summaries often consist of only a few sentences in the opening paragraph or paragraphs.

Here is the opening paragraph of a one-page test report.

In this opening, the writer summarizes a one-page report by briefly identifying the purpose of the test, test method, test results, and future action. Each topic is described in a paragraph in the rest of the report.

> On June 29 and 30, we used a computer simulation to test the prototype design for a robotic welder. In the simulation, we required the robot to spot weld front and back panels on an assembly line. We also tested the robot's ability to weld accurately throughout the full range of distances and angles in the technical specifications. The robot performed front welds accurately at all distances, but could not make back welds at certain angles. Consequently, the mountings for four actuators are being redesigned.

In the paragraphs that follow this summary, the writer describes the major features of the robotic welder, capabilities of the simulation program as well as the welding tasks given the robot, test results, and changes to be made in the design.

For longer communications, especially those that are long enough to have covers and tables of contents, the summaries are longer and often printed on a separate page.

These longer summaries are described in Chapter 11, "Writing Reader-Centered Front and Back Matter."

GUIDELINE 7 ADJUST THE LENGTH OF YOUR BEGINNING TO YOUR READERS' NEEDS

指导方针7：根据读者的需要调整开头的长度

There is no rule of thumb that tells how long the beginning should be. A good, reader-centered beginning may require only a phrase or may take several pages. You need to give your readers only the information they don't already know. Just be sure they know the following:

- The reason they should read the communication (Guideline 1)
- The main point of the communication (Guideline 2)
- The organization and scope of the communication (Guideline 3)
- The background information they need in order to understand and use the communication (Guideline 5)

What your readers need to know

If you have given your readers all this information — and have encouraged them to receive your message openly (Guideline 4) — then you have written a good beginning, regardless of how long or short it is.

Here is an opening prepared by a writer who followed all the guidelines given in this chapter.

> In response to your memo dated November 17, I have called Goodyear, Goodrich, and Firestone for information about the ways they forecast their needs for synthetic rubber. The following paragraphs summarize each of those phone calls.

Brief beginning

The following opening, from a two-paragraph memo, is even briefer:

> We are instituting a new policy for calculating the amount that employees are paid for overtime work.

Briefer beginning

At first glance, this single sentence may seem to violate all the guidelines. It does not. It identifies the topic of the memo (overtime pay), and the people to whom the memo is addressed will immediately understand its relevance to them. It also declares the main point of the memo (a new policy is being instituted). Moreover, because the memo itself is only two paragraphs long, its scope is readily apparent. The brevity of the memo also suggests its organization — namely, a brief explanation of the new policy and nothing else. The writer has correctly judged that his readers need no background information.

Figure 9.1 shows a relatively long beginning from a report written by a consulting firm hired to recommend ways to improve the food service at a hospital. Like the brief beginnings given above, it is carefully adapted to its readers and to the situation.

Examples of longer beginnings are shown in Figures 9.1 and 9.2.

Figure 9.2 shows the long beginning of a 500-page service manual for the Detroit Diesel Series 53 engine manufactured by General Motors.

FIGURE 9.1
Beginning of a Recommendation Report

The writers open their summary by stating the problem they will address. It is one that's important to their readers.

The writers detail the subparts of the problem.

The writers present themselves as the reader's problem-solving partners.

- They tell what they have done to help solve the problem.

- They tell how the report will assist their readers in doing their part of the problem-solving effort.

The writers tell how they have organized their report.

To indicate the scope of this report, the writers highlight a topic it will not cover.

They assist their readers by summarizing their main points.

INTRODUCTION

Wilton Hospital has added 200 patient beds through construction of the new West Wing. Since the wing opened, the food-service department has had difficulty meeting this extra demand. The director of the hospital has also reported the following additional problems:

1. Difficulties operating at full capacity. The equipment, some of it thirty years old, breaks down frequently. Absenteeism has risen dramatically.
2. Costs of operation that are well above average for the hospital industry nationally and in this region.
3. Frequent complaints about the quality of the food from both the patients and the hospital staff who eat in the cafeteria.

To study these problems, we have monitored the operation of the food-service department and interviewed patients, food-service employees, and staff who eat in the cafeteria. In addition, we have compared all aspects of the department's facilities and operations with those at other hospitals of roughly the same size.

In this report, we discuss our findings concerning the food-service department's kitchen facilities. We briefly describe the history and nature of these facilities, suggest two alternative ways of improving them, and provide a budget for each. In the final section of this report, we propose a renovation schedule and discuss ways of providing food service while the renovation work is being done. (Our recommendations about staffing and procedures will be presented in another report in thirty days.)

The first alternative costs about $730,000 and would take four months to accomplish. The second costs about $1,100,000 and would take five months. Both will meet the minimum needs of the hospital; the latter can also provide cooking for the proposed program of delivering hot meals to housebound persons in the city.

FIGURE 9.2
Beginning of a Service Manual

General Information   DETROIT DIESEL 53

• SCOPE AND USE OF THE MANUAL

This manual covers the basic Series 53 Diesel Engines built by the Detroit Diesel Corporation. Complete instructions on operation, adjustment (tune-up), preventive maintenance and lubrication, and repair (including complete overhaul) are covered. The manual was written primarily for persons servicing and overhauling the engine and, in addition, contains all of the instructions essential to the operators and users. Basic maintenance and overhaul procedures are common to all Series 53 engines and, therefore, apply to all Inline and Vee models.

— The writers tell what the manual is about in the first sentence.

— In the following sentences, they describe the manual's scope.

The manual is divided into numbered sections. The first section covers the engine (less major assemblies). The following sections cover a complete system such as the fuel system, lubrication system or air system. Each section is divided into subsections which contain complete maintenance and operating instructions for a specific subassembly on the engine. For example, Section 1, which covers the basic engine, contains subsection 1.1 pertaining to the cylinder block, subsection 1.2 covering the cylinder head, etc. The subjects and sections are listed in the Table of Contents on the preceding page. Pages are numbered consecutively, starting with a new Page 1 at the beginning of each subsection. The illustrations are also numbered consecutively, beginning with a new Fig. 1 at the start of each subsection.

Information regarding a general subject, such as the lubrication system, can best be located by using the Table of Contents. Opposite each subject in the Table of Contents is a section number which registers with a tab printed on the first page of each section throughout the manual. Information on a specific subassembly or accessory can then be found by consulting the list of contents on the first page of the section. For example, the cylinder liner is part of the basic engine. Therefore, it will be found in Section 1. Looking down the list of contents on the first page of Section 1, the cylinder liner is found to be in subsection 1.6.3. An Alphabetical Index at the back of the manual has been provided as an additional aid for locating information.

— The writers indicate the organization of the manual.

— They provide a guide to the usability of the manual.

SERVICE PARTS AVAILABILITY

Genuine Detroit Diesel service parts are available from authorized Detroit Diesel distributors and service dealers throughout the world. A complete list of all distributors and dealers is available in the Worldwide Distributor and Dealer Directory, 6SE280. This publication can be ordered from any authorized distributor.

CLEARANCES AND TORQUE SPECIFICATIONS

Clearances of new parts and wear limits on used parts are listed in tabular form at the end of each section throughout the manual. It should be specifically noted that the "New Parts" clearances apply only when all new parts are used at the point where the various specifications apply. This also applies to references within the text of the manual. The column entitled "Limits" lists the amount of wear or increase in clearance which can be tolerated in used engine parts and still assure satisfactory performance. It should be emphasized that the figures given as "Limits" must be qualified by the judgment of personnel responsible for installing new parts. These wear limits are, in general, listed only for the parts more frequently replaced in engine overhaul work. For additional information, refer to the paragraph entitled *Inspection* under *General Procedures* in this section.

— The writers provide background information that is implicit throughout the rest of the manual.

Bolt, nut and stud torque specifications are also listed in tabular form at the end of each section.

PARTS REPLACEMENT

Before installing a new or used part, check it thoroughly to make sure it is the proper part for the job. The quality of the replacement part must be equivalent to the quality of the original Detroit Diesel component being replaced and must meet DDC specifications for new or reusable parts.

— They provide additional background information, including cautions.

Parts must also be clean and not physically damaged or defective. For example, bolts and bolt hole threads must not be damaged or distorted. Gasketing must have all holes completly punched with no residual gasket material left clinging to the top or bottom. Flatness and fit specifications in the service manual must be strictly adhered to.

CAUTION: Failure to inspect parts thoroughly before installation, failure to install the proper parts, or failure to install parts properly can result in component or engine malfunction and/or damage and may also result in personal injury.

Page 4   May, 1990   © Copyright 1990 Detroit Diesel Corporation

Readers from different cultures may have different expectations about the ways a work-related communication will begin.

GUIDELINE 8   GLOBAL GUIDELINE: ADAPT YOUR BEGINNING TO YOUR READERS' CULTURAL BACKGROUND

整体指导方针8：根据读者的文化背景调整开头

Readers' expectations and preferences about the beginning of a communication are shaped by their culture. The suggestions you have just read are suitable for readers in the United States and some other Western countries. However, customs vary widely. For example, the French often open their business correspondence in a more formal way than do people in the United States. In some Spanish-speaking cultures, business letters begin in a flowery manner. In Japan, business letters often begin with a reference to the season. The following example shows one writer's way of adapting to the expectations of a Japanese businessperson (Human Japanese, 2005):

| Beginning of a business letter to a Japanese reader. | Here in Seattle, fall has finally arrived, and the days continue to become shorter and shorter. At night it's now cold enough that one needs a sweater to go outside. |

Next, the letter moves to the main topic:

> The reason I'm writing you is that . . . .

Clearly, you must have a good understanding of the communication customs of your readers' culture in order to create an effective opening. If you do not have this understanding, do some research or, better yet, consult with someone who is from the culture or is very familiar with it.

GUIDELINE 9   ETHICS GUIDELINE: BEGIN TO ADDRESS UNETHICAL PRACTICES PROMPTLY—AND STRATEGICALLY

道德指导方针9：迅速并有策略地揭示不道德行为

So far, the guidelines in this chapter have focused on the ways to begin a communication. In contrast, this last guideline concerns situations in which people at work sometimes hesitate to begin writing or speaking at all. Suppose you learn that your employer is engaged in an action you consider to be unethical. Or, suppose you are asked to write something that violates your sense of what is ethical. Should you speak up or express your concerns in writing? New employees are sometimes advised to wait until they have achieved security and status before trying to bring about change. But that means you could spend years before addressing a practice you regard as unethical. Ignoring an unethical act could be seen as unethical in itself.

When determining how to draw attention to something you consider to be unethical, you face a challenge similar to that of figuring out how to begin a memo in which you will recommend a course of action with which you believe your readers will disagree (see pages 287–288). Here are three strategies that could enable you to open a discussion based on your values without jeopardizing your future with your employer's organization.

- **Plant the seeds of change.** Instead of trying to alter the situation immediately, plant the seeds of change. For instance, if your employer is thinking of modifying working conditions in a factory, you might inquire, "How would this modification affect workers on the assembly line?" Or, you might ask, "Would this modification be fair to the assembly line workers?" By posing such questions, you extend the range of issues being considered, and you can subtly let others know the values that shape your understanding of the situation. In addition to asking questions, there are many other ways you can introduce your values into the discussion. Think creatively. Taking even a small step toward improving a situation is an ethical act. Moreover, in many circumstances, it's only through a long series of small steps that large improvements are achieved.
- **Use reason rather than accusation.** Your values are much more likely to prevail if you engage people with other views in a reasoned discussion than if you accuse and condemn them. It's not usually possible to persuade people by attacking them. They merely become defensive. Instead, ask them to share their sense of the values that apply to the situation. Appeal to their sense of fairness and of what is right and wrong.
- **Remain open to others' views.** One reason to avoid taking a rigid stand is that it impairs your ability to understand others' views of the situation. People regularly differ on ethical matters, and your own view is not necessarily shared by others. Strive for solutions that will satisfy both you and others. One possibility is to employ a strategy similar to that described in this chapter's discussion of Guideline 1 (see page 283): Identify the values that the other people hold that would lead them to endorse the same course of action that your values lead you to advocate.

Strategies for changing unethical practices without risking your job

You may someday witness a practice that is so outrageous that you will be willing to risk future promotions and even your job in order to stop it. If you find yourself in that situation, seek the aid of influential people inside your company. If the practice you object to violates the law or a government regulation, alert the appropriate agency. This is called *whistleblowing*. Federal law and some state laws are intended to protect whistleblowers, and some laws even reward whistleblowers by giving them a portion of any financial settlement that is made. Still, many whistleblowers do lose their jobs or continue to work under hostile conditions. If you are thinking of whistleblowing, consider the possibility of first attempting a nonconfrontational approach to the problem.

CONCLUSION 总 结

The beginning is probably the most important segment of a communication. That's because it can influence the ideas and attitudes your readers derive from the rest of your communication, and it can even determine whether or not they will read further.

This chapter has suggested that in writing a beginning you start by trying to identify your readers' attitudes toward your message and by determining what you can say to help them understand and use what follows. This reader-centered approach will enable you to create beginnings that prompt your readers to pay careful attention, encourage them to treat your information and ideas with an open mind, and help them read efficiently.

EXERCISES 练 习

EXPERTISE

1. Select a communication written to professionals in your field. This might be a letter, memo, manual, report, or article in a professional journal. (Do not choose a textbook.) Identify the guidelines from this chapter that the writer applied when drafting the communication's beginning. Is the beginning effective in achieving the writer's usability and persuasive goals? If so, why? If not, how could the beginning be improved?
2. The instructions for many consumer products contain no beginning section at all. For instance, the instructions for some lawnmowers, cake mixes, and detergents simply provide a heading that says "Instructions" and then start right in. Find such a set of instructions and — in terms of the guidelines given in this chapter — evaluate the writer's decision to omit a beginning.

ONLINE

The home page of a website typically looks very different from the opening of a printed document. Nonetheless, the home page has many of the same reader-centered goals as the printed opening. Examine the ways that two websites follow this chapter's guidelines. Consider such things as the communication functions performed by the images, layout, text (if any), and words used for buttons and links. One of the home pages you study should be for a company that sells consumer products such as cars. The other should be for a nonprofit organization or government agency. Present your analysis in the way your instructor requests.

COLLABORATION

1. The following paragraphs are from the beginning of a report in which the manager of a purchasing department asks for better-quality products from the department in the company that provides abrasives. Is this an effective beginning for what is essentially a complaint? Why or why not? Working with another student, analyze this beginning in terms of this chapter's guidelines.

   I am sure you have heard that the new forging process is working well. Our customers have expressed pleasure with our castings. Thanks again for all your help in making this new process possible.

   We are having one problem, however, with which I have to ask once more for your assistance. During the seven weeks since we began using the new process, the production line has been idle 28 percent of the time. Also, many castings have had to be remade. Some of the evidence suggests that these problems are caused by the steel abrasive supplies we get from your department. If we can figure out how to improve the abrasive, we may be able to run the line at 100 percent of capacity.

   I would be most grateful for help from you and your people in improving the abrasive. To help you devise ways of improving the abrasive, I have compiled this report, which describes the difficulties we have encountered and some of our thinking about possible remedies.

2. Form a team of two or three students. Exchange the opening sections (paragraph or longer) of a project you are now preparing for your instructor. First, suggest specific revisions that would make your partner's opening more effective at achieving his or her usability and persuasive goals. Next, suggest an alternative opening that might also be effective.

ETHICS

It can be particularly challenging to write an effective opening for a communication in which you are advocating for change based on ethical grounds. Think of some organization's practice, procedure, or policy that your values lead you to believe should be changed. Identify the person or group within the organization that has the authority to make the change that you feel is needed. Then, following the advice given in this chapter, draft the opening paragraph of a letter, memo, e-mail, report, or other communication on the topic that you could send to this person or group.

Ending a Communication
结束交流

10

GUIDELINES

1. After you've made your last point, stop *298*
2. Repeat your main point *299*
3. Summarize your key points *299*
4. Refer to a goal stated earlier in your communication *300*
5. Focus on a key feeling *301*
6. Tell your readers how to get assistance or more information *302*
7. Tell your readers what to do next *302*
8. Identify any further study that is needed *302*
9. Follow applicable social conventions *303*

CHAPTER 10

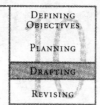

DEFINING OBJECTIVES

PLANNING

DRAFTING

REVISING

The ending of a communication can substantially increase its effectiveness. Researchers have found that readers are better able to remember things said at the end of a communication than things presented in the middle. Consequently, a skillfully written ending can increase a communication's usability by stating or reviewing points that readers will want to recall later.

In addition, an ending is a transition. It leads readers out of the communication and into the larger stream of their activities. Therefore, it provides an excellent opportunity to help readers by answering the question, "What should I do now?"

An ending is also a place of emphasis and a communication's final chance to influence readers' impressions of its subject matter. Consequently, it's an excellent place to highlight a communication's most persuasive points.

This chapter's nine reader-centered guidelines suggest specific strategies you can use to create endings that enhance your communication's usability and persuasiveness. Despite the important role that endings play, however, your best strategy sometimes will be to say what you have to say and then stop, without providing a separate ending (Guideline 1). Other times, you can use one or a combination of strategies described in Guidelines 2 through 9.

To decide which strategies to choose, focus (as always) on your readers.

> To read additional information, see more examples, and access links related to this chapter's guidelines, go to Chapter 10 at www.thomsonedu.com/english/anderson.

How to choose among possible strategies for endings

1. **Decide what you want your readers to think, feel, and do as they finish your communication.** Then select the strategy or strategies for ending that are most likely to create this response.
2. **Determine what kind of ending your readers might be expecting.** Look at what other people in your organization and your field have done in similar situations. This investigation can tell you what your readers are accustomed to finding at the end of the type of communication you are preparing.

GUIDELINE 1　AFTER YOU'VE MADE YOUR LAST POINT, STOP

指导方针1：在说清最后一点后，停止

As mentioned above, sometimes you should end your communications without doing anything special at all. That happens when you use a pattern of organization that brings you to a natural stopping place. Here are some examples:

Communications that you may want to end after the last point

- **Proposals.** You will usually end a proposal with a detailed description of what you will do and how you will do it. Because that's where your readers expect proposals to end, they will enjoy a sense of completion if you simply stop after presenting your last recommendation. Furthermore, by ending after your recommendations, you will have given them the emphasis they require.
- **Formal reports.** When you prepare a formal report (a report with a cover, title page, and binding), the convention is to end either with your conclusions or your recommendations — both appropriate subjects for emphasis.
- **Instructions.** You will usually end instructions by describing the last step.

If your analysis of your purpose, readers, and situation convinces you that you should add something after your last point, review this chapter's other guidelines to select the strategies that will best help you meet your objectives.

GUIDELINE 2 REPEAT YOUR MAIN POINT
指导方针2：重复主要观点

Because the end of a communication is a point of emphasis, you can use it to focus your readers' attention on the points you want to be foremost in their minds as they finish reading.

Consider, for instance, the ending of a classic article written to dispel a misunderstanding by family physicians about the proper way to prevent infections in wounds. The writers Mancusi-Ugaro and Rapport (1986) made their main point in the abstract at the beginning of the article, again in the fourth paragraph (where they supported it with a table), and in several other places. Nevertheless, they considered this point to be so important that they restated it in the final paragraph.

> Perhaps the most important concept to be gleaned from a review of the principles of wound management is that good surgical technique strives to maintain the balance between the host and the bacteria in favor of the host. The importance of understanding that infection is an absolute quantitative number of bacteria within the tissues cannot be overemphasized. Limiting, rather than eliminating, bacteria allows for normal wound healing.

Ending that repeats the communication's main point

The strategy of repeating your main point in your ending can also work well when you want to help your readers make a decision or persuade them to take a certain action. The following paragraph is the ending of a memo urging new safety measures:

> I cannot stress too much the need for immediate action. The exposed wires present a significant hazard to any employee who opens the control box to make routine adjustments.

Another example

GUIDELINE 3 SUMMARIZE YOUR KEY POINTS
指导方针3：总结重要观点

The strategy suggested by this guideline is closely related to the preceding one. In repeating your main point (Guideline 2), you emphasize *only* the information you consider to be of paramount importance. In *summarizing,* you are concerned that your audience has understood the general thrust of your *entire* communication.

Here, for example, is the ending of a 115-page book entitled *Understanding Radioactive Waste,* which is intended to help the general public understand the impact of the nuclear power industry's plans to open new plants (Murray, 2003):

> It may be useful to the reader for us to now select some highlights, key ideas, and important conclusions for this discussion of nuclear wastes. The following list is not complete — the reader is encouraged to add items.

Key points are summarized.

> 1. Radioactivity is both natural and manmade. The decay process gives radiations such as alpha particles, beta particles, and gamma rays. Natural background radiation comes mainly from cosmic rays and minerals in the ground.
> 2. Radiation can be harmful to the body and to genes, but the low-level radiation effect cannot be proved. Many methods of protection are available.
> 3. The fission process gives useful energy in the form of electricity from nuclear plants, but it also produces wastes in the form of highly radioactive fission products. . . .

This list continues for thirteen more items, but this sample should give you an idea of how this author ended with a summary of key points.

Notice that a summary at the end of a communication differs significantly from a summary at the beginning. Because a summary at the beginning is meant for readers who have not yet read the communication, it must include some information that will be of little concern at the end. For example, the beginning summary of a report on a quality-control study will describe the background of the study. In contrast, the ending summary would focus sharply on conclusions and recommendations.

GUIDELINE 4 REFER TO A GOAL STATED EARLIER IN YOUR COMMUNICATION

指导方针4：提及在沟通前期设定的目标

Many communications begin by stating a goal and then describe or propose ways to achieve it. If you end a communication by referring to that goal, you remind your readers of the goal and sharpen the focus of your communication. The following example comes from a seventeen-page proposal prepared by operations analysts in a company that builds customized, computer-controlled equipment used in print shops and printing plants. Notice how the ending refers to the beginning.

Beginning states a goal.

> To maintain our competitive edge, we must develop a way of supplying replacement parts more rapidly to our service technicians without increasing our shipping costs or tying up more money in inventory.

Ending refers to the goal.

> The proposed reform of our distribution network will help us meet the needs of our service technicians for rapidly delivered spare parts. Furthermore, it does so without raising either our shipping expenses or our investment in inventory.

The next example illustrates the way scientific articles often end by stating the answer to a question asked at the article's beginning. In this case, the researchers want to learn whether an electronic nose could be used to detect spoiled chicken in poultry factories and supermarkets (Rajamäki, T., et al., 2006). The spelling follows conventions in the United Kingdom.

The electronic nose is an instrument which comprises an array of electronic chemical sensors with partial specificity and an appropriate pattern-recognition system, capable of recognizing simple or complex odours. . . . The aim of this study was to determine whether it is possible to distinguish differently stored MA packaged unmarinated broiler chicken cuts with an electronic nose.	Beginning states a goal.
The results were very promising when considering the possible applications of an electronic nose as a screening tool for quality control and inspection purposes. . . . An electronic nose [developed specifically for the chicken industry] would include only a few sensors reacting to spoilage parameters of poultry meat and would therefore cost less than larger electronic nose devices developed for detecting many kinds of volatile compounds in various applications.	Ending refers to the goal.

GUIDELINE 5 FOCUS ON A KEY FEELING
指导方针5：抓住情感基调

When ending some communications, it may be more important to focus your readers' attention on a feeling rather than a fact. For instance, if you are writing instructions for a product manufactured by your employer, you may want your ending to encourage your readers' goodwill toward the product. Consider this ending of an owner's manual for a clothes dryer. Though the last sentence provides no additional information, it seeks to shape the readers' attitude toward the company.

The GE Answer Center™ consumer information service is open 24 hours a day, seven days a week. Our staff of experts stands ready to assist you anytime.	Ending designed to build goodwill

The following ending is from a booklet published by the National Cancer Institute for people who have apparently been successfully treated for cancer but do not know how long the disease will remain in remission. It, too, seeks to shape the readers' feelings.

Cancer is not something anyone forgets. Anxieties remain as active treatment ceases and the waiting stage begins. A cold or cramp may be cause for panic. As 6-month or annual check-ups approach, you swing between hope and anxiety. As you wait for the mystical 5-year or 10-year point, you might feel more anxious rather than more secure. These are feelings that we all share. No one expects you to forget you have had cancer or that it might recur. Each must seek individual ways of coping with the underlying insecurity of not knowing the true state of his or her health. The best prescription seems to lie in a combination of one part challenging responsibilities that require a full range of skills, a dose of activities that seek to fill the needs of others, and a generous dash of frivolity and laughter. You still might have moments when you feel as if you live perched on the edge of a cliff. They will sneak up unbidden. But they will be fewer and farther between if you have filled your mind with thoughts having nothing to do with cancer.	Ending designed to shape complex attitudes

Cancer might rob you of that blissful ignorance that once led you to believe that tomorrow stretched on forever. In exchange, you are granted the vision to see each today as precious, a gift to be used wisely and richly. No one can take that away.

GUIDELINE 6 TELL YOUR READERS HOW TO GET ASSISTANCE OR MORE INFORMATION
指导方针6：告诉读者如何获得帮助以及更多的信息

At work, a common strategy for ending a communication is to tell your readers how to get assistance or more information. These two examples are from a letter and a memo:

Endings that offer help

If you have questions about this matter, call me at 523-5221.

If you want any additional information about the proposed project, let me know. I'll answer your questions as best I can.

By ending in this way, you not only provide your readers with useful information, you also encourage them to see you as a helpful, concerned individual.

GUIDELINE 7 TELL YOUR READERS WHAT TO DO NEXT
指导方针7：告诉读者下一步该做什么

In some situations you can help your readers most by telling them what you think they should do next. If more than one course of action is available, tell your readers how to follow up on each of them.

Ending that tells readers exactly what to do

To buy this equipment at the reduced price, we must mail the purchase orders by Friday the 11th. If you have any qualms about this purchase, let's discuss them. If not, please forward the attached materials, together with your approval, to the Controller's Office as soon as possible.

GUIDELINE 8 IDENTIFY ANY FURTHER STUDY THAT IS NEEDED
指导方针8：明确任何需要的进一步研究

Much of the work that is done on the job is completed in stages. For example, one study might answer preliminary questions and, if the answers look promising, an additional study might then be undertaken. Consequently, one common way of ending is to tell readers what needs to be found out next.

Ending that identifies next question needing study

This experiment indicates that we can use compound deposition to create microcircuits in the laboratory. We are now ready to explore the feasibility of using this technique to produce microcircuits in commercial quantities.

Such endings are often combined with summaries, as in the following example:

Another example

In summary, over the past several months our Monroe plant has ordered several hundred electric motors from a supplier whose products are inferior to those we require in the heating and air conditioning systems we build.

> Not only must this practice stop immediately, but also *we* should investigate the situation to determine why this flagrant violation of our quality-control policies has occurred.

GUIDELINE 9 FOLLOW APPLICABLE SOCIAL CONVENTIONS
指导方针 9：遵循恰当的社会规约

All the strategies mentioned so far focus on the subject matter of your communications. When writing the endings of your communications, it is also important to observe the social conventions that apply in each situation.

Some of those conventions involve customary ways of closing particular kinds of communication. For example, letters usually end with an expression of thanks, a statement that it has been enjoyable working with the reader, or an offer to be of further help if needed. In contrast, formal reports and proposals rarely end with such gestures.

Other conventions are peculiar to specific organization. For example, in some organizations writers rarely end their memos with the kind of social gesture commonly provided at the end of a letter. In other organizations, memos often end with such a gesture, and people who ignore that convention risk seeming abrupt and cold.

Consider, too, the social conventions that apply to your relationship with your readers. Have they done you a favor? Thank them. Are you going to see them soon? Let them know that you look forward to the meeting.

CONCLUSION 总 结

This chapter has described nine reader-centered strategies for ending a communication. By considering your readers, your objectives, and the social conventions that apply in your situation, you will be able to choose the strategy or combination of strategies most likely to succeed in the particular communication you are writing.

EXERCISES 练 习

EXPERTISE

Select a communication written to professionals in your field. This might be a letter, memo, manual, technical report, or article in a professional journal. (Do not choose a textbook.) Identify the guidelines from this chapter that the writer applied when drafting that communication's ending. Is the ending effective in achieving the writer's usability and persuasive goals? If so, why? If not, how could it be improved?

ONLINE

For many websites there is no single ending point. Visitors may leave the site at any point. In fact, links in many sites lead visitors directly to other sites. Visit three different kinds of sites, such as one that provides explanations or instructions, one that enables people to purchase products, and one created by an advocacy group. Within each site, where are places that one or more of this chapter's guidelines are employed effectively?

COLLABORATION

1. The following paragraphs constitute the ending of a report to the U.S. Department of Energy concerning the economic and technical feasibility of generating electric power with a special type of windmill (Foreman). The

windmills are called diffuser augmented wind turbines (DAWT). In this ending, the writer has used several of the strategies described in this chapter. Working with another student, identify these strategies.

Section 6.0

Concluding Remarks

We have provided a preliminary cost assessment for the DAWT approach to wind energy conversion in unit systems to 150 kw power rating. The results demonstrate economic viability of the DAWT with no further design and manufacturing know-how than already exists. Further economic benefits of this form of solar energy are likely through:

- Future refinements in product design and production techniques
- Economies of larger quantity production lots
- Special tax incentives

Continued cost escalation on nonrenewable energy sources and public concern for safeguarding the biosphere environment will surely make wind energy conversion by DAWT-like systems even more attractive to our society. Promotional actions by national policy makers and planners as well as industrialists and entrepreneurs can aid the emergence of the DAWT from its research phase to a practical and commercial product.

2. Working with another student, describe the strategies for ending used in the following figures in this text:

FIGURE	PAGE	FIGURE	PAGE
1.3	14	7.3	213
2.6	52	19.1	518
2.7	53	20.3	554
5.6	138	22.7	664

ETHICS

Examine the student conduct code or values statement of your school. Which of the guidelines in this chapter does its ending follow? Why? Also, identify some of the specific values that underline the code's or values statement's provisions.

Writing Reader-Centered Front and Back Matter
以读者为中心写作正文之前和之后的部分

11

GUIDELINES

1. Review the ways your readers will use the communication *307*
2. Review your communication's persuasive goals *307*
3. Find out what's required *307*
4. Find out what's expected *308*
5. Review and revise your front and back matter *308*

CHAPTER 11

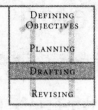

In the workplace, many communications longer than a page are held together with a paper clip or staple. Usually because of their importance or length, others have many of the features found in the books you buy for your classes. Some of these features are called *front matter* because they precede the opening chapter or section. Front matter includes the following items.

- Title Page
- Executive Summary or Abstract
- Table of Contents
- List of Figures and Tables

The other book-like features are called *back matter*, for an obvious reason.

- Appendixes
- Reference List, End Notes, or Bibliography
- Glossary or List of Symbols
- Index

Communications with front and back matter usually have covers as well. When delivered to their readers, these communications are often accompanied by transmittal letters.

In the workplace, reports and proposals with these features are often *called formal reports* and *formal proposals*, names that will be used in the chapter. Instructions with these features are usually called *instruction manuals*.

HOW TRANSMITTAL LETTERS, COVERS, AND FRONT AND BACK MATTER INCREASE USABILITY AND PERSUASIVENESS
介绍函、封面和文前、文后资料如何增加可用性和说服力

Skillfully created front matter, back matter, covers, and transmittal letters increase a communication's usability and persuasiveness in several ways.

- **They help readers find what they need.** A table of contents in the front and an index in the back guide readers to specific information they want. Even the title helps readers locate the right report or manual from a list of reports or manuals.
- **They provide an abbreviated version of the communication's main points.** The title and abstract or executive summary convey the communication's main points to executives and other busy persons who don't have time to read the entire report.

- **They create a favorable initial impression.** A reader-centered and attractive cover and other front matter foster an initial, positive impression among readers.
- **They help future readers locate the communication efficiently.** Communications with front and back matter are usually kept on hand for future use. When designed well, front matter can assist readers in the future as they look for communications that will help them perform their jobs.
- **They protect the communication from wear.** Communications with front and back matter often encounter frequent use. Their covers and bindings help them remain usable.

To assist you in creating these book-like elements, this chapter begins with four reader-centered guidelines, followed by detailed advice about writing transmittal letters, covers, front matter, and back matter.

GUIDELINE 1 REVIEW THE WAYS YOUR READERS WILL USE THE COMMUNICATION
指导方针1：考虑读者将如何使用文章

Front and back matter can make especially important contributions to a communication's usability for its readers. The way you write your title and design your table of contents can increase the efficiency with which readers can locate the information they want. To help readers in this way, you need to know what your readers will be looking for and how they will use your communication. As you begin work on the front and back matter, review the information you developed while defining your communication's usability objectives (see Chapter 3).

GUIDELINE 2 REVIEW YOUR COMMUNICATION'S PERSUASIVE GOALS
指导方针2：考虑文章说服力的目标

By thoroughly understanding your readers' goals, values, and attitudes, you can determine what should be included and emphasized in the executive summary to lead readers to make the decision or take the actions you advocate. Reviewing the information you developed while defining your communication's persuasive objectives, you can enhance the effectiveness of the executive summary and other elements of your front and back matter.

GUIDELINE 3 FIND OUT WHAT'S REQUIRED
指导方针3：找出所要求的

Many organizations distribute instructions that tell employees in detail how to prepare front and back matter. These instructions, sometimes called *style guides*, can describe everything from the maximum number of words permitted in an executive summary to the size and color of the title on a report's cover. If you are writing to one of your employer's clients, the *client's* requirements may be the ones you need to follow. Whatever the source, obtain the relevant style guide and follow its requirements precisely.

GUIDELINE 4 FIND OUT WHAT'S EXPECTED
指导方针 4：找出所期望的

Even if nothing is explicitly required, your employer and your readers probably have expectations about the way you draft front and back matter. Also, beyond what's required, there are often unspoken expectations about how the required elements will be prepared. Look at communications similar to the one you are preparing to learn what expectations you should meet.

GUIDELINE 5 EVALUATE AND REVISE YOUR FRONT AND BACK MATTER
指导方针 5：评价和修改文前及文后部分

Front and back matter are not mere formalities. Because they impact a communication's usability and persuasiveness, you should treat them seriously. Among other actions, this means including them in drafts you evaluate yourself, give to reviewers, present to readers in user testing, and carefully revise and polish.

> **Learn More**
> See Chapters 14 and 15 for guidelines on revising and testing.

CONVENTIONS AND LOCAL PRACTICE
传统及当地习俗

As mentioned above, many employers issue style guides that tell how they want their employees to write front and back matter. Of course, the instructions vary somewhat from organization to organization. For instance, one employer may want the title of any report to be placed in a certain spot on the cover, and another employer may want the title in another spot. Despite these variations, formal reports written on the job look very much alike. The formats described in this chapter reflect common practices in the workplace. You will have little trouble adapting them to other, slightly different versions when the need arises.

As you prepare front and back matter, remember that even if you are following a very comprehensive style manual, you increase your chances of achieving your communication goals by thinking continuously of your readers and applying this chapter's five guidelines.

WRITING A READER-CENTERED TRANSMITTAL LETTER
写以读者为中心的介绍函

When you prepare formal reports and proposals, you will often send them (rather than hand them) to your readers. In such cases, you will want to accompany them with a letter (or memo) of transmittal, which may be placed on top of your communication or bound into it. Transmittal letters typically contain the following elements:

- **Introduction**   In the introduction to your letter, introduce the accompanying communication and explain or remind readers of its topic. Begin on an upbeat note. Here is an example written to a client:

  > We are pleased to submit the enclosed report on evaluating three possible sites for your company's new manufacturing plant.

- **Body**   The body of a transmittal letter usually highlights the communication's major features. For example, researchers often state their main findings and the consequences of what they've learned, repeating information in their communication's abstract or summary.

- **Closing**   Transmittal letters commonly end with a short paragraph (often one sentence) that states the writer's willingness to work further with the reader or promises to answer any questions the reader may have.

Figure 11.1 shows a memo of transmittal.

> To view other examples of front and back matter, link to Chapter 11 at www.thomsonedu.com/english/anderson.

WRITING A READER-CENTERED COVER
写以读者为中心的封面

A cover typically includes the communication's title, the name or logo of the organization that created it, and the date it was issued. In some organizations, covers also include the writer's name and a document number used for filing. To write a reader-centered title, use precise, specific terms that tell your current readers exactly what the communication is about and help your future readers determine whether the communication will be useful to them.

Figure 11.2 shows the cover of a research report.

WRITING READER-CENTERED FRONT MATTER
写以读者为中心的文前部分

Depending on your readers' needs and your employer's expectations, a formal report, formal proposal, or instruction manual may include some or all of the following elements: title page, summary or abstract, table of contents, and list of figures and tables.

Title Page

A title page repeats the information on the cover and usually adds more. For instance, your employer may want you to include contract or project numbers and such cross-referencing information as the name of the contract under which the work was performed. A title page may also provide copyright and trademark notices. Note that some employers require such information on the cover instead.

Figure 11.3 shows the title page of the report whose cover is shown in Figure 11.2.

FIGURE 11.1
Memo of Transmittal Written at Work

This letter of transmittal accompanied the empirical research report shown in Figure WG4.1 (page 567).

Margaret opens with an introductory sentence that mentions the accompanying report and tells its topic.

In the body of her brief memo, Margaret summarizes the report's findings that will be of most interest to her reader. To do this, she includes very precise information, using exact percentages in the first sentence, for instance. Note that she has not included the broader range of information included in the report's executive summary (page 569).

Again tailoring her memo to her reader, an executive decision maker, Margaret describes in specific detail the next step recommended by the research team.

Margaret closes on an upbeat note and indicates that she would welcome questions.

ELECTRONICS CORPORATION OF AMERICA
MEMORANDUM

To   Myron Bronski, Vice-President, Research
           MCB
From   Margaret C. Barnett, Satellite Products Laboratory
Date   September 29, 2006
Re   REPORT ON TRUCK-TO-SATELLITE TEST

On behalf of the entire research team. I am pleased to submit the attached copy of the operational test of our truck-to-satellite communication system.

The test shows that our system works fine. More than 91% of our data transmissions were successful, and more than 91% of our voice transmissions were of commercial quality. The test helped us identify some sources of bad transmissions, including primarily movement of a truck outside the "footprint" of the satellite's strongest broadcast and the presence of objects (such as trees) in the direct line between a truck and the satellite.

The research team believes that our next steps should be to develop a new antenna for use on the trucks and to develop a configuration of satellites that will place them at least 25° above the horizon for trucks anywhere in our coverage area.

We're ready to begin work on these tasks as soon as we get the okay to do so. Let me know if you have any questions.

Encl: Report (2 copies)

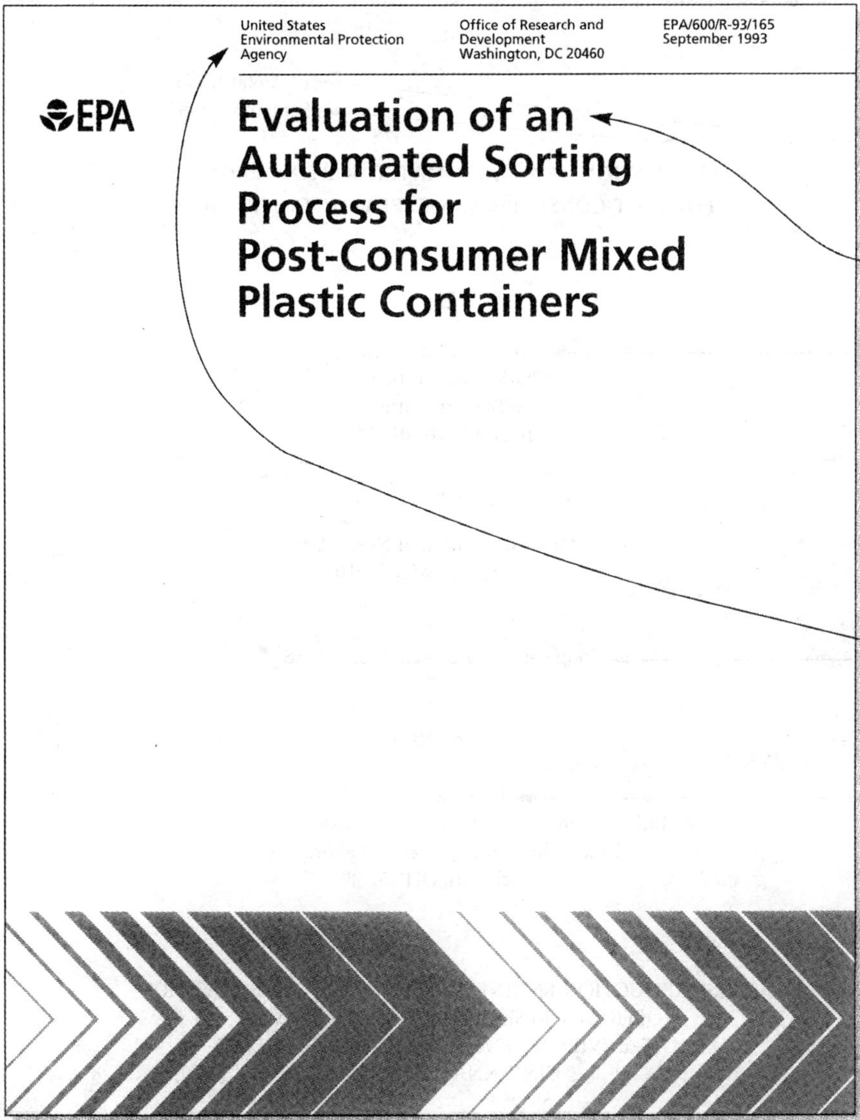

United States Environmental Protection Agency

Office of Research and Development
Washington, DC 20460

EPA/600/R-93/165
September 1993

♻EPA

Evaluation of an Automated Sorting Process for Post-Consumer Mixed Plastic Containers

FIGURE 11.2
Cover of a Formal Report

The authors give greatest visual prominence to the title of the report. Second-level prominence goes to the logo for the Environmental Protection Agency.

The title conveys very specific information about the report's contents:
- It says that the document contains an "evaluation of," rather than using the more general phrase "report on."
- It specifies that the sorting process is "automated."
- It indicates that the waste being sorted was "containers."
- It describes three specific characteristics of the containers: "post consumer," "mixed," and "plastic."

In the small type across the top of the cover, the writers provide the following:
- Full name of the EPA.
- Name of the EPA office that sponsored the study, along with its address (because this document is available to members of the general public, who might want to contact the office).
- The report's filing number.
- The report's date.

FIGURE 11.3
Title Page of the Report Whose Cover Is Shown in Figure 11.2

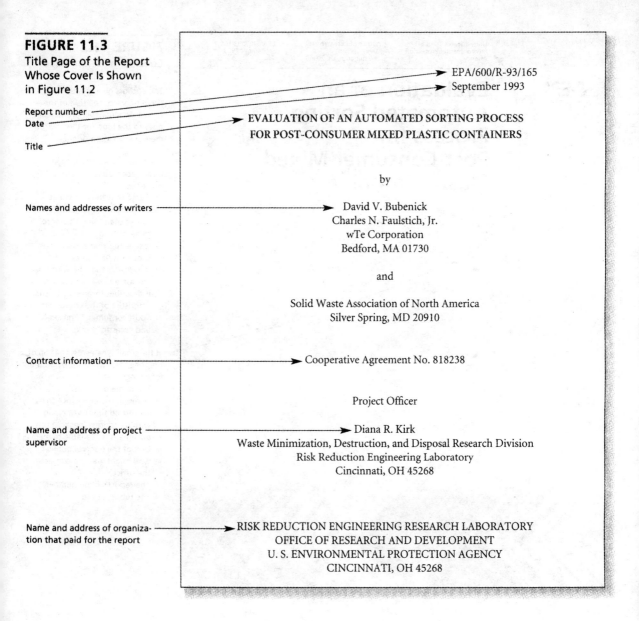

- Report number → EPA/600/R-93/165
- Date → September 1993
- Title → **EVALUATION OF AN AUTOMATED SORTING PROCESS FOR POST-CONSUMER MIXED PLASTIC CONTAINERS**

by

- Names and addresses of writers →
  David V. Bubenick
  Charles N. Faulstich, Jr.
  wTe Corporation
  Bedford, MA 01730

  and

  Solid Waste Association of North America
  Silver Spring, MD 20910

- Contract information → Cooperative Agreement No. 818238

Project Officer

- Name and address of project supervisor →
  Diana R. Kirk
  Waste Minimization, Destruction, and Disposal Research Division
  Risk Reduction Engineering Laboratory
  Cincinnati, OH 45268

- Name and address of organization that paid for the report →
  RISK REDUCTION ENGINEERING RESEARCH LABORATORY
  OFFICE OF RESEARCH AND DEVELOPMENT
  U. S. ENVIRONMENTAL PROTECTION AGENCY
  CINCINNATI, OH 45268

Summary or Abstract

Most reports and proposals that have front matter include a summary, sometimes called an *abstract*. These summaries serve three purposes:

- They help busy managers learn the main points without reading the entire document.
- They help all readers build a mental framework for organizing and understanding the detailed information they will encounter as they read on.
- They help readers determine whether they should read the full communication.

Purposes of summaries

Writing Reader-Centered Summaries

There are three types of summaries. For each communication you write, choose the one that will give your readers the most help as they perform their tasks.

- **Descriptive summaries** resemble a prose table of contents. They help readers decide whether or not to read the communication by identifying major topics covered. They do not tell the main points made about each topic. Often, descriptive summaries are used for research reports that will be placed in widely available resources, such as government databases or libraries. To aid in computerized bibliographic searches, they often contain key words that would be used by persons seeking the kind of information the document contains. Figure 11.4 shows a descriptive summary.
- **Informative summaries** distill the main points from the full document, usually in a page or less, together with enough background information about purpose and method to help readers understand the context in which the key information was developed. Informative summaries are ideally suited to readers who want to make decisions or take other action based on the findings, conclusions, and recommendations reported in the document.

Three kinds of summaries

SUMMARY

This handbook is intended to assist personnel involved with the design, construction, and installation of wells drilled for the purpose of monitoring groundwater for pollutants. It presents state-of-the-art technology that may be applied in diverse hydrogeologic situations and focuses on solutions to practical problems in well construction rather than on idealized practice. The information in the handbook is presented in both matrix and text form. The matrices use a numerical rating scheme to guide the reader toward appropriate drilling technologies for particular monitoring situations. The text provides an overview of the criteria that influence design and construction of groundwater monitoring in various hydrogeologic settings.

FIGURE 11.4
Descriptive Summary

In a descriptive summary, writers tell readers the topics discussed in a communication without telling what it says about each topic.

In this example, the writers do the following:
- Identify the intended audience and the way the handbook will assist them.
- Describe its contents.
- Tell how the information is presented.

Figure 11.5 shows an informative summary (named an abstract in this case) from the EPA report whose cover is shown in Figure 11.2.

- **Executive summaries** are a form of informative summaries tailored to the needs of executives and other decision makers who, pressed for time, want to extract the main points of a communication without reading all of it. Typically, executive summaries open by focusing on organizational questions and issues and briefly describe the investigative or research methods used by the writer. Often half or even more of the summary is devoted to precisely summarizing major conclusions and recommended actions — the type of information most helpful to decision makers. Figure 11.6 shows an executive summary.

Summaries that appear in printed and online bibliographic resources are usually called *abstracts*. In many scientific and engineering fields, the term *abstract* is also used for the summary that appears at the front of long reports and proposals.

Whether you are writing a descriptive, informative, or executive summary, follow these reader-centered guidelines.

WRITING READER-CENTERED SUMMARIES

- **Make it 100 percent redundant with the communication.** This purposeful redundancy provides a complete and understandable message to the reader who reads nothing else in the communication. It also means that the summary can't serve as the introduction, even though the introduction that follows it may seem somewhat repetitious.
- **Mirror the structure of the overall communication.** Include information from each major part of the communication, presented in the order of the parts in the overall communication.
- **Meet the needs of your readers**. For instance, if you know that your readers will be primarily interested in a novel method you used, provide more detail about the method than you would for readers who are primarily interested in your results. Likewise, in deciding what to include from any part of the full document, pick the information your specific readers will find most useful.
- **Be specific.** Replace general terms with precise ones. Instead of saying that it was "hot," say that it was "150°." Rather than saying the less expensive alternative "saved money," say that it saved "$43,000 per month." The more specific your abstract, the more useful it will be to your readers.
- **Keep it short.** Summaries are typically only 2 to 5 percent of the length of the body of the communication (not counting attachments and appendixes). That's between half a page and a whole page for every twenty pages in the body of your communication.
- **Write concisely.** Abstracts need to be lean but highly informative. Keep them short by eliminating unnecessary words, not by leaving out information important to your readers.

Learn More

For more strategies for writing concisely, see Guideline 1 for constructing sentences in Chapter 8, page 264.

FIGURE 11.5
Abstract from the Report Whose Cover Is Shown in Figure 11.2

ABSTRACT

This project evaluates a proof-of-concept, pilot-scale, automated sorting system for mixed post-consumer plastic containers developed by the Rutgers University Center for Plastics Recycling Research (CPRR). The study evaluates the system's ability to identify and separately recover five types of plastic containers representative of those found in plastics recycling programs. It also addresses the system's potential for full-scale commercial application.

Three series of tests were performed: single composition, short-term tests; mixed composition, short-term tests; and mixed composition, extended tests. A total of 82 test runs were performed during which 66,632 bottles were processed.

The five bottle types considered were natural HDPE, PVC, clear PET, green PET, and opaque HDPE. The containers recovered at each product collection station were counted and the results compared to pre-established recovery goals. Bottle counts were then converted to weight recoveries using average bottle weights. The resulting product purity/contamination weight percents were compared to allowable product contamination limits representative of industry practice. From a detailed videotape analysis of a representative test, an exact profile of bottle feed timing and sequence was reconstructed. This analysis provided valuable insight into system feed and transport dynamic as well as an understanding of how product contamination occurs.

The system produced statistically reproducible results and proved to be mechanically reliable. However, it failed to achieve all of the commercial-level container recovery and product contamination limit goals. It was concluded that bottle singulation and spacing greatly influenced the effectiveness of the identification/separation equipment.

This work was submitted by wTe Corporation in fulfillment of Contract No. 850-1291-4. The contract was administered by the Solid Waste Association of North America and sponsored by the U.S. Environmental Protection Agency. This report covers from May 1992 to July 1993.

In this abstract, the researchers included the key information from each of their report's sections.

Because the research reported in this document is for the purpose of testing a general approach to sorting waste, neither the report nor the abstract included a recommendation. (Compare with the executive summary in Figure 11.6.)

In the first sentence, the researchers announce the general **objective** of their study. Later in the paragraph, they identify its specific goals.

The researchers provide detailed information about their **method**, which is important because the method is what they were testing. They provide precise details, such as the exact number of test runs and precise number of bottles processed.

The researchers present their **results**, relating them directly to the primary research questions: Would the method work and, if so, would it work well enough to be commercially successful?

The researchers state the **conclusion** they drew from their analysis of the results.

As is often required in government-sponsored projects, the researchers provide information about the sponsors and administrators of the study.

FIGURE 11.6
Executive Summary

In this executive summary, the writers include the key information from each of the report's sections, condensing a 28-page report into fewer than 250 words.

Because an executive summary is addressed to decision makers, the writers present the information on which their readers would decide what action to take. (Compare with the abstract in Figure 11.5.)

In their first sentence, the writers state the **main point** they make in the body of their report: The airport should purchase a new system.

Because their readers would not be familiar with the details of the Accounting Department's computers, the writers provide the **background information** these readers need in order to understand the rest of the executive summary.

The writers pinpoint the **problem.**

They briefly describe the three **possible solutions** they investigated. Their language echoes the statements they made in the preceding list of the problem's sources.

The writers conclude their summary with their **recommendation and the reason for it.**

EXECUTIVE SUMMARY

The Accounting Department recommends that Columbus International Airport purchase a new operating system for its InfoMaxx Minicomputer. The airport purchased the InfoMaxx Minicomputer in 2005 to replace an obsolete and failing Hutchins computer system. However, the new InfoMaxx computer has never successfully performed one of its key tasks: generating weekly accounting reports based on the expense and revenue data fed to it. When airport personnel attempt to run the computer program that should generate the reports, the computer issues a message stating that it does not have enough internal memory for the job.

Our department's analysis of this problem revealed that the InfoMaxx would have enough internal memory if the software used that space efficiently. Problems with the software are as follows:

1. The operating system, BT/Q-91, uses the computer's internal memory wastefully.
2. The SuperReport program, which is used to generate the accounting reports, is much too cumbersome to create reports this complex with the memory space available on the InfoMaxx computer.

Consequently, we evaluated three possible solutions:

1. Buying a new operating system (BT/Q-101) at a cost of $3500. It would double the amount of usable space and also speed calculations.
2. Writing a more compact program in LINUX, at a cost of $5000 in labor.
3. Revising SuperReport to prepare the overall report in small chunks, at a cost of $4000. SuperReport now successfully runs small reports.

We recommend the first alternative, buying a new operating system, because it will solve the problem for the least cost. The minor advantages of writing a new program in LINUX or of revising SuperReport are not sufficient to justify their cost.

Table of Contents

By providing a table of contents, you help readers who want to find a specific part of your communication without reading all of it. Your table of contents also assists readers who want an overview of the communication's scope and contents before they begin reading it in its entirety.

Tables of contents are constructed from chapter or section titles and from headings. They are most useful to readers if they have two (perhaps three) levels. The highest level consists of the chapters or section titles. Often they are generic: Introduction, Method, Results, and so on. The second level consists of the major headings within each chapter or section. These second-level entries in the table of contents guide readers more directly to the information they are seeking. Using features of Microsoft Word, you can create a table of contents automatically from your communication's headings.

Creating and reviewing your table of contents can help you polish the body of your communication. If you find that your table of contents wouldn't provide as much guidance as your readers would like, that's a sign that you may need to rephrase some of your headings or add additional ones.

Figure 11.7 shows the table of contents from the report whose cover is shown in Figure 11.2. Note that the words *Table of* do not appear.

Lists of Figures and Tables

Some readers search for specific figures and tables. If your communication is more than about fifteen pages long, you can assist readers by preparing a list of figures and tables. Figure 11.8 shows the list of figures from the EPA report whose cover is shown in Figure 11.2. That report also contains a list of tables, with the same format.

WRITING READER-CENTERED BACK MATTER
写以读者为中心的文后部分

The back matter of a document may include one or more of the following elements: appendixes; reference list, works cited, or bibliography; glossary; and index.

Appendixes

Appendixes enable you to present information you want to make available to your readers even though you know it won't interest all of them. For instance, in a research report you might create an appendix for a two-page account of the calculations you used for data analysis. By placing this account in an appendix, you help readers who will want to use the same calculations in another experiment, but you

FIGURE 11.7
Table of Contents of the Report Whose Cover Is Shown in Figure 11.2

Front matter. Note that lowercase roman numerals are used for the front matter's page numbers.

Body of report. In addition to the chapter titles, the writers included the first-level headings.

Back matter

CONTENTS

Preface	iii
Abstract	iv
List of Figures	vi
List of Tables	vii
Acknowledgments	viii

1. Introduction
   - Background — 1
   - Project overview — 1
   - Technology status — 2

2. Conclusions and Recommendations
   - Conclusions — 4
   - Recommendations — 4

3. System Description — 5

4. Testing Methodology
   - Project objectives — 14
   - Quality assurance objectives — 15
   - Feed material — 15
   - Product contamination — 17
   - Tests performed — 18
   - Data reduction, calculation, and validations methods — 22

5. Test Results
   - Single-composition tests — 29
   - Mixed-composition, short-term tests — 32
   - Mixed-composition, extended (2,000 bottles) tests — 38

6. Commercial Potential
   - Pilot system design comments and suggestions — 49
   - Equipment cost estimate — 52

References — 55

Appendixes
   - A. Test Data as Collected for Extended (2,000 Bottles) Tests — 58
   - B. Extended Test Results, Outliers Not Included — 63

Glossary of Terms — 74

FIGURE 11.8
List of Figures from the Report Whose Cover Is Shown in Figure 11.2

The writers provided a list of figures to assist readers interested in finding or reviewing the information provided in them.

FIGURES

Number		Page
1	Process flow diagram	7
2	Equipment layout	8
3	Feed bin, infeed conveyor, and oversize discharge chute	9
4	Infeed arrangement viewed from C4/C5 transition	9
5	Dual discharge chutes and underside of infeed conveyor	10
6	Conveyors C4b, C4c, C5, and C6	10
7	Green PET, clear PET, and PVC identification/separation stations	11
8	PVC and clear PET product chutes, conveyor C7 in foreground	11

save readers who aren't interested from the necessity of wading through the calculations while reading the body of your report. Appendixes can also assist readers by providing important reference information in a readily accessed place. That is a function of Appendix A in the back of this text.

When you create appendixes, list them in your table of contents (see Figure 11.7) and give each an informative title that indicates clearly what it contains. Also, mention each appendix in the body of your report at the point where your readers might want to refer to it: "Printouts from the electrocardiogram appear in Appendix II."

Begin each appendix on its own page. Arrange and label the appendixes in the same order in which they are mentioned in the body of the communication. If you have only one appendix, label it simply "Appendix." If you have more than one, you may use Roman numerals, Arabic numerals, or capital letters to distinguish them.

References List, Endnotes, or Bibliography

Place your reference list, endnotes, or bibliography immediately after the body of your communication or after the appendixes. Appendix A explains which sources to cite and how to construct reference lists, endnotes, and bibliographies.

Glossary and List of Symbols

When writing at work, you will sometimes use terms or symbols that are unfamiliar to some of your readers. If you use each term or symbol only once or in only one small segment of your communication, you can explain its meaning in the text. Imagine, however, that you are writing a report in which a special term appears on pages 3, 39, and 72. If you define the term every time it occurs, your report will be repetitious. On the other hand, if you define the term only the first time it appears, your readers may have forgotten the definition by the time they encounter the term again. To solve this problem, create a glossary. It will provide the definition where readers can easily locate it if they need to but where it won't encumber their reading if they don't.

Figure 11.9 shows the first page of the glossary for the EPA report previously mentioned. The author has the terms to be defined in boldface and color so readers can find them easily. Figure 11.10 shows a list of symbols.

Index

If your communication is too long for your readers to thumb through quickly, give them a quick path to specific pieces of information by creating an index. Identify the kinds of information they might want to locate without reading the rest of the communication. If several index topics can be gathered under a single word, indent them under the main word to create second-level entries. See the example index in Figure 11.11.

Some desktop publishing programs can help you create an index by generating an alphabetized list of the words used in your communication. From this list, you can index those that will help your readers find the information they desire.

Learn More

For additional information about documenting your sources, including links to other documentation systems, go to Appendix A and to Appendix A at www.thomsonedu.com/english/anderson.

GLOSSARY OF TERMS

Availability — The probability that equipment will be capable of performing its specified function when called upon at any random point in time. Calculated as the ratio of run time to the sum of run time and downtime.

Bottle — A single plastic container, also referred to as a container.

Cascade — To sequentially increase the belt speed in a series of conveyors.

Contamination — Bottles improperly removed at a station.

Effective Bottle Feed Rate — The average rate at which a specific type of bottle is fed during a mixed composition test. Calculated as the total number of bottles of a specific type fed divided by the total run time for a specific test.

Extended Test — A test series consisting of many replicates at pre-selected conditions.

FIGURE 11.9
First Page of the Glossary of the Report Whose Cover Is Shown in Figure 11.2

In this glossary, the writers provide precise definitions for key terms in their report.

They use bold type and color to make the terms being defined stand out.

List of Symbols

a_k	allpass filter coefficients
a	vector of allpass filter coefficients
A	cross-sectional area
$A(z)$	allpass transfer function
B	area ratio
c	speed of sound
c	vector of transfer functions or of cosine functions
C	scaling coefficient
$C(z)$	transfer function of a subfilter in the Farrow structure
d	fractional part of the total delay D
D	total delay to be approximated
$D(z)$	denominator of $A(z)$

FIGURE 11.10
List of Symbols

This list of symbols, from a study concerning computer modeling of music, is several pages long.

Knowing that readers will search for symbols they have seen in the text, the writer has placed the symbols on left side — the side seen first by people who read from left to right.

To aid the readers' search, the writer has arranged the symbols in alphabetical order.

FIGURE 11.11
Index

This index is from the service manual for a diesel engine used in farm machinery.

DETROIT DIESEL 53

ALPHABETICAL INDEX

Subject	Section	Subject	Section

A

Accessory drive 1.7.7
Accumulator—Hydrostarter 12.6.1
Air box drains 1.1.2
Air cleaner 3.1
Air compressor 12.4
Air inlet restriction 15.2
Air intake system 3
Air shutdown housing .3.3
Air silencer 3.2
Alarm system 7.4.2
Alternator—battery-charging 7.1

B

Balance shaft 1.7.2
Balance weights—front 1.7
Battery—storage 7.2
Bearings:
   Camshaft and balance shaft 1.7.2
   Clutch pilot 1.4.1
   Connecting rod 1.6.2
   Connecting rod (clearance) 1.0
   Crankshaft main .1.3.4
   Crankshaft main (clearance) 1.0
   Crankshaft outboard 1.3.5.1
   Fan hub 5.4
   Idle gear—engine .1.7.4
Belt adjustment—fan .15.1
Bilge pump 12.2
Block—cylinder 1.1
Blower (In-line and 6V) 3.4
Blower (8V) 3.4.1
Blower drive gear 1.7.6
Blower drive shaft 1.7.6
Blower end plates 3.0
Bluing injector components 2.0
Breather—crankcase .4.8
By-pass valve—oil filter 4.2

C

Cam followers 1.2.1
Camshaft 1.7.2
Camshaft and balance shaft gears 1.7.3
Cap—coolant pressure control 5.3.1
Cautions . . . .*
Charging pump—Hydrostarter 12.6.1

Charts:
   Engine coolants 13.3
   Engine operating conditions 13.2
   Injector timing gage 14.2
   Lubrication 15.1
   Model description . . . .*
   Preventive maintenance 15.1
Cleaner—air 3.1
Clearance—exhaust valve 14.1
Clutch pilot bearing 1.4.1
Cold weather operation—Hydrostarter 12.6.1
Cold weather starting .12.6
Compression pressure .15.2
Compressor—air 12.4
Connecting rod 1.6.1
Connecting rod bearings 1.6.2
Converter—Torqmatic 8
Coolant—engine 13.3
Coolant—filter 5.7
Cooler—fuel 2.5.1
Cooler—oil (engine) 4.4
Cooling system 5
Coupling—drive shaft .1.4.2
Cover—engine front (lower) 1.3.5
Cover—engine front (upper) 1.7.8
Cover—valve rocker .1.2.4
Crankshaft 1.3
Crankshaft oil seals 1.3.2
Crankshaft pulley 1.3.7
Crankshaft timing gear 1.7.5
Crankshaft vibration damper 1.3.6
Cross section view of engines . . . .*
Cylinder block 1.1
Cylinder head 1.2
Cylinder liner 1.9.3
Cylinder—misfiring 15.2

D

Damper—vibration 1.3.6
Description—general . . . .*
Diesel principle . . . .*
Dipstick—oil level 4.6
Drains—air box 1.1.2
Drive—accessory 1.7.7
Drive—fuel pump 2.2.1
Drive—hydraulic governor 2.8.3
Drive—blower 3.4
Dynamometer test 13.2.1

*General Information and Cautions Section

© Copyright 1990 Detroit Diesel Corporation   May, 1990   Page 1

The writers use second-level headings to organize related topics.

To help readers scan through the index, the writers used white space and capital letters to break the index into sections.